# TORAHSCOPE
VOLUME I

# TORAHSCOPE
## VOLUME I

Life Examined and Understood
Through the Grid of the Torah

William Mark Huey

# TorahScope
## Volume I

© 2006, 2010 William Mark Huey
edited by J.K. McKee
2012 printing
first edition © 2004
All rights reserved.
No part of this book may be reproduced, stored in a retrieval system, or transmitted by any means, electronic, mechanical, photocopying, recording, or otherwise, without written permission from the author(s).

Cover photos: Istockphoto

---

Published by TNN Press, a division of Outreach Israel Ministries
1492 Regal Court
Kissimmee, Florida 34744
(407) 933-2002
www.tnnonline.net/tnnpress

---

Unless otherwise noted, Scripture quotations are from the *New American Standard, Updated Edition* (NASU), © 1995, The Lockman Foundation.

# Table of Contents

Annual Torah Reading Schedule ..................................................................vii
Introduction ..............................................................................................xi

## GENESIS
*Bereisheet* In the Beginning ..................................................................... 1
*Noach* Noah .......................................................................................... 4
*Lekh-Lekha* Get yourself out .................................................................. 9
*V'yeira* He appeared ............................................................................ 14
*Chayei Sarah* Sarah's life ...................................................................... 18
*Toldot* History ..................................................................................... 23
*V'yeitzei* He went out ........................................................................... 29
*V'yishlach* He sent ............................................................................... 33
*V'yeishev* He continued living ............................................................... 42
*Mikkeitz* At the end ............................................................................. 45
*V'yigash* He approached ...................................................................... 48
*V'yechi* He lived .................................................................................. 51

## EXODUS
*Shemot* Names .................................................................................... 55
*V'eira* I appeared ................................................................................ 58
*Bo* Go ................................................................................................ 62
*B'shalach* After he had let go ............................................................... 66
*Yitro* Jethro ........................................................................................ 70
*Mishpatim* Rulings .............................................................................. 74
*Terumah* Contribution ........................................................................ 76
*Tetzaveh* You shall command .............................................................. 79
*Ki Tisa* When you take ........................................................................ 82
*V'yakheil* He assembled ...................................................................... 87
*Pequdei* Accounts ............................................................................... 92

## LEVITICUS
*Vayikra* He called ................................................................................ 97
*Tzav* Give an order ............................................................................ 101
*Shemini* Eighth .................................................................................. 104
*Tazria* She Conceives ......................................................................... 108
*Metzora* Infected One ........................................................................ 113
*Acharei Mot* After the death ............................................................... 118
*Kedoshim* Holy Ones ......................................................................... 125
*Emor* Speak ...................................................................................... 131
*B'har* On the mount ........................................................................... 135
*B'chuqotai* By My Regulations ............................................................ 140

# NUMBERS
*Bamidbar* In the wilderness .................................................................. 145
*Naso* Take ............................................................................................... 150
*B'ha'alotkha* When you set up ............................................................. 154
*Shelakh-Lekha* Send on your behalf .................................................. 159
*Korach* Korah ......................................................................................... 166
*Chukat* Regulation ................................................................................ 170
*Balak* Destroyer ..................................................................................... 176
*Pinchas* Phinehas .................................................................................. 181
*Mattot* Tribes ......................................................................................... 184
*Mas'ei* Stages ......................................................................................... 192

# DEUTERONOMY
*Devarim* Words ..................................................................................... 197
*V'et'chanan* I pleaded .......................................................................... 202
*Ekev* Because ........................................................................................ 207
*Re'eih* See .............................................................................................. 211
*Shoftim* Judges ..................................................................................... 214
*Ki-Teitzei* When you go out ................................................................ 216
*Ki-Tavo* When you enter in ................................................................ 219
*Nitzavim* Standing ............................................................................... 223
*V'yeilekh* And he went ........................................................................ 228
*Ha'azinu* Hear ....................................................................................... 232
*V'zot Ha'berakhah* This is the blessing ............................................. 236

About the Author .................................................................................. 239
Bibliography ........................................................................................... 241

## Abbreviation Chart and Special Terms

*Special terms unique to this publication that may be used have been provided in this chart:*

Apostolic Scriptures/Writings: the New Testament
ATS: ArtScroll Tanach (1996)
b. Babylonian Talmud (*Talmud Bavli*)
BDAG: *A Greek-English Lexicon of the New Testament and Other Early Christian Literature* (Bauer, Danker, Arndt, Gingrich)
BDB: *Brown-Driver-Briggs Hebrew and English Lexicon*
CHALOT: *Concise Hebrew and Aramaic Lexicon of the Old Testament*
CJB: Complete Jewish Bible (1998)
ESV: English Standard Version (2001)
EXP: *Expositor's Bible Commentary*
Grk: Greek
HALOT: *Hebrew & Aramaic Lexicon of the Old Testament* (Koehler and Baumgartner)
HCSB: Holman Christian Standard Bible (2004)
Heb: Hebrew
KJV: King James Version

LXE: *Septuagint with Apocrypha* by Sir L.C.L. Brenton (1851)
LXX: Septuagint
LS: *A Greek-English Lexicon* (Liddell & Scott)
m. Mishnah
NASU: New American Standard Update (1995)
NEB: New English Bible (1970)
NIV: New International Version (1984)
NJPS: Tanakh, A New Translation of the Holy Scriptures (1999)
NRSV: New Revised Standard Version (1989)
RSV: Revised Standard Version (1952)
t. Tosefta
Tanakh: the Old Testament
TNIV: Today's New International Version (2005)
TWOT: *Theological Wordbook of the Old Testament*
YLT: Young's Literal Translation (1862/1898)

# Annual Torah Reading Schedule

These are the weekly Torah and Haftarah portions, as employed in both the traditional Synagogue and today's Messianic Jewish congregations

**KEY:**
A: Ashkenazic  S: Sephardic*
[] denote differences between traditional Jewish and Christian verse order

## GENESIS

**Bereisheet** "In the beginning"
Genesis 1:1-6:8
Isaiah 42:5-43:10 (A); 42:5-21 (S)

**Noach** "Noah"
Genesis 6:9-11:32
Isaiah 54:1-55:5 (A); 54:1-10 (S)

**Lekh-Lekha** "Get yourself out"
Genesis 12:1-17:27
Isaiah 40:27-41:16

**V'yeira** "He appeared"
Genesis 18:1-22:24
2 Kings 4:1-37 (A); 4:1-23 (S)

**Chayei Sarah** "Sarah's life"
Genesis 23:1-25:18
1 Kings 1:1-31

**Toldot** "History"
Genesis 25:19-28:9
Malachi 1:1-2:7

**V'yeitzei** "He went out"
Genesis 28:10-32:2
Hosea 12:12-14:10 (A); 11:7-12:12 (S)

**V'yishlach** "He sent"
Genesis 32:3-36:43
Hosea 11:7-12:12 (A); Obadiah 1:1-21 (S)

**V'yeishev** "He continued living"
Genesis 37:1-40:23
Amos 2:6-3:8

**Mikkeitz** "At the end"
Genesis 41:1-44:17
1 Kings 3:15-4:1

**V'yigash** "He approached"
Genesis 44:18-47:27
Ezekiel 37:15-28

**V'yechi** "He lived"
Genesis 47:28-50:26
1 Kings 2:1-12

## EXODUS

**Shemot** "Names"
Exodus 1:1-6:1
Isaiah 27:6-28:13; 29:22-23 (A);
Jeremiah 1:2-3 (S)

**V'eira** "I appeared"
Exodus 6:2-9:35
Ezekiel 28:25-29:21

**Bo** "Go"
Exodus 10:1-13:16
Jeremiah 46:13-28

**B'shalach** "After he had let go"
Exodus 13:17-17:16
Judges 4:4-5:31 (A); 5:1-31 (S)

**Yitro** "Jethro"
Exodus 18:1-20:23[26]
Isaiah 6:1-7:6; 9:5-6[6-7] (A); 6:1-13 (S)

**Mishpatim** "Rulings"
Exodus 21:1-24:18
Jeremiah 34:8-22; 33:25-26

---

* Ashkenazic Jews are largely those from Eastern and Northern Europe, and Sephardic Jews are largely those from Spain and Muslim lands.

**Terumah** "Contribution"
Exodus 25:1-27:19
1 Kings 5:26-6:13

**Tetzaveh** "You shall command"
Exodus 27:20-30:10
Ezekiel 43:10-27

**Ki Tisa** "When you take"
Exodus 30:11-34:35
1 Kings 18:1-39 (A); 18:20-39 (S)

**V'yak'heil** "He assembled"
Exodus 35:1-38:20
1 Kings 7:40-50 (A); 7:13-26 (S)

**Pequdei** "Accounts"
Exodus 38:21-40:38
1 Kings 7:51-8:21 (A); 7:40-50 (S)

## LEVITICUS

**Vayikra** "He called"
Leviticus 1:1-5:26[6:7]
Isaiah 43:21-44:23

**Tzav** "Give an order"
Leviticus 6:1[8]-8:36
Jeremiah 7:21-8:3; 9:22-23

**Shemini** "Eighth"
Leviticus 9:1-11:47
2 Samuel 6:1-7:17 (A); 6:1-19 (S)

**Tazria** "She conceives"
Leviticus 12:1-13:59
2 Kings 4:42-5:19

**Metzora** "Leper"
Leviticus 14:1-15:33
2 Kings 7:3-20

**Acharei Mot** "After the death"
Leviticus 16:1-18:30
Ezekiel 22:1-19 (A); 22:1-16 (S)

**Kedoshim** "Holy Ones"
Leviticus 19:1-20:27
Amos 9:7-15 (A); Ezekiel 20:2-20 (S)

**Emor** "Speak"
Leviticus 21:1-24:23
Ezekiel 44:15-31

**B'har** "On Mount"
Leviticus 25:1-26:2
Jeremiah 32:6-27

**B'chuqotai** "By My regulations"
Leviticus 26:3-27:34
Jeremiah 16:19-17:24

## NUMBERS

**Bamidbar** "In the wilderness"
Numbers 1:1-4:20
Hosea 2:1-22

**Naso** "Take"
Numbers 4:21-7:89
Judges 13:2-25

**Beha'alot'kha** "When you set up"
Numbers 8:1-12:16
Zechariah 2:14-4:7

**Shelakh-Lekha** "Send on your behalf"
Numbers 13:1-15:41
Joshua 2:1-24

**Korach** "Korah"
Numbers 16:1-18:32
1 Samuel 11:14-12:22

**Chukat** "Regulation"
Numbers 19:1-22:1
Judges 11:1-33

**Balak** "Balak"
Numbers 22:2-25:9
Micah 5:6-6:8

**Pinchas** "Phinehas"
Numbers 25:10-30:1[29:40]
1 Kings 18:46-19:21

**Mattot** "Tribes"
Numbers 30:2[1]-32:42
Jeremiah 1:1-2:3

**Mas'ei** "Stages"
Numbers 33:1-36:13
Jeremiah 2:4-28; 3:4 (A);
2:4-28; 4:1-2 (S)

## DEUTERONOMY

**Devarim** "Words"
Deuteronomy 1:1-3:22
Isaiah 1:1-27

**V'et'chanan** "And I besought"
Deuteronomy 3:23-7:11
Isaiah 40:1-26

**Ekev** "Because"
Deuteronomy 7:12-11:25
Isaiah 49:14-51:3

**Re'eih** "See"
Deuteronomy 11:26-16:17
Isaiah 54:11-55:5

**Shoftim** "Judges"
Deuteronomy 16:18-21:9
Isaiah 51:12-52:12 (or finish at 53:12)

**Ki-Teitzei** "When you go out"
Deuteronomy 21:10-25:19
Isaiah 54:1-10 (or finish at 52:13)

**Ki-Tavo** "When you come"
Deuteronomy 26:1-29:8
Isaiah 60:1-22

**Nitzavim** "Standing"
Deuteronomy 29:9[10]-30:20
Isaiah 61:10-63:9

**V'yeilekh** "He went"
Deuteronomy 31:1-30
Hosea 14:2-10; Micah 7:18-20; Joel 2:15-27

**Ha'azinu** "Hear"
Deuteronomy 32:1–52
2 Samuel 22:1–22:51

**V'zot Ha'berakhah** "This is the blessing"
Deuteronomy 33:1–34:12
Joshua 1:1–18 (A); 1:1-9 (S)


The current Torah and Haftarah reading dates, are available online
via the Outreach Israel Ministries website: www.outreachisrael.net

# INTRODUCTION

**"The secret things belong to the LORD our God, but the things revealed belong to us and to our sons forever, that we may observe all the words of this law"** (Deuteronomy 29:29).

For millennia, the diligent study of the Torah or the Law of Moses has been primarily embraced by members of the Jewish community. For a variety of reasons, many followers of Yeshua the Messiah (Jesus Christ) have not been led to pursue the Torah in a similar fashion as established by the Jewish Sages and Rabbis. Instead, the books of Moses have mostly been examined for their value in Biblical history. There is often no consistent, weekly examination of the Torah practiced in the Christian Church, unlike how it is read in Jewish synagogues worldwide.

Since the First Coming of the Messiah and the composition of the Apostolic Scriptures (New Testament), most Christians have focused their faith on these writings and their significance. After the destruction of the Temple in 70 C.E., the emerging Christian Church began to steadily separate from its Jewish Roots. These two distinct religions—which both confess to serve the God of Abraham, Isaac, and Jacob—often approach Him through two different paths: one through the "Old Testament," and one through the "New Testament." But interestingly enough, both groups are in fervent pursuit of the Law of God. One believes that the Torah is the words compiled by the teacher Moses, and the other believes that Yeshua the Messiah is the Word made flesh.

As a Believer in the Messiah of Israel, when introduced to the Torah for the first time from a Jewish perspective, I was struck by the reality that studying the Torah would actually *improve* my relationship with God. I concluded that if Yeshua is the Word made flesh (John 1:1), and if I were truly in the process of being conformed to His image (Romans 8:29; 12:2), then it would benefit me greatly to study the Torah and thus better understand who my Lord and Savior is. He Himself *did say*, after all, that Moses had written of Him (John 5:46). The books of Moses contain the foundational building blocks of the rest of Scripture, and by getting a better understanding of their eternal truths, I found that I would be able to solidify my faith.

Consequently, without a tremendous amount of encouragement, but simply the Spirit of God moving on my heart, the desire to follow the ancient paths of my spiritual forbearers in faith became a delight. Once I understood what the patterns were for a consistent study, the blessings to my family and me became very apparent to all of us. Let me tell you a little about what happened.

In 1995 on *Rosh HaShanah*, our family was first introduced to the Messianic movement. We celebrated our first Feast of Tabernacles or *Sukkot* with a Messianic Jewish congregation in Dallas, Texas that was somewhat welcoming to us a family of non-Jews. But, the congregation's stated mission was to provide a "Yeshua-oriented synagogue" for the many

Jewish people who were coming to faith in Yeshua. We did not fit this profile, but as we persevered in our attendance, we found ourselves taking a new members class that began a few months after our initial visit. In spite of not being Jewish, we were learning so much as a family that the Holy Spirit kept prompting us to continue attending.

It was during this time that we were first introduced to a traditional Jewish *Shabbat* order of service and worship, which included our initial exposure to the weekly Torah portions. Before going to this congregation, I had really never heard the word "Torah," except as the Japanese word for "attack" used in the 1970 film *Tora! Tora! Tora!* Each week as a part of the service, the congregational leader would have someone come up to the bema, deliver a short teaching, and cant from the Torah scroll. We soon discovered that the weekly bulletins informed us that we were going through the Biblical texts of Genesis through Deuteronomy, according to an already set schedule known as the annual **Torah cycle.** This was complemented by what was labeled as the Haftarah readings, which were taken from the balance of the Tanakh or Old Testament. As you can imagine, we were on a tremendous learning curve!

Within a short period of time, we were diligently following the schedule of the weekly readings. Since the congregational leader would typically refer to some aspect of the weekly Torah portion in his sermons, we were often able to read ahead to prepare for what texts would likely be preached or exposited upon. Our first year discovering the Torah cycle was fairly routine, with a nominal effort made to consider the deeper truths of God's Word. During these same early days of our Messianic walk, we were also being exposed to the richness of Messianic music, Davidic dance, and the Jewish Roots of our Christian faith.

## Torah: Instruction for Life

In the early days of our family adopting a Messianic lifestyle, we were experiencing many of the same things that the first non-Jewish Believers experienced as they turned to faith in the God of Israel. If you will recall from Acts 15, the problem of non-Jews coming to faith in the Messiah of Israel was creating some controversy. There was a debate over whether these new Believers had to be circumcised and convert to Judaism in order to be saved. In the debate as to whether the new Believers needed to be circumcised, Peter, Paul, Barnabas, and ultimately James, the brother of Yeshua, met in Jerusalem, giving their thoughts on the evidence of the Spirit of God taking up residence in the hearts of the new Believers. James, the leader of the Jerusalem Council, made the final ruling on what the new, non-Jewish Believers in Yeshua were supposed to do:

"After they had stopped speaking, James answered, saying, 'Brethren, listen to me. Simeon has related how God first concerned Himself about taking from among the Gentiles a people for His name. With this the words of the Prophets agree, just as it is written, "AFTER THESE THINGS I will return, AND I WILL REBUILD THE TABERNACLE OF DAVID WHICH HAS FALLEN, AND I WILL REBUILD ITS RUINS, AND I WILL RESTORE IT, SO THAT THE REST OF MANKIND MAY SEEK THE LORD, AND ALL THE GENTILES WHO ARE CALLED BY MY NAME,' SAYS THE LORD, WHO MAKES THESE THINGS KNOWN FROM LONG AGO. Therefore it is my judgment that we do not trouble those who are turning to God from among the Gentiles, but that we write to them that they abstain from things contaminated by idols and from fornication and from what is strangled and from blood. For Moses from ancient generations has in every city those who preach him, since he is read in the synagogues every Sabbath" (Acts 15:13-21; cf. Amos 9:11-12).

The ruling of the Jerusalem Council was that these non-Jewish Believers were to (1) abstain from pollutions of idols, (2) abstain from sexual immorality, (3) meats that were not butchered in a proper method (Deuteronomy 14:2-20), and (4) from blood (Deuteronomy 12:23-25). They were to do these things so they could enter into the Jewish community, go to the synagogue on the Sabbath day or *Shabbat*, and hear the Torah taught. Once submitting themselves to weekly Torah teachings, they could steadily learn what was acceptable and unacceptable behavior, befitting the people of God. Our family was convicted that if this was what the first non-Jewish Believers in Yeshua were anticipated to do, that we too must submit ourselves to Moses' Teaching every week.[i]

Consistent study and meditation on the Law of God is something that has certainly been admonished over the ages by many of the figures within the Tanakh (Old Testament). The Hebrew word *torah* (תּוֹרָה), meaning "teaching" or "instruction," appears 220 times in the Tanakh.[ii] When you start reading about the Torah's significance to the Biblical authors, the evidence is overwhelming that studying, applying, and obeying the Torah is paramount to walking in a way that is pleasing to the Holy One of Israel. Consider these passages that remind us of the Torah's importance:

- **Abraham, the father of faith, obeyed the Torah:** "Because Abraham obeyed My voice, and observed My safeguards, My commandments, My decrees, and My Torahs" (Genesis 26:5, ATS).

- **According to God, the Torah was to be applicable to Israel and all the strangers who attach themselves to Israel:** "Assemble the people, the men and the women and children and the alien who is in your town, so that they may hear and learn and fear the LORD your God, and be careful to observe all the words of this law" (Deuteronomy 31:12).

- **As Moses comes to the end of his life, and gives some final instructions to the people of Israel, he reminds them that observance of the Torah compliments a healthy fear of the Almighty:** "Assemble the people, the men and the women and children and the alien who is in your town, so that they may hear and learn and fear the LORD your God, and be careful to observe all the words of this law" (Deuteronomy 31:12).

- **Joshua says that meditation and observance of the Torah is required in order for Israel to be prosperous and successful:** "This book of the law shall not depart from your mouth, but you shall meditate on it day and night, so that you may be careful to do according to all that is written in it; for then you will make your way prosperous, and then you will have success" (Joshua 1:8).

- **The Psalmist reminds us to meditate upon the Torah day and night:** "How blessed is the man who does not walk in the counsel of the wicked, nor stand in the path of sinners, nor sit in the seat of scoffers! But his delight is in the law of the LORD, and in His law he meditates day and night" (Psalm 1:2).

---

[i] For a more detailed analysis, consult the commentary *Acts 15 for the Practical Messianic* by J.K. McKee.
[ii] This figure was determined using a root search of the Hebrew Tanakh (WTT) in BibleWorks 5.0.

- **The wisdom of Proverbs describes the blessings of listening to the Torah. It is stated that if you do not listen to Torah, then your prayers may be an abomination:** "He who turns away his ear from listening to the law, even his prayer is an abomination" (Proverbs 28:9).
- **The Prophets of Israel constantly point the people back to the Torah for guidelines on how to conduct their lives, and how they had fallen from the Divine will of God:** "My people are destroyed for lack of knowledge. Because you have rejected knowledge, I also will reject you from being My priest. Since you have forgotten the law of your God, I also will forget your children" (Hosea 4:6).
- **One of the final admonitions in the Hebrew Bible, from the Prophet Malachi, is that we are to remember the Instructions that God delivered from His servant Moses:** "Remember the law of Moses My servant, *even the* statutes and ordinances which I commanded him in Horeb for all Israel" (Malachi 4:4).

## TorahScope Inspired

During my initial research into the study of the Torah, I discovered that the Rabbinical community has developed a schedule that was applicable to the Jewish calendar. I found out that if you were traveling around the world, whether in London, Beijing, New York, or Jerusalem, the same Torah reading schedule would be used. This was beneficial to the Jewish person who might be away from home, but who may visit another synagogue on *Shabbat*. By following this schedule, one will know what Torah portion was being discussed, and if led, one might be able to contribute to the study or discussion. I thought this was a wonderful way of how the Jewish people were able to encourage a consistent study of the Torah. I thought that perhaps this was one of the reasons why the Jewish people were able to maintain their identity and relative cohesiveness over the centuries.

As I committed myself to a consistent study of the weekly Torah portions, I found that the Lord was using the Torah in my life for me to dig deeper into different aspects of my personal walk with Him. I found myself becoming more spiritually aware of situations and events around me. I envisioned the study of the Torah like a multi-varied optical instrument, **or a scope,** which was being used to examine a variety of nearly invisible and remote objects. I thought of a telescope and its ability to see into the stars, a microscope and its ability to magnify small objects, and even a periscope and its ability to see from beneath the darkness of the sea or objects where one did not have a direct line of sight.

Contemplating these thoughts, I coined the term **TorahScope** as my way of communicating what I was envisioning. It appeared to me that a diligent study of the Torah could be used as some kind of a scope to observe or detect the deeper, unobservable aspects of our beings. This consideration led me to start writing some observations under the byline: TorahScope. I knew how much study and diligence it takes to put something in writing. I also knew that if I would make a commitment to write a reflective commentary on the weekly Torah selection, that I would have to faithfully study the weekly Torah and Haftarah portions. I knew that in the long run, I would be the benefactor of a consistent study of the Torah. My walk with the Messiah of Israel would be blessed. After all, I concluded, if we are being conformed to the image of Messiah Yeshua, and He is the Word made flesh, **then it would probably benefit us all to develop a more comprehensive understanding of the Torah,** knowing that He is the One to whom the Torah points (Romans 10:4, Grk.)!

## Torah: Words of Life

It was not too long before I began to see many parallels between my weekly study of the Torah, and issues I was dealing with in my own life. Sometimes situations in my family could be understood better through the grid of God's Torah. At other times, circumstances in our congregational lives could be analyzed through the lens of the Torah. On a global scale, I was even able to see things happening to, or in the State of Israel, which at times reflected back on the weekly Torah or Haftarah portions. As you might imagine, every time I experienced these connections, I became more convinced that the Torah of Moses was a living document, just as the writer of Hebrews says that the Word of God is a sharp instrument:

"For the word of God is living and active and sharper than any two-edged sword, and piercing as far as the division of soul and spirit, of both joints and marrow, and able to judge the thoughts and intentions of the heart. And there is no creature hidden from His sight, but all things are open and laid bare to the eyes of Him with whom we have to do" (Hebrews 4:12-13).

As I was writing my initial TorahScope reflections, I was convinced that the Holy One was going to raise up a generation of born again Messianic Believers, who themselves could begin to write commentaries on the Torah portions. One of the challenges that any modern-day Messianic Believer has is the lack of good teaching materials from a distinct Messianic viewpoint. This is especially true when it comes to commentaries on books of the Bible, and the Torah is no exception. Libraries are filled with many Torah commentaries and writings from the Rabbis of Judaism. Much of the information that the Jewish Sages offer is very helpful and insightful. However, they have all failed to acknowledge Yeshua as the Messiah, and some of these commentaries in places make an effort to refute His Messiahship. Today, the Messianic community largely lacks Torah commentaries *from its own perspective.* (Even this TorahScope commentary, while very useful for approaching the weekly *parashot,* is only intended to provide reflections on the weekly Torah portions, and not provide you with a verse-by-verse commentary of the Pentateuch.)[iii]

My prayer for you, as you consider the relevance of studying the Torah on a regular basis, is that you will discover what I have discovered about *the blessings* of studying it. One of Moses' final exhortations to Ancient Israel describes how the words of the Torah as God's Instruction—are to be the sphere in which they live their lives:

"[H]e said to them, 'Take to your heart all the words with which I am warning you today, which you shall command your sons to observe carefully, *even* all the words of this law. For it is not an idle word for you; **indeed it is your life.** And by this word you will prolong your days in the land, which you are about to cross the Jordan to possess'" (Deuteronomy 32:46-47).

If these words do not inspire you to consider the relevance of examining God's Torah, then perhaps the words of Yeshua the Messiah will give you the encouragement you need to take the Torah to heart:

---

[iii] For a compilation of useful material, consult the *Messianic Torah Helper* by TNN Press (forthcoming).

"Do not think that I came to abolish the Law or the Prophets; I did not come to abolish but to fulfill. For truly I say to you, until heaven and earth pass away, not the smallest letter or stroke shall pass from the Law until all is accomplished. Whoever then annuls one of the least of these commandments, and teaches others *to do* the same, shall be called least in the kingdom of heaven; but whoever keeps and teaches *them*, he shall be called great in the kingdom of heaven" (Matthew 5:17-19).

The incentive to those who keep and teach God's Torah is **to be called great in the Kingdom of Heaven.** My prayer is that we will, at least, all be keepers of the Torah so that the Lord may welcome us into His Kingdom by proclaiming, "Well done good and faithful servant!"

I hope that you will be blessed by these reflective commentaries found in the pages of *TorahScope, Volume I*, as I have done my utmost to share His thoughts for us as His people.

Until the restoration of all things....

*William Mark Huey*
*Director, Outreach Israel Ministries*

# COMMENTARY ON GENESIS

## *Bereisheet* בְּרֵאשִׁית
### In the Beginning
### "Let There Be Light"

> Genesis 1:1-6:8
> Isaiah 42:5-43:10 (A); 42:5-21 (S)

The Bible begins with words that we are all too familiar with, "In the beginning God created the heavens and the earth. The earth was formless and void, and darkness was over the surface of the deep, and the Spirit of God was moving over the surface of the waters. Then God said, 'Let there be light'; and there was light" (Genesis 1:1-3). What do you think about when you read this?

The beginning of the weekly Torah cycle includes a tremendous amount of information that has been preserved down through the ages. When you consider that in these opening chapters of the Scriptures, the text takes us from the beginning of the universe all the way to the introduction of the generation of Noah, the amount of material covered is quite overwhelming. So many critical foundational aspects of our faith are mentioned, that one could easily spend a lifetime considering the topics discussed. Contemplating the concept of Creation, cosmic and human origins, the Fall, and the future new Creation—and their implications for simply living a blessed life today—has generated voluminous material that can fill countless libraries.

One of the challenges that presents itself when a Torah student approaches the opening chapters of the Bible, and the beginning of the annual Torah cycle, is to ask the Lord just what to focus *your attention* upon. Perhaps this is why Psalm 1 reminds us of the simple and practical benefits of meditating upon God's Torah, and making reflection upon it an integral part of our weekly discipline:

"How blessed is the man who does not walk in the counsel of the wicked, nor stand in the path of sinners, Nor sit in the seat of scoffers! **But his delight is in the law of the LORD, and in His law he meditates day and night.** He will be like a tree *firmly* planted by streams of water, which yields its fruit in its season and its leaf does not wither; and in whatever he does, he prospers" (Psalm 1:1-3).

As I have considered the text of *Bereisheet* many times, and have meditated upon the significance of all the different verses, one aspect of it still keeps coming to my mind. For some reason, each time I read the words, "Let there be light," the image of the benefits of illumination is something that grabs my attention. Our Creator is so powerful that He simply spoke the word "Light," and there was light dispelling darkness. Additional statements from the Psalmist may remind us of how "Your word is a lamp to my feet and a light to my path" (Psalm 119:105).

Here, the Psalmist asserts that the Word of God is indeed a lamp to our feet and a light to our paths. Without the Word of the Lord, just where would we be headed? How would we view life? What would life be like if our Creator had not given us His Word? What would we know about Creation? Would we all be evolutionists, thinking that we are a part of a comic accident with no Creator? How would we know about Him?

## A Light Unto the Nations

As I consider these questions—and a multitude of others—the corresponding Haftarah portion introduces us to the concept of light. In Isaiah 42:5-43:10, the Prophet Isaiah declares what the Most High is communicating to him about the Creation. The opening statement parallels the beginning parts of the Genesis account:

"Thus says God the LORD, who created the heavens and stretched them out, who spread out the earth and its offspring, who gives breath to the people on it and spirit to those who walk in it, 'I am the LORD, I have called you in righteousness, I will also hold you by the hand and watch over you, and I will appoint you as a covenant to the people, as a light to the nations, to open blind eyes, to bring out prisoners from the dungeon and those who dwell in darkness from the prison'" (Isaiah 42:5-7).

After the Creation account is briefly summarized, the Lord turns to His people, and reminds them of His protective hand and the covenant that He has established with them. He describes Israel in a very powerful way as "a light to the nations," *l'or goyim* (גוֹיִם לְאוֹר), meaning that this chosen people has the responsibility of bearing the love and truth of the Creator to the rest of Creation. Throughout history, Israel as a nation was able to preserve the illumination of truth that comes forth from the pages of the Holy Writ, and in particular, the Torah of Moses. Isaiah declares more of this reality, and how both Israel and Israel's Messiah are to be involved in the redemption of the world:

"He says, 'It is too small a thing that You should be My Servant to raise up the tribes of Jacob and to restore the preserved ones of Israel; I will also make You a light of the nations so that My salvation may reach to the end of the earth" (Isaiah 49:6; cf. Luke 2:32).

"Arise, shine; for your light has come, and the glory of the LORD has risen upon you. For behold, darkness will cover the earth and deep darkness the peoples; but the LORD will rise upon you and His glory will appear upon you. Nations will come to your light, and kings to the brightness of your rising" (Isaiah 60:1-3).

The Apostle Peter reiterates this concept centuries later, when he communicates the principles of being a holy nation to the Messianic community, who has been given an understanding of who and what "light" truly is:

"But you are A CHOSEN RACE, a royal PRIESTHOOD, A HOLY NATION, A PEOPLE FOR *God's* OWN POSSESSION, so that you may proclaim the excellencies of Him who has called you out of darkness into His marvelous light" (1 Peter 2:9).[1]

## Light of the World

In pondering the subject of light, I recognize that light or illumination is a concept absolutely foundational to our faith. In fact, when considering the various aspects of light, I

---

[1] Isaiah 42:20; Exodus 19:5-6; Isaiah 43:21.

am reminded of some of Yeshua's most memorable words. In His the Sermon on the Mount, Yeshua—the Light of the World—classifies His followers as also being the "light of the world":

"You are the light of the world. A city set on a hill cannot be hidden; nor does *anyone* light a lamp and put it under a basket, but on the lampstand, and it gives light to all who are in the house. Let your light shine before men in such a way that they may see your good works, and glorify your Father who is in heaven" (Matthew 5:14-15).

Juxtaposed between the Beatitudes[2] and a description about the validity of the Torah,[3] Yeshua reminds His audience that they are indeed *the light*, shining in a world that is darkened by the consequences of sin. In John's Gospel, we see further explanation concerning Yeshua, the Light of the World, and those who testify of Him:

"In Him was life, and the life was the Light of men. The Light shines in the darkness, and the darkness did not comprehend it. There came a man sent from God, whose name was John. He came as a witness, to testify about the Light, so that all might believe through him. He was not the Light, but *he came* to testify about the Light. There was the true Light which, coming into the world, enlightens every man. He was in the world, and the world was made through Him, and the world did not know Him" (John 1:4-10).

Yeshua Himself reiterates this theme about who the Light is in His talk with Nicodemus:

"This is the judgment, that the Light has come into the world, and men loved the darkness rather than the Light, for their deeds were evil. For everyone who does evil hates the Light, and does not come to the Light for fear that his deeds will be exposed. But he who practices the truth comes to the Light, so that his deeds may be manifested as having been wrought in God" (John 3:19-21).

## "Let There Be Light"

As you consider *Bereisheet*, you can focus on a great number of profound subjects that have their roots in these opening chapters of the Bible. The details of the six phases of Creation,[4] and the institution of the *Shabbat* (Sabbath) rest, are recalled.[5] The creation of Adam and Eve and their Fall from grace are articulated.[6] Aspects of the Tree of Knowledge of Good and Evil, as compared to the Tree of Life, can be contemplated.[7] The admonitions to be fruitful and multiply and to take dominion over the created order can be discussed.[8] The particulars of the introduction of sin, and the judgments brought upon Adam, Eve, and the serpent can be diagnosed.[9] The arrival of offspring in Cain and Abel, and the conflict that ensued between these brothers with contrasting sacrificial offerings, can be debated.[10] The birth of Seth and the promised seed that will carry the blessings promised to Adam and

---

[2] Matthew 5:1-12.
[3] Matthew 5:17-19.
[4] Genesis 1:1-2:1.
[5] Genesis 2:2-3.
[6] Genesis 2:7-3:24.
[7] Genesis 2:16-17; 3:1-6, 11-12.
[8] Genesis 1:28.
[9] Genesis 3:14-24.
[10] Genesis 4:1-15.

the generations that follow, could be discussed.[11] Finally, the birth of Noah and God's regret that humanity had devolved into great debauchery could be analyzed.[12]

As important as each one of these things is—in order to even begin to properly analyze these profound foundational subjects related to our faith—**you are required to have the light and illumination of the Holy Spirit.** Without the Spirit, you will certainly be in the dark. The more time you spend in the light of God's Word, the more you will be able to understand the profound aspects of it.

It is beneficial for you to spend a specified period of time in His Word every day to receive the benefits of spiritual illumination. Perhaps this is why our Jewish brethren have developed a system of study that annually takes people through the Torah, to be taught more and more about our Creator, and the light He is dispensing to His people. Perhaps as *we* study the Torah—**especially knowing that Yeshua is the Messiah**—*we* will have our hearts and minds illuminated in such a way that when we hear His voice proclaim, "Let there be light!" it will take on many profound dimensions. *The light of Yeshua dispels the darkness of sin.* Because of the Father's mercy toward us, we can then become a bearer of truth and light to all we encounter!

# Noach נֹחַ
## Noah
## "Walking by Faith"

> **Genesis 6:9-11:32**
> **Isaiah 54:1-55:5 (A); 54:1-10 (S)**

The second Torah portion begins with the words, "These are *the records of* the generations of Noah. Noah was a righteous man, blameless in his time; Noah walked with God" (Genesis 6:9). The first two Torah portions, which initiate the annual Torah cycle, each condense thousands of years of human history into six chapters of Scripture. In *Bereisheet*, the creation of Adam and Eve concludes with the introduction of Noah. *Noach* focuses intently on the life of Noah and his immediate descendants, concluding with the introduction of Abram.

As I read and meditated upon the story of Noah, his life experiences, and his interactions with the Creator God, it became apparent to me that Noah and his example of faith are recorded as an encouragement to each of us, as we deal with our own personal walks of faith and interactions with God. The author of Hebrews writes that we are required to exercise faith, as Noah did, in order to receive the righteousness that will reward our pursuit of God:

"And without faith it is impossible to please *Him*, for he who comes to God must believe that He is and *that* He is a rewarder of those who seek Him. By faith Noah, being warned *by God* about things not yet seen, in reverence prepared an ark for the salvation of his household, by which he condemned the world, and became an heir of the righteousness which is according to faith" (Hebrews 11:6-7).

---

[11] Genesis 4:25; 3:15.
[12] Genesis 5:29-6:8.

This Torah portion, devoted to the life of Noah, has been used throughout the ages as a prime example of how we, as people of faith, should behave in the wicked and perverse generations into which we have been born. No matter where we are on our personal journeys, we should each seek to emulate the walk of faith described in this reading, if we want to know how to please God.

## "God Said"

When you read this portion, you will discover that the Lord looks upon Noah as a righteous man who was blameless or perfect in his time. Our *parashah* begins with the words, "These are *the records of* the generations of Noah. Noah was a righteous man, blameless in his time; Noah walked with God" (Genesis 6:9).

The Hebrew text records that Noah was an *ish tzadiq* (אִישׁ צַדִּיק). Two important Hebrew words are introduced into the Biblical text in the opening verse of *Noach*, which become critical components of the faith system developed in the balance of the Hebrew Scriptures. The before mentioned *tzadiq* (צַדִּיק), often meaning "righteous" or "just," or various other derivatives,[13] and *tamim* (תָּמִים), often meaning "blameless,"[14] are two very important terms. As you encounter these terms in the Scriptures, you find that "righteous(ness)" and "blameless(ness)" are used liberally throughout the Tanakh, often to describe the requirements for proper communion with the Creator. A holy and righteous God imputes these attributes to the people whom He uses to accomplish His purpose:

"Then the LORD said to Noah, 'Enter the ark, you and all your household, for you *alone* I have seen *to be* righteous [*tzadiq*] before Me in this time'" (Genesis 7:1).

As you can read, Noah is apparently the only human in his generation who the Lord considered righteous before Him. What was it about Noah that made him righteous? Is it possible that when he heard the voice of God telling him to construct the ark, that his response of faithful obedience to the command resulted in righteousness? The account says that God commanded Noah, and he simply did what he was supposed to:

"Then God said to Noah, 'The end of all flesh has come before Me; for the earth is filled with violence because of them; and behold, I am about to destroy them with the earth'...Thus Noah did; according to all that God had commanded him, so he did" (Genesis 6:13, 22).

According to the closing verses of the Torah portion *Bereisheet*, as God observed the perversity and wretchedness of Noah's generation, His survey of humanity allowed Him to determine that only one man and his family were worthy to be spared:

"Then the LORD saw that the wickedness of man was great on the earth, and that every intent of the thoughts of his heart was only evil continually. The LORD was sorry that He had made man on the earth, and He was grieved in His heart. The LORD said, 'I will blot out man whom I have created from the face of the land, from man to animals to creeping things and to birds of the sky; for I am sorry that I have made them.' But Noah found favor in the eyes of the LORD" (Genesis 6:5-8).

---

[13] Cf. Harold G. Stigers, "צָדַק," in R. Laird Harris, Gleason L. Archer, Jr., and Bruce K. Waltke, eds., *Theological Wordbook of the Old Testament*, 2 vols. (Chicago: Moody Press, 1980), 2:725-755.

[14] Cf. William L. Holladay, ed., *A Concise Hebrew and Aramaic Lexicon of the Old Testament* (Leiden, the Netherlands: Brill, 1988), 391.

Apparently, Noah found favor in the eyes of the Lord. He was considered righteous and blameless because he "walked" with Him. We were introduced to the concept of "walking with God" last week in *Bereisheet* when we read about God taking Enoch:

"Then Enoch walked with God three hundred years after he became the father of Methuselah, and he had *other* sons and daughters. So all the days of Enoch were three hundred and sixty-five years. Enoch walked with God; and he was not, for God took him" (Genesis 5:22-24).

The author of Hebrews gives us more insight into why God "took" Enoch, when Enoch is also included in the chapter often called "the Hall of Faith":

"By faith Enoch was taken up so that he would not see death; AND HE WAS NOT FOUND BECAUSE GOD TOOK HIM UP; for he obtained the witness that before his being taken up he was pleasing to God" (Hebrews 11:5).

While this statement asks more questions than it answers, suffice it to say it was only because Enoch was living properly—that he was taken up by God. But as we are contemplating the life of Noah this week, we are reminded of the interconnectivity of walking by faith and living in a righteous and blameless manner. We see numerous examples in the Apostolic Scriptures (New Testament) that walking by faith is definitely something that pleases our Heavenly Father. As stated earlier, "without faith it is impossible to please God" (Hebrews 11:6, NIV).

## Pleasing Him

While digging into the subjects of walking by faith, and being righteous and blameless before the Holy One, images of different saints of old come to mind. I am reminded of Joseph, Daniel, Job, and countless others who have been listed as faithful in their respective walks of faith—many of whom are listed in Hebrews 11, but others who are seen throughout the whole of the Biblical narrative. Throughout the ages there have been others who have exhibited a steadfast walk of faith, and have been righteous and blameless, similar to Noah. There is a specific scene I think of in the Gospels, where the Lord used some people who are described just like Noah, for His redemptive purposes. One such couple is Zacharias and Elizabeth, the parents of John the Immerser:

"In the days of Herod, king of Judea, there was a priest named Zacharias, of the division of Abijah; and he had a wife from the daughters of Aaron, and her name was Elizabeth. They were both righteous in the sight of God, walking blamelessly in all the commandments and requirements of the Lord" (Luke 1:5-6).

Zacharias and Elizabeth were a couple who feared the Lord and "were upright in the sight of God, observing all the Lord's commandments and regulations blamelessly" (NIV). As a result of their Torah obedient walk, the Lord chose them to conceive and bear a child whose unique prophetic ministry would immediately precede the ministry of the Messiah.

The birth of John the Baptist, and the subsequent description of the announcement of Yeshua's birth to Joseph and Mary, have become a critical part of our faith. After all, the progressive revelation that has come forth since the days of Noah has further specified the requirements for communion with the Creator God. Believing in the atoning work of Yeshua at Golgotha (Calvary) is now necessary in the post-resurrection era in which we live. Yeshua Himself said, "I am the way, and the truth, and the life; no one comes to the Father but through Me" (John 14:6).

## Walk by Faith

In spite of the fact that we did not live multiple millennia ago during the time of Noah, one thing is certain: **the necessity to walk by faith, with the revelation that you have received, has never changed.** Enoch walked in the knowledge that he had, and it pleased the Creator. In a like manner, Noah walked in righteousness blamelessly, and because of his obedience to God, he and his immediate family were preserved from the judgment of the Flood. Millennia later, Zacharias and Elizabeth walked by faith in obedience to God's Torah, and they were used to produce the one who would be used to point others to the Messiah. Zecharias, moved by the Holy Spirit, declared at John the Immerser's circumcision,

"And you, child, will be called the prophet of the Most High; for you will go on BEFORE THE LORD TO PREPARE HIS WAYS; to give to His people *the* knowledge of salvation by the forgiveness of their sins, because of the tender mercy of our God, with which the Sunrise from on high will visit us, TO SHINE UPON THOSE WHO SIT IN DARKNESS AND THE SHADOW OF DEATH, to guide our feet into the way of peace" (Luke 1:76-79; cf. Malachi 3:1; Isaiah 9:2; 59:8).

Zacharias and Elizabeth both knew by revelation, that the coming Child, Yeshua—the yet to be born Son of Joseph and Mary—was going to be a special gift. He would have the power to bring salvation and forgiveness to those who walk in darkness.

In the post-resurrection era, further teaching has come forth from the Apostolic Writings which continue to proclaim the need to walk by faith. The Apostle Paul wrote the Corinthians the following admonition, so that they would more fully understand the meaning of "walking by faith":

"Now He who prepared us for this very purpose is God, who gave to us the Spirit as a pledge. Therefore, being always of good courage, and knowing that while we are at home in the body we are absent from the Lord—for we walk by faith, not by sight—we are of good courage, I say, and prefer rather to be absent from the body and to be at home with the Lord. Therefore we also have as our ambition, whether at home or absent, to be pleasing to Him. For we must all appear before the judgment seat of Messiah, so that each one may be recompensed for his deeds in the body, according to what he has done, whether good or bad. Therefore, knowing the fear of the Lord, we persuade men, but we are made manifest to God; and I hope that we are made manifest also in your consciences. We are not again commending ourselves to you but *are* giving you an occasion to be proud of us, so that you will have *an answer* for those who take pride in appearance and not in heart. For if we are beside ourselves, it is for God; if we are of sound mind, it is for you. For the love of Messiah controls us, having concluded this, that one died for all, therefore all died; and He died for all, so that they who live might no longer live for themselves, but for Him who died and rose again on their behalf" (2 Corinthians 5:5-15).

Here, Paul clarifies the admonition to "walk by faith, not by sight," to the Corinthians. Paul tells them that his ambition, whether in the body or absent from the Lord, is to be "pleasing to Him." It is not too dissimilar from what Enoch experienced in his life. But the big difference that makes us as post-resurrection saints different from those who preceded the arrival of the Messiah—is the fact that we now have the specific knowledge of how Yeshua died for all. **If we believe this, we can be sure to have redemption.**

Possessing faith also requires that we recognize that those who do not believe will experience punishment. The additional requirement to avoid the future judgment is absolutely critical for the Body of Messiah. As the Apostle Peter puts it, faith in the finished work of the Messiah is without substitute. In fact, he says that it was the good news to which angels long to look, only intensifying its significance:

"In this you greatly rejoice, even though now for a little while, if necessary, you have been distressed by various trials, so that the proof of your faith, *being* more precious than gold which is perishable, even though tested by fire, may be found to result in praise and glory and honor at the revelation of Yeshua the Messiah; and though you have not seen Him, you love Him, and though you do not see Him now, but believe in Him, you greatly rejoice with joy inexpressible and full of glory, obtaining as the outcome of your faith the salvation of your souls. As to this salvation, the prophets who prophesied of the grace that *would come* to you made careful searches and inquiries, seeking to know what person or time the Spirit of Messiah within them was indicating as He predicted the sufferings of Messiah and the glories to follow. It was revealed to them that they were not serving themselves, but you, in these things which now have been announced to you through those who preached the gospel to you by the Holy Spirit sent from heaven—things into which angels long to look" (1 Peter 1:6-12).

## Relevant Faith

Today, the true faith is under considerable attack from mockers who have been predicted since the days of Peter. Some in the Messianic community challenge the veracity of the Apostolic Scriptures because they were written in Greek, and not Hebrew.[15] In doing so, there has been a subtle tendency to deny or pervert the Spirit-inspired revelation that has come forth from these documents. As a sad consequence, in recent years, various people who had claimed to know the Messiah of Israel have lost their sure moorings in the Rock of Salvation. They have been cleverly convinced that a form of "works righteousness" is the only way they can walk, as found in their own human method of "Torah observance." This kind of life diminishes or discounts the atoning work of our Messiah Yeshua, as opposed to a proper obedience coming forth as we learn to walk by faith *and emulate Him.*

As each one of us seeks to "walk by faith," let us all remember that in order to please our Heavenly Father, we must recognize and believe in the work His Son performed for us at Golgotha (Calvary). We must not allow ourselves to be tempted by mockers, who will scorn and ridicule not only the life-changing message of the gospel—but most especially the declaration of the final judgment required of human beings. Peter states this predicament most clearly, relying upon the account of the Flood:

"Know this first of all, that in the last days mockers will come with *their* mocking, following after their own lusts, and saying, 'Where is the promise of His coming? For *ever* since the fathers fell asleep, all continues just as it was from the beginning of creation.' For when they maintain this, it escapes their notice that by the word of God *the* heavens existed long ago and *the* earth was formed out of water and by water, through which the world at that time was destroyed, being flooded with water. But by His word the present heavens and earth are being reserved for fire, kept for the day of judgment and destruction of ungodly men" (2 Peter 3:3-7).

Today, each one of us must "walk by faith" in the righteousness and blamelessness that has been provided for us in the work of the Messiah. May this profound truth keep us all

---

[15] Consult the publication *Scripture Under Scrutiny: Was the New Testament Really Written in Hebrew?* by TNN Press, for a detailed examination of this subject.

from the definite judgment to come! May all come to repentance, so that no one need experience such punishment!

# Lekh-Lekha לֶךְ־לְךָ
## Get yourself out
## "Trials, Faith, and Blessings"

> Genesis 12:1-17:27
> Isaiah 40:27-41:16

Our Torah portion for this week, *Lekh-Lekha*, begins with some very important words, which will guide a great deal of the Biblical story and narrative from this point onward:

"Now the LORD said to Abram, 'Go forth from your country, and from your relatives and from your father's house, to the land which I will show you; and I will make you a great nation, and I will bless you, and make your name great; and so you shall be a blessing; and I will bless those who bless you, and the one who curses you I will curse. And in you all the families of the earth will be blessed'" (Genesis 12:1-3).[16]

After the first two Torah readings have jumped through multiple millennia of human history, *Lekh-Lekha* begins to focus on Abraham, the father of faith (Romans 4:12-16). In this reading, we are told that God has chosen one man and his descendants to be either a blessing or a curse to the rest of humanity. We read that Abram experienced trials, exercised faith, and received the blessings of faithful obedience. His life, in many ways, exemplified a standard of how each of us should approach our loving Creator. We ultimately discover how in Abraham, "all the families of the earth shall bless themselves by you" (NJPS).

As you will recall, we were briefly introduced to Abram as last week's Torah portion, *Noach*, concluded. Interestingly, as you read about Abram's immediate family, you might conclude that it was actually his father Terah who was called out of Ur:

"Terah took Abram his son, and Lot the son of Haran, his grandson, and Sarai his daughter-in-law, his son Abram's wife; and they went out together from Ur of the Chaldeans in order to enter the land of Canaan; and they went as far as Haran, and settled there" (Genesis 11:31).

Abram, his wife Sarai, and his nephew Lot, were supposed to go to the Land of Canaan. But as the text indicates, they went as far as Haran, which was the crossroads in the upper Euphrates east of Assyria, and part of the trade route that connected Egypt with those in the Tigris and Euphrates River valleys. They all settled there until the death of Terah. In a cursory reading of these statements, it appears that Terah "took"[17] Abram and his other relatives. However, the Scriptures give us three specific testimonies of how the call to come out, from among the people and circumstances of Ur, was definitely made to Abram.

First, we read Nehemiah's testimony, summarizing how God chose Abram, bringing him out of Ur, and later renamed him Abraham:

---

[16] Cf. Galatians 3:8.
[17] Heb. *laqach* (לָקַח), "**take, lay hold of, seize**" (*CHALOT*, 178).

"You are the LORD God, who chose Abram and brought him out from Ur of the Chaldees, and gave him the name Abraham. You found his heart faithful before You, And made a covenant with him to give *him* the land of the Canaanite, of the Hittite and the Amorite, of the Perizzite, the Jebusite and the Girgashite—to give *it* to his descendants. And You have fulfilled Your promise, for You are righteous" (Nehemiah 9:7-8).

Second, the testimony of Stephen includes more specific information regarding Abraham's departure from Ur:

"And he said, 'Hear me, brethren and fathers! The God of glory appeared to our father Abraham when he was in Mesopotamia, before he lived in Haran, and said to him, "LEAVE YOUR COUNTRY AND YOUR RELATIVES, AND COME INTO THE LAND THAT I WILL SHOW YOU" [Genesis 12:1]. Then he left the land of the Chaldeans and settled in Haran. From there, after his father died, *God* had him move to this country in which you are now living. But He gave him no inheritance in it, not even a foot of ground, and *yet*, even when he had no child, He promised that HE WOULD GIVE IT TO HIM AS A POSSESSION, AND TO HIS DESCENDANTS AFTER HIM' [Genesis 12:7; 13:15; 15:18; 17:8]" (Acts 7:2-5).

Here, the martyr Stephen says that Abraham himself had the "God of glory" appear to him when he was in Mesopotamia, "before" he lived in Haran. The command that he was to "Depart from your land and from your kindred and go into the land which I will show you" (RSV), is spoken to Abraham when he was living in Ur.

Third, the author of Hebrews completes our Scriptural understanding of this great "father of our faith," as it relates to the mission that God gave to Abraham:

"By faith Abraham, when he was called, obeyed by going out to a place which he was to receive for an inheritance; and he went out, not knowing where he was going. By faith he lived as an alien in the land of promise, as in a foreign *land*, dwelling in tents with Isaac and Jacob, fellow heirs of the same promise; for he was looking for the city which has foundations, whose architect and builder is God" (Hebrews 11:8-10).

With this confirming evidence, we discover that the Holy One was most concerned about His choice of Abram/Abraham to be the recipient of His blessings. The Lord knew that this man would exhibit a heart of faith and the proper obedience to Him that was required. As the Prophet Isaiah points out in our complimentary Haftarah reading, He has called for men and women to be used by Him from the very beginning:

"Who has performed and accomplished *it*, calling forth the generations from the beginning? 'I, the LORD, am the first, and with the last. I am He'" (Isaiah 41:4).

As you read this week's narrative, it begins with Abram hearing a command from the Most High, which appears to be a repeat of the first appearance that occurred while the family lived in Ur. This time, Abram heard the voice of El Shaddai and obeyed, after the death of Terah. After reading Stephen's statement in Acts 7:4, it appears that Abram did not continue on his journey into Canaan until after his father's death:

"Now the LORD said to Abram, 'Go forth from your country, and from your relatives and from your father's house, to the land which I will show you'" (Genesis 12:1).

Abram hears the command to "Get thee out" (KJV) or "go forth." The Hebrew is *lekh-lekha* (לֶךְ־לְךָ), the title of this Torah portion. This is not only a command for Abraham to get out of the place where he lived, but also to remove himself from his countrymen and his own relatives. Here in this *parashah*, the trusting Patriarch begins his walk of faith. As we will learn, Abram soon realizes that representing the One True God among people is filled with trials. But because he listened, believed, and obeyed, his obedience to this God is realized by blessings he will later experience in his lifetime.

## Faith Trials

As I have pondered the opening chapters regarding the life of Abraham, I am struck by the fact that he, just like the rest of his "faith-filled" descendants, was not spared the trials of life that we all must endure. *Perhaps there is a direct connection between faith and trials?* After thinking about it, it dawns on me that perhaps *there really is* a direct correlation between faith, trials, and the blessings of responding to life's trials by faithful obedience to our Father. After all, the walk of faith we are transversing is certainly beset with personal and corporate trials. Is it possible that the Lord gives us trials so that **we can exercise our faith in order to receive more of His blessings?**

These concepts are so elementary, yet so profound to our faith in practice. After all, are not tests, trials, and even tribulations, designed by the Lord to see if we are living and walking by faith? **And does not God respond by blessing us, when we react to trials by faithfully following His instructions?** Certainly, when one considers the inevitability of trials, many Scriptures come to mind. One of the most quoted of them brings a smile to my face:

"Consider it all joy, my brethren, when you encounter various trials, knowing that the testing of your faith produces endurance. And let endurance have *its* perfect result, so that you may be perfect and complete, lacking in nothing" (James 1:2-4).

James the Just encourages his audience in the midst of the trials that they are facing. He states that responding with faith will produce an endurance that will have its perfect result in the saints. **Talk about a blessing! Can you imagine the blessing of lacking in nothing?** This is not a bad reward for joyfully considering the trials of life, and that God often uniquely uses them for each person, as he or she is being perfected in faith.

The Apostle Peter had a similar approach to handling trials:

"In this you greatly rejoice, even though now for a little while, if necessary, you have been distressed by various trials, so that the proof of your faith, *being* more precious than gold which is perishable, even though tested by fire, may be found to result in praise and glory and honor at the revelation of Yeshua the Messiah; and though you have not seen Him, you love Him, and though you do not see Him now, but believe in Him, you greatly rejoice with joy inexpressible and full of glory, obtaining as the outcome of your faith the salvation of your souls" (1 Peter 1:6-9).

Peter understood that the trials of life should be handled joyfully by Believers, because we have faith in Yeshua as the Messiah. The ultimate blessing of this is that it will result in the consummation of our salvation. Hopefully, you can readily see that there is a direct correlation between the trials you encounter, how you respond by faith, and the blessings associated with proper faith based responses.

As I consider this spiritual axiom, I think about the magnitude, severity, and frequency of trials. **Is it possible that the greater the trials we encounter, and the more faithful the response we demonstrate, the greater the blessings we will receive?** I hope this serves as encouragement for you to continue through whatever difficulties you may be facing.

Certainly, the trials endured by Abraham as narrated in the Torah, and his faithful responses, were definitely rewarded with huge blessings. Is it possible to detect some parallels in the balance of Scripture that might confirm this observation?

The entire Bible is replete with testimonies about how people have been challenged with various trials, and have responded by faith. You can go to Hebrews 11 and read about just some of the champions of faith who were blessed in a variety of ways as a result of responding to trials, tests, and tribulation. But even the author of Hebrews reminds us that there is a "cloud of witnesses" that are too numerous to try to humanly list:

"And what more shall I say? For time will fail me if I tell of Gideon, Barak, Samson, Jephthah, of David and Samuel and the prophets, who by faith conquered kingdoms, performed *acts of* righteousness, obtained promises, shut the mouths of lions, quenched the power of fire, escaped the edge of the sword, from weakness were made strong, became mighty in war, put foreign armies to flight. Women received *back* their dead by resurrection; and others were tortured, not accepting their release, so that they might obtain a better resurrection; and others experienced mockings and scourgings, yes, also chains and imprisonment. They were stoned, they were sawn in two, they were tempted, they were put to death with the sword; they went about in sheepskins, in goatskins, being destitute, afflicted, ill-treated (*men* of whom the world was not worthy), wandering in deserts and mountains and caves and holes in the ground. And all these, having gained approval through their faith, did not receive what was promised, because God had provided something better for us, so that apart from us they would not be made perfect" (Hebrews 11:32-40).

**The Biblical axiom of experiencing trials, responding in faith, and receiving the blessings of the Almighty is foundational in both Judaism and Christianity.** As I reflect on this truth, I am also reminded of the trials and persecutions that the Apostle Paul endured during his walk of faith. He writes the Corinthians, encouraging them to endure some trials, listing some of the afflictions that he had endured in his ministry for the gospel:

"Since many boast according to the flesh, I will boast also. For you, being *so* wise, tolerate the foolish gladly. For you tolerate it if anyone enslaves you, anyone devours you, anyone takes advantage of you, anyone exalts himself, anyone hits you in the face. To *my* shame I *must* say that we have been weak *by comparison*. But in whatever respect anyone *else* is bold—I speak in foolishness—I am just as bold myself. Are they Hebrews? So am I. Are they Israelites? So am I. Are they descendants of Abraham? So am I. Are they servants of Messiah?—I speak as if insane—I more so; in far more labors, in far more imprisonments, beaten times without number, often in danger of death. Five times I received from the Jews thirty-nine *lashes*. Three times I was beaten with rods, once I was stoned, three times I was shipwrecked, a night and a day I have spent in the deep. *I have been* on frequent journeys, in dangers from rivers, dangers from robbers, dangers from *my* countrymen, dangers from the Gentiles, dangers in the city, dangers in the wilderness, dangers on the sea, dangers among false brethren; *I have been* in labor and hardship, through many sleepless nights, in hunger and thirst, often without food, in cold and exposure. Apart from *such* external things, there is the daily pressure on me *of* concern for all the churches. Who is weak without my being weak? Who is led into sin without my intense concern? If I have to boast, I will boast of what pertains to my weakness. The God and Father of the Lord Yeshua, He who is blessed forever, knows that I am not lying. In Damascus the ethnarch under Aretas the king was guarding the city of the Damascenes in order to seize me, and I was let down in a basket through a window in the wall, and *so* escaped his hands" (2 Corinthians 11:18-33).

As I think about all of these trials, and Paul's faithful response to his accusers and those who personally abused him, I am again reminded of the blessings that he has received. The Apostle Paul, as a faithful servant of the Most High, will be receiving his rewards for eternity for how his writings have been used by the Ruach HaKodesh (Holy Spirit) to bring untold millions to a saving knowledge of the Messiah Yeshua! Once again, we see how a correlation between trials, faith, and blessings are all interrelated.

## Personal Application

While thinking through our Torah portion this week, and these verses I have referred to, another viable form of trial kept coming to my mind. This was the inevitability of the persecution that comes with the walk of faith that has been exercised by people like Abraham, and many other faithful followers of God throughout the ages. We know from Scripture that God's people have been persecuted throughout the ages, and many have remained steadfast to Him resisting temptation.

But now that the revelation of His Son and His completed work on the cross have been accomplished, **belief and proclamation of the gospel is guaranteed to bring persecution and trials.** After all, if you are going to walk by faith in the knowledge of Yeshua as the Savior of the world, **you will be persecuted** according to the very words of the Messiah Himself:

"Blessed are those who have been persecuted for the sake of righteousness, for theirs is the kingdom of heaven. Blessed are you when *people* insult you and persecute you, and falsely say all kinds of evil against you because of Me. Rejoice and be glad, for your reward in heaven is great; for in the same way they persecuted the prophets who were before you" (Matthew 5:10-12).

Yeshua encourages His followers to "Be glad and rejoice, because your reward is great in heaven" (HCSB). *So have you been enduring any trials lately?* Do you consider them to be great trials of the magnitude experienced by Paul, Peter, James, or any of the other Apostles? How about trials that rival the persecution experienced by the Prophets of old? Have you been stoned, filleted with a sword, or sawn in two?

For the most part, many of us have to endure an occasional mocking or putdown, but life-threatening events are few and far between for most (Western) Believers. And yet, we all do experience some tests and trials during our Earthly lives. **Is it possible that those trials are specifically designed by our Creator to give each of us an opportunity to exercise our faith?**

When the trials or tests come, do we exercise our faith by turning to the Scriptures to find the prescriptions for the trials? Do we follow God's Word, as opposed to the inclinations of our flesh? If we do, then according to the patterns established by Abraham, we will receive the blessings of faithful obedience. I think we definitely ought to look at these tests and trials as an opportunity to exercise our faith. We should examine just how well we respond, to what we might perceive as great tests or trials, gauging them against what we read in the Scriptures.

Do we follow God's instructions that are given to us in His Word? If the answer is yes, then His blessings should flow. And do you know what else? *Rejoicing will follow in due course.* When you realize that you have been chosen to endure certain trials and tests, and that by your faith you choose to follow the admonitions of His Word—you truly have something to rejoice about!

We should all be rejoicing that our faith results in the salvation of our souls. Salvation is the ultimate blessing that follows the walk of faith originally established by Abraham. May we all be found thankful for the trials, and rejoice with the blessings of the faithful!

# *V'yeira* וַיֵּרָא
## He appeared
## "A Faith that Works"

> Genesis 18:1-22:24
> 2 Kings 4:1-37 (A); 4:1-23 (S)

Some extremely important words are witnessed in our Torah reading for this week:

"Then the angel of the LORD called to Abraham a second time from heaven, and said, 'By Myself I have sworn, declares the LORD, because you have done this thing and have not withheld your son, your only son, indeed I will greatly bless you, and I will greatly multiply your seed as the stars of the heavens and as the sand which is on the seashore; and your seed shall possess the gate of their enemies. In your seed all the nations of the earth shall be blessed, because you have obeyed My voice" (Genesis 22:15-18).

The Torah portion *V'yeira* continues to explain some of the challenges that have been recorded about the life of faith exhibited by Abraham, the father of faith. The Jewish Sages have determined that during his lifetime, Abraham was given ten extremely difficult tests (m.*Avot* 5:3).[18] But no test could ever be more difficult than the one which brings this Torah reading to a close. Here we discover that Abraham has been commanded by God to actually offer up his son as a sacrifice:

"Now it came about after these things, that God tested Abraham, and said to him, 'Abraham!' And he said, 'Here I am.' He said, 'Take now your son, your only son, whom you love, Isaac, and go to the land of Moriah, and offer him there as a burnt offering on one of the mountains of which I will tell you'" (Genesis 22:1-2).

No parent could ever imagine a greater test than being commanded to offer up his or her own child—or for that matter, any child—as a burnt offering. Just the thought of human sacrifice is abhorrent for many of us to consider! And yet, we are told in this *parashah* that Abraham reacted to this command with almost immediate compliance. The very next day, early in the morning, Abraham got up and saddled his donkey. With his son Isaac in tow, he departed for the place where God had commanded him to make his offering:

"He said, 'Take now your son, your only son, whom you love, Isaac, and go to the land of Moriah, and offer him there as a burnt offering on one of the mountains of which I will tell you.' So Abraham rose early in the morning and saddled his donkey, and took two of his young men with him and Isaac his son; and he split wood for the burnt offering, and arose and went to the place of which God had told him" (Genesis 22:2-3).

As you read this account, you have to ask yourself what it was about Abraham that would have him respond so positively to God's request. After all, was not Isaac the promised child of his old age (Genesis 17:19)? Was not Isaac the child considered to be a part of the promised seed, through whom all of the nations would be blessed (cf. Genesis 22:17)?

---

[18] Cf. Nosson Scherman, ed., et al., *The ArtScroll Chumash, Stone Edition*, 5th ed. (Brooklyn: Mesorah Publications, 2000), pp 100-101.

By the time of the binding, often referred to in Jewish circles as the *aqedah* (עֲקֵדָה),[19] Abraham had already been through the great trials of his life. His first son, Ishmael, the premature product of his fleshly relations with the Egyptian handmaiden Hagar,[20] had already been sent away from the family compound. Even though Abraham was somewhat concerned about the harsh treatment of his son, he followed the demand from Sarah to banish Hagar and Ishmael, especially when God reiterated the request with further details:

"The matter distressed Abraham greatly because of his son. But God said to Abraham, 'Do not be distressed because of the lad and your maid; whatever Sarah tells you, listen to her, for through Isaac your descendants shall be named. And of the son of the maid I will make a nation also, because he is your descendant.' So Abraham rose early in the morning and took bread and a skin of water and gave *them* to Hagar, putting *them* on her shoulder, and *gave her* the boy, and sent her away. And she departed and wandered about in the wilderness of Beersheba" (Genesis 21:11-14).

A number of years later, when the command ushers forth from the Lord to take his only remaining son, Isaac, and offer him up as a burnt offering (Heb. *olah*, עֹלָה), you can imagine how perplexed Abraham could have been. And yet, Abraham complied without hesitation.

What had happened over the years to make Abraham such a compliant and obedient follower of the Living God? I would suggest that it is only through the blessing of progressive revelation, that we discover some insight into why Abraham was willing to faithfully obey without even questioning the wisdom of the Almighty. The author of Hebrews amplifies our understanding of Abraham's motives when the request came forth:

"By faith Abraham, when he was tested, offered up Isaac, and he who had received the promises was offering up his only begotten *son*; *it was he* to whom it was said, 'IN ISAAC YOUR DESCENDANTS SHALL BE CALLED.' He considered that God is able to raise *people* even from the dead, from which he also received him back as a type" (Hebrews 11:17-19; cf. Genesis 21:12).

Here it is asserted that Abraham believed how God was able to raise people from the dead, in order for Him to accomplish His promise to him. We need to remember that, by the time Abraham was asked to offer up Isaac, God had already told him that through him all of the nations of the world would be blessed. Isaac was the son born of promise:

"But God said, 'No, but Sarah your wife will bear you a son, and you shall call his name Isaac; and I will establish My covenant with him for an everlasting covenant for his descendants after him'" (Genesis 17:19).

By the time of the request to offer up Isaac, Abraham had seen the Holy One perform His promises without any deviation. Abraham obeyed the command to circumcise himself and his household (Genesis 17). Abraham had been contacted by messengers of God who had forewarned him about the judgment that was coming to Sodom and Gomorrah. He had debated with them in order to try and save any righteous (Genesis 18:20-33), and had been instrumental in helping his nephew Lot avoid the devastation of fire and brimstone (Genesis 19:1-29).

As the author of Hebrews again clarifies, Abraham had for many years, throughout his tests, been convinced that the Creator in whom he placed his faith could not possibly lie:

---

[19] Cf. Marcus Jastrow, *Dictionary of the Targumim, Talmud Bavli, Talmud Yerushalmi, and Midrashic Literature* (New York: Judaica Treasury, 2004), 1105.

[20] Genesis 16.

"For when God made the promise to Abraham, since He could swear by no one greater, He swore by Himself, saying, 'I WILL SURELY BLESS YOU AND I WILL SURELY MULTIPLY YOU.' And so, having patiently waited, he obtained the promise. For men swear by one greater *than themselves*, and with them an oath *given* as confirmation is an end of every dispute. In the same way God, desiring even more to show to the heirs of the promise the unchangeableness of His purpose, interposed with an oath, so that by two unchangeable things in which it is impossible for God to lie, we who have taken refuge would have strong encouragement to take hold of the hope set before us" (Hebrews 6:13-18; cf. Genesis 22:17).

We are reminded in these verses, from our *parashah* this week, how God could swear by no greater power than Himself:

"Then the angel of the LORD called to Abraham a second time from heaven, and said, 'By Myself I have sworn, declares the LORD, because you have done this thing and have not withheld your son, your only son, indeed I will greatly bless you, and I will greatly multiply your seed as the stars of the heavens and as the sand which is on the seashore; and your seed shall possess the gate of their enemies. In your seed all the nations of the earth shall be blessed, because you have obeyed My voice'" (Genesis 22:16-18).

This should remind us of the event years earlier when God made a unilateral covenant with Abram, before Ishmael was born, and promised Abram the land of Canaan for his descendents. At that time, all Abram could do was offer up the animals for sacrifice. Because Abram was a mere mortal, God Himself executed the covenant, in the image of a smoking fire pot and a flaming torch, by Him alone passing between the animal parts:

"Then in the fourth generation they will return here, for the iniquity of the Amorite is not yet complete. It came about when the sun had set, that it was very dark, and behold, *there appeared* a smoking oven and a flaming torch which passed between these pieces. On that day the LORD made a covenant with Abram, saying, 'To your descendants I have given this land, from the river of Egypt as far as the great river, the river Euphrates: the Kenite and the Kenizzite and the Kadmonite and the Hittite and the Perizzite and the Rephaim and the Amorite and the Canaanite and the Girgashite and the Jebusite" (Genesis 15:16-21).

Apparently, Abram/Abraham had so many personal encounters with the Lord that he had witnessed, he instinctively knew that He was entirely capable of honoring His promises. Abraham was absolutely convinced that the incredible test to offer up Isaac was another opportunity to exercise his faith in the Creator. After all the previous years of testing, Abraham was able to be an example to all people who would come after him, emulating him by his obedient works.

James the Just, attempting to encourage a First Century audience about the relationship between faith and works, uses the instance of Abraham's offering up of Isaac as a prime example of how various works reflect true faith:

"Even so faith, if it has no works, is dead, *being* by itself. But someone may *well* say, 'You have faith and I have works; show me your faith without the works, and I will show you my faith by my works.' You believe that God is one. You do well; the demons also believe, and shudder. But are you willing to recognize, you foolish fellow, that faith without works is useless? Was not Abraham our father justified by works when he offered up Isaac his son on the altar? You see that faith was working with his works, and as a result of the works, faith was perfected; and the Scripture was fulfilled which says, 'AND ABRAHAM BELIEVED GOD, AND IT WAS RECKONED TO HIM AS RIGHTEOUSNESS,' and he was called the friend of God" (James 2:17-23; cf. Genesis 15:6).

James had already been witnessing how different people in his generation were exercising their purported faith. Apparently, some were claiming a belief in Yeshua without exercising any appropriate works. He reminded them that even the demons believe that God is one, so belief in God alone is not sufficient. He said a faith without works **is really not evidence** of a faith that reckons one righteousness in covenant relationship with God, and ultimately saves one from judgment. As he concludes his exhortation, he makes a direct connection between faith and works:

"You see that a man is justified by works and not by faith alone. In the same way, was not Rahab the harlot also justified by works when she received the messengers and sent them out by another way? For just as the body without *the* spirit is dead, so also faith without works is dead" (James 2:24-26).

The ultimate summation is very concise: **faith without works is dead.** Spiritual giants like Rahab, and the others listed in Hebrews 11, have had the faith that brings life. But sadly, many throughout history have declared a faith that is was not attended by appropriate works. Such a "faith" without works is as dead as a body without spirit.

As we reflect on the faithful works of Abraham this week, we might ask ourselves if we indeed have *a faith that works.* Are we obeying the words of the Lord which we have received by faith? None of us will ever be asked to offer up one of our children as a burnt offering. But on the other hand, have we not all been asked to offer ourselves up as a living sacrifice? The Apostle Paul wrote the Romans,

"Therefore I urge you, brethren, by the mercies of God, to present your bodies a living and holy sacrifice, acceptable to God, *which is* your spiritual service of worship. And do not be conformed to this world, but be transformed by the renewing of your mind, so that you may prove what the will of God is, that which is good and acceptable and perfect" (Romans 12:1-2).

When we read these words, do we understand what Paul is urging his readers? Is he not saying that we should offer ourselves up on the altar as a living and holy sacrifice that will be acceptable to God? Would not such an offering be our spiritual service of worship, accomplishing God's Kingdom work here on Earth? *This certainly sounds like an opportunity to work as unto the Lord.* After all, Paul further states that we should not be allowing ourselves to be conformed to this world, but rather, allow our minds to be transformed by the perfect will of God! A mind empowered by God is able to fulfill His Divine tasks.

If you think about it, if we can be doing this, then our faithful works will be clearly evident—not only in our own hearts, but perhaps also in those with whom we interact *and impact* every day. Perhaps then, at the end of your life, you also could be considered a **friend of God** just like Abraham (James 2:23), all because you exercised your faith through works. This is certainly not a bad result of following in the footsteps of Abraham, who definitely had a faith that worked! He did things that are surely worthy of our emulation.

## *Chayei Sarah* חַיֵּי שָׂרָה
Sarah's life
"Life and Death Matters"

> Genesis 23:1-25:18
> 1 Kings 1:1-31

This week, we begin our Torah reading with some very perplexing verses, "Now Sarah lived one hundred and twenty-seven years; *these were* the years of the life of Sarah. Sarah died in Kiriath-arba (that is, Hebron) in the land of Canaan; and Abraham went in to mourn for Sarah and to weep for her. Then Abraham rose from before his dead..." (Genesis 23:1-3a).

When you begin to read the Torah portion *Chayei Sarah*, you are immediately struck with the oddity that although this text is named the "life of Sarah," it is not a summation of the life that Sarah lived, but is instead a record of the post-mortem activities of Abraham and his entourage. Little mention is actually made of Sarah's life, but what follows of her life is a testament to the relationship that existed between the principal Patriarch and Matriarch of our faith. Abraham's obvious grief is described along with his determination to bury her in the Promised Land.[21] Once Sarah is laid to rest, the focus turns to securing an appropriate wife for Isaac, the son of promise who was born to Abraham and Sarah in their waning years. The reading concludes with additional information about Abraham's remarriage and his final 38 years prior to his death at the age of 175.[22]

While contemplating these passages about our spiritual forbearers, a number of thoughts came to my mind. After all, it was a sovereign act of the Creator to choose Abraham and Sarah to be the couple from which the nation of Israel would be birthed. What was it about their lives that are so instructional for us today? What can we learn from this *parashah* that we can impart to our children and to other young people, so that they will follow in the faithfulness of Abraham and Sarah? In considering these questions, we will discover that when reminiscing about future deaths, we are reminded that **how we choose to live our life really does matter.**

### One Flesh

Most of us recall that it was Abram who was called out of Ur to sojourn in the Land of Canaan (Genesis 12:1). But do we remember that at the time of his calling, he was *already married* to Sarai and that she too was a part of that same calling?

"Abram and Nahor took wives for themselves. The name of Abram's wife was Sarai; and the name of Nahor's wife was Milcah, the daughter of Haran, the father of Milcah and Iscah. Sarai was barren; she had no child. Terah took Abram his son, and Lot the son of Haran, his grandson, and Sarai his daughter-in-law, his son Abram's wife; and they went out together from Ur of the Chaldeans in order to enter the land of Canaan; and they went as far as Haran, and settled there" (Genesis 11:29-31).

---

[21] Genesis 23.
[22] Genesis 25:1-11.

It may seem insignificant to consider that Abram was already married to Sarai at the time of his calling by God, but the fact remains that he was. It is also mentioned that at the time of their departure from Ur, it was already common knowledge that Sarai was barren. She was not producing any offspring or heirs for Abram, but when the time came to depart for Haran, she was among the group that traveled north up the Euphrates River. Often, as was customary in ancient cultures, barren women were set aside or abandoned if they were not producing heirs. But Abram and Sarai appear to have had a relationship that transcended the societal pressures imposed by the lack of progeny. There was something very essential about their relationship that prompted the Creator to chose them to be the first Hebrews to "cross over" the river from the old country (Genesis 14:13).

Millennia later, we can read the oracles of the Prophet Isaiah, as he describes not only the call given to Abram, but also the oneness that existed between the two progenitors of our faith:

"Listen to me, you who pursue righteousness, who seek the LORD: Look to the rock from which you were hewn and to the quarry from which you were dug. Look to Abraham your father and to Sarah who gave birth to you in pain; when *he was but* one I called him, then I blessed him and multiplied him. Indeed, the LORD will comfort Zion; He will comfort all her waste places. And her wilderness He will make like Eden, and her desert like the garden of the LORD; joy and gladness will be found in her, thanksgiving and sound of a melody" (Isaiah 51:1-3).

YLT renders this verse as, "For—one—I have called him, and I bless him, and multiply him."[23] When you consider the description asserted by Isaiah, **it claims that Abraham and Sarah were "one"** when Abram was originally called. In the Biblical understanding of marriage, the two had become *basar echad* (בָּשָׂר אֶחָד) "one flesh," as stated in Genesis 2:24: "For this reason a man shall leave his father and his mother, and be joined to his wife; and they shall become one flesh."

When Abram was called out of Ur, he was already "one flesh" with his wife Sarai. They exemplified the relationship that God had established in the Garden of Eden with Adam and Eve, and experienced some degree of mutual respect, and they no doubt loved one another deeply. A man and a woman becoming one flesh is referred to later by the Apostle Paul to be a "mystery," that in and of itself, represents the relationship between Yeshua and the *ekklēsia*:

"[B]e subject to one another in the fear of Messiah. Wives, *be subject* to your own husbands, as to the Lord. For the husband is the head[24] of the wife, as Messiah also is the head of the [assembly], He Himself *being* the Savior of the body. But as the [assembly] is subject to Messiah, so also the wives *ought to be* to their husbands in everything. Husbands, love your wives, just as Messiah also loved the [assembly] and gave Himself up for her, so that He might sanctify her, having cleansed her by the washing of water with the word, that He might present to Himself the [assembly] in all her glory, having no spot or wrinkle or any such thing; but that she would be holy and blameless. So husbands ought also to love their own wives as their own bodies. He who loves his own wife loves himself; for no one

---

[23] Heb. *ki-echad qera'tiv v'avar'keihu v'ar'beihu* (כִּי־אֶחָד קְרָאתִיו וַאֲבָרְכֵהוּ וְאַרְבֵּהוּ).

[24] Grk. *kephalē* (κεφαλή).

Editor's note: The husband being the "head" of his wife relates to him actually being *her source*, as Paul bids the husbands in Asia Minor to love their wives the same as their own bodies (Ephesians 5:28). For a more detailed examination of this, consult the commentary *Ephesians for the Practical Messianic* by J.K. McKee.

ever hated his own flesh, but nourishes and cherishes it, just as Messiah also *does* the [assembly], because we are members of His body. FOR THIS REASON A MAN SHALL LEAVE HIS FATHER AND MOTHER AND SHALL BE JOINED TO HIS WIFE, AND THE TWO SHALL BECOME ONE FLESH [Genesis 2:24]. This mystery is great; but I am speaking with reference to Messiah and the [assembly]. Nevertheless, each individual among you also is to love his own wife even as himself, and the wife must *see to it* that she respects her husband" (Ephesians 5:21-33).

It was imperative that the Lord chose a couple exemplifying the essence of oneness, to be the foundation of the one true faith—because ultimately such oneness is elementary to understanding how He relates to His people, and now His people relate to one another in mutual submission. Therefore, it is to the lives and faithfulness of Abraham and Sarah that we, their spiritual descendants, should look.

As we look at the lives of Abraham and Sarah, it is clear that he loved her very much. Even during the trials and tests of Abraham's life, there is an underlying knowledge that a true loving partnership existed between these two, called out to be the forbearers of our faith. Whether it was departing together from Haran,[25] dealing with the famine in Canaan,[26] migrating to Egypt,[27] conniving Pharaoh,[28] separating from and then rescuing Lot,[29] getting ahead of God's plan for an heir,[30] or waiting on the promises of a physical heir[31]—it appears that Abraham and Sarah were ultimately able to come into agreement as "one flesh" throughout their lives.

Of course, we always think about the faith of Abraham, who has been commonly labeled the father of our faith (Romans 4:12), and a friend of God (James 2:23). Little mention is made of the faith exhibited by Sarah, and yet, she also is listed among the faithful in the Hebrews 11 "Hall of Fame of faith":

"By faith even Sarah herself received ability to conceive, even beyond the proper time of life, since she considered Him faithful who had promised. Therefore there was born even of one man, and him as good as dead at that, *as many descendants* AS THE STARS OF HEAVEN IN NUMBER, AND INNUMERABLE AS THE SAND WHICH IS BY THE SEASHORE" (Hebrews 11:11-12; cf. Genesis 15:5; 22:17).[32]

Here, Sarah is noted as one who faithfully considered the Holy One as willing and able to complete the promises He made regarding the birth of a physical heir. When you couple this with the many more references to Abraham's faith throughout the Scriptures, you can see that the faith component of Abraham and Sarah's life together was *mutually shared*. **They**

---

[25] Genesis 12:1-5.
[26] Genesis 12:10a.
[27] Genesis 12:10b.
[28] Genesis 12:11-20.
[29] Genesis 13:1-13; 14:1-16.
[30] Genesis 16.
[31] Genesis 18:9-15.
[32] Editor's note: Do note that there are some translation disagreements for Hebrews 11:11-12, most notably reflected in the NIV rendering: "By faith Abraham, even though he was past age—and Sarah herself was barren—was enabled to become a father because he considered him faithful who had made the promise." This would reflect more on Abraham's ability to consummate the act of conception, given his old age. Obviously, both Abraham *and* Sarah had to have faith in order to conceive Isaac.

This is due to the fact that the clause *eis katabolēn spermatos* (εἰς καταβολὴν σπέρματος) is translated literally as "to the laying down of seed." For a further discussion, consult the commentary *Hebrews for the Practical Messianic* by J.K. McKee.

epitomized and exemplified the awesome power of a husband and wife working faithfully as one flesh, to accomplish what God had called them to do.

## Sarah Laid to Rest

When Sarah died and it came time to lay her body to rest, the grieving Abraham secures a gravesite for her near Hebron. Through the years of sojourning and various encounters with the Almighty, Abraham was absolutely convinced that he and his descendants would be given the land that was promised to them. He did not *even consider* burying Sarah in any other place than the Land of Canaan. He inherently knew that it was critical for Sarah to be buried in the land that was promised to them and their descendants after them.

We read that he actually purchases a cave at Machpelah, so that there would never be an argument that the land was not deeded or owned by him (Genesis 23). This is reminiscent of an oath that Abram made with the Lord years earlier regarding accepting anything from the inhabitants of the Land of Canaan:

"Abram said to the king of Sodom, 'I have sworn to the LORD God Most High, possessor of heaven and earth, that I will not take a thread or a sandal thong or anything that is yours, for fear you would say, "I have made Abram rich." I will take nothing except what the young men have eaten, and the share of the men who went with me, Aner, Eshcol, and Mamre; let them take their share'" (Genesis 14:22-24).

The scene that takes place as the transaction for a burial cave is completed with honor, and Abraham reflects the character of a man who will not just take anything for convenience's sake.

## A Wife for Isaac

In his advanced years, having observed the ways of the Canaanite peoples, Abraham knew that in order to give his son Isaac the best possible chance of maintaining a proper relationship with the Lord, it was imperative that he locate a wife for him. The best choice for a wife would not be among the native women. Abraham decided that he would send his servant Eliezer back to the land of Haran to find a suitable wife for Isaac:

"Now Abraham was old, advanced in age; and the LORD had blessed Abraham in every way. Abraham said to his servant, the oldest of his household, who had charge of all that he owned, 'Please place your hand under my thigh, and I will make you swear by the LORD, the God of heaven and the God of earth, that you shall not take a wife for my son from the daughters of the Canaanites, among whom I live, but you will go to my country and to my relatives, and take a wife for my son Isaac'" (Genesis 24:1-4).

Abraham knew the special "one flesh" relationship he had with Sarah. He understood the importance of becoming one flesh with his wife. **He intrinsically knew that the chances of becoming one flesh were greatly improved if you found a mate who had a similar background and upbringing**. As he surveyed the Canaanite field around him, he concluded that his son could best find someone like his mother among those from his own ethnic and social background. He commissioned Eliezer with an oath to find a wife from the women in Haran, who came from his family, who still lived in the region. At this time in his life, Abraham was faithfully confident that the Lord was going to send an angel ahead of his servant to find a wife for Isaac:

בראשית

"Then Abraham said to him, 'Beware that you do not take my son back there! The LORD, the God of heaven, who took me from my father's house and from the land of my birth, and who spoke to me and who swore to me, saying, "To your descendants I will give this land," He will send His angel before you, and you will take a wife for my son from there'" (Genesis 24:6-7).

This statement is evidence of Abraham's great faith in his God. Later we discover, at the end of this *parashah*, that Abraham's faith is rewarded as Rebekah returns with Eliezer and becomes the wife of Isaac. We are told that Isaac, the son of the promise, is greatly comforted by her appearance and his consequent marriage to her:

"Then Isaac brought her into his mother Sarah's tent, and he took Rebekah, and she became his wife, and he loved her; thus Isaac was comforted after his mother's death" (Genesis 24:67).

Here, the cycle of love and faith is restored as Isaac and Rebekah carry on the "one flesh" tradition of Abraham and Sarah. Another great love story unfolds, as they also become "one flesh." Their faith was also great in that Isaac had been obedient to follow Abraham to Mount Moriah for the binding.[33] Likewise, Rebekah had, without reservation, departed from her family to go to a land that she had never seen (Genesis 24:12-65). In the story of both Abraham's son and his daughter-in-law, we witness a proper model of what is expected to become one flesh, as had been modeled by Abraham and Sarah.

## Equal Yoking

As we reflect on *Chayei Sarah*, we are reminded of the benefits and the blessings of equal yoking, especially in the marriage covenant. We see examples of how the faith and love of Abraham and Sarah established a pattern that eventually blesses their descendants throughout the generations. It is also critical to understand that as parents, they had the responsibility to live a life that allowed them to have input into the life choices of their son Isaac. This is a great pattern that we should seek to emulate.

Do we take our responsibilities toward our children as seriously as Abraham and Sarah? Are we concerned about their long-term happiness and productivity in their relationship with the Lord? If we are, then we should be living a life that is pleasing to Him. By exhibiting such an example, as we approach the inevitable reality of death, we will be thankful that our lives mattered. We will be confident that our children will be able to pass on the blessings to their progeny that we have imparted to them. Hopefully, we will better understand the blessings that the Psalmist says results from walking in His ways:

"A Song of Ascents. How blessed is everyone who fears the LORD, who walks in His ways. When you shall eat of the fruit of your hands, you will be happy and it will be well with you. Your wife shall be like a fruitful vine within your house, your children like olive plants around your table. Behold, for thus shall the man be blessed who fears the LORD. The LORD bless you from Zion, and may you see the prosperity of Jerusalem all the days of your life. Indeed, may you see your children's children. Peace be upon Israel!" (Psalm 128:1-6).

Here, the Psalmist says that you will be blessed to see your children's children. But most importantly, you will be blessed if you will be able to witness your children passing on the faith *by which you lived your life*, to your grandchildren! As you approach death, you will understand that your life and how you faithfully lived it truly did matter.

---

[33] Genesis 22:1-18.

# *Toldot* תּוֹלְדֹת
## History
## "Moored to the Rock"

> Genesis 25:19-28:9
> Malachi 1:1-2:7

Our *parashah* for this week begins with the word, "Now these are *the records of* the generations of Isaac, Abraham's son: Abraham became the father of Isaac" (Genesis 25:19). Just consider a few of the thoughts in your mind when you hear the names "Isaac" and "Abraham," and what these two figures of our faith are commonly known for. Do you at all consider some of the trials that they endured, or when presented with difficult situations, how they had no choice but to place their complete trust in the Holy One?

Sometimes the Father gives us personal challenges and trials to test us, forcing us to remember where our anchor must be secured: **in Him**. Born again Believers have been firmly moored to the Rock of Salvation, Messiah Yeshua, and what He has accomplished for us via His sacrificial atonement. And, since He is the Word made flesh, I believe that it is quite beneficial that we strive to see what we can learn about the Messiah from the weekly Torah and Haftarah readings (cf. Luke 24:44), parts of the Bible that too often get overlooked by many people.

Consider the possibility that our Heavenly Father is like a huge transmitter in the universe, broadcasting His blessings that can be gleaned through a consistent study of the Torah portions on a weekly basis. I have certainly experienced the blessing of committing myself to a discipline of reading the weekly *parashah* for many years, meditating upon these passages of the Bible and integrating their distinct messages into my heart. With the added discipline of actually putting words to paper—with my TorahScope reflection commentaries—the process of delving into where He has my heart as *Shabbat* approaches becomes an exciting process. Of course, I do not want to be the only person blessed by examining the weekly *parashah*, and so one of my distinct prayers is that someone who might read these thoughts would be ministered to in a special way.

Perhaps some of the circumstances in which you presently find yourself—even some testing you might be enduring at this moment in time—needs clarity and understanding. Hopefully, you will be inspired to turn to Yeshua, the Living Word, for the answers to all of life's circumstances. We know that when we can rely upon the Lord and Him alone, because His answers to our prayers and supplications will be the perfect anecdote for seasons of consternation and affliction. James the Just sums up the trials and tribulations of life very succinctly:

"Consider it all joy, my brethren, when you encounter various trials, knowing that the testing of your faith produces endurance. And let endurance have *its* perfect result, so that you may be perfect and complete, lacking in nothing. But if any of you lacks wisdom, let him ask of God, who gives to all generously and without reproach, and it will be given to him. But he must ask in faith without any doubting, for the one who doubts is like the surf of the sea, driven and tossed by the wind. For that man ought not to expect that he will receive anything from the Lord, *being* a double-minded man, unstable in all his ways. But the brother of humble circumstances is to glory in his high position; and the rich man *is to glory* in his humiliation, because like flowering grass he will pass away. For the sun rises with a scorching wind and withers the grass; and its flower falls off and the beauty of its appearance is destroyed; so too the rich man in the midst of his pursuits will fade away. Blessed is a man who perseveres under trial; for once he has been approved, he will receive the crown of life which *the Lord* has promised to those who love Him" (James 1:2-12).

The life of faith is indeed one that includes many tests, trials, and tribulations. We know from our reading of Scripture that we should endure through whatever we face. One thing that is clear, from reading through *Toldot* this week, is that we have an intimate record of the details of a very traumatic time in the history of Abraham's descendents. In this Torah portion we see the struggle between Esau and Jacob,[34] and how Isaac and Rebekah acted and reacted to their two sons.[35]

Great lessons about God's sovereignty and human responsibility can be weighed in our meditations. Why did the Holy One select Jacob for His blessings? Why is Esau hated? *Considerable theological debates have emerged from the accounts recorded in our portion.* These, and many other questions, **should simply drive us to our knees when we recognize that God is ultimately in control of His Creation.** He chooses whom He will choose, to do whatever He has predestined them to do. And while I do not believe we are necessarily robots or mindless pawns, because personal human responsibility does have a role in this incredibly complex dichotomy of actions, we are eventually subject to the will of our Creator. We are often reduced to the dirt from whence we came, when we realize that the finite cannot even begin to comprehend the Infinite. But we must try, because He clearly states that if we seek Him, He will reveal Himself to us and we will find Him (Deuteronomy 4:29; Isaiah 51:1; 55:6; Jeremiah 29:13; Psalm 9:10; Hebrews 11:6).

I would submit that Paul adds a little clarity to this complex question about Divine sovereignty versus human responsibility. In his letter to the Romans he explains his pain over the unbelief of his fellow Jewish brethren, appealing to the account of Jacob and Esau:

> "But *it is* not as though the word of God has failed. For they are not all Israel who are *descended* from Israel; nor are they all children because they are Abraham's descendants, but: 'THROUGH ISAAC YOUR DESCENDANTS WILL BE NAMED' [Genesis 21:12]. That is, it is not the children of the flesh who are children of God, but the children of the promise are regarded as descendants. For this is the word of promise: 'AT THIS TIME I WILL COME, AND SARAH SHALL HAVE A SON' [Genesis 18:10, 14]. And not only this, but there was Rebekah also, when she had conceived *twins* by one man, our father Isaac; for though *the twins* were not yet born and had not done anything good or bad, so that God's purpose according to *His* choice would stand, not because of works but because of Him who calls, it was said to her, 'THE OLDER WILL SERVE THE YOUNGER' [Genesis 25:23]. Just as it is written, 'JACOB I LOVED, BUT ESAU I HATED' [Malachi 1:2-3]. What shall we say then? There is no injustice with God, is there? May it never be! For He says to Moses, 'I WILL HAVE MERCY ON WHOM I HAVE MERCY, AND I WILL HAVE COMPASSION ON WHOM I HAVE COMPASSION' [Exodus 33:19]. So then it *does* not *depend* on the man who wills or the man who runs, but on God who has mercy. For the Scripture says to Pharaoh, 'FOR THIS VERY PURPOSE I RAISED YOU UP, TO DEMONSTRATE MY POWER IN YOU, AND THAT MY NAME MIGHT BE PROCLAIMED THROUGHOUT THE WHOLE EARTH' [Exodus 9:16]. So then He has mercy on whom He desires, and He hardens whom He desires. You will say to me then, 'Why does He still find fault? For who resists His will?' On the contrary, who are you,

---

[34] Genesis 25:19-34; 27:1-46.
[35] Genesis 28:1-9.

O man, who answers back to God? The thing molded will not say to the molder, 'Why did you make me like this,' will it? Or does not the potter have a right over the clay, to make from the same lump one vessel for honorable use and another for common use? What if God, although willing to demonstrate His wrath and to make His power known, endured with much patience vessels of wrath prepared for destruction? And *He did so* to make known the riches of His glory upon vessels of mercy, which He prepared beforehand for glory, *even* us, whom He also called, not from among Jews only, but also from among Gentiles. As He says also in Hosea, 'I WILL CALL THOSE WHO WERE NOT MY PEOPLE, "MY PEOPLE," AND HER WHO WAS NOT BELOVED, "BELOVED."' AND IT SHALL BE THAT IN THE PLACE WHERE IT WAS SAID TO THEM, "YOU ARE NOT MY PEOPLE," THERE THEY SHALL BE CALLED SONS OF THE LIVING GOD' [Isaiah 10:22-23; Hosea 1:10]" (Romans 9:6-26).

This passage should humble us with the understanding that the Holy One of Israel is in total control of His Creation, and those He has chosen to be a part of His family. Whether one thinks that God has predestined the events of every second from eternity past, or thinks that God knows the decisions people are going to make given His Divine foreknowledge—or you simply throw your hands up in the air and consider yourself a small mortal and do not really know what to think about this passage—**further study into the Tanakh passages Paul alludes to is probably in order.**

The Apostle Paul lamented over the fact that in his day, there was a widescale Jewish rejection of Messiah Yeshua, using some foundational accounts seen in the Torah to teach the Romans. How this intertexuality actually plays into Paul's argument is something that has to be taken very seriously,[36] and may require you to not only read Romans a little closer, but also each of the series of verses he quotes from. Romans chs. 9-11 are undeniably one of the most important sections of the Bible for today's Messianic movement.

As this passage continues, Paul not only describes how those of the nations have the opportunity to come to grace through their trust in the Messiah of Israel, but are those who are largely going to benefit from it, given how the Jewish people have largely decided to reject Him:

"What shall we say then? That Gentiles, who did not pursue righteousness, attained righteousness, even the righteousness which is by faith; but Israel, pursuing a law of righteousness, did not arrive at *that* law. Why? Because *they did* not *pursue it* by faith, but as though *it were* by works. They stumbled over the stumbling stone, just as it is written, 'BEHOLD, I LAY IN ZION A STONE OF STUMBLING AND A ROCK OF OFFENSE, AND HE WHO BELIEVES IN HIM WILL NOT BE DISAPPOINTED' [Isaiah 28:16]" (Romans 9:30-33).

The Apostle Paul summarizes his thoughts about his fellow Jewish brethren and their zeal, without knowledge of Yeshua as the Savior. This passage clearly speaks to the need to demonstrate the gospel of Israel's Messiah to the people from whom He came:

"Brethren, my heart's desire and my prayer to God for them is for *their* salvation. For I testify about them that they have a zeal for God, but not in accordance with knowledge. For not knowing about God's righteousness and seeking to establish their own, they did not subject themselves to the righteousness of God. For Messiah is the [goal;

---

[36] Editor's note: For further consideration, consult N.T. Wright, "The Letter to the Romans," in Leander E. Keck, ed., et. al., *New Interpreter's Bible*, Vol. 10 (Nashville: Abingdon, 2002), pp 632-643.

culmination, TNIV][37] of the law for righteousness to everyone who believes. For Moses writes that the man who practices the righteousness which is based on law shall live by that righteousness. But the righteousness based on faith speaks as follows: 'DO NOT SAY IN YOUR HEART, 'WHO WILL ASCEND INTO HEAVEN?' (that is, to bring Messiah down), or 'WHO WILL DESCEND INTO THE ABYSS?' (that is, to bring Messiah up from the dead). But what does it say? 'THE WORD IS NEAR YOU, IN YOUR MOUTH AND IN YOUR HEART' [vs. 6-8: Deuteronomy 9:4; 30:12-14]—that is, the word of faith which we are preaching, that if you confess with your mouth Yeshua *as* Lord, and believe in your heart that God raised Him from the dead, you will be saved; for with the heart a person believes, resulting in righteousness, and with the mouth he confesses, resulting in salvation. For the Scripture says, 'WHOEVER BELIEVES IN HIM WILL NOT BE DISAPPOINTED' [Isaiah 28:16]. For there is no distinction between Jew and Greek; for the same *Lord* is Lord of all, abounding in riches for all who call on Him; for 'WHOEVER WILL CALL ON THE NAME OF THE LORD WILL BE SAVED' [Joel 2:32]. How then will they call on Him in whom they have not believed? How will they believe in Him whom they have not heard? And how will they hear without a preacher? How will they preach unless they are sent? Just as it is written, 'HOW BEAUTIFUL ARE THE FEET OF THOSE WHO BRING GOOD NEWS OF GOOD THINGS!' [Nahum 1:15] However, they did not all heed the good news; for Isaiah says, 'LORD, WHO HAS BELIEVED OUR REPORT?' [Isaiah 53:1] So faith *comes* from hearing, and hearing by the word of Messiah" (Romans 10:1-17).

A few of you might be asking, what does this specifically have to do with the Torah portion *Toldot*? Well, as stated earlier, the intention of these writings is to reflect upon our weekly readings in the Torah and Haftarah, and a principal part of the modern Messianic movement is to connect these texts with the Apostolic Scriptures (New Testament), and let the Holy Spirit minister to the personal needs of individuals. Sometimes my writings might take tangents into areas that need deeper meditation for personal repentance and reflection, and to probe where our understanding of some passages needs improvement or more investigation. *May His words have their perfect work in all of our hearts!*

This week, I would also encourage you to take a look at what the Sages for centuries have seen as an appropriate parallel passage to *Toldot*. This week's Haftarah selection is Malachi 1:1-2:7, and details some of God's dealings with the descendants of Jacob and Esau:

"The oracle of the word of the LORD to Israel through Malachi. 'I have loved you,' says the LORD. But you say, 'How have You loved us?' '*Was* not Esau Jacob's brother?' declares the LORD. 'Yet I have loved Jacob; but I have hated Esau, and I have made his mountains a desolation and *appointed* his inheritance for the jackals of the wilderness.' Though Edom says, 'We have been beaten down, but we will return and build up the ruins'; thus says the LORD of hosts, 'They may build, but I will tear down; and *men* will call them the wicked territory, and the people toward whom the LORD is indignant forever.' Your eyes will see this and you will say, 'The LORD be magnified beyond the border of Israel! A son honors *his* father, and a servant his master. Then if I am a father, where is My honor? And if I am a master, where is My respect?' says the LORD of hosts to you, O priests who despise My name. But you say, 'How have we despised Your name?' '*You* are presenting defiled food upon My altar. But you say, 'How have we defiled You?' In that you say, 'The table of the LORD is to be despised.' But when you

---

[37] Grk. *telos* (τέλος), "**the goal toward which a movement is being directed,** *end, goal, outcome*" (Frederick William Danker, ed., et. al., *A Greek-English Lexicon of the New Testament and Other Early Christian Literature*, third edition [Chicago: University of Chicago Press, 2000], 998).

present the blind for sacrifice, is it not evil? And when you present the lame and sick, is it not evil? Why not offer it to your governor? Would he be pleased with you? Or would he receive you kindly?' says the LORD of hosts. 'But now will you not entreat God's favor, that He may be gracious to us? With such an offering on your part, will He receive any of you kindly?' says the LORD of hosts. 'Oh that there were one among you who would shut the gates, that you might not uselessly kindle *fire* on My altar! I am not pleased with you,' says the LORD of hosts, 'nor will I accept an offering from you. For from the rising of the sun even to its setting, My name *will be* great among the nations, and in every place incense is going to be offered to My name, and a grain offering *that is* pure; for My name *will be* great among the nations,' says the LORD of hosts. But you are profaning it, in that you say, 'The table of the Lord is defiled, and as for its fruit, its food is to be despised.' You also say, 'My, how tiresome it is!' And you disdainfully sniff at it,' says the LORD of hosts, 'and you bring what was taken by robbery and *what is* lame or sick; so you bring the offering! Should I receive that from your hand?' says the LORD. But cursed be the swindler who has a male in his flock and vows it, but sacrifices a blemished animal to the Lord, for I am a great King,' says the LORD of hosts, 'and My name is feared among the nations. And now this commandment is for you, O priests. If you do not listen, and if you do not take it to heart to give honor to My name,' says the LORD of hosts, 'then I will send the curse upon you and I will curse your blessings; and indeed, I have cursed them *already*, because you are not taking *it* to heart. Behold, I am going to rebuke your offspring, and I will spread refuse on your faces, the refuse of your feasts; and you will be taken away with it. Then you will know that I have sent this commandment to you, that My covenant may continue with Levi,' says the LORD of hosts. 'My covenant with him was *one of* life and peace, and I gave them to him *as an object of* reverence; so he revered Me and stood in awe of My name. True instruction was in his mouth and unrighteousness was not found on his lips; he walked with Me in peace and uprightness, and he turned many back from iniquity. For the lips of a priest should preserve knowledge, and men should seek instruction from his mouth; for he is the messenger of the LORD of hosts'" (Malachi 1:1-2:7).

This section of Scripture, from the last of the Prophets, no doubt left many Jews in quite a quandary. They knew that the Holy One of Israel loved them unconditionally, but they also knew that there were obvious consequences should they sin and disobey. How many people simply go through religious motions without their hearts being in the right place? How easy was it for the ancients to promise a choice lamb to God, but bring a blemished one instead? After all, who was really going to know or care as long as the appearance of godliness was evident to one's neighbors and family?

Considering these questions from Malachi, how easy is it for modern-day followers of the Messiah to do just the same with their offerings? How many do not give what they should to those who minister to them? How many Believers do not strive for spiritual maturity? *Should we be examining our heart intentions?* Just how are we guarding the utterances from our lips? As an assemblage of those who serve God, our actions, words, and the mediations of our hearts should be pure and holy. Remember that the Lord is looking at our hearts and He is not impressed with our outward appearances. King David understood these challenges intimately:

"Also keep back Your servant from presumptuous *sins*; let them not rule over me; then I will be blameless, and I shall be acquitted of great transgression. Let the words of my mouth and the meditation of my heart be acceptable in Your sight, O LORD, my rock and my Redeemer" (Psalm 19:13-14).

בראשית

Now imagine this reality: Do you remember that there are books which record the history of humanity in Heaven? These are recordings that go into much greater detail than this week's Torah portion of *Toldot* about the lives of Isaac, Rebekah, and their twin sons Esau and Jacob. Here is a glimpse as to some of what transpires at the final judgment, when those records are considered at the Great White Throne judgment presided over by Yeshua Himself:

"Then I saw a great white throne and Him who sat upon it, from whose presence earth and heaven fled away, and no place was found for them. And I saw the dead, the great and the small, standing before the throne, and books were opened; and another book was opened, which is *the book* of life; and the dead were judged from the things which were written in the books, according to their deeds. And the sea gave up the dead which were in it, and death and Hades gave up the dead which were in them; and they were judged, every one *of them* according to their deeds. Then death and Hades were thrown into the lake of fire. This is the second death, the lake of fire. And if anyone's name was not found written in the book of life, he was thrown into the lake of fire" (Revelation 20:11-15).

For 3,300 years, we have had the testimony of the Torah to be used as an instructional tool for life. The Lord has used the lives of the Patriarchs to reveal to each of us the reality of our human condition. If we do not learn from the previous examples of those recorded for us in the Scriptures, will we face condemning judgment from the King of Kings? Or will we learn, and not have to face the damnation of the Great White Throne?

Esau made choices that he regretted years later. Jacob also made some choices that he probably questioned over time, but for some reason, the Most High made a choice and He decided to love Jacob more than Esau. To the carnal mind this does not seem fair and equitable. And logically speaking, it is not impartial. Paul states the following in Romans 9:18-23:

"So then He has mercy on whom He desires, and He hardens whom He desires. You will say to me then, 'Why does He still find fault? For who resists His will?' On the contrary, who are you, O man, who answers back to God? The thing molded will not say to the molder, 'Why did you make me like this,' will it? Or does not the potter have a right over the clay, to make from the same lump one vessel for honorable use and another for common use? What if God, although willing to demonstrate His wrath and to make His power known, endured with much patience vessels of wrath prepared for destruction? And *He did so* to make known the riches of His glory upon vessels of mercy, which He prepared beforehand for glory."

The bottom line to this saint with clay feet, after the whirlwinds of trial and testing, is a simple plea:

> **Please, Heavenly Father, do not discard this lump on the trash heap of worthless clay.** Instead, mold me into a vessel that has usefulness in Your Kingdom's work. You are the Potter and I am the clay. Let me be more moldable in your hands. Please, let me persevere so that I will receive the crown of life. Please, let my name be found in the Book of Life. Please have mercy upon me! And for those who choose to follow the inclinations of sinful flesh—have mercy on them too—and may they see the light of Your salvation.
>
> *I Bless You O LORD, my King of Kings, my Protector and my Shield! For You alone are worthy to be praised! Amein!*

# V'yeitzei וַיֵּצֵא
## He went out
## "Laban Laborers"

Genesis 28:10-32:2
Hosea 12:12-14:10 (A); 11:7-12:12 (S)

In this week's Torah reading, we are given some important images regarding the personal character of the life of the Patriarch Jacob. In his early life, it can be easily detected that unlike Abraham and Isaac who preceded him, Jacob did not necessarily place his total trust in God. On the contrary, at times Jacob tries to "bargain" with God:

"Then Jacob made a vow, saying, 'If God will be with me and will keep me on this journey that I take, and will give me food to eat and garments to wear, and I return to my father's house in safety, then the LORD will be my God. This stone, which I have set up as a pillar, will be God's house, and of all that You give me I will surely give a tenth to You" (Genesis 28:20-22).

This kind of attitude in approaching the Almighty is not unique to Jacob, nor to any other human being. In fact, in his early life, Jacob approached God the same way that he approached any mortal person. His experiences with his tasking father-in-law, Laban, would teach him some important things, causing him to rely more on God and less on himself, steadily molding him into the man of faith that the author of Hebrews considers him to be, albeit with him being known for his dying words (Hebrews 11:21-22).

*V'yeitzei* is a Torah portion that most people can identify with if they have spent any time working for others. Sadly, the world is full of people who are driven by the spirit of Laban, who are only out to serve themselves and their self interests (Genesis 29:21-35). Consider what Jacob might have felt, after laboring for seven years to marry Rachel as his wife—and then on his wedding night he got the unattractive Leah. All Laban said on the morning after was, "It is not the practice in our place to marry off the younger before the firstborn" (Genesis 29:26), flippantly annulling their previous agreement (Genesis 29:18-20). Those who make promises and conveniently forget to honor them are all over the world. *All that hard work and waiting for nothing, it would seem...* Human nature is such that interchanges and short dealings, like those between Laban and his son-in-law Jacob, are fairly common around the globe. People make promises that are easily broken because the consequences of broken vows do not necessarily surface immediately.

But before we recall some of the injustices that we may have had to endure, by the fracturing of pledges, it would probably be beneficial to first recollect all of the promises *we* have personally dishonored. It is easy to point a finger at those who twist the truth and have selective memories about their commitments, but what about our own vows that are uttered in the quieter moments of life? How about those simple promises to read the Bible, pray consistently, stop smoking or drinking, stop overeating, get more exercise, lose weight, help one's neighbors, put others' needs ahead of mine, or devote more time to one's marriage relationship? *The list could go on and on.* We have all made these types of promises to ourselves, to our spouses, to our children, or to our Creator. The problem is that it is much easier to examine the speck in our brother's eye, rather than work to remove the log that clouds our own vision of our true self. Yeshua's words are quite direct:

"Do not judge so that you will not be judged. For in the way you judge, you will be judged; and by your standard of measure, it will be measured to you. Why do you look at the speck that is in your brother's eye, but do not notice the log that is in your own eye? Or how can you say to your brother, 'Let me take the speck out of your eye,' and behold, the log is in your own eye? You hypocrite, first take the log out of your own eye, and then you will see clearly to take the speck out of your brother's eye" (Matthew 7:1-5).

Before we remove our brother or sister's speck, can we learn anything from how Jacob deals with the challenges of having "the real Laban" for his father-in-law? In so doing, can we remove any logs that we have in our eyes? Is it possible that God gave Jacob a father-in-law just like Laban to work out some issues in his life? Is it also possible that He has given each of us our own Laban-like experiences, in order to mold us into useful servants for His purposes?

I believe this is why spiritual self-examination can be so fruitful. In His economical ways, God orders all of life's circumstances so that His people can benefit from the trials and admonishments that surface. Remember that one of the benefits of being a child of the living God, guarantees that He will discipline and admonish us using a variety of means:

"You have not yet resisted to the point of shedding blood in your striving against sin; and you have forgotten the exhortation which is addressed to you as sons, 'MY SON, DO NOT REGARD LIGHTLY THE DISCIPLINE OF THE LORD, NOR FAINT WHEN YOU ARE REPROVED BY HIM; FOR THOSE WHOM THE LORD LOVES HE DISCIPLINES, AND HE SCOURGES EVERY SON WHOM HE RECEIVES' [Proverbs 3:11-12]. It is for discipline that you endure; God deals with you as with sons; for what son is there whom *his* father does not discipline? But if you are without discipline, of which all have become partakers, then you are illegitimate children and not sons. Furthermore, we had earthly fathers to discipline us, and we respected them; shall we not much rather be subject to the Father of spirits, and live? For they disciplined us for a short time as seemed best to them, but He *disciplines us* for *our* good, so that we may share His holiness. All discipline for the moment seems not to be joyful, but sorrowful; yet to those who have been trained by it, afterwards it yields the peaceful fruit of righteousness" (Hebrews 12:4-11).

Those who are legitimate sons and daughters of God will be disciplined by Him. What does this say to those who claim faith in Messiah Yeshua, but have possibly never been chastised by anything? **Let us simply pray that such people might pick up a Bible, read, and be convicted** without having to endure anything too harsh.

## The Power of Words

Remember how critical words were spoken from *Toldot* (Genesis 25:19-28:9) last week. Jacob made sure that Esau verbally swore to relinquish his birthright (Genesis 25:33), and the birthright promises were permanently transferred. Isaac, once he spoke the blessing over Jacob, was unable to rescind his words of blessing upon the younger (Genesis 27:33), and the blessings have flowed ever since to Israel rather than to Edom. These are two great examples of how powerful our words are, and how our utterances can become vows, promises, pledges, blessings, or even curses. They have an incredible impact on us and those to whom the statements are directed.

Jacob understood this principle about the power of words, having grown up in the tents of his parents Isaac and Rebekah, and hearing about his grandfather Abraham. He knew that the Most High had visited his fathers at different times and imparted some very powerful verbal promises to them. In audible and visual encounters, the Holy One had promised a multitude of descendants to each of them, and the Land of Canaan as an inheritance for their progeny. You can imagine Jacob's reaction as he was fleeing from Esau's anger, when he had a dream-vision at Bethel. Here, as his head was resting on a rock, he dreamt about seeing a ladder with angels ascending and descending from Heaven. Then, the Almighty Himself spoke these confirming words to Jacob in the dream:

"And behold, the LORD stood above it and said, 'I am the LORD, the God of your father Abraham and the God of Isaac; the land on which you lie, I will give it to you and to your descendants. Your descendants will also be like the dust of the earth, and you will spread out to the west and to the east and to the north and to the south; and in you and in your descendants shall all the families of the earth be blessed. Behold, I am with you and will keep you wherever you go, and will bring you back to this land; for I will not leave you until I have done what I have promised you" (Genesis 28:13-15).

What was Jacob's response to this exhilarating experience? He woke up and began to utter all kinds of statements and declarations. He took up the stone pillow,[38] renamed the town,[39] and uttered this recorded vow to God:

"Then Jacob made a vow, saying, 'If God will be with me and will keep me on this journey that I take, and will give me food to eat and garments to wear, and I return to my father's house in safety, then the LORD will be my God. This stone, which I have set up as a pillar, will be God's house, and of all that You give me I will surely give a tenth to You'" (Genesis 28:20-22).

As you can imagine, this was a very exciting interchange for Jacob. He had clearly been in the presence of God Himself, and his actions indicated a real desire to accomplish His will. His vow to God reveals a sincere desire to be dependent upon the Almighty who had just appeared to him in a dream—and who had been faithful to his fathers. But did you notice the "if/then" aspect of Jacob's vow? Jacob basically tells God, *"If you give me everything, then you will be my God."* This sounds like he is bargaining and expecting the Most High to perform, before he gives Him the allegiance He requires as Creator. To top it off, consider some of the stinginess of only offering 10% of all that is given—in view of everything that God has promised!

You could conclude that if one has all of his needs supplied, is given protection from enemies, and relative peace is present in his father's house, that one might be willing to give back more than just 10%. How about 20% or maybe even 35%? The problem is that the Lord ultimately requires 100%. Even if we only give 10% of our actual resources to those who serve Him on a full-time basis, we are expected to wisely use the remaining 90% of our resources and possessions, and in some way acknowledge Him as the Provider. Anything less than this and one runs the risk of taking what is holy and wasting it (cf. Matthew 7:6).

How serious is it if our time, energies, and resources are not all dedicated to God and to His purposes? *Will one fall from the ranks of the chosen?* Yeshua taught that "many are called, but few *are* chosen." You probably recall this word from reading the Scriptures, but are you aware of the larger context of where Yeshua says it? The Lord calls all to the wedding feast of His Son in the Kingdom to come:

"The kingdom of heaven may be compared to a king who gave a wedding feast for his son. And he sent out his slaves to call those who had been invited to the wedding feast, and

---

[38] Genesis 28:18.
[39] Genesis 28:19.

they were unwilling to come. Again he sent out other slaves saying, 'Tell those who have been invited, "Behold, I have prepared my dinner; my oxen and my fattened livestock are *all* butchered and everything is ready; come to the wedding feast."' But they paid no attention and went their way, one to his own farm, another to his business, and the rest seized his slaves and mistreated them and killed them. But the king was enraged, and he sent his armies and destroyed those murderers and set their city on fire. Then he said to his slaves, 'The wedding is ready, but those who were invited were not worthy. Go therefore to the main highways, and as many as you find *there*, invite to the wedding feast.' Those slaves went out into the streets and gathered together all they found, both evil and good; and the wedding hall was filled with dinner guests. But when the king came in to look over the dinner guests, he saw a man there who was not dressed in wedding clothes, and he said to him, 'Friend, how did you come in here without wedding clothes?' And the man was speechless. Then the king said to the servants, 'Bind him hand and foot, and throw him into the outer darkness; in that place there will be weeping and gnashing of teeth.' For many are called, but few *are* chosen" (Matthew 22:2-14).

In this parable Yeshua instructs His Disciples that one must be attentive to the situation at hand. When you are invited to a wedding feast, make the effort to dress like you are actually a part of the feast. If you plan to show up without any real concern for the festivities, then will you be subject to being uninvited—in this case being cast out and eternally punished? If you are only allowing a percentage of your being to attend (10% or 20%, or maybe even 50%), then you will not understand the dress code and proper protocol. Not only will you not enjoy what the Lord has invited you to, but you will be thrown out and never allowed back in.

What Jacob will discover in ensuing chapters is that only partial commitment to the Lord is not sufficient (Genesis chs. 32-33). Jacob will come to a place where he realizes that apart from Him, he can do nothing.[40] Absolute dependence upon God for not only provision and protection, but life itself, allows one to be useful for His work and purposes here on Earth. Only when Jacob is confronted with the possible slaughter of his family and his own death by the estranged Esau, is he finally willing to concede his lack of strength and cleverness in his own abilities to the Lord (Genesis 32:7-12).

At this critical juncture in his life, Jacob humbly approached Esau to receive whatever Esau determined to do (Genesis 33:1-17). Even though he has taken some precautions for the survival of at least part of his family, he placed 100% of his life in the hands of his brother, who decades before he had robbed of his birthright and the blessings of their father Isaac. Jacob, through the both literal and figurative, wrestles with the Most High (Genesis 32:24:32) and with the tools He used like Laban, and had finally come to a place where he depended on God for all things. Consider the humility Jacob demonstrated in approaching Esau:

"But he himself passed on ahead of them and bowed down to the ground seven times, until he came near to his brother" (Genesis 33:3).

Are we at such a point in our own lives, where the various Laban experiences convict us about the dark secrets we may carry? Have we gotten to the point where we are dependent upon the Lord for everything? Do we give Him 10%—or 100% of all that we have to give?

---

[40] Cf. John 15:5.

## Vows Allow

Have you made vows to the Lord that have not been kept? Do you even remember all of your commitments to not only Him, but other promises made over the years? If we would all be absolutely honest, we could probably all remember commitments made that have not been met. By remembering these things, perhaps we can begin to extend some mercy to the "Labans" of our lives who have had a larger purpose than just exemplifying ways we should not be demonstrating. If we view past, negative experiences with such "Labans" through the Father's eyes, then we might be able to understand that He frequently uses calculating and conniving people to get our attention. **He might even want to have us practice extending mercy and grace and love to those who mistreat us.** We do have some serious challenges in life when we are asked to love our enemies and to pray for those who persecute us:

"But I say to you, love your enemies and pray for those who persecute you, so that you may be sons of your Father who is in heaven; for He causes His sun to rise on *the* evil and *the* good, and sends rain on *the* righteous and *the* unrighteous" (Matthew 5:44-45).

Contemplate these words spoken by Yeshua in His Sermon on the Mount. Consider the reward for loving and praying for your enemies and those who persecute or mistreat you: you will be sons and daughters of your Father in Heaven! Imagine how tough it is for a holy and righteous God to stomach all of the sinful things He witnesses on Earth, and still each day He showers His blessings upon us in the seasons of nature—in spite of all the wretched sin that currently abounds unabated. In God's forbearance and patience, could He not be giving sinful humanity a chance to change from its wicked ways?

Was God not, in ages past, trying to get Jacob to be more like His fathers Isaac and Abraham? Was not faith the critical component that set Abraham apart from his peers? Is Abraham not the father of the faithful? Should we not be more faithful like him—even though we sometimes have the tendency to be like Jacob, or even Laban?

Rather than critique the works of the various "Labans" we have encountered in life, perhaps we should simply pray for them and love them, so that the Lord's righteousness would shine through us. If we have learned how not to be calculating and conniving, then we need to let God use us so that none will perish. The Apostle Peter admonishes us, "The Lord is not slow about His promise, as some count slowness, but is patient toward you, not wishing for any to perish but for all to come to repentance" (2 Peter 3:9).

## *V'yishlach* וַיִּשְׁלַח
### He sent
### "Silence of the Limping"

| Genesis 32:3-36:43 |
| :---: |
| Hosea 11:7-12:12 (A) |
| Obadiah 1:1-21 (S) |

Once again, students of the Torah are challenged when meditating on our weekly portions, which I have found to contain a wealth of information to contemplate. When I sit down to write my Torah commentaries, the choice of a subject matter to focus on can be overwhelming. There are many critical events to consider discussing, so one really has to search his heart and find out just what nugget of truth the Lord wants you to focus upon. After all, lengthy books have been written about certain aspects of the life and personal character of Jacob. And, my Torah commentaries are intended to be reflective, and not be like some of the technical, verse-by-verse resources that we have in our ministry library.

As I filter my life through the lens of God's Torah and plead for personally needed edification, I am magnetically drawn into the character strengths and flaws of Jacob. It is amazing how truly representative he is of so many of us! I can very easily identify with Jacob's struggles as a chosen vessel for God's Divine purposes. If you have ever endured any difficulties in your own life, then you can probably also empathize with many of Jacob's character traits—perhaps his apparent silence as he limps down the mountain trails of modern-day Samaria and Judea. Consider the following verses and Jacob's absent response:

"Shechem also said to her father and to her brothers, 'If I find favor in your sight, then I will give whatever you say to me. Ask me ever so much bridal payment and gift, and I will give according as you say to me; but give me the girl in marriage.' But Jacob's sons answered Shechem and his father Hamor with deceit, because he had defiled Dinah their sister. They said to them, 'We cannot do this thing, to give our sister to one who is uncircumcised, for that would be a disgrace to us. Only on this *condition* will we consent to you: if you will become like us, in that every male of you be circumcised, then we will give our daughters to you, and we will take your daughters for ourselves, and we will live with you and become one people. But if you will not listen to us to be circumcised, then we will take our daughter and go'" (Genesis 34:11-17).

Just contemplate this critical juncture in the family, chosen by the Lord to be a light to the world, as they reenter the Promised Land and settle around the community of Shechem. At this point in the narrative, the defiling sexual encounter with Dinah has already occurred,[41] and restitution has to be made. Now a proposition is offered by the young prince Shechem and his father Hamor, to Jacob and his sons.

What really caught my attention, after rereading this selection of verses a number of times, is that Jacob is deafeningly silent when the proposals are being discussed. In fact, the Scriptures indicate that his sons answered the requests deceitfully, and with what is ultimately demonstrated to be murder in their hearts. But for some reason, the Patriarch Jacob, who had recently been renamed Israel in an awesome encounter with the Holy One,[42] did not speak up. **Why was Jacob silent?** Can we really know what was going on in his heart and mind?

It is apparent that by the time this event occurred in Jacob's life, he was confidently aware that the God of his fathers was providing, protecting, and preserving him and his family for the fulfillment of His promises. What was it about Jacob that caused him to just bite his tongue, and not overrule his sons' conniving requests as the elder? Could it be that he was plagued with the same problem that many followers of God struggle with: the age-old battle between the Spirit and the flesh?

## Our Common Human Condition

Lamentably, many of us have different flesh patterns which exercise their influences on choices we consider and decisions we make. Jacob's life may be considered to be an "open book," which we can all benefit and learn from, if we study and contemplate the things he

---

[41] Genesis 34:1-5.
[42] Genesis 32:24-32.

did, said, and in this case *did not say*. Hopefully, if we are totally honest with ourselves, those wrestling with sinful behaviors will confess that they sometimes have about the same amount of success overcoming various flesh patterns as Jacob appears to have had.

Regrettably, confessing our faults is easier said than acted upon, considering the record we see in the Scriptures of fallen humanity. Even with the benefits of progressive revelation, many who claim a belief in the Creator God—and even His Son Messiah Yeshua—still struggle with battles of the flesh, and in experiencing victory over them. In Romans ch. 7, the Apostle Paul describes a viewpoint with which too many people can relate:

"For we know that the Law is spiritual, but I am of flesh, sold into bondage to sin. For what I am doing, I do not understand; for I am not practicing what I *would* like to *do*, but I am doing the very thing I hate. But if I do the very thing I do not want *to do*, I agree with the Law, *confessing* that the Law is good. So now, no longer am I the one doing it, but sin which dwells in me. For I know that nothing good dwells in me, that is, in my flesh; for the willing is present in me, but the doing of the good *is* not. For the good that I want, I do not do, but I practice the very evil that I do not want. But if I am doing the very thing I do not want, I am no longer the one doing it, but sin which dwells in me. I find then the principle that evil is present in me, the one who wants to do good. For I joyfully concur with the law of God in the inner man, but I see a different law in the members of my body, waging war against the law of my mind and making me a prisoner of the law of sin which is in my members. Wretched man that I am! Who will set me free from the body of this death? Thanks be to God through Yeshua the Messiah our Lord! So then, on the one hand I myself with my mind am serving the law of God, but on the other, with my flesh the law of sin" (Romans 7:14-25).

Many people are inclined to read Romans ch. 7 as Paul giving us information about himself, and that it is fairly common for Believers to have sin problems that they wrestle with and struggle to overcome. Paul seems to be telling us that he himself, even as a born again Believer and a chosen apostle of God, struggles with sin.

Certainly while we live in a sinful world and we will have to overcome temptation, is it appropriate for a Believer to use Romans 7 as an "excuse" to sin? In the recent past, many scholars have been led to think that Paul *is not*, in fact, talking about himself—but rather is speaking as a hypothetical Believer who is struggling with sin.[43] Paul himself, contrary to the Romans 7 sinner, is a relatively mature Believer who has overcome the vast majority of temptations.

Regardless of which view you take, the realities of our fallen world should force us to rely on the grace of God, because it is only by the salvation provided in Yeshua that "the requirement of the Law might be fulfilled in us, who do not walk according to the flesh but according to the Spirit" (Romans 8:4). **Only by crying out to the Lord, will we be able to overcome temptation!**

Many of the sinful temptations that we encounter as Believers are simply flesh patterns that can be easily conquered, if we reach out in faith to our Heavenly Father and learn to

---

[43] For a summary of this, consult J.M. Everts, "Conversion and Call of Paul," in Gerald F. Hawthorne, Ralph P. Martin, and Daniel G. Reid, eds., *Dictionary of Paul and His Letters* (Downers Grove, IL: InterVarsity, 1993), 158.

Do note that while many Romans commentators today recognize the possibility that the "I" in Romans 7 is not Paul speaking about himself, there are many different conclusions drawn as to what is being specifically communicated if this is not autobiographical material.

discipline ourselves. Regardless of Jacob's, or our own deceitful flesh patterns that we may still be wrestling with here or there, God is still able to accomplish His will, just as the people destined to be His own possession did this as seen throughout the Torah and Tanakh. Let us take a look.

## The Journey Home

Over twenty years have passed since Jacob left his brother Esau, and now, after reconciling with his father-in-law Laban,[44] he is faced with the prospect of facing his sibling and perceived enemy. Remember that the reason Jacob journeyed to the east was initially to depart from the wrath of his brother's rage.[45] Now with two wives, two concubines, twelve children,[46] many slaves, and much livestock, he is returning to his original home with great trepidation. He vividly recalls Esau's plans to kill him. In this illuminating *parashah*, Jacob's character is permanently altered, having the socket of his thigh dislocated by wrestling with the Divine being all night long (Genesis 32:24-32). Yet Jacob not only received the blessing of being renamed Israel (he who struggles with God) for such endurance, but for many generations following he represents the need for each of God's followers to become dependent on Him—and perhaps how people often literally or figuratively come "limping" into the Kingdom.

But before we as Believers, like Jacob, can limp—or even drag ourselves—successfully into the presence of the Most High, we need to remember that in spite of our most fervent promises and prayers, He is still in ultimate control of things. If the Lord really does have a call upon your life to serve Him and make a difference for Him, regardless of your innate inability to fulfill your part of your pledges, He is big enough to work through you to accomplish His will. In spite of all of the negative idiosyncrasies of Jacob, God was still able to use Him and Jacob will be in the Kingdom (cf. Matthew 8:11; Luke 13:28).

## Promises Made and Broken

Do you recall Jacob's vow to God to give ten percent of all that he had as payment for His provision and protection, from the previous Torah portion?

"Then Jacob made a vow, saying, 'If God will be with me and will keep me on this journey that I take, and will give me food to eat and garments to wear, and I return to my father's house in safety, then the LORD will be my God. This stone, which I have set up as a pillar, will be God's house, and of all that You give me I will surely give a tenth to You'" (Genesis 28:20-22).

Here, Jacob made a solemn vow at Bethel (Heb. *Beit'El*, בֵּיתְאֵל; meaning "house of God") to give God ten percent of his wealth, as compensation for His protection and provision. But notice one other thing that was also pledged. At this critical juncture on his journey east, in his heart, Jacob yearned to return to his father Isaac's house safely. Did Jacob at all forget about this? We know that the Lord did not, because in spite of Jacob's personal problems, he is able to return to his home country—and he even finds his brother Esau in a somewhat amicable mood:

"'Please let my lord pass on before his servant, and I will proceed at my leisure, according to the pace of the cattle that are before me and according to the pace of the

---

[44] Genesis 31:43-55.
[45] Genesis 27:42-28:5.
[46] While Benjamin had yet to be born (Genesis 35:18), Dinah was a part of this company (Genesis 30:21).

children, until I come to my lord at Seir.' Esau said, 'Please let me leave with you some of the people who are with me.' But he said, 'What need is there? Let me find favor in the sight of my lord'" (Genesis 33:14-15).

This scene occurs after Jacob's incredible experience at Peniel where he encountered, and even wrestled with, what some think was a pre-Incarnate manifestation of Messiah Yeshua. Even after this life altering experience, where he received his limp, Jacob still has a human tendency to say something that he does not really mean. Was his fear of Esau still a motivating force in his life? What about his statements made to the Lord some twenty years earlier on his trek east? Did he forget that God wanted him to return to Isaac's house, to carry on the call that He had given the Patriarchs? Surely, God would protect him. It appears that for some reason, Jacob was content to simply cross the Jordan and settle in the land around Shechem:

"Now Jacob came safely to the city of Shechem, which is in the land of Canaan, when he came from Paddan-aram, and camped before the city. He bought the piece of land where he had pitched his tent from the hand of the sons of Hamor, Shechem's father, for one hundred pieces of money. Then he erected there an altar and called it El-Elohe-Israel" (Genesis 33:18-20).

Here in Shechem, the Scriptures record that Jacob followed the family tradition established by his grandfather Abraham when he purchased the caves at Machpelah in Mamre near Hebron. How could this be? Years earlier, a fleeing Jacob indicated a hunger to be reunited with his father (Genesis 28:21), and even weeks earlier, as the broken and renamed Israel, he promises his brother that he would come to his father in Seir. So why does Jacob stop at Shechem, and not proceed any further?

## "Just Give Me Peace"

Jacob changes his mind and purchases land near Shechem. Soon, his growing family and extensive herds become permanent fixtures among the Shechemites. He even erects an altar that signifies his allegiance to the Lord, an indication that he does not plan on moving anywhere anytime soon. Does he not remember his vows to the Lord and the corresponding covenants promised to him?

Most can identify with Jacob/Israel at this point in his life. *He just wants peace*. He has just come through the trauma of encountering his brother, and certainly felt a great deal of relief that his life and the lives of his family have been spared. He knows that Esau has become very wealthy, and that Esau's holdings would perhaps create a conflict if he relocates to the area around Hebron, which includes the region of Seir to the east. He somehow justifies his decision to simply settle into the community around Shechem. The Scriptures do not indicate how long Jacob and his family had been a part of the Shechem area, but in due time, circumstances erupt that create serious tension between the indigenous population and the children of Jacob/Israel:

"Now Dinah the daughter of Leah, whom she had borne to Jacob, went out to visit the daughters of the land. When Shechem the son of Hamor the Hivite, the prince of the land, saw her, he took her and lay with her by force" (Genesis 34:1-2).

Whether Dinah was actually raped, or whether she had consensual relations with Shechem the prince because he convinced her to do so, is not the point. The fact remains that she ventured into the neighborhood, and became known among the young people of Shechem's community. In time, she attracts the attention of the young prince. Before long, whether by force or enticement, the sexual act takes place. Apparently, the prince is deeply attracted to Dinah and he asks for her hand in marriage:

"He was deeply attracted to Dinah the daughter of Jacob, and he loved the girl and spoke tenderly to her. So Shechem spoke to his father Hamor, saying, 'Get me this young girl for a wife.' Now Jacob heard that he had defiled Dinah his daughter; but his sons were with his livestock in the field, so Jacob kept silent until they came in. Then Hamor the father of Shechem went out to Jacob to speak with him. Now the sons of Jacob came in from the field when they heard *it*; and the men were grieved, and they were very angry because he had done a disgraceful thing in Israel by lying with Jacob's daughter, for such a thing ought not to be done. But Hamor spoke with them, saying, 'The soul of my son Shechem longs for your daughter; please give her to him in marriage. Intermarry with us; give your daughters to us and take our daughters for yourselves. Thus you shall live with us, and the land shall be *open* before you; live and trade in it and acquire property in it'" (Genesis 34:3-10).

Jacob was in quite a dilemma. After he heard the reports of this transgression, he waited silently to ponder his reaction. He might have recalled when he had his first encounter with Rachel at the well in Paddan-Aram many years earlier:

"Then Jacob kissed Rachel, and lifted his voice and wept. Jacob told Rachel that he was a relative of her father and that he was Rebekah's son, and she ran and told her father" (Genesis 29:11-12).

In the social mores of that day, it was not proper for a man to kiss a woman at their initial meeting, but Jacob had succumbed to the physical attraction he bore his cousin. And as it turns out, they ended up being far more than "kissing cousins." Is it possible that Jacob understood how passion and longing could be used to further God's plans for His people? He had certainly seen how it worked out in his life. He might have concluded that God was working through these unfortunate circumstances with Dinah and Shechem.

## A Deafening Silence

Hamor, the father of Shechem, makes a plea for the hand of Dinah for his son.[47] But what is interesting to note is that Jacob never responds to any of the overtures. Instead, it is his sons who retort back with the conditions of intermarriage. Why was he so silent on the matter? Did he simply consent to the arrangement that was proposed, and allow his sons to figure out the finer details? Certainly, if he disagreed with the proposal, he could have said something, and the conditions for family unions would not be acted upon. Instead, Jacob/Israel, knowing that his sons were livid, allowed the conditions to be offered. Did he know what was in their hearts, or was he more interested in maintaining peace? Here are the conditions that were determined:

"But Jacob's sons answered Shechem and his father Hamor with deceit, because he had defiled Dinah their sister. They said to them, 'We cannot do this thing, to give our sister to one who is uncircumcised, for that would be a disgrace to us. Only on this *condition* will we consent to you: if you will become like us, in that every male of you be circumcised, then we will give our daughters to you, and we will take your daughters for ourselves, and we will live with you and become one people. But if you will not listen to us to be circumcised, then we will take our daughter and go" (Genesis 34:13-17).

---

[47] Genesis 34:6ff.

Before too long, the requirement to circumcise all the men of Shechem was enacted in order for the intermarriage and assimilation to take place. But what was intended to take place did not occur. The treachery that was in the hearts of Simeon and Levi surfaced, and they completed a murderous engagement. As our Torah portion summarizes,

"Now it came about on the third day, when they were in pain, that two of Jacob's sons, Simeon and Levi, Dinah's brothers, each took his sword and came upon the city unawares, and killed every male. They killed Hamor and his son Shechem with the edge of the sword, and took Dinah from Shechem's house, and went forth. Jacob's sons came upon the slain and looted the city, because they had defiled their sister. They took their flocks and their herds and their donkeys, and that which was in the city and that which was in the field; and they captured and looted all their wealth and all their little ones and their wives, even all that *was* in the houses" (Genesis 34:25-29).

After the entire male population of Shechem is murdered—which was fairly easily to liquidate thanks to the pain of circumcision—the rest of the brothers complete the task of stealing all the wealth of the city. Can you imagine such deceitful actions being committed by the chosen people of God? Where was the compassion for the indiscretion of Dinah, and the young prince Shechem who wanted to make restitution? There was no mercy or grace found in the proud hearts of these sons of Jacob/Israel. Instead, murder and revenge prevailed. After these vile acts, the reaction of Jacob is finally recorded as he rebukes Simeon and Levi:

"Then Jacob said to Simeon and Levi, 'You have brought trouble on me by making me odious among the inhabitants of the land, among the Canaanites and the Perizzites; and my men being few in number, they will gather together against me and attack me and I will be destroyed, I and my household.' But they said, 'Should he treat our sister as a harlot?'" (Genesis 34:30-31).

The dialogue ends, and Jacob and company move.

## A Divine Response

Jacob quickly recognizes that these actions have imperiled his entire family. There is no Biblical record of Jacob responding to the pleas that Simeon and Levi offered in their defense. Instead, the next recorded statement comes from God Himself. The Lord reminds Jacob to return to Bethel to recall the promises that were made to Him:

"Then God said to Jacob, 'Arise, go up to Bethel and live there, and make an altar there to God, who appeared to you when you fled from your brother Esau'" (Genesis 35:1).

Another altar is erected, memorializing the promises received.[48] The journey continues down the hills of the Promised Land toward Hebron, and Jacob finally gets back on the trail to his father Isaac's home. But again there are challenges. His beloved wife Rachel dies at the birth of Benjamin in what is modern-day Bethlehem.[49] The love of Jacob's life is taken from him. On the journey, Jacob's eldest son Reuben sins, thus forfeiting his position to become the leader of the next generation:

"Then Israel journeyed on and pitched his tent beyond the tower of Eder. It came about while Israel was dwelling in that land, that Reuben went and lay with Bilhah his father's concubine, and Israel heard *of it*. Now there were twelve sons of Jacob" (Genesis 35:21-22).

---

[48] Genesis 35:7, 9-15.
[49] Genesis 35:16-20.

And, the journey back home continues… Finally, the full circle is completed and Jacob/Israel is back at his father's side. The promises to Abraham, Isaac, and Jacob are being fulfilled. **And, the most ironic thing occurs from our human perspective** as Isaac dies and his sons, Esau and Jacob, bury him:

"Jacob came to his father Isaac at Mamre of Kiriath-arba (that is, Hebron), where Abraham and Isaac had sojourned. Now the days of Isaac were one hundred and eighty years. Isaac breathed his last and died and was gathered to his people, an old man of ripe age; and his sons Esau and Jacob buried him" (Genesis 35:27-29).

## The Journey Completed

Regardless of all the bad decisions that Jacob made along his journey, the promise to be returned to the land of his fathers is completed. Of course, he is without the love of his life, Rachel, and is further burdened by the sinful acts of his sons in Shechem during the final leg of their trek south. But he does not forget these critical events in his life. In fact, the whole future of the nation of Israel is, in many respects, determined by some of the things which occurred during these travels down the hills of what would later be called Samaria and Judea.

In his final days, as Israel is blessing his sons, the ultimate destinies of Reuben, Simeon, and Levi are uttered. Because of their lustful and treacherous acts they lose the right to receive the blessings bestowed upon the firstborn. Instead, such a firstborn status is ultimately passed onto Judah:

"Then Jacob summoned his sons and said, 'Assemble yourselves that I may tell you what will befall you in the days to come. Gather together and hear, O sons of Jacob; and listen to Israel your father. Reuben, you are my firstborn; My might and the beginning of my strength, Preeminent in dignity and preeminent in power. Uncontrolled as water, you shall not have preeminence, because you went up to your father's bed; then you defiled *it*— he went up to my couch. Simeon and Levi are brothers; their swords are implements of violence. Let my soul not enter into their council; let not my glory be united with their assembly; because in their anger they slew men, and in their self-will they lamed oxen. Cursed be their anger, for it is fierce; and their wrath, for it is cruel. I will disperse them in Jacob, and scatter them in Israel. Judah, your brothers shall praise you; your hand shall be on the neck of your enemies; your father's sons shall bow down to you. Judah is a lion's whelp; from the prey, my son, you have gone up. He couches, he lies down as a lion, and as a lion, who dares rouse him up? The scepter shall not depart from Judah, Nor the ruler's staff from between his feet, until Shiloh comes, and to him *shall be* the obedience of the peoples. He ties *his* foal to the vine, and his donkey's colt to the choice vine; he washes his garments in wine, and his robes in the blood of grapes. His eyes are dull from wine, and his teeth white from milk'" (Genesis 49:1-12).

From these blessings and penalizations, you can see how the actions which took place in Shechem were indeed inappropriate. If the murders were consistent with God's laws and His true intention, then Simeon or Levi would have inherited the blessing of firstborn. But instead, those blessings were passed onto Judah.

## Lessons Learned

In our study of the Torah, today's challenge is to reflect upon the life of Jacob and his sons and seek a better way. What is our Heavenly Father trying to reveal to us as we contemplate the traumatic life of Jacob, and his struggle to return to the home of his father?

Regardless of Jacob's bad decisions and the consequences of them, God is still going to accomplish His will via the people He has chosen to represent Him in the world. For unknown reasons, He does not cover up or hide the transgressions of the people chosen to be His own possession. *The Biblical record includes their faults, demonstrating such a chosen people to truly be people.*

This reality should not encourage Believers to pursue things contrary to God's way. Instead, with the benefits of the Scriptural records preserved for us, we should learn to honor the verbal commitments that we have made to the Lord and to each other. We should recognize that what we say and what we do have long term consequences for us as well as our children. **We should learn from the mistakes of those who have preceded us, so we do not repeat them.** We see that Reuben, Simeon, and Levi were denied the blessing of being the chosen, main leaders of Israel.

## Spirit-Led Decisions

Like the Apostle Paul who lists the example of a sinner in Romans ch. 7, wanting to overcome temptation, if we similarly struggle, we should be willing to admit our faults and strive to do better. Jacob had faults that did hamper his effectiveness in accomplishing God's purpose for his life, and what we commonly remember him for are the good things he achieved near the end of his life—not necessarily in the time period we are considering in this *parashah*.

We each should strive to let the Spirit of God and His will prevail in our decisions, not succumbing to any excuses as to why our way might be better, and certainly not waiting until the end of our lives to be the most effective in His service. We each have choices to make, and if we are filled up with the Ruach HaKodesh we should seriously consider the negative consequences that will result if we are guided by a sinful ethic. As we mature in our walks of faith, it should be natural for us to simply choose the path that the Lord has laid out, guided by the imperative of love. Paul summarizes what God's love (*agapē*) is to chiefly embody in his words to the Corinthians:

"Love is patient, love is kind *and* is not jealous; love does not brag *and* is not arrogant, does not act unbecomingly; it does not seek its own, is not provoked, does not take into account a wrong *suffered*, does not rejoice in unrighteousness, but rejoices with the truth; bears all things, believes all things, hopes all things, endures all things. Love never fails; but if *there are gifts of* prophecy, they will be done away; if *there are* tongues, they will cease; if *there is* knowledge, it will be done away…When I was a child, I used to speak like a child, think like a child, reason like a child; when I became a man, I did away with childish things" (1 Corinthians 13:4-8, 11).

Walking in unconditional love is, at times, a difficult action to take, but one which pleases our Heavenly Father. It definitely exhibits the traits of a maturing saint who submits himself or herself to the required will of the Lord.

Secondly, when encountering those inside, and even outside of the Body of Messiah, we need to exercise grace and mercy. Yeshua the Messiah spoke specifically about our natural, fleshly proclivity to judge others:

"Do not judge so that you will not be judged. For in the way you judge, you will be judged; and by your standard of measure, it will be measured to you. Why do you look at the speck that is in your brother's eye, but do not notice the log that is in your own eye? Or how can you say to your brother, 'Let me take the speck out of your eye,' and behold, the log is in your own eye? You hypocrite, first take the log out of your own eye, and then you will see clearly to take the speck out of your brother's eye" (Matthew 7:1-5).

If we take this truth to heart, we will knowingly conclude that our flesh wants to justify itself without first examining its own faults. We might look down on others who do not see things we way we do, or who remain in immaturity. Rather than be a partial human judge—it is much better to humble ourselves, pray for those who are wrestling with issues of sin, and let the impartial Judge, God Himself, work through the issues with such people. Who in his or her right mind would want to judge another person's heart, when such a person's own heart has glaring deficiencies that need to be worked through?

Finally, we have an excellent summary remark to consider by James the Just:

"My brethren, if any among you strays from the truth and one turns him back, let him know that he who turns a sinner from the error of his way will save his soul from death and will cover a multitude of sins" (James 5:19-20).

Is it not better for Spirit-led followers of Messiah Yeshua to seek this level of restitution with those who have strayed from the truth? Such a restoration, though, needs to be tempered with the same love and mercy that saved us!

The life of Jacob and his choices have been preserved for our instruction. Jacob was always reminded of his encounter with God at Peniel as he limped through the remainder of his life (Genesis 32:25, 31-32). Have you ever had a dramatic, life altering event, that has initiated needed change away from the ways of the flesh? As you contemplate *V'yishlach* this week, what important lesson might you be overlooking? Hopefully, unlike Jacob who wrestled with God, the only limps that we have in life are those that come from bent knees **in continual prayer and humble submission to God's will**—and not any kind of reminder for chastisement from Him. In such prayer, we will learn the discernment of when to speak, and when to be silent.

## *V'yeishev* וַיֵּשֶׁב
### He continued living
### "Sovereign Choices"

**Genesis 37:1-40:23**
**Amos 2:6-3:8**

Sometimes during the course of Torah reflection, the Lord will use whatever the weekly *parashah* is to really force you to consider where you stand before Him. *V'yeishev* is just one of those readings, as the circumstances of life and the choices we have to make are brought right to the surface of our attention. Once again, the lives of our spiritual forbearers epitomize much of the perpetual struggle that humanity has had with its Creator.

In *V'yeishev* we see the emergence of Judah and Joseph, as the leaders of their generation, come to light. How they individually handled personal trials is vividly contrasted. For the Believer writing this reflective commentary, presently immersed in a very difficult trial himself (2003), the timing of this portion for reflection has been critical for making the right choice. The example of the Patriarch Joseph is a particularly encouraging one to emulate.

As Believers in the Messiah of Israel, **who must continue to endure in the Lord**, we are each given daily opportunities to make choices. We have many of the same options given to Judah and Joseph, as (1) we can either choose to follow our carnal inclinations, or (2) we can choose to let God work out all the details. Of course, we know that the former path is the natural way for the world and those who lack the indwelling presence of the Ruach HaKodesh (Holy Spirit). The second path requires faith in a Sovereign Creator, who we trust will work things out according to His perfect plan for our lives.

Years ago, in my early days in the faith, the writings of Paul helped me with some decisions I was making, which could only be prompted and executed by the Spirit of the Most High within me:

"Now we have received, not the spirit of the world, but the Spirit who is from God, so that we may know the things freely given to us by God, which things we also speak, not in words taught by human wisdom, but in those taught by the Spirit, combining spiritual *thoughts* with spiritual *words*. But a natural man does not accept the things of the Spirit of God, for they are foolishness to him; and he cannot understand them, because they are spiritually appraised. But he who is spiritual appraises all things, yet he himself is appraised by no one. For WHO HAS KNOWN THE MIND OF THE LORD, THAT HE WILL INSTRUCT HIM [Isaiah 40:13]? But we have the mind of Messiah" (1 Corinthians 2:12-16).

## Joseph's Choices

As I look at the life of Joseph, I am reminded that for some reason he made what appeared to be some very spiritual and faithful decisions, as God was preparing him for the saving work he was going to accomplish for his brothers. Why was he able to make such godly choices during his testings with his brothers (Genesis 37:18-36), while employed (Genesis 39:1-18), or incarcerated in the bowels of Egypt (Genesis 39:19-23)? Was it because of the visions he received as a youth (Genesis 37:1-17)? Without a doubt Joseph's dreams had an impact on his choices (cf. Genesis 40), as the Psalmist further articulates,

"He sent a man before them, Joseph, *who* was sold as a slave. They afflicted his feet with fetters, He himself was laid in irons; until the time that his word came to pass, the word of the LORD tested him" (Psalm 105:17-19).

It appears that from this statement "the word" that Joseph received in his dreams had a powerful impact on his future. In fact, it is evident from his actions and reactions to unprovoked abuse that he was able to choose a path of righteousness. But did you notice the additional mention of the trials or afflictions that he endured? If you look up the Hebrew verb *tzaraf* (צָרַף), you will find out that "This word describes the purifying process of a refiner, who heats metal, takes away the dross, and is left with a pure substance" (*AMG*).[50] You might ask this simple question: Why would God choose to refine Joseph with so many trials over the years until the "word" given to him came about? Perhaps the adage seen in Proverbs 3:12 was at work?

"For whom the LORD loves He reproves, even as a father *corrects* the son in whom he delights" (cf. Hebrews 12:6).

Just as the Psalmist declares, and Proverbs and Hebrews clarify, it is obvious that God loved Joseph and had a redemptive role for him to play during his life. So, a discipline delivered because of love was necessary for Joseph to fulfill his calling. Of course at this

---

[50] Warren Baker and Eugene Carpenter, eds., *The Complete Word Study Dictionary: Old Testament* (Chattanooga: AMG Publishers, 2003), 970.

point, you almost want to throw your hands up in the air and scream, "Why? Why? Why?" Then you are reminded of this very basic truth:

"'For My thoughts are not your thoughts, nor are your ways My ways,' declares the LORD. For *as* the heavens are higher than the earth, so are My ways higher than your ways and My thoughts than your thoughts" (Isaiah 55:8-9).

As students and beneficiaries of Torah reflection, we must be reminded that we are the clay and He is the Potter.[51] Let us all humbly admit that we will be works in progress before we are able to see our Lord face-to-face.

## The Right Choice

Even though God may be in ultimate control of things, reality demands that we still have to make decisions that will affect our lives, just as Joseph did in his day. If we are aware of the common struggle between our carnal inclinations, and the Spirit that indwells us, then we are in good company. This is something that the saints have always battled. The blessing is that we know we are in the war, and are hopefully making choices which relinquish our will to the will of the Holy One.

Have you ever had an encounter with the Most High? It may have been a dream like Joseph's, a voice from the Heavenly realm, or perhaps even a vision from God. Hopefully, this is a part of your testimony—because if it is, then you have the same opportunity that Joseph had to make the right choices. You can reflect upon whatever your encounter was, and remember that at some point in time, the Creator revealed Himself to you in a very unique way. You can recall that He is ultimately in control of the created order, and that He is going to accomplish His tasks.

Knowing these things, what you will learn over time is that if you can choose correctly to submit to His will, making the right spiritual choices, whatever is going on in the circumstances of life will be remedied in a more proficient manner. But if you make a choice based on your carnal proclivities, you may not only impede His speed in rectifying the situation, but you could also become encumbered by the consequences of your preferred, natural choice.

For this seeker, as *V'yeishev*'s instruction has come forth, the choice to let the Lord work out the details of my challenges is relatively easy. Of course this requires patience, one of the fruits of the Spirit that often needs to be exercised more frequently (Galatians 5:22-23). In a like manner, you can imagine how Joseph was also called to wait upon the Lord. And from the testimony of this and other passages in the Scriptures, his faith and patience were strong enough to wait for Him to move. It is encouraging to note that this challenge is not unique to Joseph or anyone of us. In fact, James the Just gives us great advice as he begins his epistle:

"Consider it all joy, my brethren, when you encounter various trials, knowing that the testing of your faith produces endurance. And let endurance have *its* perfect result, so that you may be perfect and complete, lacking in nothing. But if any of you lacks wisdom, let him ask of God, who gives to all generously and without reproach, and it will be given to him" (James 1:2-5).

Endurance can be seen as the result of a faith tempered by time and patience. Look at the results of the trials of life. How do completion and lacking in nothing sound as rewards for making the right choices during times of testing? Consistent study and meditation upon

---

[51] Cf. Isaiah 29:16; Romans 9:21.

God's Word should equip you with the wisdom you need to make the right choices, and in the Father's wisdom, His sovereign choices will be completed in the right time. Joseph waited and trusted. May we, in like manner, choose to follow his example!

# Mikkeitz מִקֵּץ
## At the end
## "To Him Be the Glory"

> Genesis 41:1-44:17
> 1 Kings 3:15-4:1

This week's *parashah* includes a very important verse that should immediately focus our attention on what God was accomplishing through the life of Joseph, when he is asked to interpret the dreams that Pharaoh has been having:

"Joseph then answered Pharaoh, saying, 'It is not in me; God will give Pharaoh a favorable answer'" (Genesis 41:16).

*Mikkeitz* allows each of us, once again, to witness the sovereign will of the Creator take its course. The sons of Jacob/Israel are once more called upon to be the principal actors in a real life drama that has been preserved for our instruction. Here, the Holy One displays His omniscient will over the affairs of the world. The Lord has a very special assignment for the people of the covenants, and He guarantees that everything that He desires goes according to His script, by deliberately selecting the cast and arranging the unique circumstances. It is abundantly clear from the record left to us in the Scriptures, that our Father wants us to learn not only from the mistakes committed by the twelve sons of Jacob/Israel—but also from the instances when proper decisions were made by them.

The protagonist in this drama is none other than the noble Joseph, who has risen from the depths of ignominious incarceration. Now positioned as the vice regent of Egypt, he finally has a golden opportunity to return the same evil upon his brothers that he received some twenty years earlier when he was sold into slavery. But something is uniquely merciful about the character of Joseph. Even though he paid a costly price for his brother's evil intentions, he does not harbor any residual bitterness toward them. Instead, he simply takes the circumstances to teach them an indelible lesson. What was it about Joseph that allowed him to extend such grace? What can modern-day Believers learn from Joseph's example?

### Dreamer of Dreams

Joseph learned as a youth that the Creator God is real. From the stories that he certainly heard from his father, he concluded that He was a personal Deity who was intimately concerned about His chosen people and the promises they had been given. His experiences with dreams certainly had an impact on his life. For years, sequestered in dank prisons, he had plenty of time to relive and analyze not only these dreams, but also the consequences of sharing them with his brothers and father. Then, this dreamer of dreams discovered in confinement that he was able to interpret others' dreams. But before listening to the dreams of others, he immediately proclaims to the cupbearer and baker that interpretations of dreams belong to his God:

"Then they said to him, 'We have had a dream and there is no one to interpret it.' Then Joseph said to them, 'Do not interpretations belong to God? Tell *it* to me, please'" (Genesis 40:8).

Joseph gives credit where credit is due. He tells the wine steward and the baker that it is only in the power of the Creator to interpret dreams. But he does have the faith to ask about the dreams, and the Lord intervenes. Joseph supernaturally receives and repeats the interpretation without any regard to the pleasant or unpleasant report (Genesis 40:9-23). What he soon discovers is that he is understanding a voice which is giving him the interpretation.

The critical thing that Joseph learned during his years in prison is that dreams and the interpretation of them can cause things to happen. For another two years (Genesis 41:1), he ponders the accuracy of his interpretation until an opportunity to interpret another dream comes forth.

## Pharaoh's Dreams

The next time Joseph is called upon to interpret something, the dreams are from the supreme ruler of Egypt, the Pharaoh himself. Now, the gifted young servant of the prison's captain of the guard is summoned to hear and interpret the dreams. He already knew that Pharaoh has exacting demands upon his servants. Remember that the baker had been hanged for no stated reason. How was he, a foreign prisoner, going to be received in a society where the Egyptians disdained Semites? Without hesitation, upon being asked whether he can once again interpret a dream (Genesis 41:15), he responds with this concise statement:

"Joseph then answered Pharaoh, saying, 'It is not in me; God will give Pharaoh a favorable answer'" (Genesis 41:16).

Joseph's first response was to give all the glory to the God of his fathers. Joseph knew that the ability to interpret dreams was not something he could just conjure up with some mystical magic. God was pleased by Joseph's attitude and he was given the proper interpretation of Pharaoh's dreams. At the conclusion of the interpretations an interesting discourse follows:

"'Now as for the repeating of the dream to Pharaoh twice, *it means* that the matter is determined by God, and God will quickly bring it about. Now let Pharaoh look for a man discerning and wise, and set him over the land of Egypt. Let Pharaoh take action to appoint overseers in charge of the land, and let him exact a fifth *of the produce* of the land of Egypt in the seven years of abundance. Then let them gather all the food of these good years that are coming, and store up the grain for food in the cities under Pharaoh's authority, and let them guard *it*. Let the food become as a reserve for the land for the seven years of famine which will occur in the land of Egypt, so that the land will not perish during the famine.' Now the proposal seemed good to Pharaoh and to all his servants. Then Pharaoh said to his servants, 'Can we find a man like this, in whom is a divine spirit?' So Pharaoh said to Joseph, 'Since God has informed you of all this, there is no one so discerning and wise as you are. You shall be over my house, and according to your command all my people shall do homage; only in the throne I will be greater than you.' Pharaoh said to Joseph, 'See, I have set you over all the land of Egypt.' Then Pharaoh took off his signet ring from his hand and put it on Joseph's hand, and clothed him in garments of fine linen and put the gold necklace around his neck. He had him ride in his second chariot; and they proclaimed before him, 'Bow the knee!' And he set him over all the land of Egypt. Moreover, Pharaoh said to Joseph,

'*Though* I am Pharaoh, yet without your permission no one shall raise his hand or foot in all the land of Egypt'" (Genesis 41:32-44).

At this critical juncture, Joseph felt the liberty to go beyond just the interpretation of Pharaoh's dream by giving him the solution to contend with the forecasted famine. Something prompted Joseph to go beyond just a strict interpretation. Is it possible that God had allowed Joseph to mature to a point in his walk with Him, that he was able to be a confident voice for Him before world leaders? It is clear from the resulting actions of Pharaoh that the solutions suggested were things that Joseph had been groomed to manage. He had been responsible for Potiphar's home and his possessions, and had done an admirable job of managing his estate. Next, he had been put in charge of the prisoners during his tenure in jail. Apparently, he was again given favor and the affairs of the prison were maintained in proper order.

Now with the wisdom implanted by the Lord, Joseph is positioned to be elevated to the second highest political rank in Egyptian society (Genesis 41:38-49). This is a remarkable rise to power—simply with the blessings of the Most High working through a unique opportunity to interpret dreams! What should we learn from the example of Joseph's life?

## Dreams and Gifts

Perhaps you are gifted with some spiritual endowment that has been freely given to you by the absolute grace of the Creator. Perhaps you have the gift of prophecy, healing, discernment, wisdom, knowledge, or any of the other gifts that our Father freely bestows upon His children for His work to be accomplished (1 Corinthians 12:28-31; Ephesians 4:11-13). You know what the gift is and have seen it operate through you at times. Just how do you operate with a recognizable supernatural gift? Your challenge is to follow the lead of Joseph.

First, remember that the gift has been given to you for purposes beyond your own personal aggrandizement. Instead, whenever you sense a spiritual gift working through you, be cautioned to give whatever glory is due to the Lord for His work to be accomplished through you. Too many times, men and women given gifts of prophecy or healing take advantage of their gifting and begin to use it for manipulative purposes. Many times this results in people who eventually bring dishonor to our Heavenly Father. Too frequently this impedes, rather than advances, His Kingdom work.

Hopefully, we can all take the life of Joseph and his humble example as the proper way to handle the spiritual giftings that are granted by the Lord to each one of us. We must use such spiritual gifts for the purposes of glorifying God, and ultimately drawing people unto Him. If you are straying in the other direction, beware!

Cry out to Him for mercy! Let Him receive the glory that He alone deserves! Ask the Lord to give you the same understanding that Joseph received. Perhaps as you give God the glory for the gifting you have received, He will give you increased responsibility in handling additional tasks in His Kingdom as others are impacted with the message of the gospel.

On the other hand, the Lord may decide to allow you to take credit for what He is doing through you. Then your reward may be here on Earth, rather than through eternity. Remember this reality: we all get the choice of when and by whom we want to be rewarded. Do you want the recognition of mere mortals, for a short season? Or would you prefer eternal favor? *It takes faith to choose the latter option.* Perhaps like Joseph, with some time in seclusion seeking the Father, we might be prepared to make the right choices. If nothing else, quietness before the Lord can certainly enhance our ability to more clearly hear His voice. Perhaps that is one of the reasons He has given us a day to rest and focus upon Him. Consider these questions as you ponder on *Mikkeitz* this *Shabbat*...

# *V'yigash* וַיִּגַּשׁ
## He approached
## "Judah and Joseph Reconciled"

> Genesis 44:18-47:27
> Ezekiel 37:15-28

In this week's Torah reading, we see how Joseph encounters his brothers, who must come to Egypt to purchase provisions. He explains to them that what they intended for evil by selling him into slavery, God has turned around into something good, as he can help them:

"God sent me before you to preserve for you a remnant in the earth, and to keep you alive by a great deliverance. Now, therefore, it was not you who sent me here, but God; and He has made me a father to Pharaoh and lord of all his household and ruler over all the land of Egypt" (Genesis 45:7-8).

When we consider God's plans to help people, through difficult circumstances, you can no doubt draw up a list of many potential applications of this—both in and outside of the Scriptures. Perhaps you yourself have seen the Lord work through terrible circumstances, which have ultimately turned out to be great blessings.

*V'yigash* is an annual reminder of the Father's plan to restore His people to a place of wholeness, just as He did the family of Jacob in ancient times. Each year Torah students have the opportunity to review these dramatic interactions between the sons of Jacob/Israel. The sovereign hand of the Creator should clearly be recognized throughout these recorded in *V'yigash*. We can be confident and assured that our Creator is still maintaining His promises to His people. The encouraging example of brothers finally being reconciled to one another at this particular juncture in the past, should give us great hope that eventually such a place of unity will be achieved among His people now. The Psalmist reminds us each of how glorious it is when we dwell together in unity.

"A Song of Ascents, of David. Behold, how good and how pleasant it is for brothers to dwell together in unity!" (Psalm 133:1).

But what is it about this Torah portion that can be so encouraging to our generation, now looking back at these events after almost four millennia of intervening history? Are there some things that we could be focusing on in light of our present circumstances as a growing and expanding Messianic movement? What about the Messiah-like qualities exemplified by the two principal characters of this familial drama? Is it possible that for our edification and instruction, we have been given excellent examples of the self-sacrifice of Judah, and then the mercy of his brother Joseph?

## The Self Sacrifice of Judah

As the previous *parashah* concludes and this one begins, we see that Judah is increasingly becoming a spokesperson for the family, seeking sustenance from the grain-rich Egyptians. Remember one distinction among the brothers from *Mikkeitz* (Genesis 41:1-

44:17) last week: Judah pledged his life to his father Israel for the life of his brother Benjamin:

"Judah said to his father Israel, 'Send the lad with me and we will arise and go, that we may live and not die, we as well as you and our little ones. I myself will be surety for him; you may hold me responsible for him. If I do not bring him *back* to you and set him before you, then let me bear the blame before you forever" (Genesis 43:8-9).

What had happened to Judah so that he was willing to lose his life for Benjamin? Could it be that his life experience with the Adullamites had softened his heart (cf. Genesis 38)? Earlier, we remember Judah urging his brothers to make a profit from the sale of Joseph rather than murdering him (Genesis 37:26-27). We also know that he has endured the loss of a wife and a son (Genesis 38:7, 10, 12), and knows the pain of those tragedies. Finally, the humbling circumstances with Tamar are obviously used to bring him into recognition of his unrighteousness (Genesis 38:26). Through it all he has developed a sincere tenderness for his father's feelings. When having to speak for the family before the yet-revealed Joseph, he makes the following declaration so that the youngest brother, Benjamin, might not be punished:

"Now, therefore, please let your servant remain instead of the lad a slave to my lord, and let the lad go up with his brothers. For how shall I go up to my father if the lad is not with me—for fear that I see the evil that would overtake my father?" (Genesis 44:33-34).

Obviously, something occurred in the life of Judah that he cannot stand to think about his father's loss of his precious son Benjamin. Here, Judah exemplifies one of the principal traits of the future Messiah of Israel: he is willing to give his life for the life of his brother (cf. John 15:13).

Is this a trait that we should consider as we address required reconciliation with those who are our literal brothers, sisters, family members, *and* fellow members of the household of faith? Are we willing to place the needs of others ahead of our own?[52] *This is admittedly difficult to do.*

## The Mercy of Joseph

In our *parashah* this week, we are also exposed to the Messiah-like characteristic of mercy that is exemplified by Joseph. By the time the famine has taken its toll on the region, Joseph is in place to extend mercy to his brothers. In his position as the viceroy of Egypt, he has the authority to do anything he wants with them, but instead of taking revenge for previous wrongs, he understands clearly that the Lord has placed him in this position for the salvation of the family of Jacob (Genesis 45:7-8).

Joseph knows that the hand of the Almighty was upon him and that he was sent ahead to enact a great deliverance. The thought of vengeance is never mentioned, but instead as we read about Joseph's actions toward his brothers and how the whole family was settled in the best land of Egypt,[53] we are able to focus on the attribute of mercy.

Just how merciful would we be to our family members, if they had committed a similar crime against us? Can we trust the sovereign hand of our Creator, who works through all the circumstances of life to accomplish His will? These, and a multitude of questions, should arise as we think about just how merciful we have been throughout our lives, or perhaps even are now, to people who have done/do us wrong.

---

[52] Philippians 2:3b.
[53] Genesis 45:9-47:12.

בראשית

## The Eventual Reconciliation

The Haftarah selection that corresponds to this Torah reading is Ezekiel 37:15-28, which deals with the future restoration of all Israel. At some point in time, our Heavenly Father is going to take the remnant of Israel from among all the nations, and make them into a single restored people of Israel in the Promised Land:

"Say to them, 'Thus says the Lord GOD, "Behold, I will take the sons of Israel from among the nations where they have gone, and I will gather them from every side and bring them into their own land; and I will make them one nation in the land, on the mountains of Israel; and one king will be king for all of them; and they will no longer be two nations and no longer be divided into two kingdoms"'" (Ezekiel 37:21-22).

Perhaps one way to expedite the eventual restoration of the Kingdom, is that followers of the God of Abraham, Isaac, and Jacob should begin extending the mercy of Joseph to each other, *and* begin exemplifying the self-sacrifice of Judah. This is imperative if one understands that the Messiah of Israel has come and has inaugurated the era of the New Covenant:

"'Behold, days are coming,' declares the LORD, 'when I will make a new covenant with the house of Israel and with the house of Judah, not like the covenant which I made with their fathers in the day I took them by the hand to bring them out of the land of Egypt, My covenant which they broke, although I was a husband to them,' declares the LORD. 'But this is the covenant which I will make with the house of Israel after those days,' declares the LORD, 'I will put My law within them and on their heart I will write it; and I will be their God, and they shall be My people. They will not teach again, each man his neighbor and each man his brother, saying, "Know the LORD," for they will all know Me, from the least of them to the greatest of them,' declares the LORD, 'for I will forgive their iniquity, and their sin I will remember no more'" (Jeremiah 31:31-34).

What is that Law written on the hearts of His people? Do mercy and self-sacrifice sound like the Torah-based qualities that they should be demonstrating, as a result of the permanent forgiveness for sin—which Yeshua's atoning sacrifice has secured us?

If you desire to be reconciled like Joseph and Judah from ages past, then an extension of mercy and self-sacrifice to others can be a good place to start. Perhaps then we will understand just how good and pleasant it is to experience the reality of brothers and sisters dwelling together in unity!

# V'yechi וַיְחִי
## He lived
### "Vowed to the Land"

> Genesis 47:28-50:26
> 1 Kings 2:1-12

While reading through *V'yechi* this week, the following words delivered by the Patriarch Jacob really stuck out at me:

"Then Jacob said to Joseph, 'God Almighty appeared to me at Luz in the land of Canaan and blessed me, and He said to me, "Behold, I will make you fruitful and numerous, and I will make you a company of peoples, and will give this land to your descendants after you for an everlasting possession"'" (Genesis 48:3-4).

*V'yechi* brings us to the end of the Book of Genesis. In just twelve readings, the Scriptures have covered thousands of years of human history. The family chosen to become a people for God's own possession, and the nation that will be a light to the world, is beginning to take shape as distinctive tribes. The life of the great Patriarch Jacob comes to a close, and his blessings bestowed upon his children and grandchildren give prophetic insight into the future characteristics and destinies of the twelve unique tribes and the emerging nation of Israel.[54]

Both Jacob and Joseph have some dying requests upon their respective deaths.[55] Both men had a sincere desire for their remains to be returned to the land of their fathers. Why was this so important? Are there some things we can learn from these examples?

## Return to the Land

As our Torah reading begins, Jacob is approaching his death and he calls for Joseph to fulfill a pledge:

"When the time for Israel to die drew near, he called his son Joseph and said to him, 'Please, if I have found favor in your sight, place now your hand under my thigh and deal with me in kindness and faithfulness. Please do not bury me in Egypt, but when I lie down with my fathers, you shall carry me out of Egypt and bury me in their burial place.' And he said, 'I will do as you have said.' He said, 'Swear to me.' So he swore to him. Then Israel bowed *in worship* at the head of the bed" (Genesis 47:29-31).

As the text continues, Jacob declares his reasons for wanting to be buried in the Land of Canaan:

"Then Jacob said to Joseph, 'God Almighty appeared to me at Luz in the land of Canaan and blessed me, and He said to me, "Behold, I will make you fruitful and numerous, and I will make you a company of peoples, and will give this land to your descendants after you for an everlasting possession"'" (Genesis 48:3-4).

In the case of Jacob, he knew that the destiny of his progeny was in the land promised to his fathers Abraham, Isaac, and ultimately him. Jacob had already prepared a burial site

---

[54] Genesis 49.
[55] Jacob: Genesis 47:28-31; 50:1-11; Joseph: Genesis 50:22-26.

בראשית

for himself next to Leah in the same cave with Abraham, Sarah, Isaac, and Rebekah.[56] He also knew from multiple declarations by God that this was a land which was destined for his descendants. Is it possible that Jacob understood that being buried in the area around Hebron would someday give additional justification for his descendants to claim that land? His request for being buried in Canaan is complied with:

"So Joseph went up to bury his father, and with him went up all the servants of Pharaoh, the elders of his household and all the elders of the land of Egypt" (Genesis 50:7).

Joseph and his brothers honored the vow they made with their father Jacob. Joseph sought and received permission from Pharaoh to place Jacob in the cave at Machpelah, and a party is sent from Egypt to Canaan after the Egyptians mourn for him and he can be mummified (Genesis 50:1-11). The pattern for honoring vows was firmly established in the hearts of the sons of Jacob. As our *parashah* concludes, we see Joseph making the same request regarding his burial to his brothers:

"Joseph said to his brothers, 'I am about to die, but God will surely take care of you and bring you up from this land to the land which He promised on oath to Abraham, to Isaac and to Jacob.' Then Joseph made the sons of Israel swear, saying, 'God will surely take care of you, and you shall carry my bones up from here.' So Joseph died at the age of one hundred and ten years; and he was embalmed and placed in a coffin in Egypt" (Genesis 50:24-26).

Why did Joseph want to be buried in the Land of Canaan, and specifically, in the land promised to him by his father Jacob? There must have been something important to them about this Promised Land. He believed the statements made by his father Jacob that this territory would be an everlasting possession for their descendants. Remember that Joseph had also received an inheritance from Jacob at the conclusion of Jacob's blessings to Ephraim and Manasseh:

"Then Israel said to Joseph, 'Behold, I am about to die, but God will be with you, and bring you back to the land of your fathers. I give you one portion more than your brothers, which I took from the hand of the Amorite with my sword and my bow'" (Genesis 48:21-22).

Notice that it is not until the end of the Book of Joshua when we finally see where the remains of Joseph are placed:

"Now they buried the bones of Joseph, which the sons of Israel brought up from Egypt, at Shechem, in the piece of ground which Jacob had bought from the sons of Hamor the father of Shechem for one hundred pieces of money; and they became the inheritance of Joseph's sons" (Joshua 24:32).

The people of Israel honored the vow made to Joseph, and transported his mummy through the wilderness experience until he was finally laid to rest at a tomb in Shechem. Is it possible that Joseph knew the importance of making the Land of Canaan, specifically Shechem, his final resting place? Did Joseph understood how this could please the Most High, because he respected his father Jacob who had given him this land for his inheritance? For those of us who study the lives of our spiritual forbearers, this embodiment of faith in the promises of the Lord is very inspirational. Even in death, the Patriarchs staked their claim on the Promised Land!

---

[56] Genesis 49:29-33.

## Testimony of Tombs

Today, the territory promised to the Patriarchs is under constant siege, and their burial memorials are a vivid reminder to us all that the final redemption of the Land is not yet complete. But, we have determined men and women who are standing today as a testimony that the Land of the Patriarchs will eventually be a permanent inheritance for those who serve Israel's God. Faithful Jewish settlers who risk life and limb to stake a claim on the land promised to Abraham, Isaac, and Jacob, are mirroring the pattern of belief exhibited by their ancestors. Many of them revere the memory of Jacob and Joseph, and the vows honored by their forefathers.

In Hebron, a city that is currently controlled by the Palestinian Authority, resides a small community of faithful Jews who are a living example of those who are holding onto the promises that have been given by God. Surrounded by a people who largely want them eliminated, the settlers of Kiryat Arba have maintained a synagogue at the tomb of the Patriarchs.

In like manner, overlooking the valley in Shechem (modern-day Nablus of the Palestinian Authority), where the remains of Joseph are (believed to be) buried, there resides another settlement of faithful Jews who are waiting for the redemption of the Promised Land. The Orthodox Jews of Elon Moreh, until the past few years (2002-2003), had a yeshiva located at the tomb of Joseph in hostile Nablus. These faithful followers are staunch defenders of the Torah and its truths. What can we learn from these faithful Jews, who are studying these very same Torah teachings, this week? Is it possible that when they read these very texts about the burial vows made to Jacob and Joseph, that they will be strengthened in their battle of will against any Palestinians who oppose the God of Israel?

Perhaps we can pray for them. and ask the Father what it is that we can do to support them in their role as witnesses to the veracity of the Scriptures. Through the ages, the very fact that these vows were kept, and are now being honored by these Jews willing to risk their lives, gives many the inspiration needed to persevere. These people are living examples of those who have been preserved through the ages because of their choices to honor vows. Do you now see how important vows can be when honored? Should we not do the same regarding our vows?

We do know that One who will maintain His vows is the Holy One of Israel. **One day the Messiah Yeshua will return, and the Land of Israel will become a place of true peace and prosperity!** So for the faithful, it is simply a matter of time before this final redemption of the Promised Land is completed. In this time as the Messianic movement grows and expands—and Jewish and non-Jewish Believers are being brought together as one people in Him—we could be witnessing the final stages in God's redemptive plan coming together. I pray that as we are all brought together, we learn to have an appreciation for the Promised Land—the same that Jacob and Joseph had.

# COMMENTARY ON EXODUS

## *Shemot* שְׁמוֹת
### Names
### "Israel, Cry Out!"

> Exodus 1:1-6:1
> Isaiah 27:6-28:13; 29:22-23 (A);
> Jeremiah 1:2:3 (S)

This week in our Torah studies we begin our examination of the Book of Exodus. In my personal meditations on the first *parashah* of Exodus, I was really hit with what the following verses communicate:

"The LORD said, 'I have surely seen the affliction of My people who are in Egypt, and have given heed to their cry because of their taskmasters, for I am aware of their sufferings. So I have come down to deliver them from the power of the Egyptians, and to bring them up from that land to a good and spacious land, to a land flowing with milk and honey, to the place of the Canaanite and the Hittite and the Amorite and the Perizzite and the Hivite and the Jebusite. Now, behold, the cry of the sons of Israel has come to Me; furthermore, I have seen the oppression with which the Egyptians are oppressing them'" (Exodus 3:7-9).

*Shemot* takes us from the death of Joseph to the time when the people of Israel begin to be delivered from the oppressing hand of the Egyptians (Exodus 6:1ff). The principal figure in the Torah narrative shifts from Joseph, who we saw at the end of Genesis, to a Levite named Moses,[1] who will be called by God to lead Israel out of its Egyptian bondage.[2]

In essence, much of our *parashah* reveals the process of how Israel will be released from the bondage of physical human slavery, and we see how its relationship to God will be more clearly described and defined. This portion has a number of interesting vignettes which can help Bible readers better understand our Creator. Moses has his burning bush experience,[3] and we see God first revealing His Divine Name to people.[4] We see in many specific ways how the Most High is a very personal God to His people, and that He talks to His servants and instructs them in what He wants them to do.

---

[1] Exodus 2:1-4:31.
[2] Exodus 3:10-22.
[3] Exodus 3:1-9.
[4] Exodus 3:14-15.

## The God Who Sees and Listens

I would like to focus your attention on two statements from *Shemot*, which reveal how our covenant-keeping God is intimately concerned about the condition of His people. In fact, we see how He saw and listened to the very groans and cries of His people:

"Now it came about in *the course of* those many days that the king of Egypt died. And the sons of Israel sighed because of the bondage, and they cried out; and their cry for help because of *their* bondage rose up to God. So God heard their groaning; and God remembered His covenant with Abraham, Isaac, and Jacob. God saw the sons of Israel, and God took notice *of them*" (Exodus 2:23-25).

"The LORD said, 'I have surely seen the affliction of My people who are in Egypt, and have given heed to their cry because of their taskmasters, for I am aware of their sufferings'" (Exodus 3:7).

Here, we are reminded how God watches over His covenant people and listens to their concerns. Like a good shepherd minding his fold of sheep, the Lord oversees His chosen flock. He is faithful to remember the promises He has made to the Patriarchs.[5] This should be very comforting not only for us to read in the Scriptures, but for those who serve the God of Abraham, Isaac, and Jacob *today*. As the Psalmist reminds us, the Holy One of Israel neither slumbers nor sleeps:

"A Song of Ascents. I will lift up my eyes to the mountains; from where shall my help come? My help *comes* from the LORD, who made heaven and earth. He will not allow your foot to slip; He who keeps you will not slumber. Behold, He who keeps Israel will neither slumber nor sleep. The LORD is your keeper; the LORD is your shade on your right hand. The sun will not smite you by day, nor the moon by night. The LORD will protect you from all evil; He will keep your soul. The LORD will guard your going out and your coming in from this time forth and forever" (Psalm 121:1-8).

The Lord is always attentive to our pleadings. The question we must ask ourselves is simply this: **Are we crying out for His presence and deliverance as in days of old?** What can you learn from our reading in *Shemot*, that you have perhaps glossed over in the past?

## The Cries of David

We know that the Holy Writ is replete with examples of faithful men and women who have cried out to God for help. Perhaps one of the most consistent "criers out" to the Lord is King David. Multiple times we are reminded in his Psalms that he cried to God for guidance, mercy, and compassion. Are there some principles we should be learning about our relationship with Him? Consider these varied quotations from the Book of Psalms:

- "Heed the sound of my cry for help, my King and my God, for to You I pray. In the morning, O LORD, You will hear my voice; in the morning I will order *my prayer* to You and *eagerly* watch. For You are not a God who takes pleasure in wickedness; no evil dwells with You" (Psalm 5:2-4).
- "In my distress I called upon the LORD, and cried to my God for help; He heard my voice out of His temple, and my cry for help before Him came into His ears" (Psalm 18:6).

---

[5] Exodus 3:6, 16.

- "Hear, O LORD, when I cry with my voice, and be gracious to me and answer me. *When You said*, 'Seek My face,' my heart said to You, 'Your face, O LORD, I shall seek'" (Psalm 27:7-8).
- "The eyes of the LORD are toward the righteous and His ears are *open* to their cry. The face of the LORD is against evildoers, to cut off the memory of them from the earth. *The righteous* cry, and the LORD hears and delivers them out of all their troubles" (Psalm 34:15-17).

Here, in just four Psalms, we can detect some important characteristics about how King David communed with the Lord. We see how David cried out to God on a regular basis. We are told that in the morning, he prayed before Him. David's words remind us that he understood how the Lord is indeed approachable through prayer and supplication. David knew that the Lord heard his pleas, and by some of the statements delivered in Psalms, we know that He would speak back to David:

"*When You said*, 'Seek My face,' my heart said to You, 'Your face, O LORD, I shall seek'" (Psalm 27:8).

Here, David says that He requests him to seek His face. Of course, when David hears God's voice, the response is an immediate affirmation of the request. Should not this be the kind of intimacy we should all be seeking?

## God's People Today

From the testimony of the Ancient Israelites and how they were eventually delivered from Egyptian bondage, we should have confidence that God will hear our groans and cries. But are we consistently offering them before the Father's throne, or are they issued before Him as *complaints*? Do we simply issue some kind of lip service to the Lord, because ultimately we are in bondage to the things of this world that are either not oppressive enough to prompt any pleadings—or that we actually *want* to be in bondage to?

We know that the whole Creation is groaning because of its slavery to sinful corruption. In a like manner, we should be groaning for the ultimate redemption of our bodies, which has been promised from the beginning. Consider the words of the Apostle Paul, who describes this reality:

"For the creation was subjected to futility, not willingly, but because of Him who subjected it, in hope that the creation itself also will be set free from its slavery to corruption into the freedom of the glory of the children of God. For we know that the whole creation groans and suffers the pains of childbirth together until now. And not only this, but also we ourselves, having the first fruits of the Spirit, even we ourselves groan within ourselves, waiting eagerly for *our* adoption as sons, the redemption of our body" (Romans 8:20-23).

Paul was writing to Believers who had been redeemed by the power of the Spirit of God, but were still waiting for the Second Coming and the complete restoration of the body. Because of Yeshua's atoning work, they were able to approach the Father much more easily and personably than the Ancient Israelites before them, and pray for the ability to overcome the struggles of life:

"But if the Spirit of Him who raised Yeshua from the dead dwells in you, He who raised Messiah Yeshua from the dead will also give life to your mortal bodies through His Spirit who dwells in you. So then, brethren, we are under obligation, not to the flesh, to live according to the flesh—for if you are living according to the flesh, you must die; but if by the Spirit you are putting to death the deeds of the body, you will live. For all who are being led by the Spirit of God, these are sons of God. For you have not received a spirit of slavery leading to fear again, but you have received a spirit of adoption as sons by which we cry out, 'Abba! Father!' The Spirit Himself testifies with our spirit that we are children of God" (Romans 8:11-16).

Here, Paul teaches that Believers have not received a spirit of slavery that leads to fear, but instead have received a spirit of adoption that leads to hope. In this case, as redeemed people we should now be crying out with even greater confidence than King David—because we have the Spirit of God testifying that we are His adopted children!

As redeemed children of God, how much more secure should we be, in knowing that our groans and cries to Him are heard? Today, it is our responsibility as God's people to be crying and groaning for the sake of Israel and our fallen world. As fellow heirs with the Messiah, we can intercede for the lost just as Yeshua interceded in prayer:

"Now if we are children, then we are heirs—heirs of God and co-heirs with Christ, if indeed we share in his sufferings in order that we may also share in his glory" (Romans 8:17, NIV).

May the Lord encourage you in your walk, as you approach Him and intercede to Him for those who have not yet been adopted by Him as a son or daughter of faith. Perhaps our groaning and cries will lead to another great deliverance for Israel, and indeed, the entire world. **Certainly, we should be rest assured that our cries will be heard!** May His deliverance occur in our lifetimes!

# *V'eira* וָאֵרָא
## I appeared
## "Proclaim His Power and Might"

> Exodus 6:2-9:35
> Ezekiel 28:25-29:21

Our Torah portion for this week begins with us seeing the Lord summarize His covenant faithfulness with His people, as He prepares to act in delivering them from Egypt:

"God spoke further to Moses and said to him, 'I am the LORD; and I appeared to Abraham, Isaac, and Jacob, as God Almighty, but *by* My name, LORD, I did not make Myself known to them. I also established My covenant with them, to give them the land of Canaan, the land in which they sojourned. Furthermore I have heard the groaning of the sons of Israel, because the Egyptians are holding them in bondage, and I have remembered My covenant'" (Exodus 6:2-5).

Throughout *V'eira* we see God reign down various judgments upon Egypt.[6] Even though Moses and Aaron constantly return to Pharaoh with the Divine plea, "Let My people go,"[7] his heart continues to be hardened.[8] Reading through our *parashah*, it seems that God's two spokespersons are actually losing ground in their role as His agents to deliver the

---

[6] Exodus 7:14-9:35.
[7] Exodus 7:16; 8:1, 20f; 9:1, 13.
[8] Exodus 7:13, 22; 8:15, 19, 32; 9:7, 12, 34-35.

Israelites from the oppression of the Egyptians. If you will remember, as the previous Torah portion, *Shemot* (Exodus 1:1-6:1), came to a close, Moses himself was perplexed about this dilemma. The people of Israel were in worse shape than when the requests to Pharaoh began. The complaints and criticism were bearing down on Moses and Aaron:

"Then Moses returned to the LORD and said, 'O Lord, why have You brought harm to this people? Why did You ever send me? Ever since I came to Pharaoh to speak in Your name, he has done harm to this people, and You have not delivered Your people at all'" (Exodus 5:22-23).

Moses was frustrated. He knew he had been called to this assignment, yet every verbal attempt to get the people released ended in greater harm for Israel. Then, God responds with a strong word that establishes the tone for the rest of what we will see during Moses' and Aaron's encounters with Pharaoh. The Lord makes the following statement that closes *Shemot*, and opens *V'eira*, definitively declaring what He was about to do:

"Then the LORD said to Moses, 'Now you shall see what I will do to Pharaoh; for under compulsion he will let them go, and under compulsion he will drive them out of his land.' God spoke further to Moses and said to him, 'I am the LORD; and I appeared to Abraham, Isaac, and Jacob, as God Almighty, but *by* My name, LORD, I did not make Myself known to them. I also established My covenant with them, to give them the land of Canaan, the land in which they sojourned. Furthermore I have heard the groaning of the sons of Israel, because the Egyptians are holding them in bondage, and I have remembered My covenant. Say, therefore, to the sons of Israel, "I am the LORD, and I will bring you out from under the burdens of the Egyptians, and I will deliver you from their bondage. I will also redeem you with an outstretched arm and with great judgments. Then I will take you for My people, and I will be your God; and you shall know that I am the LORD your God, who brought you out from under the burdens of the Egyptians. I will bring you to the land which I swore to give to Abraham, Isaac, and Jacob, and I will give it to you *for* a possession; I am the LORD"'" (Exodus 6:1-8).

Here in these words, the Lord establishes just who He is and just what He is about to do with Moses and Aaron, with Pharaoh and the Egyptians, and with the Ancient Israelites. Remember how the Almighty has established a unilateral covenant with His chosen people. It is the Lord who swore the inheritance of the Promised Land to them multiple times (Genesis 12:7; 15:18; 17:4; 26:3; 28:4), and yet for some reason or another, they still do not believe that the deliverance is coming:

"So Moses spoke thus to the sons of Israel, but they did not listen to Moses on account of *their* despondency and cruel bondage" (Exodus 6:9).

The people of Israel continue to groan, and we recall from last week that God hears their cries and groans, remembering His covenant:

"Now it came about in *the course of* those many days that the king of Egypt died. And the sons of Israel sighed because of the bondage, and they cried out; and their cry for help because of *their* bondage rose up to God. So God heard their groaning; and God remembered His covenant with Abraham, Isaac, and Jacob" (Exodus 2:23-24).

As the groaning increased with the loss of straw for the Israelites to make bricks, the Lord implements His plan for their deliverance. But as we read, this deliverance is not immediately enacted. Instead, we are told about eight different signs and judgments that are designed to judge the various gods of Egypt, and communicate to Egypt *and* to Israel His might and power. The Lord will be displaying, for the sake of Egypt *and* Israel, that He and He alone is the One True God who possesses absolute sovereignty.

In a series of dramatic encounters, Moses and Aaron begin to beseech Pharaoh to let the Israelites leave. The first sign is Aaron throwing his staff on the ground where it becomes a snake. Shortly thereafter, the Egyptian magicians do the same thing with their staffs, but soon discover Aaron's staff/snake swallowing their staffs/snakes (Exodus 7:8-13). Next, Aaron touches his staff to the Nile River and the water turns to blood. Then, the magicians again match the miracle and turn water into blood (Exodus 7:14-25). Third, Aaron waves his staff over the Nile River and a plague of frogs come up and cover the land. Interestingly, the Egyptian magicians are again able to duplicate the feat (Exodus 8:1-15). Each time as another sign takes place, Pharaoh's heart is hardened. Finally, Aaron touches his staff to the ground, and some kind of gnats or lice invade Egypt:

"Then the LORD said to Moses, 'Say to Aaron, "Stretch out your staff and strike the dust of the earth, that it may become gnats through all the land of Egypt."' They did so; and Aaron stretched out his hand with his staff, and struck the dust of the earth, and there were gnats on man and beast. All the dust of the earth became gnats through all the land of Egypt. The magicians tried with their secret arts to bring forth gnats, but they could not; so there were gnats on man and beast. Then the magicians said to Pharaoh, 'This is the finger of God.' But Pharaoh's heart was hardened, and he did not listen to them, as the LORD had said" (Exodus 8:16-19).

The magicians of Egypt could no longer counterfeit the signs and judgments. They clearly proclaimed that what they saw with the gnats was obviously the "finger of God." A comparison could be made that just like God had taken the dust of the ground to form Adam (Genesis 2:7), He now took dust and He brought forth these gnats. This inconvenience was spreading over all the land of Egypt, but in short order the Holy One was going to separate His people from the judgments to come:

"Now the LORD said to Moses, 'Rise early in the morning and present yourself before Pharaoh, as he comes out to the water, and say to him, "Thus says the LORD, 'Let My people go, that they may serve Me. For if you do not let My people go, behold, I will send swarms of insects on you and on your servants and on your people and into your houses; and the houses of the Egyptians will be full of swarms of insects, and also the ground on which they *dwell*. But on that day I will set apart the land of Goshen, where My people are living, so that no swarms of insects will be there, in order that you may know that I, the LORD, am in the midst of the land. I will put a division between My people and your people. Tomorrow this sign will occur"'" (Exodus 8:20-23).

Moses and Aaron continue delivering the plagues on God's behalf, but now as swarms of insects came over Egypt, the land of Goshen, where the Israelites were living, was not affected (Exodus 8:24). And yet, even after this plague subsides, the heart of Pharaoh was still hardened (Exodus 8:25-32).

Next, the distinctions between the Egyptians and Israel become more evident. The livestock of Egypt is separated out for death. But the Lord decides to preserve the livestock belonging to Israel (Exodus 9:1-7). The plague of sores or boils comes upon the Egyptians, and the Israelites are spared, and again the heart of Pharaoh is hardened (Exodus 9:8-17). We then get a peek into what God is actually doing to Pharaoh and Egypt, as these signs and judgments are being executed:

"But, indeed, for this reason I have allowed you to remain, in order to show you My power and in order to proclaim My name through all the earth" (Exodus 9:16).

**The Lord uses these events so that His power and greatness will be proclaimed throughout the whole world. Little did the Ancient Israelites**

**know how true this would be, as we still remember the Exodus and its awesomeness today!** The Exodus is one of the most important controlling narratives for how people read the message of the Bible, redemption in Messiah Yeshua, and how God always has worldwide intentions when He performs significant acts of salvation history.[9]

Finally, as our reading for this week comes to a close, the Egyptian people begin to get the message that the God of Moses and Aaron is not playing games. They are warned about a devastating hailstorm that is about to come (Exodus 9:18-35), and some of the Egyptians take heed to protect themselves and their livestock from certain death:

"'Now therefore send, bring your livestock and whatever you have in the field to safety. Every man and beast that is found in the field and is not brought home, when the hail comes down on them, will die.' The one among the servants of Pharaoh who feared the word of the LORD made his servants and his livestock flee into the houses; but he who paid no regard to the word of the LORD left his servants and his livestock in the field" (Exodus 9:19-21).

You would think that Pharaoh—the leader of Egypt—would be getting the message that the Lord means business, but instead he continues to harden his heart against Him (Exodus 9:35). Again, we see God making a distinction between His people and the Egyptians:

"Only in the land of Goshen, where the sons of Israel *were*, there was no hail" (Exodus 9:26).

Our Torah portion ends with this sad testimony:

"But when Pharaoh saw that the rain and the hail and the thunder had ceased, he sinned again and hardened his heart, he and his servants. Pharaoh's heart was hardened, and he did not let the sons of Israel go, just as the LORD had spoken through Moses" (Exodus 9:34-35).

We too often have to read about the sad story of individuals like Pharaoh—because even when seeing the physical results of Divine judgment, they are incapable of changing their hearts and crying out for help. They often willingly choose the judgment of God, *in order to appear humanly strong*, rather than cry out to Him for mercy.

Some reading this may have a problem with what appears to be a hardening of the heart by the Almighty Himself. Keep in mind that Pharaoh was the leader of Egypt, one who believed himself to be a god, and one who was presumably perfect. Because of these things going against him, *he may have not even had a chance at redemption*. As the Apostle Paul comments, we discover that God, who is full of mercy and compassion, actually raised up Pharaoh so that **His fame and power** could be demonstrated and proclaimed around the world:

"What shall we say then? There is no injustice with God, is there? May it never be! For He says to Moses, 'I WILL HAVE MERCY ON WHOM I HAVE MERCY, AND I WILL HAVE COMPASSION ON WHOM I HAVE COMPASSION' [Exodus 33:19]. So then it *does* not *depend* on the man who wills or the man who runs, but on God who has mercy. For the Scripture says to Pharaoh, 'FOR THIS VERY PURPOSE I RAISED YOU UP, TO DEMONSTRATE MY POWER IN YOU, AND THAT MY NAME MIGHT BE PROCLAIMED THROUGHOUT THE WHOLE EARTH' [Exodus 9:16]. So then He has mercy on whom He desires, and He hardens whom He desires" (Romans 9:14-18).

---

[9] For a further discussion, consult Christopher J.H. Wright, "God's Model of Redemption," in *The Mission of God: Unlocking the Bible's Grand Narrative* (Downers Grove, IL: InterVarsity, 2006), pp 265-323.

Paul reminded the mixed group of Believers in Rome of the example of the Egyptian Pharaoh, in describing the justice of God. Now, for those of us today who read these words and consider them for our spiritual edification, what can they possibly mean to us, over three millennia removed from the Exodus, and almost two millennia from Paul writing the Romans?

Do we really take seriously the fact that the Lord uses various trials and tribulations to declare His name and His power throughout the Earth? When we read about the events that had to occur for Ancient Israel to be delivered, do we at all praise Him for it? If we have faith in His past actions on behalf of His people, we can be confident that the Lord will be with us through whatever we face today. **To Him be the glory and the power and the honor forever and ever!**

## Bo בֹּא
### Go
### "A Perpetual Feast Forever"

> Exodus 10:1-13:16
> Jeremiah 46:13-28

This week's Torah portion, *Bo*, very much summarizes the major theme of the Book of Exodus. We witness not only the final plagues dispensed upon Egypt,[10] but we see the institution of the Passover as a memorial meal[11] to be remembered by the future generations of God's chosen people:

"For I will go through the land of Egypt on that night, and will strike down all the firstborn in the land of Egypt, both man and beast; and against all the gods of Egypt I will execute judgments—I am the LORD. The blood shall be a sign for you on the houses where you live; and when I see the blood I will pass over you, and no plague will befall you to destroy *you* when I strike the land of Egypt. Now this day will be a memorial to you, and you shall celebrate it *as* a feast to the LORD; throughout your generations you are to celebrate it *as* a permanent ordinance" (Exodus 12:12-14).

In *Bo*, the final three judgments upon Egypt are executed (locusts, darkness, firstborn), and the people of Israel are finally released to begin their journey to the Promised Land.[12] This reading gives us the first regulations about the Spring festivals of the Lord, and how His people are to commemorate the salvific events they memorialize.

Each year when *Bo* is considered, the reference to Passover being a "permanent ordinance" or "eternal decree" (ATS)[13] always creates some interesting recollections that you might be able to identify with. For years, prior to becoming Messianic, every time I read this text I paused and thought about the words "you are to celebrate it *as* a permanent ordinance."

---

[10] Exodus 10:1-11:10.
[11] Exodus 12:1-32, 42-51.
[12] Exodus 12:33-41.
[13] Heb. *chuquat olam* (חֻקַּת עוֹלָם).

## Reading Recollections

In the past, while reading through these passages, I remember going back and rereading what is stated about Passover two or three times, and thinking about what the text actually meant. After all, the words "you shall observe it as an ordinance for ever" (Exodus 12:14, RSV) are fairly easy and direct to understand. The problem I had was not in understanding the plain English text. Rather, the problem was in heeding the words spoken. I was confused because the commandment to remember the Passover was very clear—**and Passover is by no means some obscure ritual to memorialize.** Like many who have been confronted by the simple text, I first turned to my teachers for an explanation. Of course, that is where my problems were compounded.

Many years ago in the 1980s, I was at the mercy of dispensational Christian pastors and Bible teachers, who were largely repeating what they had been taught at Bible college or seminary (in this case, Dallas Theological Seminary). Because of their dispensational presuppositions—reading some parts of the Bible as only applying to Israel, and other parts as only applying to "the Church"—the command to celebrate Passover was not something that apparently applied to me. My dispensational teachers told me that Passover was something that the Jewish people did, but it was not something that Christians today were required to do, because there was a much more meaningful observance that I could participate in called Easter. To a relatively young and naïve Believer, their argument was very persuasive. As I recall, the logic went something like this:

*Remember that Jesus was our Passover Lamb. He came and was sacrificed for us. Should we not be thankful for His ultimate sacrifice and come together on the day which celebrates the resurrection of Christ?*

Of course, this justification for remembering Easter instead of Passover made good sense. Further questions I asked elicited more reasons to go along with this practice, as I was also told by my dispensational teachers:

*You need to understand that this has been going on for centuries, and certainly the ecclesiastical authorities who instituted these events knew what they were doing. The Jews will continue to do the Passover and the Christians will continue to do Easter. Just celebrate Easter and do not worry about what the Jews are doing. We live in the Church Age!*

Even though this sounded like a good argument at the time, regardless of the explanation I heard, inevitably, whenever I read these verses in Exodus, the same nagging question arose in my spirit: **What does the Scripture mean when it says "forever" or "eternal"?**

## Maturing Messianic

Sometimes, it is funny how you remember certain things in the past that prompted you to dig more into the Word of God for greater explanation. For example, the word "forever" (Heb. *olam*, עוֹלָם) seems to really stand out.[14] As I was maturing in my study and pursuit of the truth, the Lord chose to reveal more about Himself. As a seeker, I was definitely finding Him by consistently and honestly asking Him—just as Jeremiah promises:

"You will seek Me and find *Me* when you search for Me with all your heart" (Jeremiah 29:13).

---

[14] *BDB*, pp 761-763; *CHALOT*, pp 267-268; *HALOT*, 1:798-799.

James the Just's admonition, "But if any of you lacks wisdom, let him ask of God, who gives to all generously and without reproach, and it will be given to him" (James 1:5), was also something that I prayed. I did not want to find some kind of forgotten truth in the Bible, but then misuse it in the sight of those who were not ready to hear, and were not necessarily convicted by the Holy Spirit at the time the same way I was. As one who believed, and still believes, in the sovereignty of God—there is a pre-determined time for people to come to a fuller knowledge of Him.

At another reading of verses like Exodus 12:14—something dramatic occurred. One night while reading this passage, the concept of "forever" repeated itself over and over again in my spirit. All of a sudden, another thought came immediately to mind:

"All Scripture is inspired by God and profitable for teaching, for reproof, for correction, for training in righteousness; so that the man of God may be adequate, equipped for every good work" (2 Timothy 3:16-17).

When Paul wrote these words to Timothy, he was referring to the Scriptures as they knew them in the First Century, the Hebrew Tanakh (Genesis-2 Chronicles [or Malachi]).[15] Paul told the Romans a similar thing regarding the Scriptures:

"For whatever was written in earlier times was written for our instruction, so that through perseverance and the encouragement of the Scriptures we might have hope" (Romans 15:4).

I by no means thought that the writings of the Apostles were not Scripture, but I did think that perhaps too many Christians I knew were forgetting *what else* composed Scripture. Why did too many people just overlook God's revelation in the Old Testament, when the Apostles themselves did not? While thinking through Exodus 12:14 on Passover one year, a radical thought came to my mind:

*Is it possible that the very concept of obeying this commandment "forever" was something that would be profitable for teaching and training in righteousness? Why would many people overlook the Passover, and what it teaches us about the sacrifice of Jesus?*

Oftentimes when you have these types of internal debates, you are actually being instructed by the Holy Spirit. Remember that according to Yeshua, it is the Holy Spirit who has been sent to teach His followers all things:

"But the Helper, the Holy Spirit, whom the Father will send in My name, He will teach you all things, and bring to your remembrance all that I said to you" (John 14:26).

This train of thought was really stretching me away from some of the dispensational doctrines that I was being taught. When I considered this those many years ago, without any significant change with regard to the word "forever," I simply pondered these thoughts in my heart, waiting for further instruction. At the time, I was not quite ready for the transition to a Messianic lifestyle, nor would I have been led to pursue the issue further. However, with the benefit of 20/20 hindsight, it is clear now that I was definitely being set up for the next stage in my walk. In the 1980s I was thinking about things that would significantly aid me during my spiritual pursuits of the 1990s.

---

[15] The Jewish division of the Tanakh ends with 2 Chronicles, whereas the current Christian division follows the Greek Septuagint (LXX), which ends with Malachi. The LXX was used in Jewish communities of the First Century.

## The Seder Experience

In the early 1990s, just like what has happened to thousands of other evangelical Christians in recent years, I was asked to attend a *sedar* (סֵדֶר) meal to remember the Passover. Because of a tour to Israel my wife Margaret and I had been on in 1994, we were very open to the Jewish Roots of our faith, and in considering the role of the appointed times for more than just "enrichment." This *sedar* was being held at the Messianic Jewish congregation which we had started attending. For the first time in my life, I was going to keep the commandment to remember the deliverance from Egypt in a very tangible way!

The very Torah portion that we are looking at this week, *Bo*, was being discussed in the context of a Passover remembrance. The whole *sedar* experience was something to behold. As the leader of the *sedar* went through a written presentation or *haggadah*, the details of the deliverance from Egypt were thoroughly discussed. Of course, the parallels between the blood of the lamb and the Messiah Yeshua, being the ultimate blood sacrifice, were mentioned in great detail. Even the (later) Jewish traditions regarding the unleavened bread or *matzah* (מַצָּה), and how it was to be handled, all seemed to point to the work of the Messiah at Golgotha (Calvary).

Throughout the evening I thought about the commandment *to remember the Passover forever*. I considered the history of the Jewish people and how they had faithfully honored this commandment for millennia. It was apparent that this, and other remembrances of the appointed times, had kept them a unified and a separated people. And now here I was, a non-Jew participating in the very same celebration that was given not necessarily to just the Jewish people, *but to all who serve the God of Israel.*

Some of my questions from decades earlier started to resurface in my thoughts. Now, however, I was in a Messianic environment that would discuss some of the historical realities of why centuries of Christians had largely overlooked the Passover. I was finally exposed to some of the decisions made by ecclesiastical councils from the Fourth and Fifth Centuries, which forbade the Christian Church from observing the appointed times. This information, coupled with other data from my Torah studies that was being regularly assimilated, significantly altered the lifestyle of myself and my family.

As a family, we now consider it a great honor and important responsibility to remember the Passover—just as these passages remind us. We believe that we are some of the "generations" that this commandment was directed to. Of course, as we have discovered via experience, you do not get to the point where you believe that remembering the Passover is really for you until you have moved toward a Messianic lifestyle that seeks to consciously follow the Torah and its commandments. Furthermore, making the transition from a neutered Easter celebration to a full-fledged Passover remembrance is not always easy. Should you make this transition, there is a definite need to extend the Lord's love and grace to others who do not share your conviction. Rather than look at yourselves as being spiritually superior, invite your evangelical Christian family and friends to your Passover table. **Allow them to experience the goodness of Passover the same way that you have!**

## Who do you serve?

How might you figure into all of this? Have you ever really celebrated Passover? If you have, do you remember your first time at a Passover *sedar*? Did you sense that you were obeying one of God commands, for all of His people for all time? *Did you sense the Lord's presence at this* sedar *meal,* **and learn important things about your salvation in Messiah**

*Yeshua?* Do you think it would be beneficial for Believers today to remember the Passover, and for all of us to learn how we are beneficiaries of Ancient Israel's deliverance from Egypt?

By keeping Passover you will certainly be establishing a good example of obedience. You could also use this celebration as a backdrop for additional instruction about how God has miraculously acted throughout history, and how there will be a future deliverance of His people in the end-times. *We live in interesting days when our firmly held beliefs and convictions in Him will be challenged by the world.* We need to be convinced about who we are serving. By honoring and following His Instruction, we send clear signals that we are worshipping the God of Abraham, Isaac, and Jacob—and not someone or something else.

The Joshua generation that was allowed to enter into the Promised Land faced some of the same challenges that we face today. They had the words of Moses to contend with, as well as fresh memories of their parents and grandparents who were denied entrance into Canaan because they did not believe and obey the Lord. At the end of Joshua's life, he reminded the people of Israel about all the things that God had done for them over the centuries:

"Now, therefore, fear the LORD and serve Him in sincerity and truth; and put away the gods which your fathers served beyond the River and in Egypt, and serve the LORD. If it is disagreeable in your sight to serve the LORD, choose for yourselves today whom you will serve: whether the gods which your fathers served which were beyond the River, or the gods of the Amorites in whose land you are living; but as for me and my house, we will serve the LORD" (Joshua 24:14-15).

For us today, these same words need to be considered. Will we serve the Holy One of Israel with diligence—correcting previous mistakes of the past—or will we continue to be denied the blessings of remembering Passover? Hopefully, our answer will echo Joshua's admonition to Ancient Israel to serve the Lord. Today, we can visibly display our allegiance to the Lord by **continuing to make the Passover celebration** *a perpetual feast forever!* We can see people enriched in their faith, and understand all of the great lessons that the Passover and Exodus teach us.[16]

## *B'shalach* בְּשַׁלַּח
### After he had let go
### "Complaining Slaves"

Exodus 13:17-17:16
Judges 4:4-5:31 (A); 5:1-31 (S)

The previous three Torah readings of Exodus: *Shemot*, *V'eira*, and *Bo*, all detail some of the most important and memorable events in the Holy Scriptures—getting us to learn about how God miraculously involves Himself in delivering His people. Yet as important as the Exodus from Egypt is, why do we see God's chosen complaining, **immediately after they are released?** In *B'shalach* this week, we see the Ancient Israelites complaining right

---

[16] For further teaching on the themes of Passover and the Exodus, we recommend that you consult the *Messianic Spring Holiday Helper* by TNN Press.

after they have been delivered through the Red Sea, and have seen the Egyptian army defeated:

"The whole congregation of the sons of Israel grumbled against Moses and Aaron in the wilderness...and in the morning you will see the glory of the LORD, for He hears your grumblings against the LORD; and what are we, that you grumble against us?" (Exodus 16:2, 7).

In *B'shalach*, the people of Israel are finally allowed to leave Egypt and depart for the long awaited journey to the Promised Land. At last, after the ten plagues have devastated Egypt, Pharaoh succumbs to Moses' pleas and "lets the people go" to the wilderness to worship the Lord. The first few months of the trek from the bondage of slavery to freedom are recorded with some of the most memorable events in the history of Israel.

The great miracles of deliverance and provision are described in great detail. Pillars of clouds and pillars of fire lead the people from place to place.[17] The incredible parting of the Red Sea and the subsequent destruction of Pharaoh's army are highlighted and then punctuated with a memorial song and celebration.[18] Of course, in any desert trek, water and food provisions are critical, and we are told about sticks of wood that make bitter water sweet.[19] At another juncture, Moses obeys the instructions of the Lord and strikes a rock with his staff and the water flows.[20] The introduction of manna to Israel's daily diet is described in great detail.[21] Finally, quail is included for the sustenance of the people.[22]

In many respects when one remembers the events in this Torah portion, the primary thoughts are of deliverance and provision. In these Scriptures, there are many visible and tangible testimonies of God's unconditional love for Israel. On the other hand, there is another theme which cannot be overlooked. When you consider some of these events, it is easy to detect how the chosen people have one very consistent negative tendency. Even in this period of incredible signs and wonders—no matter what miracle or sign had just taken place—the people of Moses' generation would consistently whine and complain about their circumstances. This propensity was very bothersome. After all, when you consider the future of this generation, you are reminded that only two of the adults (Joshua and Caleb) actually make it into the Promised Land.

What was the problem with these people? Did they lack faith? **How could people who were firsthand witnesses to these incredible miracles be such complainers?** What was it about this group of Ancient Israelites which generated such negative tendencies?

As I thought through these questions, I kept going back to the different instances recorded in this reading to see if there was some discernable common thread that could explain this penchant for complaining. Four times, references comparing life back in Egypt seemed to surface. I asked myself if it were possible that the Israelites had developed a *slave mentality*. Right from the opening lines of our *parashah* an indication of their problem is mentioned:

---

[17] Exodus 13:17-22.
[18] Exodus 14:1-15:21.
[19] Exodus 15:22-27.
[20] Exodus 17:1-7.
[21] Exodus 16:1-7.
[22] Exodus 16:8-21.

"Now when Pharaoh had let the people go, God did not lead them by the way of the land of the Philistines, even though it was near; for God said, 'The people might change their minds when they see war, and return to Egypt'" (Exodus 13:17).

From the very beginning of Israel's transformation from bondage to liberty, the Holy One knew He was going to have to monitor His children all the way. The more direct route to Canaan would cause them to encounter the Philistines, who would aggressively resist their migration (Exodus 13:17). The Lord knew that His people did not have the stomach for war. They had just spent several centuries in Egypt, *most recently as slaves*, and they were not strong enough to encounter the hardship of conflict. Additionally, God had to demonstrate to the Israelites that it was He alone who could deliver them from their enemies. God wanted the Israelites to be dependent upon Him and Him alone.

Within a few days of them leaving, we see that the heart of Pharaoh changes and he orders his chariots to turn back the Israelites. Here is how the Israelites reacted when they were confronted by a mere 600 chariots:

"As Pharaoh drew near, the sons of Israel looked, and behold, the Egyptians were marching after them, and they became very frightened; so the sons of Israel cried out to the LORD. Then they said to Moses, 'Is it because there were no graves in Egypt that you have taken us away to die in the wilderness? Why have you dealt with us in this way, bringing us out of Egypt? Is this not the word that we spoke to you in Egypt, saying, "Leave us alone that we may serve the Egyptians"? For it would have been better for us to serve the Egyptians than to die in the wilderness'" (Exodus 14:10-12).

This is hard to imagine. At this point, the Israelites have been following a pillar of cloud and a pillar of fire, but now they are encamped by the sea without any escape route. How could several hundred thousand people be frightened by a mere 600 chariots? Is it because they had a *slave mentality* that did not give them the confidence to stand up and defend their freedom? As you read the Ancient Israelites' complaints to Moses, we see their sentiments of how they would much rather be in the comfort of their former homes in Egypt. Incredibly, the Lord uses this pitifully weak complaint to bring about His deliverance. He parts the Red Sea, and then lets the Egyptian charioteers all drown as the water returns. The Lord instructs Moses to stretch out his hand over the sea and then watch the waters part:

"Then Moses stretched out his hand over the sea; and the LORD swept the sea *back* by a strong east wind all night and turned the sea into dry land, so the waters were divided" (Exodus 14:21).

Again, in a very powerful way, God demonstrates that He wanted the Israelites to depend upon Him for salvation and deliverance. The Lord did not disappoint!

About a month later, the people complain about the lack of food. Once again a reference to their former lives in Egypt is in the forefront of their minds:

"The sons of Israel said to them, 'Would that we had died by the LORD's hand in the land of Egypt, when we sat by the pots of meat, when we ate bread to the full; for you have brought us out into this wilderness to kill this whole assembly with hunger'" (Exodus 16:3).

In order to handle this complaint, God brings down a regular supply of manna. To top this off, He also gives them a feast of quail. As the provision continues, the Israelites begin to understand that the Lord is their provider. As the Scripture relates, this specific provision continues for forty years.

Finally, the fourth major complaint again references the comparison to Egypt, when the Israelites travel to Refidim:

"Therefore the people quarreled with Moses and said, 'Give us water that we may drink.' And Moses said to them, 'Why do you quarrel with me? Why do you test the LORD?' But the people thirsted there for water; and they grumbled against Moses and said, 'Why, now, have you brought us up from Egypt, to kill us and our children and our livestock with thirst?' So Moses cried out to the LORD, saying, 'What shall I do to this people? A little more and they will stone me'" (Exodus 17:2-4).

At this point, the Israelites are again confronted with a challenge that generates grumbling, and even quarreling. This time lack of water is the issue. The Lord instructs Moses to strike a rock with his staff and the water would flow forth. Moses does this and the water flows (Exodus 17:1-7). But this scene is to be remembered very soberly, as Moses names this place Massah and Meribah, to describe the contentious attitude of the Israelites:

"He named the place Massah and Meribah because of the quarrel of the sons of Israel, and because they tested the LORD, saying, 'Is the LORD among us, or not?'" (cf. Psalm 95:8; Hebrews 3:8).

Interestingly, as we arrive at the end of our *parashah*, it appears that the Israelites are now ready for some battling with the dreaded Amalekites.[23] *Something has happened to them.* Is it possible that through the various tests and trials, they had begun to trust in the Lord for His deliverance and provision? Have they been able to dispense with just enough of the slave mentality, that they are beginning to take on the responsibilities of being the chosen nation of God?

In some respects, the challenges of the Ancient Israelites coming out of the slavery of Egypt are not too different from our individual walks with the Lord. As Believers in Yeshua the Messiah, we have all had to experience the initial difficulties of coming out of the bondage of sin. As we have struggled with sin, there have doubtlessly been times when we were prone to wander. Early in our walks with the Lord, we do not often have the intestinal fortitude or sometimes knowledge to stomach the battles against sin **that can only come with spiritual growth and experience.** In a loving way, the Father often steers us away from the temptations that He knows could cause us to return to sinful ways. He also knows that learning total dependence upon Him is crucial to handling the spiritual battles of life. At times, He will allow us to witness His deliverance from situations that might seem impossible. These victories give us greater confidence to press further into Him for even more provision and deliverance. In time, while the spiritual battles we encounter might be more serious, the ability to overcome temptation and be victorious becomes easier!

It is important that we learn from the mistakes of the Ancient Israelites in the desert (cf. 1 Corinthians 10:11, RSV). Their slave mentality gave them a propensity to complain and grumble about many of the trials and tests they faced. Even though they had eyewitness accounts of the deliverance and provision of the Lord, from their actions and statements you can conclude that many would prefer to be back in Egypt.

Let us be Believers in the God of Israel who desire to be and *function as* free people who willfully choose to be slaves to Him, and not to our former life in sin (Romans 6:16-18). In the Lord we have not only our provision, **but also our deliverance and salvation!**

---

[23] Exodus 17:1-16.

# *Yitro* יִתְרוֹ
## Jethro
## "Shema Yisrael"

> Exodus 18:1-20:23[26]
> Isaiah 6:1-7:6; 9:5-6[6-7] (A); 6:1-13 (S)

After considering what has thus far transpired in the Book of Exodus, this week's Torah portion, *Yitro*, involves one of the most memorable scenes outside of the deliverance from Egypt. It is in this reading where the Lord visits Mount Sinai and delivers the Ten Commandments.[24] The Ancient Israelites were deathly afraid of what was taking place, and so Moses has to explain what the intention of this awesome scene is intended to mean for them:

"Then they said to Moses, 'Speak to us yourself and we will listen; but let not God speak to us, or we will die.' Moses said to the people, 'Do not be afraid; for God has come in order to test you, and in order that the fear of Him may remain with you, so that you may not sin'" (Exodus 20:20).

Here at the bottom of Mount Sinai, the people of Israel actually hear the voice of the Lord. One would think that this would be a blessed event, but from the reaction recorded, we read that the people were absolutely terrified by the Voice:

"All the people perceived the thunder and the lightning flashes and the sound of the trumpet and the mountain smoking; and when the people saw *it*, they trembled and stood at a distance…So the people stood at a distance, while Moses approached the thick cloud where God *was*. Then the LORD said to Moses, 'Thus you shall say to the sons of Israel, "You yourselves have seen that I have spoken to you from heaven"'" (Exodus 20:18, 21-22).

Prior to this time since the Exodus from Egypt, the Lord had chosen to communicate to Israel through His intermediary Moses. For the most part, the Israelites were quite content with this means of communication. After all, a considerable amount of the information that came to them from Moses was very encouraging. Consider some of earlier statements from Moses just prior to the Divine declaration of the Ten Commandments:

"'"Now then, if you will indeed obey My voice and keep My covenant, then you shall be My own possession among all the peoples, for all the earth is Mine; and you shall be to Me a kingdom of priests and a holy nation." These are the words that you shall speak to the sons of Israel.' So Moses came and called the elders of the people, and set before them all these words which the LORD had commanded him. All the people answered together and said, 'All that the LORD has spoken we will do!' And Moses brought back the words of the people to the LORD" (Exodus 19:5-8).

Here, the Lord communicates a fairly simple if/then formula for Israel to become a holy nation of priests. It conveys the mission of what they are to do as intermediaries between the Creator and the rest of the Earth. It should have been something very hopeful to those who really were ready to enter into God's purpose and no longer be slaves at the behest of Egypt.

The Israelites had just witnessed a great deliverance from the Egyptians and had only been in the desert several months. *The Lord was fighting their battles.* Their basic daily

---

[24] Exodus 19:1-20:17.

nourishment was provided for by the morning arrival of manna. They were probably feeling pretty confident about their relationship with Him. Without much hesitation, upon hearing what God was calling them to do, they responded to the proposal with these affirming words:

"All the people answered together and said, 'All that the LORD has spoken we will do!' And Moses brought back the words of the people to the LORD" (Exodus 19:8).

Remarkably, the Scriptures record that *all* of the people agreed to do *all* that the Lord had spoken. *This was apparently a sincere response.* But little did the Ancient Israelites understand the magnitude of their commitment. At this point in the narrative, we see their response to the Lord, but not a huge amount of instruction on what it means to specifically follow and obey Him is given. As you can imagine, the Lord is already putting in motion a monumental event that will test the hearts of the Israelites, and ascertain whether they can really honor this pledge of obedience:

"The LORD said to Moses, 'Behold, I will come to you in a thick cloud, so that the people may hear when I speak with you and may also believe in you forever.' Then Moses told the words of the people to the LORD" (Exodus 19:9).

The Lord is going to accomplish two objectives by letting His people hear His voice. First, He will let them understand more about His holiness, and how they must consecrate themselves in order to even hear His voice. Secondly, He is going to solidify Moses' position as their intermediary before Him. Moses comes back to the people and gives them instructions on how to consecrate themselves, before the Holy One will speak to them.[25] A period of separation commences, as physical actions start preparing Israel for hearing the voice of the Lord:

"The LORD also said to Moses, 'Go to the people and consecrate them today and tomorrow, and let them wash their garments; and let them be ready for the third day, for on the third day the LORD will come down on Mount Sinai in the sight of all the people. You shall set bounds for the people all around, saying, "Beware that you do not go up on the mountain or touch the border of it; whoever touches the mountain shall surely be put to death"...So Moses went down from the mountain to the people and consecrated the people, and they washed their garments. He said to the people, 'Be ready for the third day; do not go near a woman'" (Exodus 19:10-12, 14-15).

The people begin to prepare for hearing the voice of God. Looming in the distance was a dark cloud over Mount Sinai. The people could see, and possibly even feel, the presence of the Lord. They began to cleanse themselves and did not have sexual relations for several days. Limits were set around the base of the mountain. People were told not to touch it for fear of death. Each of these actions was preparing Israel for a profound event. By performing these required things, the hearts of the Ancient Israelites were being focused on the opportunity to hear the actual voice of the Creator.

On the morning of the third day, there was thunder, lightning, a thick cloud, and the blast of a piercing *shofar*. The moment for God to speak was approaching:

"Now Mount Sinai *was* all in smoke because the LORD descended upon it in fire; and its smoke ascended like the smoke of a furnace, and the whole mountain quaked violently. When the sound of the trumpet grew louder and louder, Moses spoke and God answered him with thunder" (Exodus 19:18-19).

---

[25] Exodus 19:10-17.

It is difficult to imagine how frightening this must have been for the Ancient Israelites. The noise of the *shofar* was increasing in intensity. The top of Mount Sinai was engulfed in fire and smoke. As they stood there, the whole mountain shook violently. *The people thought they were going to die.* After all, it had been much easier to listen to the requirements of the Lord when Moses came back and reported his conversations with Him. At this juncture, Israel was fully engaged in hearing the actual voice of God—and then the Lord declares the Ten Words. **Can you imagine how petrified the people were when these commands came forth?** The intensity of the fear is recorded after the commands are declared.

With fear and trepidation the people immediately wanted to go back to the former way of communing with the Most High (Exodus 19:20). Apparently, the voice of God was so powerful that the people believed they were going to die. Even after they were consecrated before Him, the Israelites were convinced that they would rather have Moses as their mediator. **The fear was that intense!**

Interestingly, Moses immediately tells the Israelites that the Lord is using this event *to test* them: "God has come only in order to test you, and in order that the fear of Him may be ever with you, so that you do not go astray" (Exodus 19:20, NJPS). A holy fear should be instilled in them so that they would not sin and rebel against Him. God is very serious about His people not sinning—something that even until today **has not changed!**

How about today? Is there something we should be learning from the experiences of the Ancient Israelites? How should we be approaching the Lord?

The author of Hebrews refers to the events we have been considering in the past few Torah readings, imploring how Believers in Yeshua are to take seriously the Divine work of God. His admonition is to not let Believers' hearts be hardened by the deceitfulness of sin, and remember the examples of the past when God's people have had to be severely punished for their disloyalty to Him:

"Therefore, just as the Holy Spirit says, 'TODAY IF YOU HEAR HIS VOICE, DO NOT HARDEN YOUR HEARTS AS WHEN THEY PROVOKED ME, AS IN THE DAY OF TRIAL IN THE WILDERNESS, WHERE YOUR FATHERS TRIED *Me* BY TESTING *Me*, AND SAW MY WORKS FOR FORTY YEARS. THEREFORE I WAS ANGRY WITH THIS GENERATION, AND SAID, 'THEY ALWAYS GO ASTRAY IN THEIR HEART, AND THEY DID NOT KNOW MY WAYS'; AS I SWORE IN MY WRATH, "THEY SHALL NOT ENTER MY REST"' [Psalm 95:7-11]. Take care, brethren, that there not be in any one of you an evil, unbelieving heart that falls away from the living God. But encourage one another day after day, as long as it is *still* called 'Today,' so that none of you will be hardened by the deceitfulness of sin. For we have become partakers of Messiah, if we hold fast the beginning of our assurance firm until the end, while it is said, 'TODAY IF YOU HEAR HIS VOICE, DO NOT HARDEN YOUR HEARTS, AS WHEN THEY PROVOKED ME' [Psalm 95:7-8]. For who provoked *Him* when they had heard? Indeed, did not all those who came out of Egypt *led* by Moses? And with whom was He angry for forty years? Was it not with those who sinned, whose bodies fell in the wilderness? And to whom did He swear that they would not enter His rest, but to those who were disobedient? *So* we see that they were not able to enter because of unbelief" (Hebrews 3:7-19).

In this passage, the author of Hebrews reminds his audience that the generation which came out of Egypt hardened their hearts instead of listening to God's voice. By hardening their hearts, they did not know the ways of the Lord. In fact, because of their disobedience, they were not allowed to enter into the rest of the Promised Land because of their unbelief. Within his argument is the implication that if such severe punishment was enacted upon these people in Israel's past, how much more severe punishment can be guaranteed those who deny the more recent (for the First Century C.E.) and *even more serious* deliverance via the Messiah's sacrifice?

We need to remember that according to the words of Yeshua Himself, the ability to hear the voice of the Holy One is something fully accessible to His followers. Today, in this post-resurrection era, we have the privilege of hearing the voice of the Most High. Instead of exclusively having to rely on others to listen to Him for us, we should be striving to listen to the voice of the Holy One ourselves. Remember that our Heavenly Father has sent His Son Yeshua to be the Good Shepherd over His people:

"I am the good shepherd, and I know My own and My own know Me, even as the Father knows Me and I know the Father; and I lay down My life for the sheep. I have other sheep, which are not of this fold; I must bring them also, and they will hear My voice; and they will become one flock *with* one shepherd...My sheep hear My voice, and I know them, and they follow Me; and I give eternal life to them, and they will never perish; and no one will snatch them out of My hand" (John 10:14-16, 27-28).

We know that in this passage Yeshua called Himself the Good Shepherd, and His flock were the people who would hear His voice. *Are you part of His flock?* Are you hearing the Lord's voice and obeying Him? If you are, then you should be comforted by your desire to please Him. But if you are not hearing His voice and obeying Him—conforming your life to the example left by the Messiah—perhaps you need to cry out to the Lord for mercy. As the author of Hebrews reminds us concerning the ancient encounter at Mount Sinai, there is a different mountain that we should now be approaching—one even more awesome and profound—as awesome and profound as Mount Sinai enveloped in smoke surely was:

"For you have not come to *a mountain* that can be touched and to a blazing fire, and to darkness and gloom and whirlwind, and to the blast of a trumpet and the sound of words which *sound was such that* those who heard begged that no further word be spoken to them. For they could not bear the command, 'IF EVEN A BEAST TOUCHES THE MOUNTAIN, IT WILL BE STONED.' And so terrible was the sight, *that* Moses said, 'I AM FULL OF FEAR and trembling' [Exodus 19:12-13]. But you have come to Mount Zion and to the city of the living God, the heavenly Jerusalem, and to myriads of angels, to the general assembly and [congregation] of the firstborn who are enrolled in heaven, and to God, the Judge of all, and to the spirits of *the* righteous made perfect, and to Yeshua, the mediator of a new covenant, and to the sprinkled blood, which speaks better than *the blood* of Abel. See to it that you do not refuse Him who is speaking. For if those did not escape when they refused him who warned *them* on earth, much less *will* we *escape* who turn away from Him who *warns* from heaven" (Hebrews 12:18-25).

Here, the warning is to seek Yeshua as the Mediator of the New Covenant. We are reminded that we *should not refuse* His voice (cf. Hebrews 3:3). If so, the consequences for Believers today are even worse than those from the Exodus generation: **You will not enter His *eternal* rest!** So without any hesitation, dear brothers and sisters, remember: hear and obey. *Shema Yisrael!*

# Mishpatim מִשְׁפָּטִים
## Rulings
## "Blood Covenant"

> Exodus 21:1-24:18
> Jeremiah 34:8-22; 33:25-26

*Mishpatim*, beginning with the word, "These are the regulations you must present to Israel" (Exodus 21:1, NLT), is a very different kind of Torah portion than what we have read thus far in Exodus. Up until this point, our readings have been significantly dominated by events in Ancient Israel's history. Now, the specific Instruction of God will begin to be delivered to the Israelites. It is pretty serious, when you think about it, because the people will now be consecrated to the Lord's service:

"So Moses took the blood and sprinkled *it* on the people, and said, 'Behold the blood of the covenant, which the LORD has made with you in accordance with all these words'" (Exodus 24:8).

*Mishpatim* gives the Torah student a tremendous variety of images to contemplate. For three chapters (Exodus chs. 21-23), Moses delivers an array of ordinances that allow the people of Israel to, in essence, become "civilized" among the nations of the Earth. While most of the laws that are stated regulate proper ethics and morality—even until this day—other laws seem somewhat strange. The short answer is that many of the Torah's commandments were given in an Ancient Near Eastern economic and technological environment, that would not be the same environment of later centuries, and Israel's Law often ran quite contrary and subversive to the codes of their neighbors.[26]

The reason that Israel is given God's Instruction, is because in obeying God's commandments, Israel could be a kingdom of priests and a holy nation able to serve Him in the world:

"'Now then, if you will indeed obey My voice and keep My covenant, then you shall be My own possession among all the peoples, for all the earth is Mine; and you shall be to Me a kingdom of priests and a holy nation.' These are the words that you shall speak to the sons of Israel" (Exodus 19:5-6).

From the following response, you can see how Israel did sincerely desire to be a holy nation unto the Lord. As Moses delivers the various ordinances seen in *Mishpatim*, the people answer the following response with one voice (Heb. *qol echad*, קוֹל אֶחָד):

"'Moses alone, however, shall come near to the LORD, but they shall not come near, nor shall the people come up with him.' Then Moses came and recounted to the people all the words of the LORD and all the ordinances; and all the people answered with one voice and said, **'All the words which the LORD has spoken we will do!'**" (Exodus 24:2-3).

Here at the end of a very lengthy list of rulings, the Ancient Israelites conclude that they will do all that the Lord has spoken. There does not appear to be any hesitation for them to obey, and so the Lord and Israel make this covenant, and solidify it with animal sacrifices. Moses writes down what he has been given, and wakes up early the next morning

---

[26] For a further discussion, consult the article "Addressing the Frequently Avoided Issues Messianics Encounter in the Torah" by J.K. McKee.

to build an altar at the base of Mount Sinai. He builds an altar with twelve large stones that represent the twelve tribes of Israel:

"Moses wrote down all the words of the LORD. Then he arose early in the morning, and built an altar at the foot of the mountain with twelve pillars for the twelve tribes of Israel. He sent young men of the sons of Israel, and they offered burnt offerings and sacrificed young bulls as peace offerings to the LORD. Moses took half of the blood and put *it* in basins, and the *other* half of the blood he sprinkled on the altar. Then he took the book of the covenant and read *it* in the hearing of the people; and they said, 'All that the LORD has spoken we will do, and we will be obedient!' So Moses took the blood and sprinkled *it* on the people, and said, 'Behold the blood of the covenant, which the LORD has made with you in accordance with all these words'" (Exodus 24:4-8).

Moses elicits the aid of some of the Israelites, and burnt offerings and peace offerings are sacrificed to the Lord. He then takes half of the blood and sprinkles it on the altar he had just constructed (Exodus 24:5-7a). Then, Moses takes the written commandments and reads them again to the people. Once again, they respond unanimously, "All that the LORD has spoken we will faithfully do!" (Exodus 24:7b, NJPS).

In order to seal the covenant between God and Israel, Moses sprinkles the people with the blood (Exodus 24:8a). He utters this statement, "This is the blood of the covenant that the LORD has made with you in accordance with all these words" (Exodus 24:8b, NIV). This was a very critical moment for Ancient Israel as they took on the responsibility for keeping the covenant with God and obeying Him. They understood the principle that the shedding of blood was required to seal a covenant.

Is it possible that here we see a foreshadowing of the shedding of blood, which would be required in the future in order for God's people to maintain their position as His chosen kingdom of priests? As I pondered this scene, the words "blood of the covenant" (Heb. *dam-ha'b'rit*, דַּם־הַבְּרִית) kept reminding me of the Last Supper. There on the night of His betrayal, Yeshua used the same terminology:

"And He said to them, 'This is My blood of the covenant [Grk. *to aima mou tēs diathēkēs*, τὸ αἷμά μου τῆς διαθήκης], which is poured out for many'" (Mark 14:24).

What do you think went through the minds of the Disciples, who heard these words come from the mouth of the Son of God? Is it possible that they thought back to the scene from centuries earlier when their ancestors were literally sprinkled with the blood of bulls (Exodus 24:5)? At the time of the Last Supper, the thought of Yeshua's blood being the permanent atonement for sins was likely not fully understood. As you should recall from the Gospel accounts, this was a very intense time for the Apostles. When those words were spoken from the Lord, they did not fully know what was about to take place.

But we, who live today and who have heard the good news—and can look back at both the Book of Exodus and the record of Yeshua's ministry—do not have the luxury of claiming "ignorance." It has been understood ever since the crucifixion and resurrection that the shed blood of the Messiah is absolutely necessary for the final atonement of sin. The author of Hebrews reminds us of the critical need for a blood covenant:

"For when every commandment had been spoken by Moses to all the people according to the Law, he took the blood of the calves...,[27] with water and scarlet wool and hyssop,

---

[27] Editor's note: There is some doubt that "and the goats" is part of the original reading of Hebrews 9:19. The NIV notably omits this second clause, reading as, "he took the blood of calves, together with water..."

and sprinkled both the book itself and all the people, saying, 'THIS IS THE BLOOD OF THE COVENANT WHICH GOD COMMANDED YOU' [Exodus 24:8]. And in the same way he sprinkled both the tabernacle and all the vessels of the ministry with the blood. And according to the Law, *one may* almost *say*, all things are cleansed with blood, and without shedding of blood there is no forgiveness" (Hebrews 9:19-22).

Today, as we contemplate and discuss some of the ordinances given in *Mishpatim*, that were intended to make Ancient Israel a holy nation, it is far more critical to ask this profound question: Has the blood of the Messiah been shed for you, to make the New Covenant valid in your life? Without this blood of the covenant and the sprinkling of the Messiah's blood for your sin, you are without hope of permanent forgiveness and atonement. **So turn to Him and cry out for mercy!** The Apostle Paul affirms this truth:

"But God, being rich in mercy, because of His great love with which He loved us, even when we were dead in our transgressions, made us alive together with Messiah (by grace you have been saved)" (Ephesians 2:4-5).

## *Terumah* תְּרוּמָה
### Contribution
### "Willing Hearts"

> Exodus 25:1-27:19
> 1 Kings 5:26-6:13

Our Torah portion for this week, *Terumah*, begins with the command for the Ancient Israelites to contribute to the Tabernacle construction project:

"Then the LORD spoke to Moses, saying, 'Tell the sons of Israel to raise a contribution for Me; from every man whose heart moves him you shall raise My contribution. This is the contribution which you are to raise from them: gold, silver and bronze'" (Exodus 25:1-3).

In *Terumah*, the people of Israel are finally given an opportunity to give back to God for all that He has done for them—and the outpouring of material is great (cf. Exodus 36:5). With meticulous detail, Moses is given and then records the instructions for construction of a temporary Tabernacle and its components,[28] which will be used to worship the Lord during the sojourn through the desert:

"Let them construct a sanctuary for Me, that I may dwell among them" (Exodus 25:8).

Among the lengthy list of items to be contributed are not just the materials necessary for the different pieces of Tabernacle furniture, but also the materials necessary for the garments for the high priest:

"This is the contribution which you are to raise from them: gold, silver and bronze; blue, purple and scarlet *material*, fine linen, goat *hair*, rams' skins dyed red, porpoise skins, acacia wood, oil for lighting, spices for the anointing oil and for the fragrant incense, onyx stones and setting stones for the ephod and for the breastpiece" (Exodus 25:3-7).

---

Cf. Bruce M. Metzger, *A Textual Commentary on the Greek New Testament* (London and New York: United Bible Societies, 1975), pp 668-669.

[28] Exodus 25:10-27:21.

As you can deduce from this short summary list of materials, the Lord is particular about what He requires to fellowship with His chosen people in the Tabernacle that they will build for Him. He tells Moses about what this all means, stating, "See that you make *them* after the pattern for them, which was shown to you on the mountain" (Exodus 25:40). God gave Moses various Heavenly patterns, off of which the Israelites would be able to model the Tabernacle and its accoutrements.[29]

For the balance of the Book of Exodus, the specifics of the Tabernacle, its construction, and the implements to be used in it are described, and God's instructions are followed (Exodus chs. 25-40). It all culminates with the glory of God filling the Tabernacle, as the Book of Exodus concludes:

"He erected the court all around the tabernacle and the altar, and hung up the veil for the gateway of the court. Thus Moses finished the work. Then the cloud covered the tent of meeting, and the glory of the LORD filled the tabernacle" (Exodus 40:33-34).

As one reads this particular Torah portion, and contemplates the volume of the Book of Exodus that is devoted to describing the Tabernacle essentials, you should be reminded that the Lord is definitely interested in dwelling with His people. In fact, as Paul will later indicate, the concept of God dwelling with His people gets elevated to living inside human vessels, who commit themselves to Yeshua the Messiah:

"Do you not know that you are a temple of God and *that* the Spirit of God dwells in you?" (1 Corinthians 3:16).

Reflection on *Terumah* can focus on a number of different aspects detailed in the quality of materials chosen for the Tabernacle construction. Each has considerable meaning and symbolism that have ministered to me. Just as gold or silver has beauty or value—even more so, our redeemed hearts must be of a higher value and beauty—as we commit ourselves to a live of service to our Heavenly Father.

## Freewill Offering

Rather than dig into some minutiae from *Terumah*, when I read and meditated on our Torah portion this week, the Holy Spirit began to focus my attention on the importance of the freewill offering that the Israelites were commanded to give:

"Tell the sons of Israel to raise a contribution for Me; from every man whose heart moves him you shall raise My contribution" (Exodus 25:2).

As *Terumah* begins, the Hebrew verb used to describe the movement of the Israelites' hearts is *nadav* (נָדַב). In the Qal stem (simple action, active voice), it means to "**urge on, prompt**" (*CHALOT*),[30] in reference to freewill offerings and acts of heartfelt volunteering. From some other places where *nadav* is used, you can get the impression that when someone is compelled to perform an action, the personal and physical costs are not humanly considered. There is also an apparent link to gathering materials for the Tabernacle, and later the Temple, that houses the glory of God.

*Nadav* is used later in the Tanakh, in describing the freewill offerings which are given to King David for the construction of the first Temple, built during King Solomon's reign. In this passage, *nadav* appears in the Hitpael stem (intensive action, reflective voice) and

---

[29] According to Hebrews 9:23, the different components of the Earthly Tabernacle were copies of various Heavenly originals.
[30] *CHALOT*, 228.

means to "**decide voluntarily, volunteer,**" or "**offer voluntarily, give a free will offering**" (*CHALOT*)[31]:

"[O]f gold for the *things of* gold and of silver for the *things of* silver, that is, for all the work done by the craftsmen. Who then is willing to consecrate himself this day to the LORD?' Then the rulers of the fathers' *households*, and the princes of the tribes of Israel, and the commanders of thousands and of hundreds, with the overseers over the king's work, offered willingly [*nadav*]" (1 Chronicles 29:5-6).

We also see the verb *nadav* used when the materials for the Second Temple are being gathered by those of Ezra's generation:

"Then the heads of fathers' *households* of Judah and Benjamin and the priests and the Levites arose, even everyone whose spirit God had stirred to go up and rebuild the house of the LORD which is in Jerusalem. All those about them encouraged them with articles of silver, with gold, with goods, with cattle and with valuables, aside from all that was given as a freewill offering [*nadav*, Hitpael]" (Ezra 1:5-6).

In each of these recorded offerings, people whose hearts were stirred—were those who freely offered up the valuable items for the construction projects.

## Living Sacrifice

As I examined these passages and the actions of those who were moved by the Lord, I was reminded of some important things. First, I was reminded that our spiritual forbearers had an opportunity to offer gold, silver, and other precious and costly items for the construction of God's Earthly dwelling places. Whether it was the Tabernacle in the desert or the First and Second Temples, these were each unique occasions when certain persons responded in an overwhelming fashion. I was impressed with the thought that these people had their heart stirred to such a point that they did not consider the cost and high value of the items they gave.

Secondly, I was reminded of the reality that Believers today, who compose a kind of Temple for the Holy One, have much more to offer of themselves to Him. Instead of just offering gold or silver, we have the privilege of presenting ourselves as a living sacrifice before the Lord. Such a living sacrifice does not just pertain to how we individually live, *but also* how we are to function in unity accomplishing the Lord's tasks for the Earth. As the Apostle Paul puts it,

"Therefore I urge you, brethren, by the mercies of God, to present your bodies a living and holy sacrifice, acceptable to God, *which is* your spiritual service of worship" (Romans 12:1).

As children of the Most High, who should be confident that we are indwelt with the Ruach HaKodesh (Holy Spirit), we can offer ourselves up as a living sacrifice, for use by God as He so pleases. This, in and of itself, is something that each Believer must willfully choose to do. We have to contribute something so that we all function as a corporate, living sacrifice.

In order for this to be achieved, our hearts must be truly moved—without **counting the value or cost** of what we must contribute to God's service. If you do take the time to count the cost, and realize that your offering requires a total surrender to the will of God, then you just might not be willing to commit the time or energy that He requires.

---

[31] Ibid.

## A Better Sacrifice

What we all must be thankful for is that God Himself, in the Person of Yeshua, had a willing heart to offer Himself as a sacrifice for the sins of fallen humanity. As glorious as the wilderness Tabernacle, and First and Second Temples were—their service of sacrifices was not sufficient to provide us with permanent atonement, as detailed by the author of Hebrews:

"And according to the Law, *one may* almost *say*, all things are cleansed with blood, and without shedding of blood there is no forgiveness. Therefore it was necessary for the copies of the things in the heavens to be cleansed with these, but the heavenly things themselves with better sacrifices than these. For Messiah did not enter a holy place made with hands, a *mere* copy of the true one, but into heaven itself, now to appear in the presence of God for us; nor was it that He would offer Himself often, as the high priest enters the holy place year by year with blood that is not his own. Otherwise, He would have needed to suffer often since the foundation of the world; but now once at the consummation of the ages He has been manifested to put away sin by the sacrifice of Himself. And inasmuch as it is appointed for men to die once and after this *comes* judgment, so Messiah also, having been offered once to bear the sins of many, will appear a second time for salvation without *reference to* sin, to those who eagerly await Him" (Hebrews 9:22-28).

Thankfully, Yeshua's heart was stirred to the point that He was willing to be our sacrifice.

*How about you?* Is your heart being stirred to the point where you are willing to offer yourself up so that you can be useful in the Kingdom's work? If you have offered yourself up, are you encouraging others to do the same? If you are not doing these things, pray that our Heavenly Father will stir your heart to the point that the cost does not matter. Take the opportunity to offer yourself before Him.

The chance to be a willing sacrifice comes only during your lifetime. Be like those who did not miss the chance to make the offering when their time came! **Pray for the stirring of your heart!**

# *Tetzaveh* תְּצַוֶּה
## You shall command
## "Bloodied Garments"

Exodus 27:20-30:10
Ezekiel 43:10-27

*Tetzaveh* begins to stipulate many of the steps required of Ancient Israel, to become the kingdom of priests and holy nation that God wants it to be. He communicates through Moses many of the particulars that separate the Levites out from the other tribes. Aaron and his sons are specifically designated to perform some critical priestly tasks, including the consecration of the high priest. In our Torah reading for this week, we see the instruction,

"Then you shall take the other ram, and Aaron and his sons shall lay their hands on the head of the ram. You shall slaughter the ram, and take some of its blood and put *it* on the lobe of Aaron's right ear and on the lobes of his sons' right ears and on the thumbs of their right hands and on the big toes of their right feet, and sprinkle the *rest of the* blood around on the altar. Then you shall take some of the blood that is on the altar and some of the anointing oil, and sprinkle *it* on Aaron and on his garments and on his sons and on his sons' garments with him; so he and his garments shall be consecrated, as well as his sons and his sons' garments with him" (Exodus 29:19-21).

While reading this portion a number of times, I was overwhelmed by the minute details that were listed for the various garments and implements used by the high priest in his ministerial functions.[32] The variety of colors, different material types, precious metals and stones, and their locations on the specific garments, were very intriguing. Of course, all of the possible typology was not overlooked.

Much *speculation* has been given about how all of the colors and material types could be symbolic of the different aspects of the Messiah and His work as the High Priest. Some of this speculation might, however, take us away from the bigger Biblical picture—which is that in spite of such detail, the Levitical priesthood would be insufficient for offering people permanent atonement and forgiveness for sins (cf. Hebrews 9:9). The details of the Levitical priesthood, seen in *Tetzaveh* and throughout various Torah portions (notably in Leviticus and Numbers following), are to cause Believers to appreciate the priestly service of Yeshua the Messiah—which now **does offer permanent atonement and forgiveness for sins.**

It is quite beneficial for us to contemplate the symbols that we read about in *Tetzaveh*, and their foreshadowing of what was to come in the Messiah's ministry. Among the most notable of the symbols we encounter is the fact that the high priest went into the Holy of Holies once a year, with the names of the twelve tribes of Israel inscribed in two places on his apparel. First, the names of the twelve tribes were engraved on two onyx stones that were placed on the shoulders. Wearing these indicated that the high priest was bearing their weight on himself:

"You shall take two onyx stones and engrave on them the names of the sons of Israel, six of their names on the one stone and the names of the remaining six on the other stone, according to their birth. As a jeweler engraves a signet, you shall engrave the two stones according to the names of the sons of Israel; you shall set them in filigree *settings* of gold. You shall put the two stones on the shoulder pieces of the ephod, *as* stones of memorial for the sons of Israel, and Aaron shall bear their names before the LORD on his two shoulders for a memorial" (Exodus 28:9-12).

Secondly, the breastplate of judgment had twelve precious stones engraved with the names of the twelve tribes. This was placed over the high priest's heart and was a constant reminder of their presence before God:

"Aaron shall carry the names of the sons of Israel in the breastpiece of judgment over his heart when he enters the holy place, for a memorial before the LORD continually. You shall put in the breastpiece of judgment the Urim and the Thummim, and they shall be over Aaron's heart when he goes in before the LORD; and Aaron shall carry the judgment of the sons of Israel over his heart before the LORD continually" (Exodus 28:29-30).

In these two very symbolic ways, we are today reminded of the role of our High Priest, Yeshua. Yeshua the Messiah is the High Priest who is seated at the right hand of His Father in Heaven, interceding for all of those who have placed their trust in Him:

"Therefore He is able also to save forever those who draw near to God through Him, since He always lives to make intercession for them. For it was fitting for us to have such a

---

[32] Exodus 28:1-43.

high priest, holy, innocent, undefiled, separated from sinners and exalted above the heavens; who does not need daily, like those high priests, to offer up sacrifices, first for His own sins and then for the *sins* of the people, because this He did once for all when He offered up Himself. For the Law appoints men as high priests who are weak, but the word of the oath, which came after the Law, *appoints* a Son, made perfect forever. Now the main point in what has been said *is this*: we have such a high priest, who has taken His seat at the right hand of the throne of the Majesty in the heavens, a minister in the sanctuary and in the true tabernacle, which the Lord pitched, not man. For every high priest is appointed to offer both gifts and sacrifices; so it is necessary that this *high priest* also have something to offer" (Hebrews 7:25-8:3).

Further on in *Tetzaveh* we see a very dramatic event take place, when the high priest and his sons are anointed and then consecrated for their ministry service:

"You shall slaughter the ram, and take some of its blood and put *it* on the lobe of Aaron's right ear and on the lobes of his sons' right ears and on the thumbs of their right hands and on the big toes of their right feet, and sprinkle the *rest of the* blood around on the altar. Then you shall take some of the blood that is on the altar and some of the anointing oil, and sprinkle *it* on Aaron and on his garments and on his sons and on his sons' garments with him; so he and his garments shall be consecrated, as well as his sons and his sons' garments with him" (Exodus 29:20-21).

Here, the blood of the ram anoints not only the high priest and his sons, but they are also sprinkled by a mixture of the blood and anointing oil. This procedure should give us a vivid impression of the identification that the Holy One requires of the high priest and his sons, with the requirement for a blood sacrifice. As Believers, this reminds us of the Messiah's dual ministry—not just as High Priest when He ascended into Heaven—but also as *the bloody sacrifice* required to atone for the sins of fallen humanity. At the time of His crucifixion, perhaps it is possible that various disciples and followers of His were reminded of Exodus' images of the high priest and his sons being consecrated—among the many thoughts that were in their minds.

Only by appreciating the Levitical priesthood, and the sacrifices offered to consecrate Aaron and his sons—can we really appreciate the priestly service of Yeshua, and the sacrifice that He has offered for us. The author of Hebrews teaches what the blood of the Messiah is really all about, connecting it with the dedication of the Tabernacle that we read about in *Tetzaveh*:

"But when Messiah appeared *as* a high priest of the good things to come, *He entered* through the greater and more perfect tabernacle, not made with hands, that is to say, not of this creation; and not through the blood of goats and calves, but through His own blood, He entered the holy place once for all, having obtained eternal redemption. For if the blood of goats and bulls and the ashes of a heifer sprinkling those who have been defiled sanctify for the cleansing of the flesh, how much more will the blood of Messiah, who through the eternal Spirit offered Himself without blemish to God, cleanse your conscience from dead works to serve the living God?" (Hebrews 9:11-14).

May we all be thankful that Yeshua was willing to offer Himself up for us, atoning for our sins! He had much more than the bloodied garments of the high priest and his sons to contend with. It was His willingness to suffer and die for us, **that we can now have permanent forgiveness before the Father,** which the previous Levitical service *as important as it was* could not provide.

# Ki Tisa כִּי תִשָּׂא
## When you take
## "Signs of Life"

> Exodus 30:11-34:35
> 1 Kings 18:1-39 (A); 18:20-39 (S)

*Ki Tisa* covers a wide variety of topics that range from describing the half-shekel tax collected,[33] to the infamous golden calf incident,[34] and to instructions regarding the Sabbath.[35] Additional instruction is given regarding hand washing,[36] anointing oil[37] and incense formulas,[38] and how the Tabernacle is to be used.[39] Moses also relates significant interchanges that he has with the Holy One as he received the tablets of testimony, pleaded for the people of Israel, and then eventually witnessed the very glory of God.[40] These, and other events described, give students of the Torah much to ponder this week.

As one meditates upon this selection from Exodus, a multitude of impressions can be generated. For this student, three seemingly unrelated passages in the *parashah* became linked. The first Scriptural mention of the Book of Life (Exodus 32:32-33) generated some curiosity that led to some reflections about how serious the Father is about His children and their actions. These thoughts were then coupled with the passage about *Shabbat* (שַׁבָּת) or the Sabbath being a sign between God and His people (Exodus 31:12-18). Finally, the passage about Moses desiring the Lord's Divine presence struck a chord (Exodus 33:12-23). Let me explain.

## Moses' Intercession

Seeing the many things detailed in our *parashah* this week, the people of Israel are in serious trouble. Moses ascends Mount Sinai to receive God's Instruction. While there, Moses is informed that the impatient Israelites have fashioned a golden calf and are riotously worshipping it. The Lord threatens extermination of these sinners:

"Now then let Me alone, that My anger may burn against them and that I may destroy them; and I will make of you a great nation" (Exodus 32:10).

Thankfully, as a result of Moses' intercession, God decides not to do this:

"So the LORD changed His mind about the harm which He said He would do to His people" (Exodus 32:14).

At this point, we understand just how serious the Lord is about His people not worshipping other gods. Moses comes down the mountain with the tablets inscribed by the very finger of the Creator. Upon seeing the revelry over the golden calf, he shatters the tablets. Moses issues a call of loyalty to the Most High (Exodus 32:19-28a). At this point, all

---

[33] Exodus 30:11-16.
[34] Exodus 32:1-35.
[35] Exodus 31:12-17.
[36] Exodus 30:17-21.
[37] Exodus 30:22-33.
[38] Exodus 30:34-38.
[39] Exodus 31:1-11.
[40] Exodus 32:11-34:35.

the Levites respond and they are summoned to take up their swords against all who worshipped the false god. Three thousand Israelites lose their lives (Exodus 32:28b), while the Levites are consecrated for the call He has placed upon them to fulfill the obligations of priesthood:

"[T]hen Moses stood in the gate of the camp, and said, 'Whoever is for the LORD, *come to me!*' And all the sons of Levi gathered together to him. He said to them, 'Thus says the LORD, the God of Israel, "Every man *of you* put his sword upon his thigh, and go back and forth from gate to gate in the camp, and kill every man his brother, and every man his friend, and every man his neighbor."' So the sons of Levi did as Moses instructed, and about three thousand men of the people fell that day. Then Moses said, 'Dedicate yourselves today to the LORD—for every man has been against his son and against his brother—in order that He may bestow a blessing upon you today'" (Exodus 32:26-29).

The next day, God and Moses get into a debate. Moses offers himself as "an atonement" for the sins of the Israelites. (I believe that this offer is reminiscent of what Yeshua would later accomplish, actually being the permanent atonement for the sins of humanity.) The dialogue between Moses and the Lord continues:

"On the next day Moses said to the people, 'You yourselves have committed a great sin; and now I am going up to the LORD, perhaps I can make atonement for your sin.' Then Moses returned to the LORD, and said, 'Alas, this people has committed a great sin, and they have made a god of gold for themselves. But now, if You will, forgive their sin—and if not, please blot me out from Your book which You have written!' The LORD said to Moses, 'Whoever has sinned against Me, I will blot him out of My book'" (Exodus 32:30-33).

Interestingly, this is the first mention of the Book of Life in the Holy Writ, a record of those who stand under God's favor. The most important place we see the Book of Life mentioned, though, is in the final judgment recorded by John in the Book of Revelation:

"And I saw the dead, the great and the small, standing before the throne, and books were opened; and another book was opened, which is *the book* of life; and the dead were judged from the things which were written in the books, according to their deeds. And the sea gave up the dead which were in it, and death and Hades gave up the dead which were in them; and they were judged, every one *of them* according to their deeds. Then death and Hades were thrown into the lake of fire. This is the second death, the lake of fire. And if anyone's name was not found written in the book of life, he was thrown into the lake of fire" (Revelation 20:12-15).

One thing is very certain from the interchange between God and Moses, when seen through the filter of Revelation 20:12-15: **a person does not want his or her name to be missing from the Book of Life.** The consequence of sinning against the Most High by worshipping another god (Exodus 32:33), and then being among those judged "according to their works" (Revelation 20:12, NRSV), *is a very frightening concept.*

Another important thing is mentioned when the Lord speaks to Moses. God alone has the ability to blot out or erase a name from the Book of Life (Exodus 32:33). We should simply recognize that He has given His children ample understanding throughout the Scriptures to take loyalty to Him seriously. It is not impossible to truly be loyal to God, but demonstrating loyalty to Him is not something that is entirely passive, either.

While pondering the gravity and reality of the Book of Life, reflecting on *Ki Tisa*, two passages came to my mind from this *parashah*. First, God describes an action that can serve as a tangible sign between us and Him, that we are striving to be His. Secondly, the evidence of His presence in our midst, as sought by Moses, is a definite sign that we are His. One is an action we can take, and the other is an action God takes.

## Shabbat Observance

Earlier in this Torah portion (Exodus 31:12-18), the Lord gives His people some specific instruction about how to remember *Shabbat*, or the seventh-day Sabbath. This day of rest was to be an important sign between Israel and the Lord, which was to distinguish them among the nations. Remembering *Shabbat* was to serve as a tangible sign, for future generations, that Israel was His chosen people and that God created the universe by His supreme hand:

"The LORD spoke to Moses, saying, 'But as for you, speak to the sons of Israel, saying, "You shall surely observe My sabbaths; for *this* is a sign between Me and you throughout your generations, that you may know that I am the LORD who sanctifies you. Therefore you are to observe the sabbath, for it is holy to you. Everyone who profanes it shall surely be put to death; for whoever does any work on it, that person shall be cut off from among his people. For six days work may be done, but on the seventh day there is a sabbath of complete rest, holy to the LORD; whoever does any work on the sabbath day shall surely be put to death. So the sons of Israel shall observe the sabbath, to celebrate the sabbath throughout their generations as a perpetual covenant." It is a sign between Me and the sons of Israel forever; for in six days the LORD made heaven and earth, but on the seventh day He ceased *from labor*, and was refreshed.' When He had finished speaking with him upon Mount Sinai, He gave Moses the two tablets of the testimony, tablets of stone, written by the finger of God" (Exodus 31:12-18).

Here in these verses, as the finger of God has completed inscribing the Decalogue, He twice mentions within the span of a few verses two important things. First, the remembrance of *Shabbat* is a sign between the Lord and His people "throughout your/their generations" (Exodus 31:13, 16). Secondly, the Ancient Israelites were told that anyone who profanes or works on *Shabbat* would receive the penalty of capital punishment (Exodus 31:14b, 15b). This is extremely serious, and the fact that it is reiterated compounds the gravity of the statute.

Here in the Book of Exodus, we see how important the Lord considered the institution of the Sabbath to be. It is considered a Creation ordinance (Exodus 31:15), as we remember how God Himself rested after His six periods of creating the universe (Genesis 2:2). Even if we believe in this post-resurrection era that the capital punishment for not remembering the Sabbath has been absorbed by the sacrifice of Yeshua the Messiah (cf. Colossians 2:14), why does it seem that many Christians today want to overlook the Biblical imperative to rest on the seventh day? At most, the being "cut off" they would experience would not be participating in all of the good things that *resting for a complete day* naturally offers us.

Much of the negativity that today's Messianic Believers encounter, when telling Christian family or friends that they are keeping the Sabbath, comes from various encounters we read in the Gospels (i.e., Matthew 12:9-14; Mark 2:23-28; 3:1-6; Luke 6:1-5, 6-11; 13:10-17; John 5:10, 15-16; 7:22-23), and how they have been too commonly read. We see scenes where Yeshua the Messiah is either seen arguing with some of the religious officials in His day, or how He is rebuked by them for doing "unauthorized" things on the Sabbath. Bible scholars today are not all agreed that Yeshua opposed the keeping of the Sabbath, as much as He opposed the different streams of Jewish tradition present in His day that made it difficult for the Sabbath to be a legitimate day of rest for the normal person—and how some authorities opposed the legitimate doing of good on the Sabbath, as He was rebuked for healing people.[41] And notable to also remember, is how Yeshua did not oppose all tradition—just those traditions that specifically took away from accomplishing the purpose of His Father.

Yeshua's ministry and teachings clarified much of what the Torah originally intended profaning the Sabbath to be. In His Sermon on the Mount, Yeshua spends a considerable amount of time working through various Torah commandments as they related to one's heart intent (Matthew chs. 5-7). He **did not** come *to fulfill and thus abolish* the Law, as many may inaccurately teach—but instead to fulfill the Law by showing people how to live out its intentions properly in human life (Matthew 5:16ff). When it came to the issues concerning *Shabbat*, our Lord demonstrated that healing and doing good was appropriate. Yeshua stated how "The sabbath was made for humankind, and not humankind for the sabbath" (Mark 2:27, NRSV), and how its rest is something which can benefit all people.

## The Presence of God

A little further on in our *parashah*, we encounter a second visible sign that clearly marks the people of God. **God's presence is to be among His people:**

"'Now therefore, I pray You, if I have found favor in Your sight, let me know Your ways that I may know You, so that I may find favor in Your sight. Consider too, that this nation is Your people.' And He said, 'My presence shall go *with you*, and I will give you rest.' Then he said to Him, 'If Your presence does not go *with us*, do not lead us up from here. For how then can it be known that I have found favor in Your sight, I and Your people? Is it not by Your going with us, so that we, I and Your people, may be distinguished from all the *other* people who are upon the face of the earth?'" (Exodus 33:13-16).

Here, the Hebrew word *panim* (פָּנִים) or "face" is actually translated as "presence." When the face of God Himself shines upon His people, it is evidence of His favor and blessing toward them. Such favor was to be so tangible toward Ancient Israel, that in their comings and goings, they would be distinguished among all others on Earth. As further detailed, this would involve God being merciful to His people:

"The LORD said to Moses, 'I will also do this thing of which you have spoken; for you have found favor in My sight and I have known you by name.' Then Moses said, 'I pray You, show me Your glory!' And He said, 'I Myself will make all My goodness pass before you, and will proclaim the name of the LORD before you; and I will be gracious to whom I will be gracious, and will show compassion on whom I will show compassion.' But He said, 'You cannot see My face, for no man can see Me and live!' Then the LORD said, 'Behold, there is a place by Me, and you shall stand *there* on the rock; and it will come about, while My glory is passing by, that I will put you in the cleft of the rock and cover you with My hand until I have passed by. Then I will take My hand away and you shall see My back, but My face shall not be seen'" (Exodus 33:17-23).

Here, as Moses pleads for the presence of the Most High, He concedes that His glory will be evident, but that neither Moses nor any other would see His specific "face." Instead, God's glory, goodness, grace, and compassion would be evident among the people of Israel—demonstrating the substance of what His "face" really is. His attributes, which are

---

[41] Cf. S. Westerholm, "Sabbath," in Joel B. Green, Scot McKnight, and I. Howard Marshall, eds., *Dictionary of Jesus and the Gospels* (Downers Grove, IL: InterVarsity, 1992), pp 716-719, for a summary of some of the opinions present in academic thought.

frequently embodied in the later New Testament term *agapē* (ἀγάπη), would manifest themselves among the Ancient Israelites. In due time, the presence of His very Spirit would move beyond the Tabernacle or Temple, and would be fully dwelling within the hearts of His people (cf. Ezekiel 35:25-27). We see some of the specific aspects of God's "face" listed, as He passes beside Moses on Mount Sinai:

"Then the LORD passed by in front of him and proclaimed, 'The LORD, the LORD God, compassionate and gracious, slow to anger, and abounding in lovingkindness and truth; who keeps lovingkindness for thousands, who forgives iniquity, transgression and sin; yet He will by no means leave *the guilty* unpunished, visiting the iniquity of fathers on the children and on the grandchildren to the third and fourth generations'" (Exodus 34:6-7).

How much do these attributes sound like the summarizations of the *agapē* love demonstrated by Messiah Yeshua, who offered Himself up for our sins? Consider the Apostle Paul's description of what Believers are to embody, as a direct result of Yeshua's atoning work:

"So, as those who have been chosen of God, holy and beloved, put on a heart of compassion, kindness, humility, gentleness and patience; bearing with one another, and forgiving each other, whoever has a complaint against anyone; just as the Lord forgave you, so also should you. Beyond all these things *put on* love [*agapē*], which is the perfect bond of unity" (Colossians 3:12-14).

The Apostle John also writes about the great love of God manifested toward us:

"In this is love, not that we loved God, but that He loved us and sent His Son *to be* the propitiation for our sins. Beloved, if God so loved us, we also ought to love one another. No one has seen God at any time; if we love one another, God abides in us, and His love is perfected in us. By this we know that we abide in Him and He in us, because He has given us of His Spirit" (1 John 4:10-13).

We know that unlike Moses, whose offer of personal atonement was not acceptable (cf. Exodus 32:30), Yeshua's offer, as the Son of God, is acceptable (Hebrews 9:26-28).

## Two Signs

Today as Believers in Yeshua the Messiah, who have been washed of our sins by His work, we should be experiencing the presence of our Creator, as originally revealed to Moses on Mount Sinai (Exodus 34:6-7). We should have His love and His blessings enveloping us, ever-reminding us of how much the Lord really does care for us and wants us to commune with Him! This presence of God should fill us up with His love, which we are surely to demonstrate to all people we encounter.

Yet if we possess the presence of God inside of us, are there any *specific* actions we can demonstrate which reflect on the goodness He has showered? I would submit to you that remembering *Shabbat* or the seventh-day Sabbath (Exodus 31:12-18), a day each week when we can rest and experience refreshment in Him, is something that we need to be considering. *Shabbat* is a time when we get to focus on the Lord in a very unique way, ceasing from our labors, and allowing Him to reveal His presence to us.

How do we learn to balance the value of these two aspects of our faith? How do we remember the many imperatives we see in the Scriptures to demonstrate love toward others (i.e., 1 Corinthians 13:4-8; Romans 12:9-17)?

Many generations of Jewish people faithful to the Lord's ways have experienced the blessings of *Shabbat*, and we can hope that many who truly pressed into Him on the seventh-day were supernaturally revealed the truth of Messiah Yeshua as they sought God for answers. Similarly—and whether or not today's Messianics really want to admit it—many generations of Christians faithful to the Old Testament have also experienced the blessings of the Sabbath, albeit they have observed it on the first day. Even though a "Sunday Sabbath" was not our Father's original intention, He has still honored the dedication of many Christians in past history who strived to make Sunday a day of abstention from work and commerce—something which only in the latter-half of the Twentieth Century was really lost.

In our day as the Father restores His people through the growth of the Messianic movement, not only will Jewish Believers get to experience the blessedness of the Sabbath by their faith in Messiah Yeshua—but many non-Jewish Believers will get to experience some of the things that have made Jewish remembrance of *Shabbat* so special. The edifying traditions that enable us to really focus on who the Lord is, and which bring us together as families and communities where He dwells, can help focus our remembrance of the Sabbath as we consider who we all are as His *redeemed* people. We all await the return of our King, and the much greater rest He will bring to us in the future (Hebrews 4:9-11).[42]

## *V'yakheil* ויקהל
### He assembled
### "Stirred and Willing Hearts"

> Exodus 35:1-38:20
> 1 Kings 7:40-50 (A); 7:13-26 (S)

*V'yakheil* describes the beginning phases of the construction of the Tabernacle and its furnishings. You should recall that the specific description of the *mishkan* (מִשְׁכָּן) or Tabernacle had been given to Moses several months earlier, as recorded in previous Torah portions. *Terumah* (Exodus 25:1-27:19) has detailed the offerings and contributions that were made by the people for its construction. *Tetzaveh* (Exodus 27:20-30:10) goes into great elaboration about worship related articles and the specific dedication instructions. *Ki Tisa* (Exodus 30:11-34:35) relates the trials endured by the Israelites, as they could not patiently wait for Moses to come down from the mountain with this wealth of information. Our reading for this week begins with the word,

"Then Moses assembled all the congregation of the sons of Israel, and said to them, 'These are the things that the LORD has commanded *you* to do: For six days work may be done, but on the seventh day you shall have a holy *day*, a sabbath of complete rest to the LORD; whoever does any work on it shall be put to death'" (Exodus 35:1-2).

If you attempt to understand the chronology between the end of *Mishpatim* (Exodus 21:1-24:18) and the beginning of the construction phase, you see that two forty-day periods had passed (Exodus 24:16-18; 34:28), and probably a number of other days. Various Jewish sources have noted that the construction began on the 11th of Tishri, right after Moses had descended from Mount Sinai after the second set of forty days and forty nights. It occurred on what would later become the Day of Atonement:[43]

---

[42] For a further discussion, consult the *Messianic Sabbath Helper* by TNN Press.
[43] A. Cohen, ed., *The Soncino Chumash* (London: Soncino Press, 1983), 565.

"The glory of the LORD rested on Mount Sinai, and the cloud covered it for six days; and on the seventh day He called to Moses from the midst of the cloud. And to the eyes of the sons of Israel the appearance of the glory of the LORD was like a consuming fire on the mountain top. Moses entered the midst of the cloud as he went up to the mountain; and Moses was on the mountain forty days and forty nights... So he was there with the LORD forty days and forty nights; he did not eat bread or drink water. And he wrote on the tablets the words of the covenant, the Ten Commandments" (Exodus 24:16-18, 28).

Without dissecting the specifics about the actual timing, the Israelites were certainly being prepared for the Lord to dwell in their presence. They had already experienced the trauma at the base of the mountain when the thunder sounded, the lightning flashed, the ground shook, and the blast of *shofar*s issued great warnings. They had already determined that Moses needed to be their spokesperson and representative before the Creator.

In recent weeks, they had impatiently rebelled against the Lord and had worshipped a golden calf. Upon Moses' first descent from the mountain, judgment came in the form of death by either sword-wielding Levites or the ensuing plague. After Moses' second descent, the hearts of Israel were definitely prepared for making an offering for the construction of the Tabernacle and its furnishings. At this point in the narrative of Exodus, our Torah portion *V'yakheil* begins.

## A Shabbat Reminder

Interestingly, as Moses assembled the people of Israel to begin bringing their freewill offerings and start the construction of the Tabernacle, the admonition to remember *Shabbat* is declared and further defined.[44] In spite of His dwelling being built, the Lord is very concerned about the need for the people to have a weekly day of rest so they do not get worn out, otherwise He would not have instructed Moses to mention the Sabbath again.

Even a project as significant as the construction of the Tabernacle, and the other implements of worship, does not take precedence over the observance of *Shabbat*. The Lord declares *Shabbat* to be a holy day or *yom qodesh* (יוֹם קֹדֶשׁ), and told the Ancient Israelites that those working shall be put to death. The Lord further defines work for them by stating that the kindling of a fire in one's habitation was also a violation. We see some of the instructions from our previous *parashah* (Exodus 31:12-18) repeated:

"But as for you, speak to the sons of Israel, saying, 'You shall surely observe My sabbaths; for *this* is a sign between Me and you throughout your generations, that you may know that I am the LORD who sanctifies you. Therefore you are to observe the sabbath, for it is holy to you. Everyone who profanes it shall surely be put to death; for whoever does any work on it, that person shall be cut off from among his people'" (Exodus 31:13-14).

**Is the Lord trying to make Ancient Israel aware of the importance of Shabbat?** For those of us who are studying the Torah today, the constant repetitions about *Shabbat* should begin to sink into our hearts. Obviously, our Father is very serious about this sign that is supposed to set His people apart. Even though the sacrifice of His Son may have taken away the physical death penalty originally prescribed to ancient Sabbath-breakers, by not taking a day of rest—could we find that we are cutting ourselves off from being able to rest and bask in His presence?

---

[44] Exodus 35:1-3.

## Collection for Construction

After the *Shabbat* warning, the whole community of Israel is assembled and the collection of articles for the construction project begins.[45] It is evident from the outpouring that is recorded, that the hearts of the people were tenderized for the moment of giving. Certainly, a degree of solemnity circulated among the people as their hearts were beginning to stir toward their freewill offerings. Just where was their treasure going to be found? *It was surely going to be with the purposes of Israel's God.* We can consider the applicability of Yeshua's later word: "for where your treasure is, there your heart will be also" (Matthew 6:21).

Throughout Exodus 35, the Hebrew term *lev* (לֵב) or "heart" is used nine different times.[46] This is very significant, because as we know, the Lord is most concerned about the hearts of His people and how they are to be turned toward Him. Of course, the "heart" is very complicated to understand because it has multiple meanings or an array of applications throughout the Scriptures. The word *lev* is "usually rendered as heart but whose range of meaning is extensive…it usually refers to some aspect of the immaterial inner self or being since the heart is considered to be the seat of one's inner nature as well as one of its components" (*AMG*).[47]

In these passages we are introduced to at least two different kinds of hearts, if not more. First, we see the "willing heart" that is inclined to make offerings without any strings attached. Here, the Hebrew verb *nadav* (נָדַב), or a derivative like the adjective *nadiv* (נָדִיב), is coupled in some way with *lev*. *Nadav* means "voluntary desire of the heart to give of oneself or of one's resources to the service of the Lord" (*AMG*).[48] The following verses bring forth the absolute willingness of the people of Israel to freely offer all that was necessary for the construction project:

"Take from among you a contribution to the LORD; whoever is of a willing [adj. *nadiv*] heart, let him bring it as the LORD's contribution: gold, silver, and bronze…Everyone whose heart stirred him and everyone whose spirit moved [verb *nadav*] him came *and* brought the LORD's contribution for the work of the tent of meeting and for all its service and for the holy garments. Then all whose hearts moved [adj. *nadiv*] them, both men and women, came *and* brought brooches and earrings and signet rings and bracelets, all articles of gold; so *did* every man who presented an offering of gold to the LORD…The Israelites, all the men and women, whose heart moved [verb *nadav*] them to bring *material* for all the work, which the LORD had commanded through Moses to be done, brought a freewill offering to the LORD" (Exodus 35:5, 21-22, 29).

The other type of heart that is mentioned in this section of Scripture is a heart of wisdom, which some versions render with either "skill" (NASU) or "ability" (RSV). Here, one of the most common Hebrew terms for wisdom, *chokmah* (חָכְמָה), is coupled with *lev*.[49] *Chokmah* means "wisdom, skill, experience, shrewdness" (*AMG*).[50] The following are examples of it being employed in Exodus 34. You can detect from these passages that God

---

[45] Exodus 35:4-9, 20-35.
[46] Exodus 35:5, 10, 21, 22, 25, 26, 29, 34, 35.
[47] Baker and Carpenter, 536.
[48] Ibid., 708.
[49] Exodus 35:26, 31, 35.
[50] Baker and Carpenter, 337.

Himself endowed these artisans with hearts of wisdom to help produce the diverse parts of the Tabernacle:

"All the women whose heart stirred with a skill [*chokmah*] spun the goats' *hair*... He also has put in his heart to teach, both he and Oholiab, the son of Ahisamach, of the tribe of Dan. He has filled them with skill [*chokmah*] to perform every work of an engraver and of a designer and of an embroiderer, in blue and in purple *and* in scarlet *material*, and in fine linen, and of a weaver, as performers of every work and makers of designs" (Exodus 35:26, 34-36).

The people of Israel responded to not only the offering of materials, but also the construction project from what skill or "wisdom" issued forth from their hearts:

"Now Bezalel and Oholiab, and every skillful person in whom the LORD has put skill [*chokmah*] and understanding to know how to perform all the work in the construction of the sanctuary, shall perform in accordance with all that the LORD has commanded. Then Moses called Bezalel and Oholiab and every skillful person in whom the LORD had put skill [*chokmah*], everyone whose heart stirred him, to come to the work to perform it. They received from Moses all the contributions which the sons of Israel had brought to perform the work in the construction of the sanctuary. And they still *continued* bringing to him freewill offerings every morning. And all the skillful men who were performing all the work of the sanctuary came, each from the work which he was performing" (Exodus 36:1-4).

Many hearts had been stirred during the preceding months. When the opportunity to give to the Lord had arrived, they willfully gave abundantly. In fact, the offering was *so overwhelming* that Moses had to tell the people to stop bringing materials:

"[A]nd they said to Moses, 'The people are bringing much more than enough for the construction work which the LORD commanded *us* to perform.' So Moses issued a command, and a proclamation was circulated throughout the camp, saying, 'Let no man or woman any longer perform work for the contributions of the sanctuary.' Thus the people were restrained from bringing *any more*. For the material they had was sufficient and more than enough for all the work, to perform it" (Exodus 36:5-7).

## Heart Condition

As you consider *V'yakheil* this week, with its focus on the heart, it might be a good time to reflect upon your own heart condition. The examples I have listed above show how the Ancient Israelites *whole*-heartedly responded to the challenge of building the Tabernacle. Perhaps what they demonstrated in ancient times can be used to bring some introspection into our own hearts, at this hour of great turmoil in the world. Think of such an examination of the heart like your annual physical, or your car's regular oil change.

It is not by chance that we are considering this section of Scripture as the world suffers diverse, and rather serious conflicts. Hearts all over the globe are challenged by decisions that are made in high government circles, often without their consent. Many people are filled with questions for which they think there are no answers. Perhaps the Lord will position *you* to be available to those who are asking about life's big issues. Be prepared to share the "hope that is in you" (1 Peter 3:15), this hope being the gospel message of salvation. We should seriously consider having our *hearts stirred* toward the Holy One of Israel, while imploring Him to give us *hearts of wisdom*.

Just how do we respond to the opportunities presented each day, to offer ourselves for the work of the Kingdom? Are you mustering, by your freewill, to choose to serve the Lord with your resources and talents? What about those of you who have been given a heart of wisdom with the innate ability to skillfully create things for the King's use? Are you using your God-given talents for your own benefits, or for the edification of His Kingdom?

These and a flood of questions might come to mind as we ponder our hearts, wills, inclinations, resolutions, and determinations. We also might be reminded that a hardened heart is wickedly deceitful, as described by the Prophet Jeremiah:

"The heart is more deceitful than all else and is desperately sick; who can understand it? I, the LORD, search the heart, I test the mind, even to give to each man according to his ways, according to the results of his deeds" (Jeremiah 17:9-10).

Even if you have received salvation in Messiah Yeshua and have a regenerated and transformed heart, we still live in a world where most people do not have regenerated and transformed hearts. *We are surrounded by these people every day*, and whether we acknowledge it or not, we can be affected by them. The Psalmist reminds us that we have a need to treasure God's Word in our hearts, so we remain unaffected by the power of sin:

"With all my heart I have sought You; do not let me wander from Your commandments. Your word I have treasured in my heart, that I may not sin against You" (Psalm 119:10-11).

We are similarly instructed in Proverbs how God's Word is to be imprinted onto our psyche, as we trust in Him and are led by Him:

"My son, do not forget my teaching, but let your heart keep my commandments; for length of days and years of life and peace they will add to you. Do not let kindness and truth leave you; bind them around your neck, write them on the tablet of your heart. So you will find favor and good repute in the sight of God and man. Trust in the LORD with all your heart and do not lean on your own understanding. In all your ways acknowledge Him, and He will make your paths straight" (Proverbs 3:1-6).

Trusting in God with all your heart, and not relying upon your own limited human "wisdom," is critical in maintaining a good life. Letting God direct your path as you acknowledge Him in all your ways, gives Him preeminence in your heart and the course upon which you walk. *Such will be a long life of peace and tranquility.* It will be a life certainly guided by love for God and neighbor, the foremost of the Torah's commandments. Yeshua, when asked about the greatest commandment of all, responded to this end:

"'Teacher, which is the great commandment in the Law?' And He said to him, '"YOU SHALL LOVE THE LORD YOUR GOD WITH ALL YOUR HEART, AND WITH ALL YOUR SOUL, AND WITH ALL YOUR MIND."' This is the great and foremost commandment. The second is like it, 'YOU SHALL LOVE YOUR NEIGHBOR AS YOURSELF.' On these two commandments depend the whole Law and the Prophets" (Matthew 22:36-40; cf. Deuteronomy 6:5; Leviticus 19:18).

Clearly, the Lord wants all of our hearts, all of our souls, and all of our minds. His description of the greatest commandment expresses the need for one's heart to be totally dedicated to the imperatives of love—*because saying and thinking are not enough*. The Apostle John emphasizes how we must let our love for God manifest itself by our positive actions of service:

"But whoever has the world's goods, and sees his brother in need and closes his heart against him, how does the love of God abide in him? Little children, let us not love with word or with tongue, but in deed and truth. We will know by this that we are of the truth, and will assure our heart before Him in whatever our heart condemns us; for God is greater than our heart and knows all things" (1 John 3:17-20).

Here as you read and reflect on these words, the contrast between "with word or with tongue" versus "in deed and in truth" are quite sobering. How are we measuring up to these strong words? How does your heart respond when you see needs among those in the assembly? If we fall short of extending compassion to others, perhaps we need to cry out to the Lord for more of Him and His stirring our hearts. We know that if we are His and we ask in faith, He will pour Himself out for us:

"[A]nd whatever we ask we receive from Him, because we keep His commandments and do the things that are pleasing in His sight" (1 John 3:22).

*We thank you, Father, that we can confess to you the condition of our hearts! Stir our hearts, O God! Soften our hearts with the oil of gladness! Fill us with your Ruach! Make us willing vessels that depend upon You for all things. Use us that You may be glorified through all that You do through us.*

## Pequdei פְּקוּדֵי
### Accounts
### "The Glory of God"

Exodus 38:21-40:38
1 Kings 7:51-8:21 (A); 7:40-50 (S)

This week's Torah portion, *Pequdei*, concludes the Book of Exodus. Although some important things occur in our selected reading, Exodus ends with some very meaningful words, as the Tabernacle is completed and the Ancient Israelites prepare to enter into the purpose that the Lord has set for them:

"Then the cloud covered the tent of meeting, and the glory of the LORD filled the tabernacle. Moses was not able to enter the tent of meeting because the cloud had settled on it, and the glory of the LORD filled the tabernacle. Throughout all their journeys whenever the cloud was taken up from over the tabernacle, the sons of Israel would set out; but if the cloud was not taken up, then they did not set out until the day when it was taken up. For throughout all their journeys, the cloud of the LORD was on the tabernacle by day, and there was fire in it by night, in the sight of all the house of Israel" (Exodus 40:34-38).

In *Pequdei*, we see the appearance of the glory of God in the completed Tabernacle:

"[T]he cloud covered the Tent of Meeting, and the Presence of the LORD filled the Tabernacle" (Exodus 40:34, NJPS).

For the past ten readings, since the introduction of Moses in *Shemot*, the Israelites have been on a somewhat soul-searching journey in the wilderness. Their emotional "roller coaster" that began with their deliverance from Egypt, has now culminated with God's glory residing in their very midst. If you did not know any better, you might think that a considerable amount of time has passed, because the people of Israel have been through an intense period of getting to know their God. But instead, it has really just been a little over one year since Moses first appeared and asked Pharaoh to let the people go. We are told that the Tabernacle was finally assembled on the first day of the first month of the second year:

"Now in the first month of the second year, on the first *day* of the month, the tabernacle was erected" (Exodus 40:17).

In just over a year, these several hundred thousand Israelites, coupled with the mixed multitude that had joined themselves to them (Exodus 12:38), now constituted the nation of Israel. This former rabble of slaves were now free men and women chosen by God to be "a kingdom of priests and a holy nation" (Exodus 19:6), in order to be His light unto the other nations of the world. The Prophet Isaiah will later declare,

"I am the LORD, I have called you in righteousness, I will also hold you by the hand and watch over you, and I will appoint you as a covenant to the people, as a light to the nations" (Isaiah 42:6).

Of course, even though Israel now has many of the things that will form its national identity, the new nation has a way to go. Through His servant Moses, the Lord has revealed *enough* about Himself and what He requires for His glory (Heb. *kavod*, כָּבוֹד; Grk. *doxa*, δόξα) to reside among mortals, that for the first time since the Garden of Eden, His glory can now more tangibly dwell among people. The instructions for construction of the Tabernacle, its implements, and the courtyard have been followed. At the right time, Moses anoints and consecrates the Tabernacle and everything in it. He washes Aaron and his sons, and anoints them in their holy garments.[51] Exodus 40:16 summarizes, "Thus Moses did; according to all that the LORD had commanded him, so he did."

One can only imagine the excitement that was running through the hearts of the Ancient Israelites as the construction project is completed. Remember, over the course of the previous year, the Lord through Moses had revealed a tremendous amount about who He is and what He requires of His people. During that time, Israel had witnessed the judgment upon Egypt. They saw the ten plagues and their devastation, and avoided the death of their firstborn children and livestock. The miracles of the Red Sea crossing were still etched in their memories. The trauma of hearing the voice of God Himself from the trembling mountain, and the unanimous decision to let Moses be their mediator, could never be forgotten. Receiving the Ten Commandments, precepts, and other instructions started to outline rules and regulations for human interactions.

Of course, the golden calf incident of rebellion against their Deliverer God had horrific consequences. Not only did judgment fall upon the Israelites by sword-wielding Levites, but a plague sent by the Lord, judged all whose hearts were not right (Exodus 32:35). If you will recall, various material needs for the Tabernacle were actually mentioned in the text (Exodus 25:13-31:11) before the rebellion of idol worship occurred (Exodus 32:1-35). The Holy One used the remorse, and perhaps even guilt of these incidents, to generate an overwhelming response when the material was finally gathered. Hearts were stirred and the outpouring was so great that the people were ordered to stop (Exodus 35:21; 36:5-7).

## The Glory of God

When I meditated upon *Pequdei* this week, a summary of the Book of Exodus kept coming to mind. It was surely incredible to tally what happened to the Ancient Israelites in just *a little over a year* of real time. From the bonds and burden of human slavery—to encampment around the newly constructed Tabernacle of the Lord—was quite a journey! Now His glory was in their midst, rather than the yoke of heavy servitude. We are told that once God's glory fell, Moses was unable to enter into the Tent of Meeting:

---

[51] Exodus 38:1-40:33.

"Moses was not able to enter the tent of meeting because the cloud had settled on it, and the glory of the LORD filled the tabernacle" (Exodus 40:35).

Apparently, the presence of the Lord was so intense, that human interaction with it was difficult to achieve. Even the beloved Moses was unable to enter the Tent of Meeting. As I thought about this, I wondered about other recorded times that the glory of God fell upon Israel. The completion of Solomon's Temple came to mind, when the glory once again fell upon those gathered. In these two passages, the same basic report is articulated: no one could stand because of the intensity of God's presence:

"It happened that when the priests came from the holy place, the cloud filled the house of the LORD, so that the priests could not stand to minister because of the cloud, for the glory of the LORD filled the house of the LORD" (1 Kings 8:10-11).

"[I]n unison when the trumpeters and the singers were to make themselves heard with one voice to praise and to glorify the LORD, and when they lifted up their voice accompanied by trumpets and cymbals and instruments of music, and when they praised the LORD *saying,* 'He indeed is good for His lovingkindness is everlasting,' then the house, the house of the LORD, was filled with a cloud, so that the priests could not stand to minister because of the cloud, for the glory of the LORD filled the house of God'" (2 Chronicles 5:13-14).

Apparently, according to these statements about when the Tabernacle was completed, and the testimonies from when the Temple of Solomon was dedicated, the appearance of the glory of God was so intense **that one was either prevented from getting in His presence, or one is forced to prostrate before Him**—because of its greatness. While considering these passages, I wondered about the times I have felt His glory during my lifetime. Of course, we know that God inhabits the praises of His people, as the Psalmist attests:

"Yet You are holy, O You who are enthroned upon the praises of Israel" (Psalm 22:3).

There have been times during praise and worship when I have felt His glory in the room where I was worshipping. These have been very special times, and as a spirit of unity among those gathered prevails, the presence of the Lord is more noticeable. We should all consider the vision of the Prophet Isaiah, and how serious it is to be invited into His presence, even if just for a short while:

"In the year of King Uzziah's death I saw the Lord sitting on a throne, lofty and exalted, with the train of His robe filling the temple. Seraphim stood above Him, each having six wings: with two he covered his face, and with two he covered his feet, and with two he flew. And one called out to another and said, 'Holy, Holy, Holy, is the LORD of hosts, the whole earth is full of His glory.' And the foundations of the thresholds trembled at the voice of him who called out, while the temple was filling with smoke. Then I said, 'Woe is me, for I am ruined! Because I am a man of unclean lips, and I live among a people of unclean lips; for my eyes have seen the King, the LORD of hosts'" (Isaiah 6:1-5).

For some reason, whenever I think of this passage, I envision Isaiah prostrating on the floor, looking up at the throne of God, imploring Him for mercy. *Here, he confesses his state of mortal sinfulness.* It is interesting that Isaiah focuses on his unclean lips, and the unclean lips of those among whom he dwells.

Thinking about these verses from Isaiah, I was reminded about the title of our Torah portion for this week, *Pequdei* or "Accounts." As our reading begins, we see meticulous details about the amount of actual weight in the precious metals used for the Tabernacle project. For some reason, is God reminding us that He is mindful of particulars? Without hesitation, I recalled a passage in the Gospels from Yeshua:

"But I tell you that every careless word that people speak, they shall give an accounting for it in the day of judgment. For by your words you will be justified, and by your words you will be condemned" (Matthew 12:36-37).

Then, I wondered to myself about *careless words that come from unclean lips.* I looked at some of the verses surrounding Matthew 12:36-37. Yeshua warned against idle words when He was being accused of being demon possessed:

"But if I cast out demons by the Spirit of God, then the kingdom of God has come upon you. Or how can anyone enter the strong man's house and carry off his property, unless he first binds the strong *man*? And then he will plunder his house. He who is not with Me is against Me; and he who does not gather with Me scatters. Therefore I say to you, any sin and blasphemy shall be forgiven people, but blasphemy against the Spirit shall not be forgiven. Whoever speaks a word against the Son of Man, it shall be forgiven him; but whoever speaks against the Holy Spirit, it shall not be forgiven him, either in this age or in the *age* to come. Either make the tree good and its fruit good, or make the tree bad and its fruit bad; for the tree is known by its fruit. You brood of vipers, how can you, being evil, speak what is good? For the mouth speaks out of that which fills the heart. The good man brings out of *his* good treasure what is good; and the evil man brings out of *his* evil treasure what is evil" (Matthew 12:28-35).

I remembered a previous incident in my life, hearing about a particular individual who believed that when a gospel presentation was given—it was actually from Satan! This was an interesting attack, because he made his accusations from solely viewing a videotape, and perhaps not even that closely. If he looked closely at the video—which I also watched—he would have seen a number of people *prostrated on the floor and on their knees* as the gospel presentation went forth. When I saw this, I thought: Was the glory of God present at this message? There certainly were many evidences of His presence from the testimonies that came forth.

Then as I thought about this reality, the concepts of God's glory, how He "inhabits our praises," and a new thought about not properly discerning the Body of Messiah, all came into focus. I wanted to tell the man who haphazardly judged the work of the Lord: Do you remember the words of Paul as he was instructing the Corinthians about properly examining oneself before taking of the bread and wine at Passover? Paul states,

"But a man must examine himself, and in so doing he is to eat of the bread and drink of the cup. For he who eats and drinks, eats and drinks judgment to himself if he does not judge the body rightly. For this reason many among you are weak and sick, and a number sleep. But if we judged ourselves rightly, we would not be judged. But when we are judged, we are disciplined by the Lord so that we will not be condemned along with the world" (1 Corinthians 11:28-32).

While reflecting on these truths, I often catch myself and pray for any person who believes that the work of the Holy Spirit is demonic. He or she is usually unable to discern the Body of Messiah, or to differentiate between the works of the Devil and the Spirit of the Most High—making judgments about things with insufficient information.

I also find myself confessing any unloving or improper thoughts I can have when I hear improper accusations. I know that I can also misunderstand the ways of the Lord and make incorrect conclusions. Steadfast is the admonition, "If we confess our sins, He is faithful and righteous to forgive us our sins and to cleanse us from all unrighteousness" (1 John 1:9).

## Concluding Thoughts

As you can see from this final Torah portion of Exodus, the Ancient Israelites have come a long way from their deliverance from Egypt and to seeing the glory of God fall upon them in the Tabernacle in the wilderness. When we consider what we have read from this *parashah*, and the work it took to prepare God's dwelling place—how much work has He had to conduct you through, preparing you to be an effective Believer in His service? Even with the permanent atonement and forgiveness from sins available in Messiah Yeshua, we still have to be readied for His service—following the proverbial "cloud" wherever it may lead us (Exodus 40:38).

My prayer is that each of us would seek the place where His glory would be upon us continually, as our lips offer Him praise! *And what should we praise Him for?* The fact that there are more people who have been reconciled with Him, who He can likewise inhabit!

# COMMENTARY ON LEVITICUS

## *Vayikra* וַיִּקְרָא
### He called
### "Sacrificial Identification"

> Leviticus 1:1-5:26[6:7]
> Isaiah 43:21-44:23

The Torah portion *Vayikra* begins the Book of Leviticus, and serves as the Hebrew name (וַיִּקְרָא) for the entire text. Chs. 1-7 detail sacrificial laws for individuals, for the congregation of Israel, and for priests. This is followed by chs. 8-10 describing the worship in the completed Tabernacle. Chs. 11-17 focus on the laws of clean and unclean, purity and purification, and conclude with the institution of the Day of Atonement. Chs. 18-26 compose laws of marriage, personal and social ethics, the appointed times, land tenure, and national welfare. The final chapter of Leviticus, ch. 27, deals with oath making and tithes.

If you will recall from *Pequdei's* closing verses from the end of Exodus, the Tabernacle was completed and the glory of God took up residence in the midst of Israel (Exodus 40:34-38). Now that the means to offer sacrifices were available, a description of the sacrificial system is given. Please note how the Pentateuch is not necessarily narrated for us in absolute chronological order, because if this were the case, then Exodus 40 should be followed by Numbers 7, which records the consecration of the Tabernacle. Instead, the different books of the Pentateuch have been organized for us the way they have because of theological and literary reasons.

With the Tabernacle now in place at the end of Exodus, the Book of Leviticus begins by describing the sacrificial system which would be able to cover the sins of the Ancient Israelites. In our *parashah* for this week, the differentiations between the burnt offering,[1] grain offering,[2] peace offering,[3] sin offering,[4] and guilt offering[5] are described. There is also some clarification between unintentional sins and intentional sins, and how different people are supposed to handle the different offerings in order to receive forgiveness. One of the verses that immediate jumped out at me, when I started reading *Vayikra*, was Leviticus 1:4:

---

[1] Leviticus 1:1-17.
[2] Leviticus 2:1-16.
[3] Leviticus 3:1-17.
[4] Leviticus 4:1-35.
[5] Leviticus 5:1-6:7.

"He shall lay his hand on the head of the burnt offering, that it may be accepted for him to make atonement on his behalf."

## Offerings Defined

In contemplating all the different offerings, and the distinctions between the intentional and unintentional sins, seen in *Vayikra*, I thought about a number of things. Making free will offerings to God was an expected "given" among the Ancient Israelites. These offerings were to be presented before the Lord as a token of their appreciation of His goodness toward them. Perhaps, I reckoned, the people knew that as limited mortals they were not necessarily in right relationship with an Eternal God, and so they would feel led *to just give something* to Him. Such an innate desire to offer up the best of one's flocks or herds as burnt offerings, or simply a sacrifice to please the Lord, might salve one's conscience for a short time.

Early in our Torah reading, we encounter the Hebrew word *qorban* (קָרְבָּן), used for "offering," and simply means "offering, oblation" (*BDB*):[6]

"Speak to the sons of Israel and say to them, 'When any man of you brings an offering [*qorban*] to the LORD, you shall bring your offering of animals from the herd or the flock. If his offering is a burnt offering [*qorban*] from the herd, he shall offer it, a male without defect; he shall offer it at the doorway of the tent of meeting, that he may be accepted before the LORD'" (Leviticus 1:2-3).

Apparently, there is not a completely accurate English word to describe all the things that *qorban* could fully entail. The term *qorban* is derived from the root *qarav* (קָרַב), basically meaning "*come near, approach, enter into*" (*TWOT*).[7] When an Israelite brought forth a *qorban* offering, it was designed by God to draw His people closer to Him. The physical act, of offering up a farm animal that had economic value, was a far greater "sacrifice" than simply taking the time to pray or observe the daily worship of the Tabernacle. **There was a realized cost associated with offering up one's prized agricultural possession.** Some of the individual's "treasures" or assets were losing their lives.

Millennia later, Yeshua described how one could tell where a heart was located. He taught, "for where your treasure is, there your heart will be also" (Matthew 6:21).

When one of the Ancient Israelites would make an offering of a prized animal, the individual was tangibly displaying his or her desire to be in communion with the Creator, frequently having to make restitution for some kind of sin or error committed. And on another level, by offering a living animal as a covering for sin, the message of substitution would be visibly communicated. The one who was offering up the animal had to identify with it, by laying his hands upon it right before it is killed:

"He shall lay his hand on the head of the burnt offering, that it may be accepted for him to make atonement on his behalf. He shall slay the young bull before the LORD; and Aaron's sons the priests shall offer up the blood and sprinkle the blood around on the altar that is at the doorway of the tent of meeting" (Leviticus 1:4-5).

In the Book of Leviticus, now that the Tabernacle was constructed and the sacrificial altar was erected, the priests had the venue and the God-given directions on how to

---

[6] Francis Brown, S.R. Driver, and Charles A. Briggs, *A Hebrew and English Lexicon of the Old Testament* (Oxford: Clarendon Press, 1979), 898.

[7] Leonard J. Coppes, "קָרַב," in *TWOT*, 2:811.

properly offer sacrifices. Here in *Vayikra*, we are reminded once again that our Creator has required a blood sacrifice for the atonement of sin. As it will be later stated, animals' lives will have to be offered before God in order to (temporarily) cover the errors committed by humans (Leviticus 17:11).

## Identification

The next thing that really seemed to catch my attention, in reading through *Vayikra* this week, was the overwhelming reminder that various Israelites were frequently having to lay their hands on the heads of animals being sacrificed. By doing so, they were having to identify with these animals, and recognize that the shed blood of the animals were, in essence, covering for punishment that was rightfully *theirs*. Whether one was offering a bull, lamb, or goat, the laying on of hands was standard procedure. Consider the following passages from our selection:

> "He shall lay his hand on the head of his offering and slay it at the doorway of the tent of meeting, and Aaron's sons the priests shall sprinkle the blood around on the altar" (Leviticus 3:2).

> "If he is going to offer a lamb for his offering, then he shall offer it before the LORD, and he shall lay his hand on the head of his offering and slay it before the tent of meeting, and Aaron's sons shall sprinkle its blood around on the altar" (Leviticus 3:7-8).

> "Moreover, if his offering is a goat, then he shall offer it before the LORD, and he shall lay his hand on its head and slay it before the tent of meeting, and the sons of Aaron shall sprinkle its blood around on the altar" (Leviticus 3:12-13).

> "He shall bring the bull to the doorway of the tent of meeting before the LORD, and he shall lay his hand on the head of the bull and slay the bull before the LORD. Then the anointed priest is to take some of the blood of the bull and bring it to the tent of meeting, and the priest shall dip his finger in the blood and sprinkle some of the blood seven times before the LORD, in front of the veil of the sanctuary" (Leviticus 4:4-6).

What you also might have noticed is that after the identification with the animal by the laying on of hands, the person making the confession has to watch it being killed, and then witness its blood sprinkled. This method of covering for sin should have left a lasting impression on the one who has brought the live animal to the priest. Even if one became somewhat desensitized to seeing animals killed, the animal still had economic value—an economic value which in some way was being *thrown away* as a punishment for improper deeds.

It is difficult for us living in the Twenty-First Century to often identify with what is recorded in much of Leviticus. Most of us have never even seen a farm animal slaughtered, and then butchered so that we might enjoy some fresh, homegrown meat. But if you ever have seen this occur, then you should vividly remember how, as the blood drained from the animal, its life force leaves. By the laying on of hands for identification purposes, and then watching the blood being sprinkled around the altar and various places, the *qorban* achieves its purpose to bring some person a covering for sins.

## From Shadow to Reality

For the most part, in order to really study the sacrificial system as described in this *parashah*, I had to turn to the Rabbinical authorities for answers. My examination did not uncover too many Messianic interpretations of these procedures, and evangelical Christian sources are often most concerned about what the sacrificial system meant within the religious milieu of the Ancient Near East. While such historical information is good, what does a Torah portion like *Vayikra* really communicate to Messianic Believers today?

I simply remembered how the Apostolic Scriptures have some excellent things to say about the sacrificial system seen in the Torah. The author of Hebrews summarizes the need for the ultimate sacrifice, only available through the shed blood of the Lamb. He asserts how the animal sacrifices of the Torah, because they have to be repeated over and over again, do not provide the permanent covering for sins that the sacrifice of Messiah Yeshua provides for us:

"For the Law, since it has...a shadow of the good things to come *and* not the very form of things, can never, by the same sacrifices which they offer continually year by year, make perfect those who draw near. Otherwise, would they not have ceased to be offered, because the worshipers, having once been cleansed, would no longer have had consciousness of sins? But in those *sacrifices* there is a reminder of sins year by year. For it is impossible for the blood of bulls and goats to take away sins. Therefore, when He comes into the world, He says, 'SACRIFICE AND OFFERING YOU HAVE NOT DESIRED, BUT A BODY YOU HAVE PREPARED FOR ME; IN WHOLE BURNT OFFERINGS AND *sacrifices* FOR SIN YOU HAVE TAKEN NO PLEASURE. THEN I SAID, "BEHOLD, I HAVE COME (IN THE SCROLL OF THE BOOK IT IS WRITTEN OF ME) TO DO YOUR WILL, O GOD"' [Psalm 40:6-8]. After saying above, 'SACRIFICES AND OFFERINGS AND WHOLE BURNT OFFERINGS AND *sacrifices* FOR SIN YOU HAVE NOT DESIRED, NOR HAVE YOU TAKEN PLEASURE *in them*' [Psalm 40:6] (which are offered according to the Law), then He said, 'BEHOLD, I HAVE COME TO DO YOUR WILL' [Psalm 40:7]. He takes away the first in order to establish the second. By this will we have been sanctified through the offering of the body of Yeshua the Messiah once for all. Every priest stands daily ministering and offering time after time the same sacrifices, which can never take away sins; but He, having offered one sacrifice for sins for all time, SAT DOWN AT THE RIGHT HAND OF GOD [Psalm 110:1], waiting from that time onward UNTIL HIS ENEMIES BE MADE A FOOTSTOOL FOR HIS FEET [Psalm 110:1]. For by one offering He has perfected for all time those who are sanctified" (Hebrews 10:1-14).

Here, the author of Hebrews reminds his audience of the need for a sacrifice, so that one can draw near to the Lord. And of course, what we find in this passage is that Yeshua Himself willingly became the offering for those who believe in Him, inaugurating a Melchizedkian priesthood before the Father in Heaven. In this post-resurrection era, animal sacrifices would at best be redundant reminders of how He had to come and provide a permanent sacrifice for sinful humanity. Our author plainly tells us, "by one sacrifice he has made perfect forever those who are being made holy" (Hebrews 10:14, NIV).

The challenge for us is that, *by faith*, we must believe the report that the Messiah has come and has died for our sins—providing permanent restitution that the animal sacrifices of *Vayikra* could not provide. We have to believe that He is seated at the right hand of the Father in Heaven, waiting for that day when His enemies will be made a footstool for His feet. *We have to identify with Him, lay our hands upon His head, and let His blood atone for our sins.* For many, confessing their sins before the Lord is very difficult, as it forces them to recognize that they are yet to be perfected. **We are limited mortals in need of the mercy of an Eternal God!**

As you consider the varied offerings of *Vayikra*, we need to pray for others who need to accept the precious blood of the Messiah of Israel and His willing sacrifice! We need to pray that as people read through these chapters of Leviticus, they might recognize how animal sacrifices can only go so far.

# *Tzav* צַו
### Give an order
### "Holy Unto Him"

> Leviticus 6:1[8]-8:36
> Jeremiah 7:21-8:3; 9:22-23

In *Tzav*, our Torah readings shift from being general instructions for the people of Israel, to more specific directions for the priests of Israel. Leviticus chs. 6-7 are particularly concerned with the details for sacrificial offerings and the instructions for various procedures. The Hebrew term *torah* (תּוֹרָה) appears in Leviticus 6:2, 7, 18; 7:1, 7, 11, 37—and so in essence, "instruction" becomes one of the themes of this *parashah*. Not only are the priests of Israel commanded to perform these regulations, but God has also given specific instructions on how they should be performed. *Tzav* begins with the word,

"Then the LORD spoke to Moses, saying, 'Command Aaron and his sons, saying, "This is the law for the burnt offering: the burnt offering itself *shall remain* on the hearth on the altar all night until the morning, and the fire on the altar is to be kept burning on it"'" (Leviticus 6:8-9).

After this, our selection turns to detailing specific instructions on how Aaron as high priest, and his sons, were to be anointed in their Levitical service. We may see how the anointing oil used represents the Ruach (Spirit), and how blood symbolic of the required atonement for human sin—are both used to separate out these priests for their sacred ministry to the Lord:

"So Moses took some of the anointing oil and some of the blood which was on the altar and sprinkled it on Aaron, on his garments, on his sons, and on the garments of his sons with him; and he consecrated Aaron, his garments, and his sons, and the garments of his sons with him" (Leviticus 8:30).

## A Continual Fire or a Living Sacrifice?

As you read and contemplate the statutes listed in *Tzav* this week, you might be wondering about the symbolism of the various sacrifices, or how a continual burnt offering, would represent something important to those in the camp of Ancient Israel. You might get the impression that after a while these activities and requirements may become somewhat mundane and routine for those chosen or privileged to perform them. After all, the text states that these sacrifices are to burn continually:

"The fire on the altar shall be kept burning on it. It shall not go out, but the priest shall burn wood on it every morning; and he shall lay out the burnt offering on it, and offer up in smoke the fat portions of the peace offerings on it. Fire shall be kept burning continually on the altar; it is not to go out" (Leviticus 6:12-13).

In some ways, the service of the Levitical priests always offering burnt sacrifices, is not too dissimilar from a bar-b-que pitmaster today. Animal meat has to be continually tended to. Someone needs to be there watching that the fire does not go out. Specific procedures have to be followed to make sure that the directions are complied with.

What might happen if some of the priests were just not fully committed to their mission? Could the work of laying fires and sacrificing animals get a little boring or redundant? Could a priest get so accustomed to the procedures involved, that the spiritual component of what the animal sacrifices represented to the people be overlooked?

When reflecting on Leviticus' requirement for the priests to offer up a perpetual sacrifice, the concept of being a living sacrifice, as described by the Apostle Paul to the Romans, came to my mind.

"Therefore I urge you, brethren, by the mercies of God, to present your bodies a living and holy sacrifice, acceptable to God, *which is* your spiritual service of worship. And do not be conformed to this world, but be transformed by the renewing of your mind, so that you may prove what the will of God is, that which is good and acceptable and perfect. For through the grace given to me I say to everyone among you not to think more highly of himself than he ought to think; but to think so as to have sound judgment, as God has allotted to each a measure of faith. For just as we have many members in one body and all the members do not have the same function, so we, who are many, are one body in Messiah, and individually members one of another. Since we have gifts that differ according to the grace given to us, *each of us is to exercise them accordingly*: if prophecy, according to the proportion of his faith; if service, in his serving; or he who teaches, in his teaching; or he who exhorts, in his exhortation; he who gives, with liberality; he who leads, with diligence; he who shows mercy, with cheerfulness. *Let* love *be* without hypocrisy. Abhor what is evil; cling to what is good. *Be* devoted to one another in brotherly love; give preference to one another in honor; not lagging behind in diligence, fervent in spirit, serving the Lord; rejoicing in hope, persevering in tribulation, devoted to prayer, contributing to the needs of the saints, practicing hospitality. Bless those who persecute you; bless and do not curse. Rejoice with those who rejoice, and weep with those who weep. Be of the same mind toward one another; do not be haughty in mind, but associate with the lowly. Do not be wise in your own estimation" (Romans 12:1-16).

Here, in this often quoted passage from the Apostolic Scriptures, Paul exhorts the Romans to offer themselves up as a living sacrifice, which will serve as evidence that they are accomplishing the Lord's calling for them. This is not just individuals' service as a living sacrifice, *but the Body of Messiah itself* functioning together as a living sacrifice. Paul reminds all of us today that we are each uniquely created with different measures of faith, different offices, different gifts, unique talents, and diverse abilities. And yet, as Believers in the Kingdom of God—we are each going to be responsible for conducting ourselves in a manner that is acceptable to our Creator. Each one of the different skills we possess as individuals is to be used for the purposes of a united Body of Messiah (Romans 12:4). All of us have a responsibility, in some way or another, to be constantly ministering—just like the original Levitical priests who were called to perform various duties as anointed servants of the Most High.

Reading this assessment from the Apostle Paul, I noted that he reminded his audience of one of the major problems that seems to frequently arise with those called to be God's representatives on Earth. He says, "Be not wise in your own conceits" (Romans 12:16, KJV). For some reason, there can be a tendency for God's people to think that they have become wise, because of their presumed position before Him. When we do this, we often run the risk of not accomplishing His purposes, because we have lost focus on what it means to live as a "sacrifice."

## Glory in *This*

Thinking through the proclivity to sacrifice as a mundane routine, but one devoid of any true meaning, I was reminded of how the Prophet Jeremiah addresses some of this problem in our Haftarah reading. After describing the way that the Levitical priests of his day were abusing their roles, he lambastes them with very vivid language:

"'Yet they did not listen to Me or incline their ear, but stiffened their neck; they did more evil than their fathers. You shall speak all these words to them, but they will not listen to you; and you shall call to them, but they will not answer you. You shall say to them, "This is the nation that did not obey the voice of the LORD their God or accept correction; truth has perished and has been cut off from their mouth. Cut off your hair and cast *it* away, and take up a lamentation on the bare heights; for the LORD has rejected and forsaken the generation of His wrath." For the sons of Judah have done that which is evil in My sight,' declares the LORD, 'they have set their detestable things in the house which is called by My name, to defile it. They have built the high places of Topheth, which is in the valley of the son of Hinnom, to burn their sons and their daughters in the fire, which I did not command, and it did not come into My mind. Therefore, behold, days are coming,' declares the LORD, 'when it will no longer be called Topheth, or the valley of the son of Hinnom, but the valley of the Slaughter; for they will bury in Topheth because there is no *other* place. The dead bodies of this people will be food for the birds of the sky and for the beasts of the earth; and no one will frighten *them away*'" (Jeremiah 7:26-33).

Here, we find that the priests had followed some of the vile practices of the neighboring pagan nations, including child and human sacrifice as the most wicked. Punishment for this sinful behavior is declared by Jeremiah as God's Prophet. But what is most interesting, is that as the Haftarah selection concludes—in the tradition of not departing a teaching on a negative note—two verses from Jeremiah 9 are considered:

"Thus says the LORD, 'Let not a wise man boast of his wisdom, and let not the mighty man boast of his might, let not a rich man boast of his riches; but let him who boasts boast of this, that he understands and knows Me, that I am the LORD who exercises lovingkindness, justice and righteousness on earth; for I delight in these things,' declares the LORD" (Jeremiah 9:23-24).

Just as Paul had warned the Romans about being wise in their own estimation, Jeremiah declared earlier that a wise person should not boast out of human achievement or possession. What delights the Lord is that people exercise the virtues of lovingkindness, justice, and righteousness. Doing these things constitute not only holiness, but will always draw us back to what it means to serve the Lord in some kind of priestly capacity—either in what the Levites were originally called to do, or in what His people as intermediaries between Him and the world at large are called to do.

Whether the Levitical priests were required to offer up the morning and evening sacrifices on the altar, or whether they were to minister to the poor, afflicted, down hearted, and imprisoned of their day—they were to perform their function faithfully unto Him. God's people today are to still perform the acts of good service that testify of His love and mercy to all! *Such a "priestly" service is even more imperative in this post-resurrection era where permanent atonement has been offered.* Yet as today's born again Believers accomplish this priestly service, we must have the indwelling power of the Ruach HaKodesh (Holy Spirit) to guide us, so the actions we perform for Him do not become mundane or lose their importance.

**Are you fulfilling God's call upon your life to be a part of the Body of Messiah, as a living sacrifice?**

## *Shemini* שְׁמִינִי
### Eighth
### "True Shock and Awe"

> Leviticus 9:1-11:47
> 2 Samuel 6:1-7:17 (A); 6:1-19 (S)

The title of our Torah portion for this week, *Shemini* or "Eighth," points one to the chronological context of the "eighth day" that begins this section of Leviticus. A glance at the concluding statements from *Tzav* last week, notes how the seven days of consecration which God required of Aaron and his sons has just been completed. Aaron and his sons had been very busy anointing and consecrating the Tabernacle, various implements for sacrifice, different accoutrements for the Tent of Meeting, and even themselves:

"At the doorway of the tent of meeting, moreover, you shall remain day and night for seven days and keep the charge of the LORD, so that you will not die, for so I have been commanded. Thus Aaron and his sons did all the things which the LORD had commanded through Moses" (Leviticus 8:35-36).

Our selection in *Shemini* begins with, "Now it came about on the eighth day that Moses called Aaron and his sons and the elders of Israel" (Leviticus 9:1). Now that the seven days of consecration are completed, the glory of God is ready to manifest itself before the Ancient Israelites. The Tabernacle's system of offerings and sacrifices is ready to begin its designated function:

"Then Aaron lifted up his hands toward the people and blessed them, and he stepped down after making the sin offering and the burnt offering and the peace offerings. Moses and Aaron went into the tent of meeting. When they came out and blessed the people, the glory of the LORD appeared to all the people. Then fire came out from before the LORD and consumed the burnt offering and the portions of fat on the altar; and when all the people saw *it*, they shouted and fell on their faces" (Leviticus 9:22-24).

This is a very dramatic and exciting section of Scripture to contemplate and imagine in one's mind's eye. Now that the anointing and consecration of the Tabernacle have been completed, and all of the required sacrifices have been offered, the glory of the Lord, *kavod-ADONAI* (כְּבוֹד־יְהוָה), appears.

Aaron first lifts up his hands, and then Moses blesses the people. Then, God's glory falls upon the Tent of Meeting. In a powerful way, a fire comes down and consumes the burnt offering and portions of fat on the altar. The appearance of the all-consuming fire was so overwhelming that the people shouted for joy that their offerings were acceptable and fell on their faces in awe.[8]

## Aaron's Sons Consumed

Following Leviticus ch. 9, there is a distinct break as the scene of the Tabernacle changes from readers seeing the glory of God manifested—to a very tragic incident involving the deaths of Nadab and Abihu. For some unstated reason in the text, the two eldest sons of Aaron decided to offer up some "strange fire" (Heb. *eish zarah*, אֵשׁ זָרָה) that was unauthorized by the Holy One of Israel. They soon discover that unsanctioned activities at this sacred place—based on their own volitional choices—have terminal consequences:

"Now Nadab and Abihu, the sons of Aaron, took their respective firepans, and after putting fire in them, placed incense on it and offered strange fire before the LORD, which He had not commanded them. And fire came out from the presence of the LORD and consumed them, and they died before the LORD" (Leviticus 10:1-2).

The death of these two men was a stunning and unexpected tragedy. It was a clear display of God's apparent displeasure with the actions of Nadab and Abihu. Moments before in the text, a holy fire consumes sacrificial offerings. But then, for offering up "unholy fire" (RSV) or "unauthorized fire" (NIV), the heirs-apparent of Aaron are consumed. As the Hebrew verb *akal* (אָכַל) describes it, they were "eat[en], devour[ed], consume[d]" (*AMG*).[9] This is the same verb used previously for the consumption of the offering (Leviticus 9:24). The same God who demonstrated His pleasure with the presentation of offerings before Him in Leviticus 9, is now displeased with the presentation of inappropriate fire before Him in Leviticus 10.

Aaron was in *total shock* after seeing his two sons die by the force of God. Because of the severity of the Levitical service, Moses communicates these direct commands to Aaron, which he had received from the Lord:

"Then Moses said to Aaron, 'It is what the LORD spoke, saying, "By those who come near Me I will be treated as holy, and before all the people I will be honored."' So Aaron, therefore, kept silent" (Leviticus 10:3).

Certainly, these words from God spoken by Moses, struck a chord with Aaron. Could it have been possible that Aaron thought back to the admonition uttered just before the Decalogue was received at Mount Sinai? Here the instruction was, "Also let the priests who

---

[8] As an aside, it is interesting to note two things from this account. First, witnessing supernatural actions *in person* can generate enough fear to buckle the stiffest of knees. Second, the witnesses to God's glory falling and the fire consuming the offerings caused the Ancient Israelites to fall on their faces. This incident, and others throughout the Scriptures (i.e., Genesis 17:3; Numbers 16:4; Joshua 5:14; Daniel 8:17; Matthew 17:6), indicate how people generally respond to the genuine presence of God.

Back in the early to mid-1990s, a phenomenon was moving through various charismatic circles known by a variety of names such as the "Toronto blessing" or "holy laughter." As people claimed to have been blessed by various speakers, etc., many were falling down under the supposed power of the Holy Spirit. In many cases, as they were being prayed for, the typical response was to see people fall on their backs as they were being touched—rather than fall forward on the face, as is typical from the Scriptural examples.

Things like this should make one pause and ask just what kind of a "spirit" was being served. If more of the participants had been conscious of the Biblical examples where people *fall on their faces* before God, there could have been a recognition that these actions needed to be viewed with a more critical eye. Thankfully today, as more and more Believers become better acquainted with the basic principles of God's Torah, He will equip us to more properly question the origins of the various spiritual phenomenon we encounter.

[9] Baker and Carpenter, 49.

come near to the LORD consecrate themselves, or else the LORD will break out against them" (Exodus 19:22).

At this juncture, Moses was warning not just the Levites, but by extension all of the Ancient Israelites, to not be presumptuous about approaching their Creator. The priests needed to be reminded about the necessity of personal consecration, lest they be punished for presenting something unholy or inappropriate before the Lord.

Leviticus 10:3 is clear how "Aaron remained silent" (NIV) as Moses delivered instruction following the deaths of Nadab and Abihu. Can you imagine what was going through his mind? He was responsible for the golden calf incident in Exodus 32, and yet here he was still standing, in spite of three thousand Israelites slaughtered. For what could seem to be a far lesser offense than committing idolatry against the Holy One, he had to look at the charred remains of his sons. Aaron understood in a very visible way that in order to be in the presence of the Lord, one must be sanctified unto Him.

What can we learn from this today, in the era of New Covenant when Yeshua's sacrifice has offered permanent forgiveness from sins? *The Lord **still requires** His people to be holy in order for them to access to His presence.* He demands that He be glorified and properly honored by His creatures. It is quite possible that Aaron was terrified into thinking that he could be the next victim of the consuming fire of God. While Believers today might have the sacrifice of Yeshua covering their transgressions, even the Apostolic Scriptures admonish us, "work out your salvation with fear and trembling" (Philippians 2:12).

## Pleasing the Holy One

There is speculation by the Jewish Rabbis that Nadab and Abihu were perhaps under the influence of alcohol when they made the bad decision to offer up strange fire on the altar.[10] This is a possibility, as they could have been intoxicated so as to not properly follow the procedures that the Lord required of them as consecrated priests. The mention of this prohibition, several verses later in Leviticus 10, is a good textual clue that they could have indeed been drunk:

"Do not drink wine or strong drink, neither you nor your sons with you, when you come into the tent of meeting, so that you will not die—it is a perpetual statute throughout your generations—and so as to make a distinction between the holy and the profane, and between the unclean and the clean, and so as to teach the sons of Israel all the statutes which the LORD has spoken to them through Moses" (Leviticus 10:9-11).

The problem with alcohol may provide some explanation, but we need not overlook some of the verses which appear between the description of Nadab and Abihu's death (Leviticus 10:1-3) and then the description of how priests were not to drink while on duty (Leviticus 10:9-11). Some intriguing statements are made in Leviticus 10:6-7, succinctly describing how holy God considers the priestly office to be:

"Then Moses said to Aaron and to his sons Eleazar and Ithamar, 'Do not uncover your heads nor tear your clothes, so that you will not die and that He will not become wrathful against all the congregation. But your kinsmen, the whole house of Israel, shall bewail the burning which the LORD has brought about. You shall not even go out from the doorway of the tent of meeting, or you will die; for the LORD's anointing oil is upon you.' So they did according to the word of Moses" (Leviticus 10:6-7).

---

[10] J.H. Hertz, ed., *Pentateuch & Haftorahs* (London: Soncino Press, 1960), 445.

Aaron's other two sons, Eleazar and Ithamar, will take the place of Nadab and Abihu as priests. They are all instructed not to mourn for the untimely deaths of their brothers. Then they are told to not even leave the Tent of Meeting, because "the anointing oil of the LORD is upon you" (RSV).

The God of Israel was very serious about His chosen priests honoring the office in which they were to serve. In some respects, you can ascertain that from the shock of the consuming deaths of Nadab and Abihu, a genuine awe and reverence of the Lord has settled in the hearts of Aaron and his other sons. Obedience to these directives was adhered to without question. As this section of Leviticus closes, Moses asks Aaron and his sons why they have not followed the instructions to partake of the "holy" offerings that were clear instructions from the Most High:

"'Why did you not eat the sin offering at the holy place? For it is most holy, and He gave it to you to bear away the guilt of the congregation, to make atonement for them before the LORD. Behold, since its blood had not been brought inside, into the sanctuary, you should certainly have eaten it in the sanctuary, just as I commanded.' But Aaron spoke to Moses, 'Behold, this very day they presented their sin offering and their burnt offering before the LORD. When things like these happened to me, if I had eaten a sin offering today, would it have been good in the sight of the LORD?' When Moses heard *that*, it seemed good in his sight" (Leviticus 10:17-20).

Aaron responds to this rebuke with a very heartfelt reply, which indicates that the circumstances of his sons' deaths, in his mind, prohibited them from eating the sin offering. Having seen his two sons die in a very tragic way, and having heard the admonitions about mourning and leaving the presence of the Lord while under the anointing, Aaron's heart seems to finally be in the right place.

Even with the potential for immediate Divine retribution, Aaron's contrite response was, "would the LORD have approved?" (NJPS). Apparently, this was what the Lord was looking for from His high priest and his sons, and Moses was satisfied with the response (Leviticus 10:20). Since Aaron was not consumed for disregarding the requirements for the sin offering, the Lord was pleased with his service as high priest of Israel.

In *Shemini*, God makes it clear through a very dramatic episode, what He required of the Levitical priesthood. As exemplified in Aaron and his sons, He desires a set-apart people who understand the call upon their lives, and who put His interests as Creator ahead of their own as mortals. Aaron learns from the shocking deaths of Nadab and Abihu that being presumptuous with how someone approaches God can bring significant consequences. *Aaron was a changed man.* Is it possible that he went through some kind of a mental checklist, asking the question of whether or not God would approve, before every priestly action he took? These initial scenes had to be preparatory for the great responsibility that being the high priest of Israel would entail.

## Conforming to His Image

Today, as representatives of the God of Israel in the Earth, we need to approach our service unto Him with the same kind of sobriety that Aaron developed. We need to understand His ways, a very important part of which involves personal Torah study. So much knowledge and understanding about God's holiness can be imparted to us by a review of the weekly *parashah*, as we contemplate not only the continuing trajectory of God's Word, but also His mission and calling for our individual lives.

In Leviticus 11, a part of our Torah portion for this week, we encounter the first major instruction detailing the kosher dietary laws. Many Believers today will casually dismiss these directions given by God, because they think they were only for a previous time or age. But at the same time, several prominent evangelical Christians today—because of the poor health of many in our society—have spoken in favor of the *health benefits* that are derived from not eating certain meats. Are God's people to be regulated by Him in simple matters like their diet? Can you learn anything about God's holiness by what you eat?[11]

As we search our own hearts in these days of "shock and awe,"[12] perhaps we should ask the Lord to give us hearts that are reminiscent of Aaron's heart—hopefully without having to witness the same kind of dramatic encounters that he saw! Learning from *Shemini*, before we take actions, we should learn to ask the simple question **of whether or not God would approve.** By training our hearts and minds to such a pattern of behavior, those called into His service can demonstrate how they are being conformed to the image of Yeshua:

"For those whom He foreknew, He also predestined *to become* conformed to the image of His Son, so that He would be the firstborn among many brethren; and these whom He predestined, He also called; and these whom He called, He also justified; and these whom He justified, He also glorified" (Romans 8:29-30).

Let us be reminded that Yeshua only did what the Father instructed Him to do:

"So Yeshua said, 'When you lift up the Son of Man, then you will know that I am *He*, and I do nothing on My own initiative, but I speak these things as the Father taught Me'" (John 8:28).

By His grace, may we also be reminded that we, as obedient servants, should be doing only that which the Lord has instructed us. By being sensitive to His will, not only will He be glorified—but we might find ourselves truly in awe of His work *through us*. If we choose otherwise, we may be in for an unexpected shock!

## *Tazria* תַזְרִיעַ
### She Conceives
### "What Did Yeshua Do?"

Leviticus 12:1-13:59
2 Kings 4:42-5:19

One of the many blessings that today's Messianic Believers receive in committing themselves to a consistent, weekly examination of the Torah portion, is the much fuller perspective that they naturally receive of the Scriptures. Too frequently, people who read the Apostolic Scriptures or New Testament, when reading references about the Mosaic Law, have very little idea about what is being talked about. This week as we encounter *Tazria*, "She Conceives," we actually see some interesting commandments that directly

---

[11] For a further discussion, consult the articles "To Eat or Not to Eat?" and "How Do We Properly Keep Kosher?" by J.K. McKee.

[12] The wars in Afghanistan and Iraq (2002-2003).

relate to the birth of Yeshua and how Joseph and Mary were obedient to the Torah. Our *parashah* begins by saying,

"Then the LORD spoke to Moses, saying, 'Speak to the sons of Israel, saying: "When a woman gives birth and bears a male *child*, then she shall be unclean for seven days, as in the days of her menstruation she shall be unclean. On the eighth day the flesh of his foreskin shall be circumcised. Then she shall remain in the blood of *her* purification for thirty-three days; she shall not touch any consecrated thing, nor enter the sanctuary until the days of her purification are completed"'" (Leviticus 12:1-4).

In many years *Tazria* is coupled with the following *parashah*, *Metzora* (Leviticus 12:1-15:33), as both of these selections continue to focus on Leviticus' theme of holiness. In this section of the Pentateuch, we see various regulations regarding what it means for something to be "clean" (Heb. *tahor*, טָהוֹר), rather than "unclean" (Heb. *tamei*, טָמֵא). Our previous *parashah*, *Shemini*, actually ended with God delivering instructions on clean and unclean meats, and how following them would contribute to His people being holy:

"'For I am the LORD who brought you up from the land of Egypt to be your God; thus you shall be holy, for I am holy.' This is the law regarding the animal and the bird, and every living thing that moves in the waters and everything that swarms on the earth, to make a distinction between the unclean and the clean, and between the edible creature and the creature which is not to be eaten" (Leviticus 11:45-47).

Now that the Lord has laid out the restrictions on what is to be considered edible food, some further instruction is given regarding cleanliness and uncleanliness. The two specific sets of commandments given in *Tazria* regard the blood of childbirth (Leviticus 12:1-8) and the handling of leprosy (Leviticus 13:1-59).

## Proper Parental Influence

While reflecting on *Tazria*, and how little I knew about postnatal care or the intricacies of various skin afflictions, the most dominant thoughts that came to mind were recollections from the Apostolic Scriptures on the birth of Yeshua and what His parents did. Joseph and Mary followed the Torah's commandments with what were to be done with a newborn child. Examining Luke's record of what took place after Yeshua was born, we see that Joseph and Mary followed the instructions we see in this Torah portion, having brought the infant Messiah to the Temple in Jerusalem for dedication:

"And when eight days had passed, before His circumcision, His name was *then* called Yeshua, the name given by the angel before He was conceived in the womb. And when the days for their purification according to the law of Moses were completed, they brought Him up to Jerusalem to present Him to the Lord (as it is written in the Law of the Lord, 'EVERY *firstborn* MALE THAT OPENS THE WOMB SHALL BE CALLED HOLY TO THE LORD' [Exodus 13:2, 12, 15]), and to offer a sacrifice according to what was said in the Law of the Lord, 'A PAIR OF TURTLEDOVES OR TWO YOUNG PIGEONS' [Leviticus 12:8]" (Luke 2:21-24).

In this account, we note that Joseph and Mary were obeying the instructions regarding the circumcision of a male child, and his dedication before the Lord. Luke makes some direct quotations from the Torah, detailing the commandments that Joseph and Mary were following:

"Sanctify to Me every firstborn, the first offspring of every womb among the sons of Israel, both of man and beast; it belongs to Me…you shall devote to the LORD the first offspring of every womb, and the first of every beast that you own; the males belong to the LORD" (Exodus 13:2, 12).

"But if she cannot afford a lamb, then she shall take two turtledoves or two young pigeons, the one for a burnt offering and the other for a sin offering; and the priest shall make atonement for her, and she will be clean" (Leviticus 12:8).

We can discern that Joseph and Mary were relatively humble in their means, because of the reference to the turtledoves and/or pigeons that were made. But, they did follow the Law of Moses, and they raised Yeshua—as well as their sons James and Jude—in a Torah-keeping environment. Luke later summarizes the kind of home in which Yeshua was reared, noting how they went to Jerusalem on a regular basis to keep the appointed times:

"When they had performed everything according to the Law of the Lord, they returned to Galilee, to their own city of Nazareth. The Child continued to grow and become strong, increasing in wisdom; and the grace of God was upon Him. Now His parents went to Jerusalem every year at the Feast of the Passover. And when He became twelve, they went up *there* according to the custom of the Feast" (Luke 2:39-42).

## Yeshua's Torah Obedience

As you read through *Tazria*, you are given a very detailed account of instruction regarding how to deal with the disease commonly referred to as leprosy (Heb. *tzara'at*, צָרַעַת), although other forms of skin eruptions are also described. As I read these passages, my mind flashed forward to scenes where Yeshua healed lepers during His ministry. The ability to heal a leper would have been a sign that the Messiah had come:[13]

"Now when John, while imprisoned, heard of the works of Messiah, he sent *word* by his disciples and said to Him, 'Are You the Expected One, or shall we look for someone else?' Yeshua answered and said to them, 'Go and report to John what you hear and see: *the* BLIND RECEIVE SIGHT and *the* lame walk, *the* lepers are cleansed and *the* deaf hear, *the* dead are raised up, and *the* POOR HAVE THE GOSPEL PREACHED TO THEM. And blessed is he who does not take offense at Me'" (Matthew 11:2-6; cf. Isaiah 35:5-6; 42:18; 61:1).

As Yeshua healed lepers of their illness, He instructed them to follow the Torah's instruction—specifically so that those healed could testify of their cleansing:

"And a leper came to Yeshua, beseeching Him and falling on his knees before Him, and saying, 'If You are willing, You can make me clean.' Moved with compassion, Yeshua stretched out His hand and touched him, and said to him, 'I am willing; be cleansed.' Immediately the leprosy left him and he was cleansed. And He sternly warned him and immediately sent him away, and He said to him, 'See that you say nothing to anyone; but go, show yourself to the priest and offer for your cleansing what Moses commanded, as a testimony to them'" (Mark 1:40-44).

"And a leper came to Him and bowed down before Him, and said, 'Lord, if You are willing, You can make me clean.' Yeshua stretched out His hand and touched him, saying, 'I am willing; be cleansed.' And immediately his leprosy was cleansed. And Yeshua said to him, 'See that you tell no one; but go, show yourself to the priest and present the offering that Moses commanded, as a testimony to them'" (Matthew 8:2-4).

Yeshua knew the instructions that had been given in *Tazria*. Even though He knew that lepers had been completely healed of the debilitating disease, He upheld the Torah's instruction so that the priests might inspect the cleansing:

---

[13] The "lepers are cleansed" was "not a specific OT expectation, but implied in general statements, e.g., Isa 53:4; Matt 8:1-4" (Donald A. Hagner, *Word Biblical Commentary: Matthew 1-13*, Vol 33a [Nashville: Thomas Nelson, 1993], 301).

"If in his sight the scale has remained, however, and black hair has grown in it, the scale has healed, he is clean; and the priest shall pronounce him clean" (Leviticus 13:37).

As we read and reflect upon *Tazria*, we can be reminded that Yeshua, as well as His parents, followed the commandments in the selection that we are reviewing this week. It does not appear from these testimonies that Yeshua attempted to annul the importance of these commandments because of His ministry—even though the lepers who were healed would no doubt speak to the priests of the One who healed them!

## WWJD?

Many of us in the community of faith are aware of the popular acronym **WWJD** that has been fashioned into bracelets, t-shirts, and a variety of other commercially viable forms for sale in the evangelical world. I do not at all want to belittle those who have used the simple admonition **What Would Jesus Do?** I am convinced that many people have been prompted to do many positive things from the WWJD acronym. It has been an easy way to promote holiness among many Christians, who need a visible reminder of the Lord we serve.

As Messianic Believers, though, our engagement level with who the Messiah is and how He lived—goes a little beyond the simple commands to love God and neighbor, as important as those are.[14] This week, many of us are taking a look at *Tazria* (Leviticus 12:1-13:59), a selection of text which for most people might seem pretty dry and boring, detailing things that are really not that applicable in the Twenty-First Century. Yet, in studying this part of Scripture, we can learn more of the details of how Joseph and Mary, and how the Messiah Himself, lived their lives in the First Century.

If I did not take the time to read and study passages like this from the Book of Leviticus, I might not know how God is concerned about mothers who give birth to children, or those who are afflicted with leprosy. I would not have any idea what the commandments were that Yeshua directed healed lepers to follow, as they would go and testify to the priests at the Temple of the Messiah who had healed them. By not reading *Tazria*, I might not know of the simple fact of how our Heavenly Father is concerned about our hygiene, and how He surely does not want us to contract diseases like leprosy.

In His Sermon on the Mount, Yeshua the Messiah was clear that He did not come to abolish, but to fulfill, the Law of Moses (Matthew 5:17-18). He also stated how "Whoever then annuls one of the least of these commandments, and teaches others *to do* the same, shall be called least in the kingdom of heaven; but whoever keeps and teaches *them*, he shall be called great in the kingdom of heaven" (Matthew 5:19). The commandments we read about this week in *Tazria* can largely not be followed today, because of the lack of a Temple in Jerusalem—but most importantly because of the fact that leprosy is not as rampant as it once was in past centuries (for which we should all praise God!). But not following largely inapplicable commandments is different than teaching against them, and how they instruct us as God's people. By reading *Tazria* this week, I am sure that we have all learned some things about the character of our Heavenly Father that we have not known, or at least thought about, before.

Yeshua the Messiah came to fulfill the Torah of Moses, meaning that He came to show people how to live it properly. As Believers in Him, we can actually learn things about His

---

[14] Deuteronomy 6:5; Leviticus 19:18; cf. Matthew 19:19; 22:39; Mark 12:31; Luke 10:27; Romans 13:9; Galatians 5:14; James 2:8.

life and His ministry in the Gospels by studying the Torah. Obscure parts like healed lepers going to the Temple, actually make much more sense.

Unfortunately, many Christians (but thankfully not all!) who wear the WWJD bracelets conclude that Yeshua "fulfilled and thus abolished" the Torah of Moses. From this vantage point, what we are considering in *Tazria* this week has largely nothing to do with Yeshua's birth or with His ministry. As it is often said, "We as New Testament Believers do not have to be concerned with any of restrictions on our lives, imposed by adherence to an antiquated list of do and don'ts." **How far from the truth is this?** The New Covenant actually involves God supernaturally writing the Torah's instructions onto our heart for our remembrance (Jeremiah 31:31-34; Ezekiel 36:25-27). A view of holiness, *emulating the Lord Yeshua the Messiah*, that excludes any kind of obedience to the Law, **has done considerable harm to the Body of Messiah.** Simply look at all of the people who claim to be following the Messiah, but have very little concept of Biblical ethics or morality. To them, WWJD is just a cloth bracelet, but not really a committed lifestyle.

I am not trying to unfairly criticize those who are unaware about some of the finer details of the Torah as seen in readings like *Tazria*. There are plenty of things in the Torah that today's evangelical Christians and Messianics **all agree need to be followed.**[15] The high standard that Yeshua gives us in His Sermon on the Mount—a teaching firmly rooted within Moses' Teaching—is a place where we can come together with Christians, and learn what it means to fulfill the Law. When we get to areas like *Shabbat*, the appointed times, or kosher as detailed last week—how can we approach these areas in a constructive, investigative spirit? How can today's Messianics demonstrate that emulating the Messiah Yeshua means not only treating others with love, but also deriving the blessings that other parts of the Torah will undeniably bring to one's life?[16]

Today's Messianic Believers need to learn to demonstrate, as Yeshua instructed, a proper Torah obedience by good works (Matthew 5:16; cf. Ephesians 2:10). When evangelical Christians who wear that What Would Jesus Do? bracelet witness our actions of faith, will they be able to really see some of the things that Yeshua did? *What about Jewish people who need to know the salvation available in the Messiah Yeshua, and inquire of our good deeds?* I certainly hope and pray that we can see a generation of Messianic Believers come forth who can provide answers to the question **What Did Yeshua Do?** in a manner that brings honor and glory to Him.[17]

---

[15] For a summary, consult Walter C. Kaiser, "The Law as God's Gracious Guidance for the Promotion of Holiness," in Wayne G. Strickland, ed., *Five Views on Law and Gospel* (Grand Rapids: Zondervan, 1996), pp 177-199.

[16] For a further discussion, consult the book *Torah In the Balance, Volume I* by J.K. McKee.

[17] For some further thoughts, consult the author's article "Our Messianic Future," appearing in the November 2009 issue of Outreach Israel News.

# *Metzora* מְצֹרָע
## Infected One
## "The Evil Tongue"

> Leviticus 14:1-15:33
> 2 Kings 7:3-20

In *Tazria* last week, I did not discuss the different aspects of leprosy that are detailed. Instead, I decided to focus on what Yeshua did in terms of following the Torah. In *Metzora*, being considered this week, the subject of leprosy is again up for review. So with the gentle prodding of the Ruach (Spirit), let us dig a little deeper into this issue. The instructions we encounter include what a cleansed leper was to do, in order to be restored to the community of Ancient Israel:

"The one to be cleansed shall then wash his clothes and shave off all his hair and bathe in water and be clean. Now afterward, he may enter the camp, but he shall stay outside his tent for seven days. It will be on the seventh day that he shall shave off all his hair: he shall shave his head and his beard and his eyebrows, even all his hair. He shall then wash his clothes and bathe his body in water and be clean" (Leviticus 14:8-9).

Generally, these Torah portions which deal with the various states of being unclean, are considered right before the season of Passover. In this time of cleaning the leaven out of our houses—and hopefully also the sin out of our lives—are there any unseen transgressions that inevitably fly undiscovered below the spiritual radar? Is it possible that the Lord might want you to personally deal with a matter that has a negative influence on your family life, the people at your congregation, or the greater Body of Messiah?

One subject that has been traditionally associated with *Metzora* has been contemplating a spiritual affliction known as *lashon ha'ra* (לְשׁוֹן הָרַע) or "the evil tongue." The Jewish Rabbis have taught that the more profound issue which is being addressed in either *Tazria* or *Metzora* is not the physical condition of a skin affliction, but instead a spiritual affliction. Baruch A. Levine summarizes,

"Playing on the linguistic similarity of the Hebrew for 'leper' (*m'tzora*) and the Hebrew for 'one who gossips' (*motzi shem ra*), the sages considered leprosy to be a punishment for the sins of slander and malicious gossip (Lev. R. 16:11). They teach that gossip is like leprosy because it is highly contagious. One infected person can spread a malicious rumor to many others."[18]

## *Lashon Ha'ra*

In the chapters of *Tazria* and *Metzora* we encounter the Hebrew noun *tzara'at* (צָרַעַת) and verb *tzara* (צָרַע),[19] which are difficult to translate into English. The medical term "leprosy" is used in most Bibles. As interpreters have searched for additional meaning of these terms, they inevitably went to the other times where they appear in the Torah,

---

[18] Baruch A. Levine, "Leviticus," in David L. Lieber, ed., *Etz Hayim: Torah and Commentary* (New York: Rabbinical Assembly, 2001), 652.

[19] *BDB*, pp 863, 864.

comparing them to how they are used in this *parashah*. There are two notable incidents considered.

The first time we see leprosy referred to regards the Ancient Israelites' deliverance from Egypt. The subject at hand concerns the results of speaking against someone, questioning one's motives and creating doubt, and/or holding suspicion toward someone:

"Then Moses said, 'What if they will not believe me or listen to what I say? For they may say, "The LORD has not appeared to you"'…The LORD furthermore said to him, 'Now put your hand into your bosom.' So he put his hand into his bosom, and when he took it out, behold, his hand was leprous [*tzara*] like snow" (Exodus 4:1, 6).

In the first instance we encounter, Moses questions whether the people of Israel will even believe him and follow his guidance, as the Lord has chosen him to lead them out of Egypt. Moses' reaction is to question Ancient Israel's ability to follow the explicit instructions of the Lord. So, the Lord gives him the sign of having his hand turn leprous. Leprosy, and the ability for it to appear and disappear, would be a sign that a spiritual condition of unbelief was plaguing the Israelites.

The second time we see leprosy referred to, and probably the most influential reference outside of *Tazria-Metzora*, is when Moses' sister Miriam speaks against him to Aaron. While it appears that both Miriam and Aaron are speaking against their brother, Miriam receives the judgment of becoming leprous:

"Then Miriam and Aaron spoke against Moses because of the Cushite woman whom he had married (for he had married a Cushite woman)…But when the cloud had withdrawn from over the tent, behold, Miriam *was* leprous, as *white as* snow. As Aaron turned toward Miriam, behold, she *was* leprous [*tzara*]" (Numbers 12:1, 10).

Only the pleas that Moses makes to God restore his sister to normalcy (Numbers 12:13ff). Seeing these usages of "leprosy," the Sages concluded that slander and malicious gossip were a major cause of leprosy. *Their opinion should be well taken.* Consider the connections that can be made by killing someone with words that emanate from your heart. Yeshua spoke of how a wickedness which generates death and destruction—comes forth from an evil mouth:

"The good man out of the good treasure of his heart brings forth what is good; and the evil *man* out of the evil *treasure* brings forth what is evil; for his mouth speaks from that which fills his hear" (Luke 6:45).

Here, the connection is very obvious. When the human heart is filled with evil thoughts, the mouth and what ushers forth from it are simply verbal manifestations. God knows all about this common human problem, and the potentially devastating consequences of the spoken word—especially when the spoken word is used maliciously *to deliberately* harm someone.

We need to remember that at God's spoken command, the universe came into being (Genesis 1). He knows the power that words spoken can have. He omnisciently knew that the common schoolyard colloquialism used to defend oneself from verbal abuse was/is not at all accurate: *"Sticks and stones will break my bones, but words will never hurt me!"* **Words do hurt,** especially when they are designed by a wicked heart to deliberately insult and damage another person.

Here is what the Lord says about things He hates:

"There are six things which the LORD hates, yes, seven which are an abomination to Him: Haughty eyes, a lying tongue, and hands that shed innocent blood, a heart that devises wicked plans, feet that run rapidly to evil, a false witness *who* utters lies, and one who spreads strife among brothers" (Proverbs 6:16-19).

These seven things include:
1. haughty eyes
2. a lying tongue
3. hands that shed innocent blood
4. a heart that devises wicked plans
5. feet that run rapidly to evil
6. a false witness that utters lies
7. one who spreads strife among brothers

If you consider what these seven abominations actually are, you will note that three of them concern spoken utterances which originate with the tongue (#s 1, 6, 7). There might be a good case to include the evil heart that devises wicked plans (#4) with the tongue, because in order to execute evil plans, such thoughts have to be formulated. Almost half of the things which the Lord despises and considers abominable relate to an evil tongue, or to a wicked heart that causes the tongue to speak forth dark things. It should not be difficult for us to see why the Lord wants His people to be very careful about what they say with their mouths.

Is it possible that during the early years of the nation of Israel, as the people were wandering in the desert and preparing to enter into the Promised Land—that there were many skin eruptions that warned this community that various people were using their tongues to tear the fabric of the maturing society? When we read about the wilderness journeys of the Israelites, we often do not think of them as people enjoying themselves. There was complaining toward, suspicion of, and also distrust of both God and Moses on the part of many of the Ancient Israelites. There were people who spoke against the directives issued by Moses and the leaders he appointed.

The Lord knew that nothing could be more detrimental to a community than rumors, gossip, slander, and outright lies. Perhaps the opportunity for a person to be set outside of the camp for seven days, or even fourteen days, would cause perpetrators to reconsider their transgressions. Is it possible that as someone dealt with the guilt of using his or her tongue *to murder the character* of another person, that the offender might be healed and the leprous signs could have disappeared? On the other hand, if the evil heart and its intentions continued to dwell on wickedness, then would the result have been a life wandering around outside the camp—and when people saw you they would utter "Unclean, unclean!"?

## Further Tongue Lashings

The problems associated with dark utterances from the tongue were by no means just confined to the early stages of Israel's development. *Speaking slanderous or spiteful words is a common human problem, after all.* It is not at all surprising to see the Apostles addressing proper speech. We are all familiar with the Apostle Paul's word, "Let no unwholesome word proceed from your mouth, but only such *a word* as is good for edification according to the need *of the moment*, so that it will give grace to those who hear" (Ephesians 4:29), something that guided me since I was a young Believer.[20] This week, though, I was led to

---

[20] For further consideration, consult the exegesis paper on Ephesians 4:29, "How Are Messianics to Properly Communicate?" by J.K. McKee.

read through the Epistle of James, and see how James the Just handles the ability for the spoken word to have a catastrophic impact on the community of faith.

James comments extensively about the challenges of being in a position of teaching, and how the use of one's tongue can have a variety of consequences:

"Let not many *of you* become teachers, my brethren, knowing that as such we will incur a stricter judgment. For we all stumble in many *ways*. If anyone does not stumble in what he says, he is a perfect man, able to bridle the whole body as well. Now if we put the bits into the horses' mouths so that they will obey us, we direct their entire body as well. Look at the ships also, though they are so great and are driven by strong winds, are still directed by a very small rudder wherever the inclination of the pilot desires. So also the tongue is a small part of the body, and *yet* it boasts of great things. See how great a forest is set aflame by such a small fire! And the tongue is a fire, the *very* world of iniquity; the tongue is set among our members as that which defiles the entire body, and sets on fire the course of *our* life, and is set on fire by hell. For every species of beasts and birds, of reptiles and creatures of the sea, is tamed and has been tamed by the human race. But no one can tame the tongue; *it is* a restless evil *and* full of deadly poison. With it we bless *our* Lord and Father, and with it we curse men, who have been made in the likeness of God; from the same mouth come *both* blessing and cursing. My brethren, these things ought not to be this way" (James 3:1-10).

In this passage, James admonishes the teachers of his day with how serious it is when they use their tongues. He declares that an evil tongue "pollutes our whole being; it keeps the wheel of our existence red-hot, and its flames are fed by hell" (NEB). This is how powerful an unbridled and undisciplined tongue can be, and it is something that we should be mindful to control by relinquishing its activity to the Holy Spirit. If you keep reading James' words you begin to understand some of the ways the enemy uses the human tongue to create division:

"What is the source of quarrels and conflicts among you? Is not the source your pleasures that wage war in your members? You lust and do not have; *so* you commit murder. You are envious and cannot obtain; *so* you fight and quarrel. You do not have because you do not ask... Do not speak against one another, brethren. He who speaks against a brother or judges his brother, speaks against the law and judges the law; but if you judge the law, you are not a doer of the law but a judge *of it*...Do not complain, brethren, against one another, so that you yourselves may not be judged; behold, the Judge is standing right at the door" (James 4:1-2, 11; 5:9).

Fighting, quarreling, speaking against one another, judging one another, complaining against one another—and the list goes on. Do these things sound like the works of the Spirit or works of the flesh (cf. Galatians 5:19-21)? **Well, the answer is simple and obvious to spiritual persons guided by the Lord.** In fact, in the midst of his warnings, James contrasts what inappropriate and appropriate wisdom are:

"Who among you is wise and understanding? Let him show by his good behavior his deeds in the gentleness of wisdom. But if you have bitter jealousy and selfish ambition in your heart, do not be arrogant and *so* lie against the truth. This wisdom is not that which comes down from above, but is earthly, natural, demonic. For where jealousy and selfish ambition exist, there is disorder and every evil thing. But the wisdom from above is first pure, then peaceable, gentle, reasonable, full of mercy and good fruits, unwavering, without hypocrisy. And the seed whose fruit is righteousness is sown in peace by those who make peace" (James 3:13-18).

James compares the wise and understanding with those who are Earthly, natural, and demonic. *The contrast is obvious.* Just like the priests who could look at a skin affliction in the time of Moses and Joshua, in James' day it was readily apparent by behavioral actions who was living a life of the Spirit and who was living a life of jealousy and selfish ambition. And these things were not difficult to see: one can generally discern simply by listening to what is spoken from the various mouths whether one has godly or demonic wisdom. **These indicators have not changed in our generation, some two thousand years later.** We have the same responsibility to speak forth, and listen to, godly wisdom.

## The Doers: Slow to Speak

Earlier in the instructional words of James, he makes it very simple for those who have the ears to hear:

"*This* you know, my beloved brethren. But everyone must be quick to hear, slow to speak *and* slow to anger; for the anger of man does not achieve the righteousness of God. Therefore, putting aside all filthiness and *all* that remains of wickedness, in humility receive the word implanted, which is able to save your souls. But prove yourselves doers of the word, and not merely hearers who delude themselves. For if anyone is a hearer of the word and not a doer, he is like a man who looks at his natural face in a mirror; for *once* he has looked at himself and gone away, he has immediately forgotten what kind of person he was. But one who looks intently at the perfect law, the *law* of liberty, and abides by it, not having become a forgetful hearer but an effectual doer, this man will be blessed in what he does. If anyone thinks himself to be religious, and yet does not bridle his tongue but deceives his *own* heart, this man's religion is worthless" (James 1:19-26).

Here, James gets to the heart of the matter. He talks about the ability to control the tongue and the anger that bubbles up from the heart. He admonishes his readers to be quick to hear, but be slow to become angry and slow to speak. James knew that if people can just give their hearts and minds some time to catch up with their emotions—that may have been stirred by some fallacious lies, slander, gossip, or false witness—then they can willingly give the situations over to the Lord. Then, with a sound heart and mind, Believers will exhibit the reality that they are more than just hearers of God's Word, but most importantly, are doers of His Word.

Such admonitions are critical in our day and age, as we have *so many more ways* to do damage to people than just the spoken word. Now with the advances of technology, one can slander another person on video, DVD, cassette, CD, or with lightning speed to the world over via the increasingly ubiquitous Internet. Now with the simple click of a mouse on some personal blog, someone with a wicked heart can commit murder without any bloodletting. *People can find their character assassinated with little or no warning.* Bullets are no longer required…

**Think again** about how you are using your tongue as you enter into *Shabbat* this week and are probably preparing yourself for Passover. Is there any leaven in this area of your life that needs some confession and repentance? We know that He is faithful and just to forgive us of our sins *if* we confess them. We know that He will cleanse us of all unrighteousness *if* we are truly repentant (1 John 1:9). But in order to receive the forgiveness God offers us, we must come before Him with a broken and contrite spirit, and humbly confess our errant ways. We must also confess with our mouths. **Consider it today.** We must learn to control our tongues:

"For we all stumble in many *ways*. If anyone does not stumble in what he says, he is a perfect man, able to bridle the whole body as well" (James 3:2).

If we can acknowledge our faults, then we should be able to enter into the assembly of the redeemed, and speak edifying words that are able to build up people in the Lord. The words we speak should be evidence of God's love inside of us (cf. 1 Peter 4:8), and should be used only to help others. If we speak anything negative, it should be only in the form of admonishing people from staying away from sin, and what takes them away from the salvation we possess in Messiah Yeshua. In so doing, we can hopefully accomplish James' final admonition to his readers, and bring known sinners back from death and exile from God:

"My brethren, if any among you strays from the truth and one turns him back, let him know that he who turns a sinner from the error of his way will save his soul from death and will cover a multitude of sins" (James 5:19-20).

**As you remember the blood of the Lamb that redeems us from eternal judgment, let that same love be extended to your brothers and sisters with an edifying word rather than an evil tongue!**

# *Acharei Mot* אַחֲרֵי מֹת
## After the death
## "Blood Life"

> **Leviticus 16:1-18:30**
> **Ezekiel 22:1-19 (A); 22:1-16 (S)**

Just like the double Torah portions of *Tazria-Metzora* (Leviticus 12:1-15:33) that are separated for leap year readings, *Acharei Mot* is usually coupled with the following portion, *Kedoshim* (Leviticus 19:1-20:27). Our selection for this week starts out with describing the meticulous requirements the high priest is to perform on the Day of Atonement or *Yom Kippur* (יוֹם כִּפּוּר).[21] It is followed by general instruction about sacrificial offerings and blood,[22] and various kinds of inappropriate sexual relations.[23]

The instructions detailing *Yom Kippur* naturally get your attention in reading *Acharei Mot*. This observance is stated to be a permanent statute for God's people, and a special High Sabbath, when people contemplate their humanity by humbling themselves:

"*This* shall be permanent statute [*chuqat olam*, חֻקַּת עוֹלָם] for you: in the seventh month, on the tenth day of the month, you shall humble your souls and not do any work, whether the native, or the alien who sojourns among you; for it is on this day that atonement shall be made for you to cleanse you; you will be clean from all your sins before the LORD. It is to be a sabbath of solemn rest for you, that you may humble your souls; it is a permanent statute" (Leviticus 16:29-31).

Once a year, the Lord really does want His people to think about their sins—both individual and corporate—and what it takes to provide restitution for them. While

---

[21] Leviticus 16:1-34.
[22] Leviticus 17:1-16.
[23] Leviticus 18:1-30.

Believers today might not think that this is really necessary, because we have the blood covering and sacrifice of Messiah Yeshua, there are still things to pray about on *Yom Kippur* **such as those who do not have the blood covering of Messiah Yeshua over their hearts.** We can also consider how we ourselves have been maturing, *or not*, in Him. By fasting and humbling ourselves on this solemn day, we can reflect on where we stand before the Lord, acknowledging those areas before Him in prayer where we need to improve. We can reflect on how the original sacrifice offered at *Yom Kippur* has now given way to the supreme of sacrifices in what the Son of God has accomplished for us, as is summarized by the Apostles:

- "[B]eing justified as a gift by His grace through the redemption which is in Messiah Yeshua; whom God displayed publicly as a propitiation in His blood through faith. *This was* to demonstrate His righteousness, because in the forbearance of God He passed over the sins previously committed" (Romans 3:24-25).
- "In Him we have redemption through His blood, the forgiveness of our trespasses, according to the riches of His grace" (Ephesians 1:7).
- "[A]ccording to the foreknowledge of God the Father, by the sanctifying work of the Spirit, to obey Yeshua the Messiah and be sprinkled with His blood: May grace and peace be yours in the fullest measure" (1 Peter 1:2).
- "[B]ut if we walk in the Light as He Himself is in the Light, we have fellowship with one another, and the blood of Yeshua His Son cleanses us from all sin" (1 John 1:7).

If Paul, Peter, and John understood and reflected upon the need for a blood sacrifice to cover sin—with Yeshua's own blood now permanently covering sin—it is obviously beneficial for us to reflect on what this all means, and what He endured for us on the cross. In this week's Torah portion, the principle of an animal giving of itself and its blood *to cover (temporarily) a human transgression*, is articulated:

"For the life of the flesh is in the blood, and I have given it to you on the altar to make atonement for your souls; for it is the blood by reason of the life that makes atonement" (Leviticus 17:11).

Here, our Heavenly Father explains that an atonement for sin can only be accomplished by the substitution of life-for-life or blood-for-blood. In the Torah, God originally required various animals (cf. Leviticus 17:2) to provide some kind of covering for human sin. Of course, these sacrifices had to be repeated over and over, because an animal sacrifice is incomplete to cover a human sin. When Yeshua finally came and offered Himself up for fallen humanity, a permanent covering became available. In fact, according to the author of Hebrews, Yeshua's sacrificial work is tied directly to His priestly work, and the inauguration of the age of New Covenant[24]:

"But when Messiah appeared *as* a high priest of the good things to come, *He entered* through the greater and more perfect tabernacle, not made with hands, that is to say, not of this creation; and not through the blood of goats and calves, but through His own blood, He entered the holy place once for all, having obtained eternal redemption. For if the blood of goats and bulls and the ashes of a heifer sprinkling those who have been defiled sanctify for the cleansing of the flesh, how much more will the blood of Messiah, who through the

---

[24] Cf. Hebrews 8:7-13; 10:14-18; and Jeremiah 31:31-34; Ezekiel 36:25-27.

eternal Spirit offered Himself without blemish to God, cleanse your conscience from dead works to serve the living God? For this reason He is the mediator of a new covenant, so that, since a death has taken place for the redemption of the transgressions that were *committed* under the first covenant, those who have been called may receive the promise of the eternal inheritance...For when every commandment had been spoken by Moses to all the people according to the Law, he took the blood of the calves...with water and scarlet wool and hyssop, and sprinkled both the book itself and all the people, saying, 'THIS IS THE BLOOD OF THE COVENANT WHICH GOD COMMANDED YOU' [Exodus 24:8]. And in the same way he sprinkled both the tabernacle and all the vessels of the ministry with the blood. And according to the Law, *one may* almost *say*, all things are cleansed with blood, and without shedding of blood there is no forgiveness. Therefore it was necessary for the copies of the things in the heavens to be cleansed with these, but the heavenly things themselves with better sacrifices than these. For Messiah did not enter a holy place made with hands, a *mere* copy of the true one, but into heaven itself, now to appear in the presence of God for us; nor was it that He would offer Himself often, as the high priest enters the holy place year by year with blood that is not his own. Otherwise, He would have needed to suffer often since the foundation of the world; but now once at the consummation of the ages He has been manifested to put away sin by the sacrifice of Himself. And inasmuch as it is appointed for men to die once and after this *comes* judgment, so Messiah also, having been offered once to bear the sins of many, will appear a second time for salvation without *reference to* sin, to those who eagerly await Him" (Hebrews 9:11-16, 19-28).

In this passage from Hebrews, the author talks about entrance into the Holy of Holies and the blood that is required to cover sin. He uses the Levitical priesthood and sacrifices as a point of comparison and contrast for the Melchizedekian priesthood and sacrifice of Yeshua. Twice within his treatise, he interweaves the reality of the New Covenant now being available by the Messiah's work (Hebrews 8:7-13; 10:14-18). Yeshua's obedience to offer Himself up as the sacrificial Lamb, initiated the permanent atonement and forgiveness promised in Jeremiah 31:31-34:

"'Behold, days are coming,' declares the LORD, 'when I will make a new covenant with the house of Israel and with the house of Judah, not like the covenant which I made with their fathers in the day I took them by the hand to bring them out of the land of Egypt, My covenant which they broke, although I was a husband to them,' declares the LORD. 'But this is the covenant which I will make with the house of Israel after those days,' declares the LORD, 'I will put My law within them and on their heart I will write it; and I will be their God, and they shall be My people.'"

When you read the Messianic Scriptures, you realize that the Apostles were very much aware of the serious, salvation-historical impact of Yeshua's death. They understood that His shed blood was critical for the salvation of human beings and the inauguration of the New Covenant and the permanent atonement and forgiveness it entails. By reading their epistles and knowing what parts of the Tanakh they either were quoting from or alluding to, you can conclude that they definitely knew how the New Covenant also involved **the Lord writing His Law onto our hearts.**[25]

While thinking through this in light of *Acharei Mot*, it dawned on me that the principles discussed in our Torah portion were also referenced at a crucial and important juncture in the development of the early Body of Messiah. In the early years after the ascension of

---

[25] For a further examination, consult the article "What is the New Covenant?" by J.K. McKee.

Yeshua into Heaven, the gospel was going forth in power and people from a diverse array of backgrounds and cultures were coming to knowledge and acceptance of the gospel. A contention arose among the early Believers, because in certain areas as the good news went forth, some of the Jewish Believers demanded that the new, non-Jewish Believers become circumcised as proselytes in order to be considered "saved" (Acts 15:1).

When was the last time you read through Acts 15? From the testimonies we see recorded by Luke, if the controversy over the inclusion of non-Jews as equals into the fledgling *ekklēsia* was not resolved—it would erupt into a divided Body of Messiah. The non-Jewish Believers were saved the same way as Jewish Believers, **by the grace of the Lord Yeshua** (Acts 15:11), but not all agreed. The mixed assembly at Antioch, Paul and Barnabas' hub of operation, seemed to not really have any problems until some highly conservative Jewish Believers from Judea came to make a visit. *They insisted* that without the non-Jewish Believers becoming ethnic Jews, they could not be saved (Acts 15:1-2). Knowing how the gospel was spreading out into the Mediterranean, a fair-minded solution to a potential crisis would have to be found. Paul and Barnabas are sent to Jerusalem to determine what should be done (Acts 15:3-4). The Jerusalem Council that was convened, was presided over by James, the half-brother of Yeshua, and Peter, who was the first Jewish Believer to share the good news with a non-Jew (cf. Acts chs. 10-11; 15:7-11).

If you follow the proceedings that are described in Acts 15, you will note that James seemed to sit back and listen to the different testimonies and arguments that were presented (Acts 15:7-12), before he issued his ruling. There is no doubt that James understood—as well as many of his contemporaries—that Yeshua had inaugurated the New Covenant with His sacrificial death. James would have certainly known that the New Covenant of Jeremiah 31 and Ezekiel 36 was to be made with a restored people of Israel, and that God's salvation was to go forth to the nations. He agrees with the testimony of Peter, and confirms how "God…concerned Himself about taking from among the Gentiles a people for His name," and "With this the words of the Prophets agree" (Acts 15:14-15).

James recognized the Biblical reality that the salvation of the nations was a part of the restoration of the Kingdom to Israel. A specific Tanakh passage he appealed to was Amos 9:11-12, from this week's Haftarah selection. This appears within a larger prophecy detailing the restoration of all Israel:

"'In that day I will raise up the fallen booth of David, and wall up its breaches; I will also raise up its ruins and rebuild it as in the days of old; that they may possess the remnant of Edom and all the nations who are called by My name,' declares the LORD who does this" (cf. Acts 15:16-18).

There is a noticeable difference with what James says in Acts 15, as Luke narrates his quote with, "SO THAT THE REST OF MANKIND MAY SEEK THE LORD, AND ALL THE GENTILES WHO ARE CALLED BY MY NAME" (Acts 15:17). James does not follow the Hebrew text in Amos which reads *sh'eirit Edom* (שְׁאֵרִית אֱדוֹם), but the Septuagint which reads with *hoi kataloipoi tōn anthrōpōn* (οἱ κατάλοιποι τῶν ἀνθρώπων). The LXX Jewish translators understood *Edom* (אֱדוֹם) to be connected to *adam* (אָדָם), the Hebrew word for **"mankind, people"** (*HALOT*),[26] and they rendered it into Greek as "the remnant of men"

---

[26] Ludwig Koehler and Walter Baumgartner, eds., *The Hebrew & Aramaic Lexicon of the Old Testament*, 2 vols. (Leiden, the Netherlands: Brill, 2001), 1:14.

(Apostle's Bible),[27] referring to God's faithful remnant that would come forth out of humanity's masses.

James recognizes that by the work of the Messiah, the Tabernacle of David has been rebuilt—representative of the prophetic/charismatic worship ministry that King David had once established (cf. 1 Chronicles 25). Such a ministry was now manifested in the gospel going forth and changing lives, and was going to affect far more than just the First Century Jews. People from the world at large were going to be impacted with the salvation of Israel's Messiah. And, not only would they come to welcome the gospel, but the Prophets of Israel recognized how they would seek being taught from God's Torah (Isaiah 2:3; Micah 4:2). Even though there were more details to be considered in the wider selection of Amos 9:7-15, and James makes a specific appeal to "the words of the Prophets" (Acts 15:15)—meaning that there are many more Tanakh passages he could have affirmed—Amos 9:11-12 itself is quite loaded.[28]

The Jewish Apostles and leaders of the early *ekklēsia* had a great command of the Scriptures. There is every reason to believe that James could have had the entire Torah, and large parts of the Tanakh, memorized. After all, both he and Yeshua grew up in the same home together. Here, Yeshua was instructed, in all truth and righteousness, by His Earthly father Joseph. The other siblings received the same instruction from their Torah obedient parents (cf. Jude 1). As James presided over the Jerusalem Council, listening to all of the arguments made, you will note by his conclusions how *three* of the four specific things James concludes **must be adhered to** by the new, non-Jewish Believers, are derived from this week's Torah portion. While circumcision and proselyte conversion were not required of them for inclusion in the faith community, there were some things that the non-Jewish Believers had to do which were non-negotiable. The decree issued by James was,

"Therefore it is my judgment that we do not trouble those who are turning to God from among the Gentiles, but that we write to them that they abstain from things contaminated by idols and from fornication and from what is strangled and from blood. For Moses from ancient generations has in every city those who preach him, since he is read in the synagogues every Sabbath" (Acts 15:19-21).

James listed four sinful activities that he knew needed to be immediately stopped in order for the new, non-Jewish Believers to be allowed to come in among Jewish Believers for fellowship and instruction. Three of these restrictions are considered in *Acharei Mot*, and the fourth is mentioned and further discussed in the next Torah portion, *Kedoshim* (Leviticus 19:1-20:27). According to the conclusions agreed upon by those at the Jerusalem Council, the four things that had to be adhered to in order to minimize the possible tension between the Believers included:

1. Abstinence from pollutions of idols
2. Abstinence from fornication
3. Abstinence from things strangled
4. Abstinence from blood

As the non-Jewish Believers would follow these four prohibitions, each of which is rooted within the Torah, they would be able to fellowship with Jewish Believers. James' concluding statement in Acts 15:21, "For from the earliest times, Moshe has had in every

---

[27] Or, "those remaining of humans" (New English Translation of the Septuagint).
[28] For further consideration of Amos 9:11-12 within Acts 15:16-18, consult the commentary *Acts 15 for the Practical Messianic* by J.K. McKee.

city those who proclaim him, with his words being read in the synagogues every *Shabbat*" (CJB), implies that these new Believers would need to be instructed in the godly principles of God's Torah, accessible at the local synagogue. They would have to submit to some kind of Torah teaching simply to know what the four prohibitions were, and as a result, they would learn more about the kinds of changes that the God of Israel required of them.

These four requirements would help take the pagan culture out of the lives of the new, non-Jewish Believers. In time, as they would become familiar with the Torah's instructions, these former idol-worshipping pagans would begin to receive further understanding about how God's Torah is to guide Messiah followers in holiness (cf. Matthew 5:16). By the power of the New Covenant supernaturally writing God's commandments onto the heart—and not some demand of Torah-keeping for salvation (Acts 15:1, 5)—would the early, non-Jewish Believers learn to appreciate Moses' Teaching.

*What are some of the things these new Believers would learn from the Torah?* Simply consider how three of the prohibitions delivered by James are specific negative commandments seen in *Acharei Mot* (and the fourth is talked about in *Kedoshim*).

> **(1)** The first, and most obvious of the prohibitions that James issued, regarded the practice of idolatry. In *Acharei Mot*, the Torah addresses the problem of sacrifices to goat demons, which God commanded the Israelites to stop. In *Kedoshim*, the idols of molten gods are mentioned. James' instruction would have prohibited any of the non-Jewish Believers from participating in social and civic events at the local shrine, where people could have conducted business activities, seeking the favor of the gods, or participated in some kind of festal rites. This section of Leviticus, the Torah commands,
>
>> "They shall no longer sacrifice their sacrifices to the goat demons with which they play the harlot. This shall be a permanent statute to them throughout their generations" (Leviticus 17:7).
>
>> "Do not turn to idols or make for yourselves molten gods; I am the LORD your God" (Leviticus 19:4).
>
> **(2)** The second admonition from James related to sexual immorality, a major theme of Leviticus ch. 18. While temple prostitution could definitely be in view, a whole host of sexual sins from fornication to adultery to homosexuality and bestiality are included. *Acharei Mot* lists many vile acts of sexual sin. The consequences of these sins for the Ancient Israelites was ejection from the Promised Land. For Believers, James could have considered violation of these commandments as grounds for excommunication from the assembly:[29]
>
>> "Do not defile yourselves by any of these things; for by all these the nations which I am casting out before you have become defiled. For the land has become defiled, therefore I have brought its punishment upon it, so the land has spewed out its inhabitants. But as for you, you are to keep My statutes and My judgments and shall not do any of these abominations, *neither* the native, nor the alien who sojourns among you (for the men of the land who

---

[29] This is something that the Apostle Paul has to specifically instruct in 1 Corinthians 5.

have been before you have done all these abominations, and the land has become defiled); so that the land will not spew you out, should you defile it, as it has spewed out the nation which has been before you" (Leviticus 18:24-28).

**(3)** The third prohibition James issued regarded strangled meats, or animals that were killed by either choking or suffocation, with the specific intent of keeping large quantities of blood coagulated within the meat. He knew how serious the warnings were against consuming blood, as seen in the Torah, as animals killed for human food were to be properly respected (cf. Genesis 9:4). The non-Jewish Believers were expected to eat properly butchered meat, and by implication a kosher-style of diet, for fellowship with Jewish Believers. As our *parashah* this week details,

> "And any man from the house of Israel, or from the aliens who sojourn among them, who eats any blood, I will set My face against that person who eats blood and will cut him off from among his people...For *as for the* life of all flesh, its blood is *identified* with its life. Therefore I said to the sons of Israel, 'You are not to eat the blood of any flesh, for the life of all flesh is its blood; whoever eats it shall be cut off.' When any person eats *an animal* which dies or is torn *by beasts*, whether he is a native or an alien, he shall wash his clothes and bathe in water, and remain unclean until evening; then he will become clean" (Leviticus 17:10, 14-15).

While there were many areas of the Torah where the Jewish Believers recognized that the new, non-Jewish Believers would not change instantly—and they needed time—James' decree in Acts 15:19-21 listed four prohibitions where the Jewish Believers could not be forbearing. *Change was* ***required.*** With the agreement of the others gathered in Jerusalem (Acts 15:22), the admonitions of James were made a "standard policy" during the early stages of building the Body of Messiah (Acts 21:25). But, the testimony of the Apostolic Scriptures indicates that such a policy, *with just four areas requiring mandated change*, was not always easy.[30]

We read later about problems that arose in Corinth from eating meat sacrificed to idols. The Apostle Paul, confronting a Corinthian assembly who had people claiming "Everything is permissible for me" (1 Corinthians 6:12, NIV)[31] and committing a wide

---

[30] For further reading on the scene of Acts 15, and its role for Messianic Believers today, consult *Acts 15 for the Practical Messianic* by J.K. McKee.

[31] Editor's note: A few things are to be noted with the slogan, "All things are lawful for me" (1 Corinthians 6:12, NASU).

First of all, the term often rendered as "lawful" from the Greek, does not have *nomos* (νόμος) or "law" as a root. It is the term *exesti* (ἔξεστι), appropriately meaning, "*it is allowed, it is in one's power, is possible*" (H.G. Liddell and R. Scott, *An Intermediate Greek-English Lexicon* [Oxford: Clarendon Press, 1994], 273). Anthony C. Thiselton considers this to best relate to "Liberty to do anything" (*New International Greek Testament Commentary: The First Epistle to the Corinthians* [Grand Rapids: Eerdmans, 2000], pp 458, 461).

Secondly, while not noted by the NASU, versions like the RSV, NIV, NRSV, ESV, HCSB, NLT, CJB, et. al., all place what is said in quotation marks " ". This reflects the view, also held by most modern 1 Corinthians commentators, that Paul *is not saying* this, but rather it is something that the Corinthians concocted, which he had to make an effort to refute. In the estimation of Richard B. Hays, "'I am free to do anything' must have been a favorite slogan of the Corinthians" (*Interpretation, A Bible Commentary for Teaching and Preaching: 1 Corinthians* [Louisville: John Knox Press, 1997], 101).

variety of sins (cf. 1 Corinthians 5:1), notes to them: "Therefore, if food causes my brother to stumble, I will never eat meat again, so that I will not cause my brother to stumble" (1 Corinthians 8:13). This was pretty serious, not only because they could bring meat sacrificed to idols to fellowship meals—but also because many of the Corinthians were still engaged in the social circle of the pagan temple! The Apostolic decree of Acts 15:19-21 was precisely designed for the non-Jewish Believers to be **cut off from the social sphere of the pagan temple**, and for them to be associated with their fellow Jewish Messiah followers *or* at least those who recognized Israel's One God.

Of all of the things that the new, non-Jewish Believers would have doubtlessly been exposed to, as they began submitting themselves to a weekly hearing of Moses' Teaching, is the role that blood plays as a covering for sin. They would hear the Torah's instructions on how animals were to be sacrificed at specific times and in specific ways to provide a temporary atonement for human transgression. *This might have been different from the sacrificial offerings made in Greco-Roman temples*, often provided to just appease the gods or curry their favor. The non-Jewish Believers, seeing how the Levitical priesthood would have to offer sacrifices over and over again, would hopefully realize how the most important blood shed was that of the Messiah Yeshua. In hearing the Torah read, **they would understand how His shed blood offered permanent atonement for all humanity.**

Today's Messianic community has attracted many evangelical Christians wanting to embrace their Hebraic Roots. They are not like the first non-Jewish Believers, who were originally raised in paganism. They already know Messiah Yeshua, and they have a basic idea about the Bible's morality. But they do need to learn more about the Torah and the Tanakh, in an effort to appreciate why Yeshua has come and died for our sins. *We all need to learn to appreciate—non-Jewish* **and** *Jewish—why He came and shed His blood for us.* For, it is only by His sacrifice, that permanent atonement and forgiveness are truly available! Only by what He has accomplished, can we have eternal life and restored communion with the Father!

## *Kedoshim* קְדֹשִׁים
### Holy Ones
### "Holiness and the Golden Rule"

> Leviticus 19:1-20:27
> Amos 9:7-15 (A); Ezekiel 20:2-20 (S)

The overriding theme of *Kedoshim* begins and closes with the admonition for Israel to be holy. Found within these bookends is a list of important rules that promote the pursuit of holiness. These range from simple ways to handle the harvest,[32] labor,[33] and foreign relations,[34] to restrictions about the occult[35] and deviant sexual activity.[36] This wide variety

---

[32] Leviticus 19:9-10, 23-25.
[33] Leviticus 19:13.
[34] Leviticus 19:33-34.
[35] Leviticus 19:26; 20:1-8, 27.
[36] Leviticus 20:10-26.

of instructions is all designed to sanctify God's people unto Himself. Our *parashah* for this week begins and closes with the following verses, clearly requiring holiness:

- "Then the LORD spoke to Moses, saying: 'Speak to all the congregation of the sons of Israel and say to them, "You shall be holy, for I the LORD your God am holy"'" (Leviticus 19:1-2).
- "Thus you are to be holy to Me, for I the LORD am holy; and I have set you apart from the peoples to be Mine" (Leviticus 20:26).

As one reflects upon the various commandments detailed in *Kedoshim*, a sense of protection from the wickedness of the sinful world in which we live should come to mind. Even though the thought of participating in many of these activities *should never have been considered by us as born again Believers*—the sad reality is that these depraved activities do occur in many civilizations *today*, and not only those of the ancient past. And, even in the largely Judeo-Christian culture of the West, the laxity of moral codes and basic human ethics has been fostering some proliferation, of many of these formerly illegal actions, in various degrees. One could readily conclude from observing the society that surrounds us, that we are approaching the Last Days that Paul warned Timothy about. As he informed his student,

"But realize this, that in the last days difficult times will come. For men will be lovers of self, lovers of money, boastful, arrogant, revilers, disobedient to parents, ungrateful, unholy, unloving, irreconcilable, malicious gossips, without self-control, brutal, haters of good, treacherous, reckless, conceited, lovers of pleasure rather than lovers of God, holding to a form of godliness, although they have denied its power; avoid such men as these" (2 Timothy 3:1-5).

When you take a look at this list of how human beings will behave in the Last Days, you can readily detect that each of these despicable characteristics is almost part and parcel with people ignoring the list of commandments detailed in *Kedoshim*. But rather than focus on all of the negative aspects of *Kedoshim* this week, I would instead like you to consider one small section of our reading that relates to the actions among the people, brethren, and neighbors of Israel. The positive commandments about how people should treat their neighbors is something quite significant to the rest of the Biblical story, as demonstrating love and respect for others is definitive evidence that we are indeed pursuing holiness and a proper walk with the Lord. The Torah instructs,

"You shall do no injustice in judgment; you shall not be partial to the poor nor defer to the great, but you are to judge your neighbor fairly. You shall not go about as a slanderer among your people, and you are not to act against the life of your neighbor; I am the LORD. You shall not hate your fellow countryman in your heart; you may surely reprove your neighbor, but shall not incur sin because of him. You shall not take vengeance, nor bear any grudge against the sons of your people, but **you shall love your neighbor as yourself;** I am the LORD" (Leviticus 19:15-18).

The Biblical requirement for people to treat their neighbors, and fellow brothers and sisters—with love, respect, and forbearance—is something that is sorely needed not only among those who believe in Jesus in the Christian community, **but most especially within our still-maturing Messianic community of faith.** Sadly, it has been my experience that many people who profess to be pursuing a Torah-based lifestyle, often struggle with adhering to the basic commandments of how God's people are to properly relate to their neighbors. This is very troubling, because unlike some of the more obscure commandments buried in the Torah that are easy to overlook, perhaps with little or no reference made in the Messianic Scriptures, both Yeshua and the Apostles amplify how we should treat our neighbors. Leviticus 19:18 is one of the most recognizable Torah verses quoted in the New Testament.[37] Perhaps the most quoted reference where Leviticus 19:18 appears is in the Synoptic Gospels, where Yeshua is asked what the greatest commandment in the Torah is. He logically appealed to the *Shema* (Deuteronomy 6:4-5) and to the need for people to love their neighbors:

> "Yeshua answered, 'The foremost is, "HEAR, O ISRAEL! THE LORD OUR GOD IS ONE LORD; AND YOU SHALL LOVE THE LORD YOUR GOD WITH ALL YOUR HEART, AND WITH ALL YOUR SOUL, AND WITH ALL YOUR MIND, AND WITH ALL YOUR STRENGTH." The second is this, "YOU SHALL LOVE YOUR NEIGHBOR AS YOURSELF." There is no other commandment greater than these.' The scribe said to Him, 'Right, Teacher; You have truly stated that HE IS ONE, AND THERE IS NO ONE ELSE BESIDES HIM; AND TO LOVE HIM WITH ALL THE HEART AND WITH ALL THE UNDERSTANDING AND WITH ALL THE STRENGTH, AND TO LOVE ONE'S NEIGHBOR AS HIMSELF, is much more than all burnt offerings and sacrifices.' When Yeshua saw that he had answered intelligently, He said to him, 'You are not far from the kingdom of God.' After that, no one would venture to ask Him any more questions" (Mark 12:29-34).

> "'Teacher, which is the great commandment in the Law?' And He said to him, '"YOU SHALL LOVE THE LORD YOUR GOD WITH ALL YOUR HEART, AND WITH ALL YOUR SOUL, AND WITH ALL YOUR MIND." This is the great and foremost commandment. The second is like it, "YOU SHALL LOVE YOUR NEIGHBOR AS YOURSELF." On these two commandments depend the whole Law and the Prophets'" (Matthew 22:36-40).

> "And a lawyer stood up and put Him to the test, saying, 'Teacher, what shall I do to inherit eternal life?' And He said to him, 'What is written in the Law? How does it read to you?' And he answered, 'YOU SHALL LOVE THE LORD YOUR GOD WITH ALL YOUR HEART, AND WITH ALL YOUR SOUL, AND WITH ALL YOUR STRENGTH, AND WITH ALL YOUR MIND; AND YOUR NEIGHBOR AS YOURSELF.' And He said to him, 'You have answered correctly; DO THIS AND YOU WILL LIVE'" (Luke 10:25-28).

There are some slight differences between the questions asked among these three accounts, but the same basic answer is given. The concept of loving God with all of one's heart, mind, soul, and strength **is paramount in order to consider the thrust of the Torah's instruction.** The requirement to love one's neighbor is the second greatest of the Torah's commandments, and is a benchmark to see if the first greatest commandment is really being followed. After all, it has been observed that if you love an invisible God, then what about your neighbor who is visible? One has the opportunity to display love for a seen neighbor, by the same actions that should be made toward an unseen God.

## Loving our Neighbors

As you dig deeper into our Torah portion, you will detect that Leviticus 19:15-18 has a more explicit way of extending love for neighbor. First, you should note how God admonishes His people to judge fairly, as circumstances will arise in life which require us to make decisions or rulings:

---

[37] Matthew 19:19; Mark 12:31; Luke 10:27; Romans 13:9; Galatians 5:14; James 2:8.

"You shall do no injustice in judgment; you shall not be partial to the poor nor defer to the great, but you are to judge your neighbor fairly" (Leviticus 19:15).

The Prophet Zechariah clarifies how impartiality is critical to administering proper justice:

"'These are the things which you should do: speak the truth to one another; judge with truth and judgment for peace in your gates. Also let none of you devise evil in your heart against another, and do not love perjury; for all these are what I hate,' declares the LORD" (Zechariah 8:16-17).

It is clear that if one judges with evil present in the heart, that one will be opposing the Lord and His established ways. Those who judge with evil motives will demonstrate themselves to be those who do not truly love God and neighbor.

A second major principle seen in our *parashah* addresses the chronic problem of human slander. As God instructed Ancient Israel,

"You shall not go about as a slanderer among your people, and you are not to act against the life of your neighbor; I am the LORD" (Leviticus 19:16).

There is nothing more damaging to a person, short of physical harm, than the wickedness of defaming someone by slander and gossip. Sadly, this is one of the most prevalent sins in the contemporary Body of Messiah—either Christian *or* Messianic. Notably, the Jewish theological tradition is well aware of the damage that an evil tongue can bring to the faith community, and specific prayers are to be offered each day from the *siddur* against speaking guile.[38]

The Biblical admonition against slander is coupled with the command to not "stand aside while your fellow's blood is shed" (Leviticus 19:16, NJPS). With this being the case, how should we react when we hear our neighbor's name or character being slandered *or murdered*? Would it not make sense to stand up for a brother or sister and prevent one's character being assassinated? Sadly, many Believers today largely do not know how to employ these commands in real life situations. We would benefit greatly if we simply came to the defense of someone who is slandered.

Following this, the concept of harboring hatred in the heart for one's neighbor is considered. God commands,

"You shall not hate your fellow countryman in your heart; you may surely reprove your neighbor, but shall not incur sin because of him" (Leviticus 19:17).

We have all heard our fellow Believers in Messiah talk about the intentions of the human heart. Here in the Torah text, the Lord amplifies the issue about what might occur in the heart. It is very clear that His people are not supposed to hate their fellow, but by including *b'levavekha* (בִּלְבָבֶךָ) or "in your heart" with the command, the need to take this seriously is intensified. The need to not hate one's fellow is also quite severe, as it is something that has to be commented on later by the Apostles. Consider what the Apostle John candidly says:

"The one who says he is in the Light and *yet* hates his brother is in the darkness until now. The one who loves his brother abides in the Light and there is no cause for stumbling in him. But the one who hates his brother is in the darkness and walks in the darkness, and does not know where he is going because the darkness has blinded his eyes" (1 John 2:9-11).

---

[38] Joseph H. Hertz, ed., *The Authorised Daily Prayer Book*, revised (New York: Bloch Publishing Company, 1960), pp 25-29; cf. Nosson Scherman and Meir Zlotowitz, eds., *Complete ArtScroll Siddur, Nusach Sefard* (Brooklyn: Mesorah Publications, 1985), 23.

If anyone holds any hatred toward a brother or sister, such a person should check to see whether he or she is living in darkness. While we might struggle with negative feelings toward non-Believers at times, **we have no legitimate reason to hold continual malice toward anyone in the community of faith.** The reality of life may be that we will have disagreements with fellow Believers, but such disagreements need to be tempered with love and respect, and if we have to rebuke or admonish someone—then it needs to be done tactfully. The Torah's instruction gives us a very solemn warning about reproving one's neighbor without incurring sin (Leviticus 19:17b). The Apostle Paul further amplifies our understanding of how to lovingly rebuke a brother or sister in the Lord:

"Do not receive an accusation against an elder except on the basis of two or three witnesses. Those who continue in sin, rebuke in the presence of all, so that the rest also will be fearful *of sinning*. I solemnly charge you in the presence of God and of Messiah Yeshua and of *His* chosen angels, to maintain these *principles* without bias, doing nothing in a *spirit of* partiality. Do not lay hands upon anyone *too* hastily and thereby share *responsibility for* the sins of others; keep yourself free from sin" (1 Timothy 5:19-22).

Paul gives Timothy instruction about how to properly handle a problem with an elder in the congregation. If one has to rebuke an elder, then the key is to do it soberly and without falling into sin. Too often, though, people level charges against others for the slightest provocation and the most ridiculous reasons. In this account, as should be practiced with others, the necessity for multiple witnesses to a charge must be observed. Claiming something without legitimate proof will lead to slander and character defamation. The sin of a spirit of partiality is sternly warned against—because obviously, if you have ought in your heart, then you will not be able to be impartial and objective in your deliberations and cross-examinations.

Finally, while love for neighbor is one of the most important commandments in the Torah, notice how the concept of loving is coupled with the prohibition against taking "revenge" (NIV) against one's neighbor:

"You shall not take vengeance, nor bear any grudge against the sons of your people, but you shall love your neighbor as yourself; I am the LORD" (Leviticus 19:18).

The Apostle Paul teaches that if someone does wrong to you, that repaying evil with evil will not achieve anything. Rather, evil must be overcome with doing good:

"Never pay back evil for evil to anyone. Respect what is right in the sight of all men. If possible, so far as it depends on you, be at peace with all men. Never take your own revenge, beloved, but leave room for the wrath *of God*, for it is written, 'VENGEANCE IS MINE, I WILL REPAY' [Leviticus 19:18], says the Lord. 'BUT IF YOUR ENEMY IS HUNGRY, FEED HIM, AND IF HE IS THIRSTY, GIVE HIM A DRINK; FOR IN SO DOING YOU WILL HEAP BURNING COALS ON HIS HEAD' [Proverbs 25:21-22]. Do not be overcome by evil, but overcome evil with good" (Romans 12:17-21).

Paul links Leviticus 19:18, which we are having to consider in our Torah portion, with a well-known proverb:

"If your enemy is hungry, give him food to eat; and if he is thirsty, give him water to drink; for you will heap burning coals on his head, and the LORD will reward you" (Proverbs 25:21-22).

## The Final Measure

When you consider the referenced verses in *Kedoshim*, they lay the foundation for one of the most important commandments in the Holy Writ. Many refer to this as the Golden

Rule: "In everything, therefore, treat people the same way you want them to treat you, for this is the Law and the Prophets" (Matthew 7:12; cf. Luke 6:31; 10:25-28). After loving God, we are supposed to love our neighbors as we should love ourselves. So, as you meditate upon *Kedoshim* this week, you might ask yourself just how well you are loving your neighbor.

If married, do you consider your spouse to be your closest neighbor? Are you looking out for his or her needs? Are you putting his or her needs ahead of yours? Are you trying to find new ways to serve him or her, and make your relationship better? Are you coming to the defense of him or her when he or she is being wronged? *The list of what husbands and wives can do for one another can go on and on.* What about your close family members or friends? What about your colleagues at work? The point is, when considering the closest and most familiar of relationships, you need to exercise love by being sensitive to others' needs, and always be trying to help people in unexpected ways.

Here is a real sobering thought that I would like you meditate upon: **imagine the Golden Rule like a measuring rod that determines your degree of holiness.** If you are honest with yourself, you may think that you are not very holy. When analyzing our interactions with various "neighbors" over the years, just about all of us can recall times when we were impartial in judgment. *We spoke without thinking.* How about those times when we actually committed slander? What about times we hated someone in our hearts, because of something done to us? Is it possible that we have not loved our neighbors as ourselves? *Where might we need to make restitution?*

If you take the time to do some introspection, you might conclude that this is a very well-needed spiritual exercise. You might realize that obedience to the second greatest commandment is more theory than reality in your life. But this is why the faithful Torah student is blessed. Every year we have the opportunity to let the Spirit of the Most High instruct us about loving our neighbors. And, we have the Spirit to convict us where we need to change, cry out for help, and in changing we can then serve as a positive example to others. The Lord bids us to be holy in more than just outward doings, but in the heart attitude that we carry inside of us!

Do you remember how Yeshua, when addressing His followers, dealt with the "loving your neighbors" issue? He raised it to a much higher level! In fact, He taught that His followers are to love their enemies and to pray for those who persecute them:

"You have heard that it was said, 'YOU SHALL LOVE YOUR NEIGHBOR and hate your enemy.' But I say to you, love your enemies and pray for those who persecute you, so that you may be sons of your Father who is in heaven; for He causes His sun to rise on *the* evil and *the* good, and sends rain on *the* righteous and *the* unrighteous. For if you love those who love you, what reward do you have? Do not even the tax collectors do the same? If you greet only your brothers, what more are you doing *than others*? Do not even the Gentiles do the same? Therefore you are to be perfect, as your heavenly Father is perfect" (Matthew 5:43-48).

There is no Biblical commandment *anywhere* that instructs God's people to hate their enemies, although hatred for enemies is something that is quite common to the human condition.[39] To combat this problem, Yeshua concludes His admonition by instructing His

---

[39] The Dead Sea Scrolls do, in fact, include an injunction that hating one's enemies was acceptable:

"He is to teach them both to love all the Children of Light—each commensurate with his rightful place in the council of God—and to hate all the Children of Darkness, each commensurate with his guilt and the vengeance

listeners that they need **to be perfect, just as the Father is perfect.** Of course, such a degree of perfection can only be obtained from supernatural work of God within a redeemed heart.

Do you have a redeemed heart? Have you appropriated the shed blood of the Messiah, being forgiven of your sins? Do you walk in the holiness that the Lord requires of His people—by demonstrating love and mercy toward others? I hope that you truly are of the redeemed, and you are reflecting such redemption to all those you encounter and meet. **May His name and works be revered beyond measure!**

## Emor אֱמֹר
### Speak
### "Timing is Everything"

> Leviticus 21:1-24:23
> Ezekiel 44:15-31

As you consider *Emor* this week, more commandments are listed that carry on the theme of holiness which we have been considering in the past few Torah portions. Called into a priestly service for the Most High, the people of Israel continue to receive more instructions about how to maintain a state of separateness before the Creator. The Lord gives His people more details on what it means to be a holy nation and a kingdom of priests. He really does want them to be "holy ones," which we reviewed last week in *Kedoshim* (Leviticus 19:1-20:27), in all that they do.

When you look at the four chapters of Scripture composing *Emor*, as the Book of Leviticus prepares to wind down, one detects three distinct Hebrew verbs—which indicate to me that God is trying to communicate some important concepts to His people. The Hebrew verb *amar* (אָמַר) is seen throughout this portion.[40] *Amar* "is translated in various ways depending on the context...In addition to vocal speech, the word refers to thought as internal speech" (*AMG*).[41] A similar Hebrew term used in our *parashah* is the verb *davar* (דָּבַר).[42] *Davar* has a variance of meanings, including: "to speak, to say," "to promise," "to sing or chant," "think," "pronounce judgment" (*AMG*),[43] obviously each contingent on context. A final Hebrew verb that stands out is *qara* (קָרָא), used various times,[44] and means "to call, to declare, to summon, to invite, to read, to be called, to be invoked, to be named" (*AMG*).[45] When seeing this, the issue witnessed is not that God is speaking—but are His people even hearing, listening, and most of all, heeding His instructions? Leviticus 23:2 is one significant place where these three terms are all used together:

---

due him from God" (1QS 1.9-11; Michael Wise, Martin Abegg, Jr., and Edward Cook, trans., *The Dead Sea Scrolls: A New Translation* [San Francisco: HarperCollins, 1996], 127).

[40] Leviticus 21:1, 16-17; 22:1, 3, 17-18, 26; 23:1-2, 9-10, 23-24, 26, 33-34; 24:1, 13, 15.
[41] Baker and Carpenter, 72.
[42] Leviticus 23:1-2, 9-10, 23-24, 26, 33-34, 37, 44; 24:1, 13, 15, 23.
[43] Baker and Carpenter, 223.
[44] Leviticus 23:2, 4, 21, 37.
[45] Baker and Carpenter, 1009.

"Speak [*davar*] to the sons of Israel and say [*amar*] to them, 'The LORD's appointed times which you shall proclaim [*qara*] as holy convocations—My appointed times are these.'"

## The Appointed Times

The most striking feature you will encounter, seen in reading *Emor*, is the list given of the *moedim* (מוֹעֲדִים) or appointed times. Leviticus 23 includes a summary of the appointed times and the significance that they have for God's people. This chapter begins with the word,

"The LORD spoke again to Moses, saying, 'Speak to the sons of Israel and say to them, "The LORD's appointed times which you shall proclaim as holy convocations—My appointed times are these: For six days work may be done, but on the seventh day there is a sabbath of complete rest, a holy convocation. You shall not do any work; it is a sabbath to the LORD in all your dwellings. These are the appointed times of the LORD, holy convocations which you shall proclaim at the times appointed for them"'" (Leviticus 23:1-4).

The appointed times of the Lord are things to be taken very seriously, as they are labeled by Him to be *miqra'ei qodesh* (מִקְרָאֵי קֹדֶשׁ) or "sacred occasions" (NJPS). These special seasons will help to establish the yearly cycles for Ancient Israel, as they will continue to be formed and molded as God's special people throughout the rest of the Torah. These appointed times will notably tell a story not only of God's dealings in delivering His people in times past, but also of how He will deliver His people in the future via mighty acts of salvation. The appointed times will serve to not only give structure to each new year, but will teach future generations of God's people about what it means to come together and join in a very special and reverent time of communion with Him.

It is notable that the first of the appointed times listed in Leviticus 23 is the weekly Sabbath or *Shabbat*:

"For six days work may be done, but on the seventh day there is a sabbath of complete rest, a holy convocation. You shall not do any work; it is a sabbath to the LORD in all your dwellings" (Leviticus 23:3).

There is disagreement among Jewish interpreters as to whether or not the Sabbath can really be considered among the appointed times. One view, indicated in the *Soncino Chumash*, is that "The Sabbath is not included among *the appointed seasons of the Lord*...[because] The reason is that the Sabbath is a day fixed by God, whereas the actual date for the observance of the festivals had to await the proclamation of the Sanhedrin."[46] Contrary to this, the *ArtScroll Chumash* thinks, "The Sabbath is mentioned with the festivals to teach that anyone who desecrates the festivals is regarded as if he had desecrated the Sabbath, and anyone who observes the festivals is regarded as if he had observed the Sabbath."[47] Regardless of which position one takes, a person, who remembers the appointed times in Leviticus 23:5ff, is automatically expected to be remembering *Shabbat* every week. The Prophet Ezekiel declares that by sanctifying *Shabbat*, it would be a sign between God and His people:

---

[46] Cohen, *Chumash*, 749.
[47] Scherman, *Chumash*, 683.

"I am the LORD your God; walk in My statutes and keep My ordinances and observe them. Sanctify My sabbaths; and they shall be a sign between Me and you, that you may know that I am the LORD your God" (Ezekiel 20:19-20).

The willingness to take one day out of seven, in order to spend time with our Creator, is recognized to be a sign between God and His people. It is a time not only to rest and be refreshed, but also consider God's goodness and provision for us.[48]

## The Spring and Fall Feasts

With God's people considering His goodness and blessing every week with *Shabbat*, the significance of the other appointed times seen in Leviticus 23—remembered throughout the year—can only be highlighted. Jewish interpreters of Leviticus 23 are agreed that seven specific holidays are listed:

1. *Pesach* (פֶּסַח) or Passover (Leviticus 23:5)
2. *Chag HaMatzah* (חַג הַמַצָּה) or the Festival of Unleavened Bread (Leviticus 23:6-8)
3. *Shavuot* (שָׁבֻעוֹת) or the Feast of Weeks (Leviticus 23:9-21)[49]
4. *Yom Teruah* (יוֹם תְּרוּעָה) or the Day of Blowing (Leviticus 23:23-25)[50]
5. *Yom Kippur* (יוֹם כִּפּוּר) or the Day of Atonement (Leviticus 23:26-32)
6. *Sukkot* (סֻכּוֹת) or the Feast of Tabernacles (Leviticus 23:33-44)
7. *Shemini Atzeret* (שְׁמִינִי עֲצֶרֶת) or the Eighth Day Assembly (Leviticus 23:39b)

Why do these seven appointed times, observed throughout the year, bear significance for God's people? What do they teach us about important things in the past history of God's people, but also important things to come in the future?

- **Passover** or *Pesach* is to specifically teach of God's past and future dealings in salvation history. Deliverance from Ancient Israel's bondage to slavery in Egypt and from the clutches of Pharaoh is recalled, and for Believers today the reality of our freedom in Yeshua from the condemnation of sin, are all to be remembered at this time of great celebration.

- The **Festival of Unleavened Bread** or *Chag HaMatzah* and the eight days of avoiding leaven is an important time to not only reflect upon the Ancient Israelites having to eat the bread of haste, but also for Believers to reflect and deal with some of the sin that can often creep into our lives. Purification from the stains of transgression, and turning ourselves toward the Bread of Life, Messiah Yeshua, is a beneficial exercise.

- *Shavuot* or the **Feast of Weeks** honors two wonderful events. On this day during Moses' era, the Decalogue was given from the heights of Mount Sinai. Some 1,300 years later, after the ascension of Yeshua into Heaven, the Holy Spirit was poured out upon the Believers assembled in Jerusalem. Each year on this special day, Messianic Believers can

---

[48] For more information and teaching on *Shabbat*, consult the *Messianic Sabbath Helper* by TNN Press.

[49] Also commonly known by the Greek-derived term Pentecost.

[50] *Yom Teruah* is observed in the Jewish tradition, of both the First Century C.E. and today, as *Rosh HaShanah* or the Civil New Year (m.*Rosh HaShanah* 1:1).

- remember these two powerful events, and pray for additional power and revelation.[51]

- In Jewish tradition, **Yom Teruah** is observed as *Rosh HaShanah* or the Civil New Year, with the blowing of the *shofar* (שׁוֹפָר) or ram's horn. Historically, this has been a season for the Jewish community to do *teshuvah* (תְּשׁוּבָה),[52] or perform a return to God for His faithfulness and blessing. But it is also a time to mark the beginning of the ten days that lead up to the Day of Atonement. *Rosh HaShanah* begins the Ten Days of Awe, a season of special reflection on the previous year.

- **Yom Kippur** or the **Day of Atonement** is considered the holiest day on the Hebrew calendar. Originally, the high priest of Israel bore the sins of the people and presented himself in the Holy of Holies for forgiveness. On this unique day God's people are instructed to deny themselves, or afflict their souls. Fasting and prayer are the major parts of this day. Today as Believers in Yeshua, we can reflect upon His finished work as not only the required sacrifice for our sins, but also His unique service for us as our High Priest. We can also use *Yom Kippur* as a specific time to offer up prayers and intercession for the lost of Planet Earth—especially Jewish people who do not yet know the Messiah.

- The **Feast of Tabernacles** or **Sukkot** is an eight-day celebration where we build our temporary *sukkah* (סֻכָּה) and reflect on God dwelling among His people. Here, thankfulness, praise, and special consideration for the provisions made for us by Him should be the focus. It is also beneficial to look forward to the coming days when the Messiah Himself will come to tabernacle with us in His Kingdom on Earth.[53]

If you are a Jewish Believer in Yeshua, have the appointed times at all taken on new significance and depth, as you now remember them every year? What are the similarities and differences between a traditional Jewish observance, and your new Messianic Jewish observance? If you are a non-Jewish Believer from an evangelical Christian background, how have the appointed times added richness to your understanding of the gospel and your faith in Jesus? Do you think that today's Christians can learn much more about the Messiah from the *moedim*?

Today's Messianic movement has been uniquely positioned to help all of God's people learn to appreciate both the Sabbath and appointed times. We get to show others that these were not ordinances exclusively for His people in the past, but can have continuing relevance and value for His people right now. They are "a shadow of the things to come...the substance [of which] belongs to Christ" (Colossians 2:17, ESV).[54]

---

[51] For more information and teaching on the Spring appointed times, consult the *Messianic Spring Holiday Helper* by TNN Press.

[52] The term *teshuvah*, itself based on the verb *shuv* (שׁוּב), means "return to God, repentance" (*Jastrow*, 1703).

[53] For more information and teaching on the Fall appointed times, consult the *Messianic Fall Holiday Helper* by TNN Press.

[54] Consult the article "Does the New Testament Annul the Biblical Appointments?" by J.K. McKee.

## Concluding Thoughts

As you consider *Emor* this week, it is my hope and prayer that the Holy One of Israel is speaking directly to you. How do you approach the Lord's appointed times? Do you truly bask in His presence on *Shabbat*? Do you glory in the accomplishments of Yeshua at each one of the feasts? Are you truly interested in allowing the appointed times of the Lord to instruct you in His ways and His ongoing progress of salvation history? What do the appointed times teach you about the future?

God's people get to visibly demonstrate that they are His by remembering the appointed times. Each one of us makes up His Kingdom of priests, serving as His representatives among the masses of sinful humanity (cf. 1 Peter 2:9). Does your Messianic congregation or fellowship make *Shabbat* and the appointed feasts a time for reaching out to others, and in demonstrating the goodness of our Heavenly Father to others? Are they used as times to bless others with what He has done for us? Or, are the appointed times used to condemn and harass those who presently do not keep them, or think that they are unimportant? **If timing is everything**, then position yourself to be a beacon of His light and salvation to all you encounter—not only during the appointed times—but during all times!

# *B'har* בְּהַר
## On the mount
## "The Faithful Jubilee"

> Leviticus 25:1-26:2
> Jeremiah 32:6-27

In our short *parashah* for this week, various commandments are given about the Sabbatical years for the Promised Land, the jubilee,[55] and more instruction about how God's people are to treat their neighbors.[56] As you read and reflect upon this selection, you can readily conclude that the Lord is very serious about molding a faithful people who would depend upon Him for His provision. *B'har* opens by detailing the main instruction about Sabbatical years:

"The LORD then spoke to Moses at Mount Sinai, saying, 'Speak to the sons of Israel and say to them, "When you come into the land which I shall give you, then the land shall have a sabbath to the LORD. Six years you shall sow your field, and six years you shall prune your vineyard and gather in its crop, but during the seventh year the land shall have a sabbath rest, a sabbath to the LORD; you shall not sow your field nor prune your vineyard"'" (Leviticus 25:1-4).

The commandment to take one day in seven, to rest and remember the weekly *Shabbat*—is now mirrored on an annual cycle. Every seventh year all of the arable land is to have a rest from crop production. Furthermore, after seven sets of seven weeks of years (or forty-nine years), a fiftieth year of jubilee is to be proclaimed (Leviticus 25:8). On the

---

[55] Leviticus 25:1-22.
[56] Leviticus 25:35-55.

fiftieth year or year of jubilee, the land is again to remain fallow and have its rest from crop production:

"You shall have the fiftieth year as a jubilee; you shall not sow, nor reap its aftergrowth, nor gather in *from* its untrimmed vines. For it is a jubilee; it shall be holy to you. You shall eat its crops out of the field" (Leviticus 25:11-12).

During the season of jubilee it would be almost three years before a crop could be harvested (years 49 and 50 with fallow land, and year 51 for the growing season). These commandments were obviously designed to develop a faithful people who trust and depend upon God for their provision and well being (cf. Leviticus 25:20-22).

After watching the Most High provide for His people for seven consecutive Sabbatical years, the year of jubilee (Heb. *yoveil*, יוֹבֵל) was to be proclaimed (Leviticus 25:10). *But what was this year of jubilee to be?* Beyond simply letting the land remain fallow on this year, the entire economic system would go through a significant adjustment (Leviticus 25:23-34). Once every fifty years, the restoration of Israel to its original tribal boundaries, coupled with the annulment of labor contracts, is commanded:

"You shall thus consecrate the fiftieth year and proclaim a release through the land to all its inhabitants. It shall be a jubilee for you, and each of you shall return to his own property, and each of you shall return to his family" (Leviticus 25:10).

The Lord obviously knew the propensity of many in Ancient Israel to take advantage of weaker or less-gifted people, and every fifty years it was His intention to restore the Promised Land and its inhabitants to a degree of the way it was when they originally took possession. By restoring property to their original families, and releasing people from debt or indentured servitude, proper relationships can be restored between the Land and the people of Israel. The proclamation of the year of jubilee, in essence, would level the playing field for successive generations of Israelites. The human tendency to want to control and accumulate power by possession would be minimized, if not periodically eliminated.

The Lord instituted these commandments because He knew, that in their own strength, the exact opposite of what He requires for a nation of priests—who are supposed to serve others—would likely be prevailing. He knew that fallen humanity's predisposition is to **wrong neighbor** rather than to **love neighbor**.[57] A secular humanist or Darwinist would conclude that people just have a tendency to gravitate toward a "survival of the fittest" mentality. However, in God's goodness to Ancient Israel, these cyclical ordinances were enacted so that His people could return a kind of normalcy every fifty years and during each future generation, with much concern for the poor and destitute (Leviticus 25:35-55). To further insure proper relationships among the Israelites' neighbors, the instruction following speaks against various kinds of wrongdoing (cf. Leviticus 26).

## Do No Wrong

Two times in *B'har*, admonitions against wrongdoing are strongly asserted. The Hebrew verb *yanah* (יָנָה), meaning "to oppress, to treat violently" (*AMG*),[58] suggests that this was a part of the reason why the jubilee year was instituted:

"If you make a sale, moreover, to your friend or buy from your friend's hand, you shall not wrong [*yanah*] one another. Corresponding to the number of years after the jubilee, you shall buy from your friend; he is to sell to you according to the number of years of

---

[57] Cf. Leviticus 19:18.
[58] Baker and Carpenter, 451.

crops. In proportion to the extent of the years you shall increase its price, and in proportion to the fewness of the years you shall diminish its price, for *it is* a number of crops he is selling to you. So you shall not wrong [*yanah*] one another, but you shall fear your God; for I am the LORD your God" (Leviticus 25:14-17).

Earlier in the Torah, the verb *yanah* is employed to refer to the treatment that was **not to be done** to the sojourner or stranger within the midst of Israel:

"You shall not wrong [*yanah*] a stranger or oppress him, for you were strangers in the land of Egypt" (Exodus 22:21).

"When a stranger resides with you in your land, you shall not do him wrong [*yanah*]" (Leviticus 19:33).

"He shall live with you in your midst, in the place which he shall choose in one of your towns where it pleases him; you shall not mistreat [*yanah*] him" (Deuteronomy 23:16).

As you read a little further in *B'har*, you will detect that the Israelites are not only told to do no wrong, but they are also specifically commanded to help or assist others who are less fortunate. In other words, we might say, **instead of wronging their neighbors, they were to love their neighbors:**

"If a fellow countryman of yours becomes so poor he has to sell part of his property, then his nearest kinsman is to come and buy back what his relative has sold…Now in case a countryman of yours becomes poor and his means with regard to you falter, then you are to sustain him, like a stranger or a sojourner, that he may live with you. Do not take usurious interest from him, but revere your God, that your countryman may live with you. You shall not give him your silver at interest, nor your food for gain…You shall not rule over him with severity, but are to revere your God" (Leviticus 25:25, 35-37, 43).

The legal principles of setting aside contracts for various time periods, redemption rights, forgoing interest on loans or debts, bankruptcy codes, and a variety of other business activities in modern times—may be able to trace their roots to some of the commandments in *B'har* that were to regulate Ancient Israel's economy. In various respects, you can even see links between these verses and the creation of some welfare states in the West.[59] In fact, when you study the history of the Jewish people and the Jewish tendency to often be "liberal" on many social issues, these positions have some of their roots in this very Torah portion.[60]

## Lack of Faith

Even though we can make various links and comparisons between modern-day legal and economic systems, and Israel's legal and economic system in the Ancient Near East, one thing is quite clear: **Ancient Israel had a difficult time following the basic tenets of the Sabbatical year and the year of jubilee.** When you examine history of Israel as recorded in the Tanakh, noticeably absent is the record that the Sabbatical years or jubilee years were ever remembered. Something must have been misunderstood for these

---

[59] Editor's note: Be aware of how much of the socialized medicine seen in places like Western Europe and Canada was originally promoted by many Christian clergy, who thought it was a Biblical and moral duty to provide free healthcare to the masses. Only the interference of government bureaucracy saw quality of care suffer, being unable to serve all people.

If the faith community itself would make an effort to help the sick and destitute, using their resources wisely in sponsoring clinics and education for healthy living, then a government administrated health system would be largely unnecessary.

[60] Cf. Levine, in *Etz Hayim*, pp 742-746.

commandments to not be followed. Was the faith required to let the ground remain fallow for a Sabbatical year just missing? Were the positions of agricultural influence too valuable for some to give up? It cannot be avoided that God declares how the Promised Land was His to give the Israelites, and how He definitely has the right to tell them how to administer it:

"The land, moreover, shall not be sold permanently, for the land is Mine; for you are *but* aliens and sojourners with Me. Thus for every piece of your property, you are to provide for the redemption of the land" (Leviticus 25:23-24).

God owned the Land, and simply allowed Israel to occupy it in order to produce crops or tend their livestock. If this principle had been understood and complied with, then many of the problems about owning and controlling land—and much of the oppression of the poor spoken against in the Prophets—could have been minimized. The problem is that the Ancient Israelites largely did not have the faith or confidence to follow these precepts. They may have believed the Word of God, but for some reason or another, found it difficult to implement following many of the commandments, which we are considering this week in *B'har*.

We need to remember that the God of Israel desires a people who will manifest faith and trust in Him. Abraham, Isaac, and Jacob were all figures of faith who modeled the appropriate actions that pleased Him. And, we know that without faith, it is impossible to please Him:

"And without faith it is impossible to please *Him*, for he who comes to God must believe that He is and *that* He is a rewarder of those who seek Him" (Hebrews 11:6; cf. 11:8-16).

## The Faithful Jubilee

As you ponder the instructions described in *B'har*, you can consider how many of our spiritual forbearers seemed to lack the faith to keep these commands. You should be reminded that it was because of a longstanding disobedience to them that Jeremiah's warning, about the required punishment for not obeying the Sabbatical year, was fulfilled by the exile of the Southern Kingdom to Babylon for seventy years:

"This whole land will be a desolation and a horror, and these nations will serve the king of Babylon seventy years...For thus says the LORD, 'When seventy years have been completed for Babylon, I will visit you and fulfill My good word to you, to bring you back to this place'" (Jeremiah 25:11; 29:10).

"Those who had escaped from the sword he carried away to Babylon; and they were servants to him and to his sons until the rule of the kingdom of Persia, to fulfill the word of the LORD by the mouth of Jeremiah, until the land had enjoyed its sabbaths. All the days of its desolation it kept sabbath until seventy years were complete" (2 Chronicles 36:20-21).

While the Southern Kingdom was punished for not observing the statutes of the Lord, consider how He must have been quite patient in allowing the people to ignore the command to let the Promised Land rest, for many centuries. Even though He had to issue judgment, Jeremiah's words continue with the promise of restoration: "'I know the plans that I have for you,' declares the LORD, 'plans for welfare and not for calamity to give you a future and a hope" (Jeremiah 29:11). The theme of Israel's restoration from captivity, and a return to the favor of God, is a consistent one seen throughout the Prophets.[61]

---

[61] For further consideration, consult the various entries on the Prophets in *A Survey of the Tanach for the Practical Messianic* by J.K. McKee.

The concept of a year of jubilee is one that resonates quite well with people of faith, hearing that all debts will be paid in full, and that those in bondage or captivity will be released. The announcement of the year of jubilee was to be delivered to Ancient Israel on *Yom Kippur*. It would symbolize that all debts to the Lord and one's fellow were completely gone. Just as the corporate sins of Israel were being dealt with, so every fifty years was it God's intention for the people to experience various physical releases and a fresh start:

"You are also to count off seven sabbaths of years for yourself, seven times seven years, so that you have the time of the seven sabbaths of years, *namely*, forty-nine years. You shall then sound a ram's horn abroad on the tenth day of the seventh month; on the day of atonement you shall sound a horn all through your land. You shall thus consecrate the fiftieth year and proclaim a release through the land to all its inhabitants. It shall be a jubilee for you, and each of you shall return to his own property, and each of you shall return to his family" (Leviticus 25:8-10).

The concept of a jubilee is expounded upon by the Prophet Isaiah, who declared that a *sh'nat-ratzon l'ADONAI* (שְׁנַת־רָצוֹן לַיהוָה) would come, along with considerable restoration to the downtrodden:

"The Spirit of the Lord GOD is upon me, because the LORD has anointed me to bring good news to the afflicted; He has sent me to bind up the brokenhearted, to proclaim liberty to captives and freedom to prisoners; to proclaim **the favorable year of the LORD** and the day of vengeance of our God; to comfort all who mourn, to grant those who mourn *in* Zion, giving them a garland instead of ashes, the oil of gladness instead of mourning, the mantle of praise instead of a spirit of fainting. So they will be called oaks of righteousness, the planting of the LORD, that He may be glorified. Then they will rebuild the ancient ruins, they will raise up the former devastations; and they will repair the ruined cities, the desolations of many generations" (Isaiah 61:1-4).

This prophecy is highly important, because when Yeshua stood up in the synagogue at Nazareth, and quoted from this text, He made an affirmative declaration that He was indeed the Messiah of Israel:

"And He came to Nazareth, where He had been brought up; and as was His custom, He entered the synagogue on the Sabbath, and stood up to read. And the book of the prophet Isaiah was handed to Him. And He opened the book and found the place where it was written, 'THE SPIRIT OF THE LORD IS UPON ME, BECAUSE HE ANOINTED ME TO PREACH THE GOSPEL TO THE POOR. HE HAS SENT ME TO PROCLAIM RELEASE TO THE CAPTIVES, AND RECOVERY OF SIGHT TO THE BLIND, TO SET FREE THOSE WHO ARE OPPRESSED, TO PROCLAIM THE FAVORABLE YEAR OF THE LORD.' And He closed the book, gave it back to the attendant and sat down; and the eyes of all in the synagogue were fixed on Him. And He began to say to them, '**Today this Scripture has been fulfilled in your hearing**'" (Luke 4:16-21).

As is quite frequent with Messianic fulfillment of prophecy, the essential reality of the year of jubilee—only here regarding a great release of the debt of sins—is now present in the lives of Believers. More by far is yet to come, as we do await Yeshua's Second Coming, His return to judge the world, and the establishment of His Kingdom from Zion. But in order to be a part of His coming Kingdom, we have to be those who have had the good news of salvation proclaimed to us, and the release from bondage to sin enacted within our lives!

Many questions arise in my heart as I meditate on *B'har*. I think the key to evaluating these questions is whether we each have greater faith than those who preceded us. Would we have honored the Sabbatical years and the jubilee had we been one of the Ancient Israelites?

More importantly, has a release from the penalty of sins been declared over us (cf. Colossians 2:14)? Can we rejoice in that the Lord has given us a new life of communion and fellowship with Him? Can we declare with confidence what He has done within us, and how Yeshua's work at Golgotha (Calvary) has transformed us? Are we at all committed to making sure that people are not consumed by that future day of vengeance foretold in the Scriptures?

If your faith in the Holy One of Israel is real, then your personal jubilee has been secured by the sacrificial death of the Messiah. **Your thankfulness can be exemplified by leading others to their own personal faithful jubilee!**

## *B'chuqotai* בְּחֻקֹּתַי
### By My Regulations
### "Remember the Land"

> Leviticus 26:3-27:34
> Jeremiah 16:19-17:24

*B'chuqotai* brings the Book of Leviticus to completion. For ten portions, the Torah student has been learning about many aspects of the Levitical priesthood. This includes instructions about the various offerings,[62] the establishment of the priesthood,[63] the laws of purification,[64] the Day of Atonement,[65] various prohibitions about heathen customs,[66] laws of holiness,[67] and the appointed times of the Lord.[68] Now, as the listing of instructions comes to a close, ch. 26 focuses our attention on the blessings of obedience versus the consequences of disobedience, and ch. 27 closes with details about voluntary contributions for the maintenance of the sanctuary. Among the things we are considering in our Torah portion for this week, one verse really jumped out at me:

"[T]hen I will remember My covenant with Jacob, and I will remember also My covenant with Isaac, and My covenant with Abraham as well, and I will remember the land" (Leviticus 26:42).

While reflecting on *B'chuqotai*, the reality of God's covenantal faithfulness to His chosen people kept coming to my mind. We are reminded that in spite of Israel's frequent disobedience to God, **He is still faithful** to keep the promises He originally made with the Patriarchs. According to the Scriptures, He will fulfill His Word and bring these promises to their eventual fruition. But here in *B'chuqotai*, we find that God's people too have some responsibility, and they too must act in order to receive of God's blessings.

---

[62] Leviticus 1:1-7:38.
[63] Leviticus 8:1-10:20.
[64] Leviticus 11:1-15:33.
[65] Leviticus 16:1-34.
[66] Leviticus 17:1-18:30.
[67] Leviticus 19:1-22:33.
[68] Leviticus 23:1-26:3.

## To Bless or To Curse

As *B'chuqotai* begins, Moses relays to the Israelites that if they obey the Lord, that He will bless and prosper them, saying:

"If you walk in My statutes and keep My commandments so as to carry them out, then I shall give you rains in their season, so that the land will yield its produce and the trees of the field will bear their fruit...Moreover, I will make My dwelling among you, and My soul will not reject you. I will also walk among you and be your God, and you shall be My people" (Leviticus 26:3-4; 11-12).

The main benefit of obeying God is that the Israelites would experience Him dwelling and walking among them. The Lord would be Israel's God, and Israel would be His special people. Obeying God is not something that people do out of some legalistic obligation or burden, but it is something that comes because of an intimate relationship one desires with the Creator. *This does not mean obedience is optional, though.* Moses must also speak God's words about disobedience to the Israelites, which are fairly severe:

"But if you do not obey Me and do not carry out all these commandments, if, instead, you reject My statutes, and if your soul abhors My ordinances so as not to carry out all My commandments, *and* so break My covenant, I, in turn, will do this to you: I will appoint over you a sudden terror, consumption and fever that will waste away the eyes and cause the soul to pine away; also, you will sow your seed uselessly, for your enemies will eat it up. I will set My face against you so that you will be struck down before your enemies; and those who hate you will rule over you, and you will flee when no one is pursuing you. If also after these things you do not obey Me, then I will punish you seven times more for your sins. I will also break down your pride of power; I will also make your sky like iron and your earth like bronze. Your strength will be spent uselessly, for your land will not yield its produce and the trees of the land will not yield their fruit. If then, you act with hostility against Me and are unwilling to obey Me, I will increase the plague on you seven times according to your sins. I will let loose among you the beasts of the field, which will bereave you of your children and destroy your cattle and reduce your number so that your roads lie deserted. And if by these things you are not turned to Me, but act with hostility against Me, then I will act with hostility against you; and I, even I, will strike you seven times for your sins. I will also bring upon you a sword which will execute vengeance for the covenant; and when you gather together into your cities, I will send pestilence among you, so that you shall be delivered into enemy hands. When I break your staff of bread, ten women will bake your bread in one oven, and they will bring back your bread in rationed amounts, so that you will eat and not be satisfied. Yet if in spite of this you do not obey Me, but act with hostility against Me, then I will act with wrathful hostility against you, and I, even I, will punish you seven times for your sins. Further, you will eat the flesh of your sons and the flesh of your daughters you will eat. I then will destroy your high places, and cut down your incense altars, and heap your remains on the remains of your idols, for My soul shall abhor you. I will lay waste your cities as well and will make your sanctuaries desolate, and I will not smell your soothing aromas. I will make the land desolate so that your enemies who settle in it will be appalled over it. You, however, I will scatter among the nations and will draw out a sword after you, as your land becomes desolate and your cities become waste. Then the land will enjoy its sabbaths all the days of the desolation, while you are in your enemies' land; then the land will rest and enjoy its sabbaths. All the days of *its* desolation it will observe the rest which it did not observe on your sabbaths, while you were living on it" (Leviticus 26:14-35).

As you read this lengthy list of punishments—some of which are quite grotesque—the gravity of disobeying God is very apparent.[69] **The Lord does not desire His people to disobey Him,** yet each time Israel will refuse to obey Him, the severity of the punishment against them will increase. First comes illness, followed by defeat from the enemies of Israel. Next, a famine ravages the Land. Then, wild beasts are sent to devour children and livestock. A siege comes from a foreign power that imposes incredible hardship on Israel, including people eating their own children. Finally, when obedience is not achieved, God will scatter or exile Israel among the nations.

What is interesting to note is that during this listing of punishments for disobedience—no less than four times—Moses is instructed to communicate that the judgments will be "seven times more" (Leviticus 26:18; 21, 24, 28) for the sins. God serves as a Judge issuing the sentence for breaking a law. In His justice system regarding the proper treatment of the Promised Land, a seven-fold payment is required to satisfy severe sins of disobedience. This section concludes with a reminder to Ancient Israel about the requirement for Sabbath rests to the Land.

When reading through this, you can see how the Lord is very interested in the Promised Land receiving its Sabbath rest. One way or another, He is going to make sure that His Land has its rest. Then, while the Land is enjoying its Sabbath rest, His people will be separated from it in exile:

"As for those of you who may be left, I will also bring weakness into their hearts in the lands of their enemies. And the sound of a driven leaf will chase them, and even when no one is pursuing they will flee as though from the sword, and they will fall. They will therefore stumble over each other as if *running* from the sword, although no one is pursuing; and you will have *no strength* to stand up before your enemies. But you will perish among the nations, and your enemies' land will consume you. So those of you who may be left will rot away because of their iniquity in the lands of your enemies; and also because of the iniquities of their forefathers they will rot away with them" (Leviticus 26:36-39).

## Remember the Land

As you read further on in our *parashah*, you see how the covenant-keeping God of Israel is prophetically declaring His plan to restore His exiled people to the Promised Land after it experiences its years of Sabbath rest. But it is not enough for the Promised Land to just lay fallow for a period of time, as there are some requirements His exiled people will have to demonstrate. In order for them to be returned to the Promised Land, the Lord requires His scattered people **to confess and repent of the sins that exiled them out of it in the first place:**

"If they confess their iniquity and the iniquity of their forefathers, in their unfaithfulness which they committed against Me, and also in their acting with hostility against Me—I also was acting with hostility against them, to bring them into the land of their enemies—or if their uncircumcised heart becomes humbled so that they then make amends for their iniquity, then I will remember My covenant with Jacob, and I will remember also My covenant with Isaac, and My covenant with Abraham as well, and I will remember the land. For the land will be abandoned by them, and will make up for its sabbaths while it is made desolate without them. They, meanwhile, will be making amends for their iniquity, because they rejected My ordinances and their soul abhorred My statutes.

---

[69] For even more prophetic details, read the curses of Deuteronomy 28.

Yet in spite of this, when they are in the land of their enemies, I will not reject them, nor will I so abhor them as to destroy them, breaking My covenant with them; for I am the LORD their God. But I will remember for them the covenant with their ancestors, whom I brought out of the land of Egypt in the sight of the nations, that I might be their God. I am the LORD" (Leviticus 26:40-45).

God's exiled people are required to acknowledge the wrong that they have committed before Him (Leviticus 26:40). They must recognize how their transgressions have kept them from a right relationship before Him. Israel must acknowledge that its ancestors committed evil and acted with hostility against God, and desire corporate forgiveness and restoration.

The Lord does acknowledge that as Israel repents of its sin, "I walked contrary to them and brought them into the land of their enemies" (Leviticus 26:41, RSV). This *qeri* (קְרִי), or "opposition, contrariness" (*BDB*),[70] was required because the severe sins of Israel had to be judged—although we do not see any implication here *that God wanted* to judge His people. Quite contrary to this, Moses communicates how the Lord will remember His covenants with the Patriarchs, and that He will remember His covenant with the Land (Leviticus 26:42). Then, the blessings of remembrance and the mercy and faithfulness of Him toward His people can again be bestowed (Leviticus 26:43-45).

After the Promised Land has had its Sabbath rests, the Lord will restore it to Israel. God says He will not reject, abhor, or destroy Israel for breaking the covenants with Him (Leviticus 26:44). Instead, this great restoration will be done *l'einei ha'goyim* (הַגּוֹיִם לְעֵינֵי) or "before the eyes of the nations" (Leviticus 26:45, YLT), as a great testimony of His faithfulness to those who are repentant.

## The Promised Land Today

It is interesting to see how the words of *B'chuqotai* do not just compose some kind of farfetched idealism—but they involve prophecies being fulfilled in our day. In the past century, the Land of Israel went from being largely desolate and underdeveloped, to now being a place of great agricultural and economic prosperity. Via the advent of the Zionist movement, and many Jews wanting to return home to the Promised Land, we can certainly consider how much (or at least some) of their attention was directed to words like Leviticus 26:35-38 in wanting to once again have a safe Jewish homeland.

Throughout Jewish history we see how many lived in the lands of their enemies, or at least those of people who were not always neighborly to them. There was often very little strength to stand up to the authorities, and Jewish communities were frequently harassed, restricted, regulated, and subjected to various degrees of persecution. Is it possible that after all of the persecutions, pogroms, inquisitions, and the Holocaust—some of the inheritors of God's promises began to confess their sins and the iniquities of their ancestors? It appears that in God's mercy toward His people, He heard their pleas and responded by making a way to restore them to the Promised Land. The creation of the modern-day State of Israel in the Middle East is a great testimony to God honoring His word to "remember the land" (Leviticus 26:42). Today, the Jewish people have their own state and homeland, that is a regional power quite capable of defending itself, and has great respect in the eyes of many nations.

---

[70] *BDB*, 899.

Much more regarding Israel, of course, may be said to be transpiring. Today in the Messianic movement, not only have we witnessed thousands upon thousands of Jewish people come to faith in Messiah Yeshua—but also a great number of evangelical Believers embrace their Hebraic Roots and consider the value of following God's Torah. *God is bringing His people together in a unique way.*

The emerging Messianic community we see forming in our generation has a way to go, involving a great deal of Bible study and consideration for the mission that the Father wants us to perform. I think people are beginning to see that as important as the formation of the State of Israel has been, there is much more on God's agenda that needs to be accomplished. **He will remember the Promised Land.** But in order for any of us, whether we be Jewish Believers who can become Israeli citizens, or non-Jewish Believers who become part of the Messianic movement—*the key is that we confess and repent of our sins.* Only by acknowledging that we have committed things abominable and unacceptable in the eyes of our Creator, can we be restored to His purpose. Individual redemption must precede corporate redemption.

**Have you offered the necessary prayers of confession?** Only when we have all done this, can all of the great promises, the Father has issued regarding His Land, come to pass! Only then can Yeshua the Messiah return to take up His throne from Jerusalem.

# COMMENTARY ON NUMBERS

## *Bamidbar* בְּמִדְבַּר
### In the wilderness
### "More Than Just a Number"

> Numbers 1:1-4:20
> Hosea 2:1-22

*Bamidbar* is the first Torah portion of the Book of Numbers, from which this text takes its traditional Hebrew name. The first words in this *parashah* describe how Israel is going to spend the next thirty-eight years "in the wilderness" (Heb. *b'midbar*, בְּמִדְבָּר). During this journey Israel will learn to depend upon the Lord and follow Him, eventually being able to occupy the Promised Land. Great trials are on the horizon, as the nurturing process will mold Israel into a set-apart people uniquely chosen to be God's light to the nations:

"Then the LORD spoke to Moses in the wilderness of Sinai, in the tent of meeting, on the first of the second month, in the second year after they had come out of the land of Egypt, saying, 'Take a census of all the congregation of the sons of Israel, by their families, by their fathers' households, according to the number of names, every male, head by head from twenty years old and upward, whoever *is able to* go out to war in Israel, you and Aaron shall number them by their armies'" (Numbers 1:1-3).

As you consider *Bamidbar* this week, you can readily appreciate why it is commonly called "Numbers."[1] There are many facts and figures transcribed, as Moses is requested to take a census of the male population eligible for military service. As I spent some time considering various aspects of the tabulation process, what came to my mind was the reality **that the Ancient Israelites were more than just "numbers" to God.** The Holy One demonstrated some concern for not only these people, but also demonstrates concern up until today—for the destinies of each one of His human children and how they fit into His plan for the ages.

Although there has been a previous census mentioned in the collection of finances for the Tabernacle (Exodus 38:26), it was not the specific reckoning of people that we see in the Book of Numbers. We get to finally see some of details of how large the Israelite Exodus was from Egypt, and obviously how they needed the Lord's provision. We have to remember that these events took place over 3,300 years ago in the general area today

---

[1] The English title "Numbers" is a carryover from the Greek Septuagint. The LXX's Jewish translators chose the name *Arithmoi* (ΑΡΙΘΜΟΙ), meaning "numbers."

known as the Sinai Peninsula.[2] Now that we will begin to focus in on the actual people involved in the Exodus, it is difficult to imagine how, given the primitive conditions, Israel could make its trek. As the accounting begins and you contemplate the numbers, you realize that we are easily dealing with several hundred thousand people.[3] Moving these people through a wilderness environment for a total of forty years was indeed a miraculous achievement. Here in *Bamidbar*, we can begin to appreciate the level of organization and cooperation that made much of this possible.

## Organizational Structure

It might be difficult for us to fathom several hundred thousand people with various belongings and livestock, bivouacked in the desert. The logistical needs including food, water, and basic sanitation for this amount of people is overwhelming (even though it might not be that much bigger than a giant sports stadium filled to capacity along with thousands of tailgaters). Thankfully, God was responsible for providing the basic sustenance, water, and there were instructions in place to deal with the sanitation problems (cf. Deuteronomy 23:13). *Some degree of organization had already been implemented.*

In *Bamidbar*, we witness that the Ancient Israelites are very much structured by various tribal, clan, and family units. When the Israelites left Egypt, they had the accommodating will to depart in a kind of martial array (Exodus 13:18), requiring people to know their place within the social framework. A group of people as large as Israel does not move in this manner, without a substantial degree of cooperation among the different families, clans, and tribes. But, if we remember back to some of the early challenges experienced during Moses' tenure of leadership, we should recall how his father-in-law Jethro was very instrumental in helping establish some specific organizational structure to the mass of Israelites:

"Furthermore, you shall select out of all the people able men who fear God, men of truth, those who hate dishonest gain; and you shall place *these* over them *as* leaders of thousands, of hundreds, of fifties and of tens…So Moses listened to his father-in-law and did all that he had said. Moses chose able men out of all Israel and made them heads over the people, leaders of thousands, of hundreds, of fifties and of tens" (Exodus 18:21, 24-25).

As this advice was instituted, the people of Israel began to have different levels of leadership, which brought additional order into the camp, and alleviated much of the stress that was upon Moses and the elders. It seems, from a practical standpoint, that by the time

---

[2] There is debate over the exact route of the Exodus, with some favoring different sites in the modern-day Sinai Peninsula, and others alternative locations, perhaps even in modern-day Saudi Arabia. Consult Duane A. Garrett, ed., et. al., *NIV Archaeological Study Bible* (Grand Rapids: Zondervan, 2005), pp 108-109, 112; and the FAQ on the TNN website, "Exodus, Route of."

[3] Editor's note: In Numbers 2:32 we are told "the total of the numbered men of the camps by their armies, [was] 603,550," which according to some would make the total population of the Israelites somewhere in the range of 2-3 million. There are many conservative scholars who have difficulty with this conclusion, pointing out how the Semitic term *elef* (אֶלֶף), often rendered as "thousand," does have cognates that can regard it meaning "troop" or "company." If 603 *elef* 550 is taken to mean something less than 603,550, then the total population of the Israelites is reduced to somewhere probably in the hundreds of thousands. Bible translations, though, tend to stay on the safe side with the rendering of "thousand."

For a further discussion, consult K.A. Kitchen, *On the Reliability of the Old Testament* (Grand Rapids: Eerdmans, 2003), 264; and the "Excursus on Large Numbers," in Timothy R. Ashley, *New International Commentary on the Old Testament: The Book of Numbers* (Grand Rapids: Eerdmans, 1993), pp 60-66. Also see the FAQ on the TNN website, "Exodus, numbers of."

the census seen in Numbers takes place—thirteen months after the departure from Egypt—that the Israelites have already positioned themselves around the Tent of Meeting according to their tribes. At this point, Moses and Aaron formalize the specific directives from God, delivered in our Torah portion. Now, even more order is established between the different tribal units:

"Now the LORD spoke to Moses and to Aaron, saying, 'The sons of Israel shall camp, each by his own standard, with the banners of their fathers' households; they shall camp around the tent of meeting at a distance'" (Numbers 2:1-2).

After processing some of the logistical thoughts, and wondering how this mass of people could function in the wilderness, I concluded that it was simply **the miraculous intervention of God Himself** which ultimately had to sustain Israel.

## Everybody Counts!

As I reread the opening statements of *Bamidbar*, one expression really caught my attention. Moses and Aaron, in conducting the census, were to count each eligible male by their heads, *l'gulgelotam* (לְגֻלְגְּלֹתָם), "every male individually" (Numbers 1:2, NRSV) or "one by one" (NIV). **What did God mean by having these people counted "head-to-head"?**

I looked up the Hebrew term *gulgolet* (גֻּלְגֹּלֶת), frequently translated as "head," and naturally did a word study. In my reading, it seemed to me that the Lord was really interested in each individual person who was being numbered for service. When you speak to a person face-to-face—or head-to-head as it is here—you tend to have a very sincere and intimate conversation with one. You acknowledge the most recognizable part of the person with your most recognizable part. Note how much Moses wanted to see the face of the Most High, but was denied:

"The LORD said to Moses, 'I will also do this thing of which you have spoken; for you have found favor in My sight and I have known you by name.' Then Moses said, 'I pray You, show me Your glory!' And He said, 'I Myself will make all My goodness pass before you, and will proclaim the name of the LORD before you; and I will be gracious to whom I will be gracious, and will show compassion on whom I will show compassion.' But He said, 'You cannot see My face, for no man can see Me and live!' Then the LORD said, 'Behold, there is a place by Me, and you shall stand *there* on the rock; and it will come about, while My glory is passing by, that I will put you in the cleft of the rock and cover you with My hand until I have passed by. Then I will take My hand away and you shall see My back, but My face shall not be seen'" (Exodus 33:17-23).

Here, the Lord acknowledges that He knows Moses by his name, but He is not able to let Moses see His face—because according to this testimony, Moses would die. Apparently, a mortal cannot look directly upon the sight of pure holiness and live.

But as we contemplate this head-to-head experience of Numbers 1:2, we note that each of the Israelites may have had to look into the eyes of either Moses or Aaron, or at least would probably have had to see them as the census took place. *Do we see a desire from the Lord to recognize each person in the camp?* Certainly, the opportunity to present yourself to Moses and Aaron either at, or near the Tent of Meeting, would have been a great privilege. By this time in the wilderness journey, both Moses and Aaron had certainly distinguished themselves as anointed servants of God. Now as representatives of God, they are instructed to count each male who was twenty years old and over, who was eligible for military service.

I imagine how one would feel when it was his turn to be personally counted and be recognized by either Moses and Aaron, or at least some of those in Moses' and Aaron's close confidence. These were the two chosen representatives of God Himself who would hear your name, and see that it was tabulated for the purpose of the census. Thinking about this, what came to my mind was that this could have been like a graduation from school, or even a military commissioning ceremony. It could also be thought of as some kind of spiritual *ordination* in the minds of those who received the recognition of being counted, being listing for their responsibilities concerning the future journeys of Israel, and the battles, up ahead.

The Hebrew word *gulgolet* simply means "**skull**," in reference "for each person" or "enrolment by head count" (*HALOT*).[4] You are probably familiar with this term because the location where Yeshua was crucified outside Jerusalem was called Golgotha,[5] derived from either *gulgolet* (גֻּלְגֹּלֶת) or the Aramaic *Gulgulta* (גֻּלְגָּלְתָּא), meaning Place of a Skull (likely due to some kind of rock formation).[6] Does the counting in Numbers 1:2 reveal anything more than what appears on the surface?

The term *gulgolet* appears twelve times in the Tanakh: five times it appears in this Torah portion,[7] and it is seen twice in Exodus,[8] when the manna was gathered for each family and when the statute for the poll or head tax was being declared:[9]

"This is what the LORD has commanded, 'Gather of it every man as much as he should eat; you shall take an omer apiece [*l'gulgolet*, לְגֻלְגֹּלֶת] according to the number of persons each of you has in his tent'" (Exodus 16:16).

"[A] beka a head [*l'gulgolet*] (*that is*, half a shekel according to the shekel of the sanctuary), for each one who passed over to those who were numbered, from twenty years old and upward, for 603,550 men" (Exodus 38:26).

Within the Torah portion *Bamidbar*, the Lord calls upon Moses to count the eligible men head-to-head:

"[A]nd they assembled all the congregation together on the first of the second month. Then they registered by ancestry in their families, by their fathers' households, according to the number of names, from twenty years old and upward, head by head [*l'gulgelotam*, לְגֻלְגְּלֹתָם]...Now the sons of Reuben, Israel's firstborn, their genealogical registration by their families, by their fathers' households, according to the number of names, head by head [*l'gulgelotam*], every male from twenty years old and upward, whoever *was able to* go out to war...Of the sons of Simeon, their genealogical registration by their families, by their fathers' households, their numbered men, according to the number of names, head by head [*l'gulgelotam*], every male from twenty years old and upward, whoever *was able to* go out to war" (Numbers 1:18, 20, 22).

You can assume that each of the remaining tribes was also recognized and numbered by its "skulls." The leadership of Israel, in the census taking, has some kind of face-to-face

---

[4] *HALOT*, 1:191.
 This is different from another word commonly rendered as "head," *rosh* (רֹאשׁ), which dependent on context can regard authority in various places.
[5] Mark 15:22; Matthew 27:33; John 19:17.
[6] The common term Calvary is derived from the Latin rendering *Calvariae*.
[7] Numbers 1:2, 18, 20, 22; 3:47.
[8] Exodus 16:16; 38:26.
[9] The other times *gulgolet* appears in the Tanakh are: Judges 9:53; 2 Kings 9:35; 1 Chronicles 10:10; 23:3, 24.

encounter with the people numbered—letting them know that they have value as appreciated members of the community. *There is certainly something impressive about having a leader recognize your existence.* In a representative way, the Holy One is letting Moses, Aaron, and the elders perform a vital function in encouraging the Israelites. What this said to me is that the Lord is very interested in the individual, and that He looks upon each person as a unique creation. **Everybody counts to Him!**

Continuing in this Torah portion, you read about the different people mentioned and realize that the men listed are not just numbers, but instead are names with distinct tribal identifications (Numbers 2). Each of them descended from named fathers, and each has been granted a position among his peers—something truly encouraging if you were an Egyptian slave only thirteen months prior. If you read and think about the names, recognize how the Father often allows people to live out the etymological meaning of their names. Realize that each individual has worth and value in *His eyes*, even if one does not mean very much to others. Here, the Lord appreciates the roles of the Exodus generation so much, that a special census is taken of them for posterity.

It is rather amazing to think that the Lord would have taken the time to record who these Israelites were—when many people today do not often know who their great-grandparents were, and do not have genealogical records in their possession. Was this census like a selective service registration for the military draft? How would this have affected the individual Israelites' place in society? How would it have influenced Israel's transition from a disparate nation of slaves into an organized nation of priests?

As I contemplated these things, I had a very sobering thought: of all the names I was looking at among the Israelites, *only two* of this generation actually made it into the Promised Land. We will learn in later Torah readings that only Joshua and Caleb, because of their faith, are spared from dying in the wilderness. All of the rest perish and do not make it across the Jordan River.

## The Rock of Our Salvation

Remember that King David, and other Psalmists and Prophets, have often referred to the Lord the Rock (Heb. *tzur*, צוּר):

"The LORD is my rock and my fortress and my deliverer, My God, my rock, in whom I take refuge; My shield and the horn of my salvation, my stronghold" (Psalm 18:2).

"And they remembered that God was their rock, and the Most High God their Redeemer" (Psalm 78:35).

I believe these passages are all about the Messiah of Israel. *He is the Head. He is the Chief Cornerstone.* Thinking about Yeshua, and my earlier examination of the word *gulgolet*, one cannot help but think about His execution—atoning for our sins:

"They took Yeshua, therefore, and He went out, bearing His own cross, to the place called the Place of a Skull, which is called in Hebrew, Golgotha. There they crucified Him, and with Him two other men, one on either side, and Yeshua in between" (John 19:17-18).

This event is what every person must look to for salvation. We all are counted and numbered among the people of the world, **but it is imperative that you be counted among the company of the redeemed!** It does not matter if a person is of the numbers of the bloodlines of Israel, because ultimately only a remnant of Israel and humanity at large will probably decide to believe in the finished work of the Messiah. The author of Hebrews observes,

"For we who have believed enter that rest, just as He has said, 'AS I SWORE IN MY WRATH, THEY SHALL NOT ENTER MY REST' [Psalm 95:11], although His works were finished from the foundation of the world" (Hebrews 4:3).

Remember, the Israelite males who were recognized, numbered, and commissioned in *Bamidbar* lacked the faith in God to believe—and consequently perished in the wilderness. Only a remnant of two believed and entered into the Promised Land.

Today, many in the Messianic community believe that claiming some kind of identity in either Judaism or Israel is sufficient enough to be tallied among the redeemed. *Do not be deceived!* According to Isaiah's prophecies, only a remnant avoids the judgment that will be unleashed upon the unrighteous:

"A remnant will return, the remnant of Jacob, to the mighty God. For though your people, O Israel, may be like the sand of the sea, *only* a remnant within them will return; a destruction is determined, overflowing with righteousness. For a complete destruction, one that is decreed, the Lord GOD of hosts will execute in the midst of the whole land" (Isaiah 10:21-23).

Brothers and sisters, make sure that you believe in the atoning work accomplished by Yeshua at the rock of Golgotha! Make sure that you are not just numbered among community of Israel because you make a profession of faith in Israel's Messiah—but that **you are actually counted among the redeemed remnant** who knows Him as Lord and Savior!

# *Naso* נָשֹׂא
## Take
## "Blessings and Shalom"

| Numbers 4:21-7:89 |
|---|
| Judges 13:2-25 |

The most striking feature in this week's Torah portion, *Naso*, is the reciting of what has become known as the Aaronic Benediction. While a standard feature of the Jewish liturgical tradition and of the weekly *Shabbat* service, Christians are certainly familiar with this blessing as well:

"Then the LORD spoke to Moses, saying, 'Speak to Aaron and to his sons, saying, "Thus you shall bless the sons of Israel. You shall say to them: The LORD bless you, and keep you; the LORD make His face shine on you, and be gracious to you; the LORD lift up His countenance on you, and give you peace." So they shall invoke My name on the sons of Israel, and I *then* will bless them'" (Numbers 6:22-27).

*Naso*, of course, includes much more information than just its record of the Aaronic Benediction. *Naso* is a rather interesting Torah reading because it gives meticulous instruction about a wide variety of topics. Initially, as Numbers 4 concludes, the *parashah* begins by summarizing additional details about the priestly functions of two of the Levitical families numbered and responsible for specific duties concerning the Tabernacle and the altar. The Gershonites and the Merarites are explicitly selected for transporting and constructing the Tabernacle.[10] What is interesting to note, just as we saw in *Bamidbar* last week, is how the Lord is very concerned about each individual and the task that is assigned to them: "Assign to each man the specific things he is to carry" (Numbers 4:32b, NIV). This level of detail allows one to understand more clearly why the God of Israel is not some remote or distant Deity, but is instead a very personal God who is intimately involved in the details of life.

In Numbers 5, after describing some conditions that require removal from the camp,[11] the narrative shifts to an instructional overview of the law of jealousy and how Israelite men were to handle perceived or real jealousy with their wives.[12] In Numbers 6, the ritual of the Nazirite vow is explained,[13] culminating with what has been traditionally labeled the instruction for declaring forth the Aaronic Benediction (Numbers 6:22-27). Finally in Numbers 7, our selection then moves ahead in time to the events that occurred when the Tabernacle was first built and its dedication was celebrated by the tribes of Israel.[14] The final crescendo for our *parashah* this week comes when Moses is given the privilege of hearing the voice of God:

"Now when Moses went into the tent of meeting to speak with Him, he heard the voice speaking to him from above the mercy seat that was on the ark of the testimony, from between the two cherubim, so He spoke to him" (Numbers 7:89).

With this wide range of instruction and information seen in *Naso*, it is normal for us to ask God about what He is trying to communicate. From the minute detail regarding which individuals will handle specific implements, to the dedication of the Tabernacle and the presence of the Lord in the camp, much is covered. As each piece of instruction is recorded, one might begin to remember how one of the great challenges of Ancient Israel's departure from Egypt was their transition into becoming a nation of priests *from among a population of slaves*. Many of *Naso*'s instructions were designed to bring an increasing degree of order into the assembly of these people.

As I meditated upon the wide variety of instructions, the significance of the Aaronic Benediction seemed to come to mind the most often—because we do certainly hear it at every *Shabbat* service. Here, in the midst of discussing a variety of ways to bring a semblance of order into the emerging nation of Israel, the Lord instructed Moses on how to have Aaron and his sons bless the people. **Have you ever considered the blessing of having this prayer spoken over you?** Let us look at the text.

---

[10] Numbers 4:21-49.
[11] Numbers 5:1-4.
[12] Numbers 5:5-31.
[13] Numbers 6:1-21.
[14] Numbers 7:1-89.

## The Power of the Name

The Aaronic Benediction, appearing in Numbers 6:22-27, states,

Y'varekh'kha ADONAI v'yishmerekha.
Ya'er ADONAI panav eleikha
   vichunekha.
Yissa ADONAI panav eleikha v'yasem
   l'kha shalom.

יְבָרֶכְךָ יְהוָה וְיִשְׁמְרֶךָ
יָאֵר יְהוָה פָּנָיו אֵלֶיךָ וִיחֻנֶּךָ
יִשָּׂא יְהוָה פָּנָיו אֵלֶיךָ וְיָשֵׂם
לְךָ שָׁלוֹם

**And the LORD spoke to Moses, saying, "Speak to Aaron and to his sons, saying, 'Thus shall you bless the Israelites. Say to them: May the LORD bless you and guard you. May the LORD light up His face to you and grant grace to you; may the LORD lift up His face to you and give you peace.' And they shall set My name over the Israelites, and I Myself shall bless them"** (Numbers 6:22-27, Alter).

God instructed Moses in a very succinct way on how Aaron and his sons were to bless the people of Israel. If you dig a little bit closer into some of the terms used in this blessing, you might begin to understand how significant it was for them to be spoken over the Israelites. We certainly do see how the Hebrew text is clear about the proper use of the Divine Name of God, and how powerful it can be. The priests were to tell the people that the Lord would: keep them, shine upon them, be gracious to them, lift His countenance upon them, and give them peace. When thinking about this, we might consider the vision of the Prophet Isaiah being taken up into Heaven, seeing the Holy One high and lifted up upon His throne:

"In the year of King Uzziah's death I saw the Lord sitting on a throne, lofty and exalted, with the train of His robe filling the temple. Seraphim stood above Him, each having six wings: with two he covered his face, and with two he covered his feet, and with two he flew. And one called out to another and said, 'Holy, Holy, Holy, is the LORD of hosts, the whole earth is full of His glory.' And the foundations of the thresholds trembled at the voice of him who called out, while the temple was filling with smoke" (Isaiah 6:1-4).

Recognize that when the Scriptures employ the same word three times—like *qadosh qadosh qadosh* (קָדוֹשׁ קָדוֹשׁ קָדוֹשׁ) in Isaiah 6:3—it is probably time for a Bible reader to pay close attention. *The Lord is trying to show us something very significant.*

In the Aaronic Benediction, the most holy name of God Himself, YHWH/YHVH (יהוה), is spoken over Israel **three times**—with some tremendous blessings attached. If you read the summary verse at the end of Numbers ch. 6 you are reminded of a great blessing: "Thus they shall link My name with the people of Israel, and I will bless them" (Numbers 6:27, NJPS). Here in this final verse of the prayer (which in the traditional liturgy is often not considered to be a part of the prayer, but only the narrative of Numbers), God describes the fact that His Divine Name will be placed upon the people of Israel.

When I read through Numbers 6:27, it made me think about how important our identification with God truly is, and how He uses His name to bring distinctiveness to His people. The *shem* (שֵׁם) of God often relates to "his reputation, fame...esp. as embodying the (revealed) character of" (*BDB*)[15] Him. But as I contemplated this concept, I was reminded of some of the age-old problems associated with the use of the Divine Name of our Creator, and how the enemy has cleverly, *and sometimes frequently*, made it a cause of division.

Many questions arise in some parts of today's broad Messianic community because Judaism has historically not pronounced the Divine Name of God. There is no doubt that it is clearly written in the Hebrew texts of the Tanakh. *Just looking at these verses in Numbers attests to that reality.* The Divine Name of God, YHWH/YHVH (יהוה), appears 6,828 times in the Hebrew Bible. The authors, compilers, or editors of the Tanakh did not have a difficult time declaring who they received their revelation from or the Creator they wished to specifically identify. However, following the Babylonian Diaspora, the Jewish people began to consider the Divine Name so holy that it was to be reserved only for the high priest to speak on *Yom Kippur* or the Day of Atonement. The Mishnah attests to this tradition:

"And the priests and people standing in the courtyard, when they would hear the Expressed Name [of the Lord] come out of the mouth of the high priest, would kneel and bow down and fall on their faces and say, 'Blessed be the name of the glory of his kingdom forever and ever'" (m.*Yoma* 6:2).[16]

There was a protocol established in Second Temple times for speaking the Divine Name of God—and those who would speak it out of place could be condemned to death for blasphemy.[17] When reviewing the text of the Apostolic Scriptures, it is clear that Yeshua and the Apostles adhered to this protocol. In the Gospels, Yeshua actually spends more time calling His Father, "Father" or "Abba"—than actually referring to Him as God or Lord. If Yeshua considered not speaking the name YHWH aloud to be an error of the Second Temple Judaism in which His ministry functioned, then there would be plenty of evidence in the Apostolic Scriptures supporting this, including charges of blasphemy against Him for verbalizing the name YHWH. If anything, though, it was Yeshua's claim of being the "I AM"—to actually be YHWH (Mark 14:63; Matthew 26:64-65; Luke 22:71; cf. Exodus 3:14)[18]—that condemned Him to death.

As Messianic Believers who are trying to return to the theology of the First Century Believers, who operated within the context of Second Temple Judaism, we must recognize that while our Heavenly Father has a proper name, **it was not used by Yeshua and the Apostles.** We must have the same kind of respect for the holiness of the name YHWH that they had. We should not hesitate to use appropriate titles for our Creator such as God or Lord, just as they were employed by Yeshua and the Apostles.

In recent years, some have claimed that the Father is "restoring" the usage of the Divine Name to His people. While this is interesting to consider, in most cases the enemy has gotten into the mix and made the Sacred Name a point of great contention and ultimately division. The Sacred Name sub-sector, not only in demanding widespread usage of the name YHWH, also claims that the English name Jesus errantly derives from "Zeus," even

---

[15] *BDB*, 1028.

[16] Jacob Neusner, trans., *The Mishnah: A New Translation* (New Haven and London: Yale University Press, 1988), 275.

[17] Cf. "God, names of," in Jacob Neusner and William Scott Green, eds., *Dictionary of Judaism in the Biblical Period* (Peabody, MA: Hendrickson, 2002), 259.

[18] For a further discussion, consult G.M. Burge, "'I Am' Sayings," in *Dictionary of Jesus and the Gospels*, pp 354-356.

though the Greek transliteration of *Yeshua* (יֵשׁוּעַ), *Iēsous* ('Iησοῦς), appears throughout the Septuagint—a Greek translation of the Hebrew Bible *of Jewish origin*. Having been in Messianic ministry now for well over a decade, I have had to interact with many Sacred Name Only people, and am sad to report that they have brought a great deal of problems into our young and fledgling Messianic faith community.

Should we not be wiser about the wiles of the Devil, and be better prepared and informed to handle the privilege of being called the people of God? Are we ready to really use His name? Considering all of the division and disrepute the Sacred Name Onlyists have often brought to the Messianic movement, *if you use the Divine Name regularly*, would it be appropriate to step back for a moment and (re)consider its usage?[19]

I believe we all need to more fully comprehend who the Lord is and how great His love for us actually is, so we can be a people who are really called by *and are worthy of* His name. Most importantly, we need to understand Him as our Heavenly Father, and have an intimate relationship with Him. **May this come quickly as we strive to know Him in deeper and more profound ways!**

## *B'ha'alotkha* בְּהַעֲלֹתְךָ
### When you set up
### "Arise, O Lord!"

> Numbers 8:1-12:16
> Zechariah 2:14-4:7

*B'ha'alotkha* conveys a variety of details about the early days of the wilderness journey of Ancient Israel. From a description of use of the *menorah* (מְנוֹרָה),[20] to amplification about the role of the Levites,[21] to alternative Passover allowances,[22] to the Israelites following the cloud,[23] to instructions about blowing twin silver trumpets,[24] to encampment movement procedures,[25] to selecting seventy elders to distribute the workload,[26] to the infamous incident when Moses is challenged by Aaron and Miriam[27]—this *parashah* is indeed "loaded" with a wide variety of topics to consider. Each descriptive scenario contains insight on how the Lord was firmly molding this unique group of people into a special nation for His own possession and purposes.

---

[19] For a further discussion, consult the articles "Sacred Name Concerns" and "Anti-Semitism in the Two-House Movement" by J.K. McKee.
  Some other useful thoughts, to witness how the Sacred Name agenda has caused severe problems with many of today's Messianic Jews, are seen in Aaron Eby and Toby Janicki, *Hallowed Be Your Name: Sanctifying God's Sacred Name* (Marshfield, MO: First Fruits of Zion, 2008).
[20] Numbers 8:1-4.
[21] Numbers 8:5-26.
[22] Numbers 9:1-14.
[23] Numbers 9:15-23.
[24] Numbers 10:24-10.
[25] Numbers 10:11-36.
[26] Numbers 11:16-30.
[27] Numbers 12:1-16.

As I pondered some of these things, I was reminded of how Israel was to be set-apart as a people of faith, relying on the Lord for its provision and guidance. I thought about how each of the distinctive things seen in our *parashah* this week communicate different aspects of God's holiness and/or involvement in the lives of the Israelites—but I also reflected on how these would be considered each year as the Torah cycle is read through once again. *Time and space limit us in being able to focus on every one of the above listed aspects.* The visual impressions of all of these activities is certainly vivid. Considering each of these circumstances, I tried to place myself among the masses of Israel, and I contemplated how I would have reacted to hearing the various instructions and whether or not I would learn from them.

For some reason, the proclamation which Moses declared prior to every wilderness departure became a definite point of focus. While it is frequently a part of the traditional liturgy in the Synagogue on *Shabbat*, it also points to the Lord's greatness as one who defends His people:

"Then it came about when the ark set out that Moses said, 'Rise up, O LORD! And let Your enemies be scattered, and let those who hate You flee before You.' When it came to rest, he said, 'Return, O LORD, *to* the myriad thousands of Israel'" (Numbers 10:35-36).

The simple statement, "Advance, O LORD! May Your enemies be scattered, and may Your foes flee before You!" (NJPS), seemed to take on more significance for me this year, as I have reflected on a few of the current conflicts in the Middle East, and how the enemies of Israel have been especially vociferous. I thought about the Ark of the Covenant, and pictured how the Levites would carefully lift it up, move it forward, and all of Israel would march with it—following the ubiquitous cloud that led their way. Naturally, what takes place in a traditional *Shabbat* service is that as Numbers 10:26 is read, a congregational ark is opened, and the Torah scroll is brought forth to be canted.[28] The comparison was not exactly overwhelming, but after further reflection I realized that my even knowing about what occurs in a traditional *Shabbat* service was, in itself, something to be very thankful for.

I began to realize that as a non-Jewish Believer in Messiah Yeshua, for the first time in perhaps many generations, I was actually considering some of the tangible events that took place in the history of the infancy of Israel. *I was not just looking at them as dusty Biblical history*, or as a part of the Scriptures to just quickly read through. The text I was studying and contemplating from Numbers was very meaningful—especially as our sovereign God has seen to its preservation for over three millennia! Certain procedures discussed in *B'ha'alotkha* began to take on some more significance. The thought of actually participating in these activities—even if just as a theoretical, ancient person—became real. Application of these instructions in modern times on some level became something to seriously consider, rather than simply reading and appreciating these as past historical events.

How should I apply what we are reading in this week's *parashah* to my own personal life? How do I appreciate their ancient setting, and do more than just be knowledgeable of what is recorded?

## Seven Pillars of Wisdom

At this point, wanting to focus on the significance of Numbers 10:35-36, I uncovered something that those who are only reading English Bibles are often not aware of. Those of

---

[28] Cf. Hertz, *Authorised Daily Prayer Book*, pp 473-475; Jules Harlow, ed., *Siddur Sim Shalom for Shabbat and Festivals* (New York: Rabbinical Assembly, 2007), 139.

you who have a Hebrew Bible can probably see that bracketing in Numbers 10:35-36 are two inverted *nun*s (נ).²⁹ This is not normal punctuation that one typically sees in the Bible. What do these *nun*s mean?

*V'yehi binso'a ha'aron v'yomer Moshe, "Qumah ADONAI v'yafutzu o'vekha v'yanusu mesanekha mipanekha," u'venuchoh yomar, "Shuvah ADONAI riv'vot alfei Yisrael"*

וַיְהִי בִּנְסֹעַ הָאָרֹן וַיֹּאמֶר מֹשֶׁה
כ
קוּמָה יְהוָה וְיָפֻצוּ אֹיְבֶיךָ וְיָנֻסוּ
מְשַׂנְאֶיךָ מִפָּנֶיךָ
וּבְנֻחֹה יֹאמַר שׁוּבָה יְהוָה רִבְבוֹת
אַלְפֵי יִשְׂרָאֵל כ

Numbers 10:35-36 are important verses in the Torah, communicating how Ancient Israel would move in the desert, and imploring God to protect Israel from its enemies. Seeing the two inverted *nun*s, I naturally wanted to know what they represented. Were these markings originally made by Moses, or were they later scribal notations to point out something to readers? J.H. Hertz, the editor of *Pentateuch and Haftorahs*, summarizes our options:

"These two verses are enclosed in inverted 'Nuns' to indicate either that they are not here in their original place (Talmud); or that they are taken from another source (possibly from 'the Book of the Wars of the Lord', see 21:14) and form a distinct section, scroll, or even 'book' of the Torah. Some of the Rabbis held that the Book of Numbers consisted of three sections...and accordingly, they counted a total of seven books of the Torah. Thus, according to Rabbi Johanan, 'Wisdom hath hewn out her seven pillars' (Proverbs 9:1) referred to the 'Seven' books of the Torah."³⁰

The textual explanation is that the two inverted *nun*s signify that there is some doubt as to whether or not Numbers 10:35-36 are actually in their correct place within the Hebrew text, being dislocated. The resource *Masorah of the Biblia Hebraica Stuttgartensia* observes how, "This suggestion is supported by the LXX [Septuagint] where verses 35-36 have been inserted between verses 33 and 34 (i.e., the order is 33, 35, 36, 34)."³¹ And in fact, the Greek Septuagint does include what we read as Numbers 10:33-36 in a different verse order from the Hebrew Masoretic Text:

[33] And they departed from the mount of the Lord a three days' journey; and the ark of the covenant of the Lord went before them a three days' journey to provide rest for them. [35] **And it came to pass when the ark set forward, that Moses said, Arise, O Lord, and let thine enemies be scattered: let all that hate thee flee.** [36] **And in the resting he said, Turn again, O Lord, the thousands** *and* **tens of**

---

²⁹ Karl Elliger and Wilhelm Rudolph, et. al., eds., *Biblica Hebraica Stuttgartensia* (Stuttgart: Deutche Bibelgesellschaft, 1977), 231; Aron Dotan, ed., *Biblia Hebraica Leningradensia* (Peabody, MA: Hendrickson, 2001), 213.

³⁰ Hertz, *Pentateuch & Haftorahs*, 613.

³¹ Page H. Kelley, Daniel S. Mynatt, and Timothy G. Crawford, eds., *The Masorah of Biblia Hebraica Stuttgartensia* (Grand Rapids: Eerdmans, 1998), pp 34-35.

Ashley also states, "scholars generally agree that [the inverted *nun*s] indicate that the early scribes thought verses so enclosed were displaced from their original context" (p 199).

**thousands in Israel.** [34] And the cloud overshadowed them by day, when they departed from the camp.[32]

If some textual witnesses of Numbers 10:33-36 have placed vs. 35-36 in a slightly different order, it does not change our understanding of anything at all in the wider narrative. Moses still implored the Lord to fight on behalf of Israel, and that His enemies would flee at His power.

Of course, the theological explanation offered by Hertz, for the inverted *nun*s, is also something quite interesting to ponder. Referencing Proverbs 9:1, we see, "Wisdom has built her house, she has hewn out her seven pillars." From this line of reasoning, the two *nun*s do more than just highlight the importance of Numbers 10:35-36, but they might actually serve to represent Numbers 10:35-36 as a kind of separate "book" of the Torah. Rather than the Pentateuch or Chumash only composing Genesis, Exodus, Leviticus, Numbers, and Deuteronomy—Numbers can be thought to compose a Numbers$^1$, Numbers 10:35-36, and then a Numbers$^2$ (for lack of better titles)—concurrent with the seven pillars. Certainly, this is an interesting point of view that one might consider in Torah study, and I do think that the logic has some merit. **Numbers 10:35-36 is something important that people of faith need to take notice of.**

## The Ark of Testimony

Going before the Lord in prayer, and querying the Holy Spirit about what *B'ha'alotkha* should instruct me this week, I was simply reminded of some of the previous Torah teachings about the importance of the Ark of the Covenant (or, Testimony). The last verse of *Naso*, examined last week, indicated that the voice of the Lord spoke to Moses from above the mercy seat, which sat right on top of the Ark of the Covenant:

"Now when Moses went into the tent of meeting to speak with Him, he heard the voice speaking to him from above the mercy seat that was on the ark of the testimony, from between the two cherubim, so He spoke to him" (Numbers 7:89).

It is not difficult to be reminded of how many important events in the Tanakh are related to the Ark of the Covenant. The proper movement of the Ark of the Covenant precipitated the splitting of the Jordan River (Joshua chs. 3-4). The Ark of the Covenant being present was instrumental in the destruction of the walls of Jericho (Joshua 6). In the later history of Israel, the location of the Ark of the Covenant is noticeably important, to receive the blessings of the Holy One. The Prophet Samuel heard the voice of God as he slept near the Ark (1 Samuel 3:3). Later on, the Ark's capture by the Philistines, and the glory departing Israel as a result of its loss, are described. The Philistines were judged by improperly withholding the Ark (1 Samuel 6). Eventually, the Ark is recovered and returned to Israel, but not without some dire consequences for some of the transporters (2 Samuel 6). Finally, the Ark is placed in the Tabernacle provided by King David in Jerusalem, and King Solomon builds the First Temple which ultimately houses it.

As you recollect the recorded history of the Ark of the Covenant, you should be reminded of its significance in the life of Ancient Israel. After all, the tablets of the Ten Commandments, written by the very finger of God, were placed in the Ark. These are

---

[32] Sir Lancelot C. L. Brenton, ed & trans., *The Septuagint With Apocrypha* (Peabody, MA: Hendrickson, 1999), 188.

some of the most tangible objects of our Creator's involvement with the development of His chosen people:

"When He had finished speaking with him upon Mount Sinai, He gave Moses the two tablets of the testimony, tablets of stone, written by the finger of God" (Exodus 31:18).

When we realize that the Ark contained these tablets of stone, we can more fully comprehend its significance. But as I considered and meditated upon this truth, I was reminded of some of the greater benefits which have been promised to and have been received by followers of the Messiah of Israel. The Prophets Jeremiah and Ezekiel both detail a promised New Covenant, where God's Instruction would be supernaturally transcribed upon redeemed human hearts:

"'Behold, days are coming,' declares the LORD, 'when I will make a new covenant with the house of Israel and with the house of Judah, not like the covenant which I made with their fathers in the day I took them by the hand to bring them out of the land of Egypt, My covenant which they broke, although I was a husband to them,' declares the LORD. 'But this is the covenant which I will make with the house of Israel after those days,' declares the LORD, 'I will put My law within them and on their heart I will write it; and I will be their God, and they shall be My people'" (Jeremiah 31:31-33).

"And I will give them one heart, and put a new spirit within them. And I will take the heart of stone out of their flesh and give them a heart of flesh, that they may walk in My statutes and keep My ordinances and do them. Then they will be My people, and I shall be their God...Moreover, I will give you a new heart and put a new spirit within you; and I will remove the heart of stone from your flesh and give you a heart of flesh. I will put My Spirit within you and cause you to walk in My statutes, and you will be careful to observe My ordinances" (Ezekiel 11:19-20; 36:26-27).

As you read these parallel passages, I sincerely pray that your old, stony heart has been removed. Being forgiven and cleansed of sin by the sacrifice of Yeshua, such a heart should now be replaced by a new heart of flesh. This heart of flesh loves God and neighbor, and wants to obey Him as a result of the presence of the Holy Spirit. Such an obedience is able to serve the community of faith, and make a difference in the world so that others might come to know the goodness and grace of God. This obedience is by no means stirred on by some drive to "earn salvation," but comes from a Divine empowerment by the supernatural activity inaugurated by the gospel.[33]

## New Covenant Arks

Being given a new heart of flesh, by the salvation work of the Messiah, is it appropriate for Believers to consider themselves as functioning like an ark of testimony for the Living God? The Apostle Paul did teach that Believers compose a temple of the Most High:

"Do you not know that you are a temple of God and *that* the Spirit of God dwells in you?" (1 Corinthians 3:16).

If we compose a kind-of temple of God today, with His Instruction supernaturally written on redeemed hearts—then perhaps it would be prudent for us to employ some of the same techniques that Moses used as he followed the cloud leading Ancient Israel. *Believers are supposed to be led by the Spirit and walk by the Spirit.* Is there a parallel between the cloud that led Ancient Israel, and how we are supposed to be led by the Holy Spirit?

"For all who are being led by the Spirit of God, these are sons of God" (Romans 8:14).

---

[33] For further consideration, consult the exegesis paper "What is the New Covenant?" by J.K. McKee.

"But I say, walk by the Spirit, and you will not carry out the desire of the flesh" (Galatians 5:16).

Moses certainly knew that the enemies of God were everywhere, and that they hated everything that His people stood for and represented. Should we not internalize this same reality as Messiah followers today? By faith, just prior to moving the Ark of the Covenant, Moses declared **"Rise O LORD"**—summoning the Most High to take note that Israel was preparing to move. Then he exclaimed, **"and let Your enemies scatter, and Your foes flee before You!"** (Numbers 10:35, Alter). With great authority, Moses calls upon God to establish who He is, as he prepares the people to follow the cloud. The Lord then clears a path for the movement of the Ark of the Covenant so that the enemies of Israel would not be allowed to disrupt its transport.

The inverted *nun*s seen in the Masoretic Text of Numbers 10:35-36 certainly do set these two verses apart, so that readers can take notice of them. Likewise, Numbers 10:35 is canted in the traditional liturgy of the Synagogue as the Torah scroll is removed from its ark during the *Shabbat* service, a practice also adhered to in much of the Messianic community.[34] But might there be something more for us to realize?

Born again Believers, with God's Instruction written on their hearts by His Spirit, do make up a kind of "ark." Do we ever personally pray the protection of Numbers 10:35-36 as we move from location-to-location or place-to-place? We certainly know that we will be hated for being Messiah's followers. Should we not know that the enemy and his minions often lie in wait for us? In going out into our sinful world, do we go out with the confidence of Moses who appealed to the Lord for His power to strike down Israel's enemies? Or, either forgetting or being ignorant of words like Numbers 10:35-36, do we just go out into the world unprepared and forgetting to appeal to the Holy One for His protection?

Perhaps if we thought of ourselves as a kind-of ark, we might be more mindful of the responsibility we have to protect ourselves from the schemes of the Devil. Then, in God's faithfulness toward us, He will truly be able to return to us, *and shower us with His blessings*, after the enemy flees! I simply encourage you to walk by the Spirit, and be confident in the Lord that He does go before us, protecting us from all those who would seek to harm or destroy us.

# *Shelakh-Lekha* שְׁלַח־לְךָ
## Send on your behalf
### "Scriptural Equality"

| Numbers 13:1-15:41 |
|---|
| Joshua 2:1-24 |

*Shelakh-Lekha* is best known for the account of the twelve spies who are sent into Canaan to scout out the opportunities for the Israelites, so they can occupy the Promised Land.[35] We witness the classic scene of how two spies, Joshua and Caleb, came back with a good

---
[34] Consult "A Traditional Morning Shabbat Service" in the *Messianic Sabbath Helper* by TNN Press (forthcoming paperback edition).
[35] Numbers 13:1-24.

report—and the ten spies who reported negatively.[36] Our Torah portion for this week records a critical part of Ancient Israel's history, which must be studied properly today. Great lessons on faith can be *contrasted* with an inherent lack of faith—and negative consequences which can ensue for not believing the promises of God.[37] While the messages seen in *Shelakh-Lekha* have been the substance of much theological and spiritual reflection for over three millennia, I think we can also see how it likely inspired many in the Zionist movement of the Nineteenth and Twentieth Centuries to want to return to the Land of Israel. **For this, we must be very grateful!**

Now after over a half-century of existence, the modern-day State of Israel is a viable country, uniquely existing as a testimony to the validity of the promises made by God contained in the Holy Writ. We all know that the Scriptures are replete with statements and prophecies which indicate that Israel would eventually be reconstituted, as a fulfillment of the promises given by the Lord to the Patriarchs.[38] Many of the promises seen in the Tanakh were used to inspire the original Zionist settlers to make the necessary sacrifice, and perform the hard work and labor, required to establish a Jewish homeland in the Middle East.

As you read our *parashah*, I would urge you to not exclusively reflect on some of its positive aspects as they concern the Promised Land and the vibrancy of Israel today. Consider the reaction of Moses when he hears that God is planning to wipe Israel out because of rebellious attitudes toward Him (Numbers 14:11-12). Will God be known as being cruel and despicable, who led His chosen people out of Egypt only to slaughter them mercilessly in the desert (Numbers 14:13-16)? Even with the promise of Moses' seed being made into a nation mightier than the Israelites set before him (Numbers 14:12), Israel's humble leader intercedes on their behalf, appealing to God as One who is slow to anger and abundant in lovingkindness:

"But now, I pray, let the power of the Lord be great, just as You have declared, 'The LORD is slow to anger and abundant in lovingkindness, forgiving iniquity and transgression; but He will by no means clear *the guilty*, visiting the iniquity of the fathers on the children to the third and the fourth *generations*. Pardon, I pray, the iniquity of this people according to the greatness of Your lovingkindness, just as You also have forgiven this people, from Egypt even until now.' So the LORD said, 'I have pardoned *them* according to your word; but indeed, as I live, all the earth will be filled with the glory of the LORD'" (Numbers 14:17-21).

*Shelakh-Lekha* is an appropriate point in our Torah readings where we should reflect upon the humility of Moses as Israel's leader. Not only do we see Moses plead before God on behalf of the people, but the burden of service he carries for Israel cannot be denied. Moses is willing to stand as an advocate for the people before the Lord, even when they might prefer to stone Him to death (Numbers 14:10).

---

[36] Numbers 13:25-33.
[37] Numbers 14:1-38.
[38] These prophecies may include, but are not limited to:
 Deuteronomy 30:1-5; Isaiah 14:1, 34:16-17, 35:10, 65:9-10; Jeremiah 3:18, 16:14-15, 29:14, 30:2-3, 31:16-18, 50:19; Ezekiel 11:17, 20:41-42, 34:13-15, 36:8-12, 36:24-28, 38:8; Amos 9:14-15; Micah 4:6-8; Zephaniah 2:7; Zechariah 2:11-12, 8:7-8, 10:8-10.

## Entering the Land

While the Lord does not wipe out the people of Israel, "starting over" with Moses' descendants, it is nevertheless decreed that all of those twenty years and over—save Joshua and Caleb—will die in the wilderness. *Only the children of the Exodus generation are qualified to enter into the Promised Land* (Numbers 14:29-31). With this said, the remainder of our Torah portion narrates some of the instructions and laws that are to be observed when Canaan is eventually occupied by Israel.[39] Of particular importance will be how the Israelites will offer various animal sacrifices to the Lord, doubtlessly as an expression of their thanksgiving to Him for His bounty and provision in the Land He has granted them:

"Now the LORD spoke to Moses, saying, 'Speak to the sons of Israel and say to them, "When you enter the land where you are to live, which I am giving you, then make an offering by fire to the LORD, a burnt offering or a sacrifice to fulfill a special vow, or as a freewill offering or in your appointed times, to make a soothing aroma to the LORD, from the herd or from the flock"'" (Numbers 15:1-3).

The bulk of what is seen in Numbers 15 elaborates upon the various procedures for offering grain, rams, and bulls before the Lord. Within these instructions some specific statements stand out, regarding who they apply to:

"All who are native shall do these things in this manner, in presenting an offering by fire, as a soothing aroma to the LORD. If an alien sojourns with you, or one who may be among you throughout your generations, and he *wishes to* make an offering by fire, as a soothing aroma to the LORD, just as you do so he shall do. *As for* the assembly, there shall be one statute for you and for the alien who sojourns *with you*, a perpetual statute throughout your generations; as you are, so shall the alien be before the LORD. There is to be one law and one ordinance for you and for the alien who sojourns with you...You shall have one law for him who does *anything* unintentionally, for him who is native among the sons of Israel and for the alien who sojourns among them. But the person who does *anything* defiantly, whether he is native or an alien, that one is blaspheming the LORD; and that person shall be cut off from among his people" (Numbers 15:13-16, 29-30).

Here, we see two categories of people referred to, who exist within the community of Israel: the *ezrach* (אֶזְרָח) or "native," and the *ger* (גֵּר) or "alien." While the instruction here specifically concerns "an offering by fire" and "a sin offering" (Numbers 15:13, 27), it does lay the important legal precedent that the same standard will be adhered to by those within the Promised Land, regardless of if they are native born Israelites or those who have entered in from outside to the community. As the NIV renders Numbers 15:16, "The same laws and regulations will apply both to you and to the alien living among you." Dennis T. Olson explains how "non-Israelite groups are welcomed into the center [of the sanctuary] to offer their sacrifices and offerings. In this way, they are given the same status as native Israelites before God."[40] In today's Messianic community, the idea that there is to be "one law" for both Jewish and non-Jewish Believers to regard as having the same spiritual relevance, has certainly caused a great deal of discussion—and even some controversy.

---

[39] Numbers 15:1-41.

[40] Dennis T. Olson, *Interpretation, A Bible Commentary for Teaching and Preaching: Numbers* (Louisville: John Knox Press, 1996), 93.

## A Few Challenges Seen in Today's Messianic Community

The reasons why Numbers 15:15, 29-30, and other Torah passages that use the terminology "one law"[41] are controversial, are too lengthy to be discussed in this brief commentary—because they carry a great deal of complex emotions for people in significant sectors of the Messianic movement. It is undeniable that the Lord has been moving in the past thirty to forty years, as the number of Jewish people who have come to publicly acknowledge Yeshua as the Messiah has exploded. There are now Messianic Jewish congregations all over North America and English-speaking countries, with some also in Europe and Latin America. Yet as this has occurred, many non-Jewish Believers have been drawn into Messianic congregations in an effort to be enriched by their Hebraic and Jewish Roots.

It is understandable, given the complex history of the relations between Judaism and Christianity, why many Messianic Jews want to have their own congregations separated out from the wider Body of Messiah. Yet, with the majority of people in most Messianic congregations *not Jewish*, is it acceptable for there to be special treatment and ministry given to Jewish Believers, and less attention given to non-Jewish Believers? Our family's experience in Messianic Judaism in the late 1990s was that while we were welcome to attend congregational services, our place in Messianic Judaism was not one as full equals in Messiah. We were told on several occasions by leaders we encountered that our place was to pray for and financially support Jewish ministry, and that we could be associate members. *Perhaps this was just our experience,* and the experience of other non-Jewish Believers in Messianic Judaism is a little different. Certainly, we do not want to broad brush entire sectors of Messianic Judaism, as progress has doubtlessly been made in the time since, in many places, to see that all brothers and sisters in Yeshua are welcome in Messianic assemblies—and that all feel like they belong and that they can contribute to the vitality of the Body of Messiah. *The Messianic movement is definitely a work in progress…*

In his letter to the Galatians, the Apostle Paul acknowledges how a great level of equality has been brought about by the sacrifice of Messiah Yeshua:

"For all of you who were baptized into Messiah have clothed yourselves with Messiah. There is neither Jew nor Greek, there is neither slave nor free man, there is neither male nor female; for you are all one in Messiah Yeshua. And if you belong to Messiah, then you are Abraham's descendants, heirs according to promise" (Galatians 3:27-29).[42]

All people, regardless of ethnicity, social status, or even gender, **stand equal before the Father because of the work of His Son.** What Paul says here was absolutely radical for the First Century, as it directly subverted an ancient Jewish prayer (t.*Berachot* 6:18), that is even seen in the Orthodox Jewish *siddur* today. The observant Jew proclaims, as it appears in the *The Authorised Daily Prayer Book*,

> Blessed art thou, O Lord our God, King of the universe, who hast not made me a **heathen** [*nakri*, נָכְרִי].

> Blessed art thou, O Lord our God, King of the universe, who hast not made me a **bondman** [*aved*, עֶבֶד].

---

[41] Exodus 12:48-49; Leviticus 7:7; 24:22; 24:22; Numbers 9:14.
For a detailed analysis of these passages, consult the exegesis paper "One Law for All" by J.K. McKee.
[42] Referenced by Olson, 93, after his comments on Numbers 15:15.

Blessed art thou, O Lord our God, King of the universe, who hast not made me a **woman** [*ishah*, אִשָּׁה].[43]

Paul's words in Galatians 3:28 not only subvert the message of this errant prayer—but attack its message of assumed superiority in the same order in which someone would pray it![44] Noting these distinctions, F.F. Bruce concludes, "It is not unlikely that Paul himself had been brought up to thank God he was born a Jew and not a Gentile, a freeman and not a slave, a man and not a woman. If so, he takes up each of these three distinctions which had considerable importance to Judaism and affirms that in Christ they are all irrelevant."[45] Certainly while there are natural distinctions that exist for people who acknowledge Yeshua as Savior—any ethnic or gender differences are insignificant compared to who He is and what He has accomplished for us. While the post-resurrection era is dominated by an equality not necessarily seen in the previous era, it does not mean that the distinctions of ethnicity, social standing, or gender are entirely erased, **but instead they are to be things which are to contribute to the vitality of the *ekklēsia*.** The theme of much of Paul's letters (i.e., Ephesians 4:11-12) is how Jewish and non-Jewish Believers can come together as one in the Lord, and *all can be encouraged* to use their gifts and talents to His glory! While in a Messianic setting the virtues and edifying traits of Judaism are emphasized, the same courtesy is often not granted to those of us from evangelical Christian backgrounds.

The Messianic movement where the value of *all* of God's people is emphasized, and all are encouraged to be everything they can be, really does not exist at this point in history. Our broad faith community has little or no understanding of what it means for us to all be in mutual submission to one another, where someone else's needs are regarded as more important than your own (cf. Ephesians 5:21; Philippians 2:3-4). Even in the independent Messianic movement, much of which has arisen because of the various issues seen in Messianic Judaism, the concept of "mutual submission" is quite foreign.[46] Yet, it is something that will definitely guide the Messianic movement of the future, as the Father's plan of restoring His people comes into greater focus. I have confidence that regardless of some of our current limitations, what lies ahead is going to be a significantly exciting time of growth and maturity![47]

## Only the Noahide Laws?

The conviction of many of today's non-Jewish Messianic Believers is that they are a part of the community of Israel via their faith in Messiah Yeshua. As the Torah itself communicates, "One law and one standard applies for you and for the alien residing with you" (Numbers 15:15, Keter Crown Bible). This would seem to mean that non-Jewish

---

[43] Hertz, *Authorised Daily Prayer Book*, pp 19, 21; Scherman and Zlotowitz, *Complete ArtScroll Siddur*, 21.
[44] For a further discussion, consult the exegesis paper on Galatians 3:28, "Biblical Equality and Today's Messianic Movement" by J.K. McKee.
[45] F.F. Bruce, *New International Greek Testament Commentary: Galatians* (Grand Rapids: Eerdmans, 1982), 187.
[46] Editor's note: This is because being mutually submissive does not just affect the interactions of those within the local assembly, but how husbands and wives are to serve one another as co-leaders of the home.
[47] For some additional thoughts, consult the article "Is God's Purpose Bigger?" by J.K. McKee, appearing in the October 2009 issue of Outreach Israel News.

Believers should be following the Torah no differently than Jewish Believers.[48] They should consider the Law of Moses to have relevance and blessing for their lives, informing them how the Lord wants all of His people to be holy and set-apart unto Him. In fact, while the Torah originally communicated to Ancient Israel that there was to only be one standard for the native or sojourner, in the post-resurrection era non-Jewish Believers are to be regarded "no longer [as] strangers and aliens, but...fellow citizens with the saints, and...of God's household" (Ephesians 3:6). Such a classification of native, sojourner, or even "God-fearer"—is to be largely regarded as a part of the pre-resurrection era. If anything, all Believers in Messiah Yeshua are sojourners and aliens *in the world*, their citizenship in Heaven (1 Peter 2:11; Philippians 3:20).

Many of today's Messianic Jews eagerly embrace non-Jewish Believers as their fellow brothers and sisters, and are more than happy for them to be considering God's Torah as relevant instruction. They want the Messianic movement to be the "one new humanity" (Ephesians 2:15, NRSV/CJB). They know that the enemy wants to keep Jewish Believers and non-Jewish Believers divided as much as he can. They know that a Messianic Judaism off to itself, with an evangelical Christianity still often disregarding the Law of Moses, is not at all a good thing. Even if there are some obstacles and difficulties along the way, many of my Messianic Jewish friends recognize that we all have to work together to see a restoration of Israel come forth that is more all-encompassing than just involving the Jewish people; it is something that involves the entire world.

Contrary to the thought that the Torah is relevant for all of God's people is the Jewish theological construct that the Torah is only to be followed by the Jews. The nations at large are thought to only have to really follow seven precepts affecting the *b'nai Noach* or children of Noah, derived from Genesis 9.[49] Much of this concept has made its way into parts of Messianic Judaism as well, which has thought that non-Jewish Believers can become "righteous Gentiles" by only following the seven Noahide laws. By extension, some even think that the Apostolic Decree of Acts 15:19-21 is based in these Noahide laws, which include:

1. a prohibition against idolatry
2. a prohibition against blasphemy
3. a prohibition against bloodshed/murder
4. prohibitions against incest and adultery
5. a prohibition against robbery
6. the need to establish courts of law
7. a prohibition against eating flesh cut from a living animal[50]

While these seven prohibitions are surely righteous injunctions to be observed by all Messiah followers, suggesting that these are the *only* "commandments" that non-Jewish Believers are to follow today is a bit of a hasty conclusion. The Apostolic Scriptures include

---

[48] Editor's note: This does not, however, mean that such non-Jewish Believers need to live as *culturally "Jewish"* in all aspects of their lives. While Jewish tradition should have a role in one's Torah observance, there are many aspects of Jewish culture that do not have to be followed by non-Jewish Believers, mostly regarding non-congregational related issues.

For a further discussion, consult the relevant chapters of the *Messianic Torah Helper* by TNN Press (forthcoming).

[49] Cf. "Noahides," in *Dictionary of Judaism in the Biblical Period*, 456.

[50] Cf. Nahum M. Sarna, *JPS Torah Commentary: Genesis* (Philadelphia: Jewish Publication Society, 1989), pp 376-377.

clear instruction to mixed assemblies of Jewish and non-Jewish Believers that goes well beyond these seven issues—as important as they are.[51] But more problematic for those Messianic Jews who might want to view someone like me as only being some kind of a "Noahide," is the fact that these so-called Noahide laws were likely not formulated until after the destruction of the Second Temple. There are two lists of these different regulations found in Jewish literature (*Jubilees* 7:20-21;[52] t.*Avodah Zarah* 8:4[53]), and as David Instone-Brewer points out, "The two versions of the list in Jubilees and in later rabbinic texts have so little in common that we cannot know what this list contained in the first century or even if such a list existed."[54]

## Moving Forward by the Will of the Spirit

I think it is safe to say that with the Holy Spirit dictating the enactment of the New Covenant (Jeremiah 31:31-34; Ezekiel 36:25-27), **the Lord wants non-Jewish Believers to follow more than just seven injunctions.** While non-Jewish Believers should be very sensitive to the needs of Jewish Believers, it is unfortunate that too many people—such as myself and my family—have been "unwelcomed" in various Messianic Jewish congregations at times. If, for a season, we have to be a part of independent Messianic congregations and fellowships, let us not be unwelcoming of *anyone* who may enter in. Let us not reciprocate any rejection by Messianic Judaism, and desire unity and reconciliation in the future.

Many of us, regardless of whether we are Jewish or non-Jewish, know that following God's Torah need not be a burden, but can be a great delight! *To know that one is obeying his or her Heavenly Father is very encouraging.* As we are molded by Him to accomplish His tasks, let us truly be those who can make a difference by our obedience to God, building bridges and bringing His people together. Our world—and even many religious people in Judaism and Christianity—lacks a firm ethical and moral compass. Having a foundation in the Torah will help many people return to the path of obedience and holiness, and enable them to appreciate more fully why Messiah Yeshua came to die in their place.

---

[51] The prohibitions of the Apostolic Decree of Acts 15:19-21 are best thought of as being those areas where the First Century Jewish community was unwilling to compromise or be lenient toward outsiders. The prohibitions issued by James the Just would require the new, non-Jewish Believers to effectively cut themselves off from their old, pagan spheres of social interaction, making their new spheres of social interaction those who followed Israel's Messiah (Jewish Believers) or at least Israel's One God (the Jewish community).
Consult the commentary *Acts 15 for the Practical Messianic* by J.K. McKee for more information.

[52] "And in the twenty-eighth jubilee Noah began to command his grandsons with ordinances and commandments and all of the judgments which he knew. And he bore witness to his sons so that they might do justice and cover the shame of their flesh and bless the one who created them and honor father and mother, and each one love his neighbor and preserve themselves from fornication and pollution and from all injustice. For on account of these three the Flood came upon the earth. For (it was) because of fornication which the Watchers, apart from the mandate of their authority, fornicated with the daughters of men and took for themselves wives from all whom they chose and made a beginning of impurity" (O.S. Wintermute, "Jubilees," in James H. Charlesworth, ed., *The Old Testament Pseudepigrapha*, Vol 2 [New York: Doubleday, 1985], pp 69-70).

[53] "Concerning seven religious requirements were the children of Noah admonished: setting up courts of justice, idolatry, blasphemy [cursing the Name of God], fornication, bloodshed, and thievery" (Jacob Neusner, trans., *The Tosefta: Translated from the Hebrew With a New Introduction*, 2 vols. [Peabody, MA: Hendrickson, 2002], 2:1291-1292).

[54] David Instone-Brewer, "Infanticide and the Apostolic Decree of Acts 15" in Journal of the Evangelical Theological Society Vol. 52 No. 2 (2009):308.

None of us should exhibit any pride about our heritage or lineage, blinding us to the necessary service we should offer as Messiah followers. As witnessed here in *Shelakh-Lekha*, we should strive to have the humility of Moses, who stood up for an entire generation of Israelites that really did not want him around. Some of us may not be wanted in various sectors of the Messianic community. But rather than moving aside and letting God judge, or at least penalize, others, for their inappropriate behavior—**let us stand and defend them.** Let us be patient and stand in awe as He really does promise a grand restoration of all Israel before His Son's return!

# *Korach* קֹרַח
## Korah
## "Falling on Faces"

> Numbers 16:1-18:32
> 1 Samuel 11:14-12:22

When most people think of our Torah portion for this week, the title *Korach* naturally reminds them of the insurrection that Korah initiated when he challenged the leadership of Moses and Aaron. Unsatisfied with their delegated responsibilities, Korah and some two hundred and fifty leaders in the congregation asked Moses and Aaron why they "exalted," or lifted themselves up, above the rest of the assembly. This accusation came without any known warning. The question in Moses' mind was so astounding that his initial reaction was **to simply fall on his face before the Lord:**

"Now Korah the son of Izhar, the son of Kohath, the son of Levi, with Dathan and Abiram, the sons of Eliab, and On the son of Peleth, sons of Reuben, took *action*, and they rose up before Moses, together with some of the sons of Israel, two hundred and fifty leaders of the congregation, chosen in the assembly, men of renown. They assembled together against Moses and Aaron, and said to them, 'You have gone far enough, for all the congregation are holy, every one of them, and the LORD is in their midst; so why do you exalt yourselves above the assembly of the LORD?' When Moses heard *this*, he fell on his face" (Numbers 16:1-4).

This dramatic response to Korah's indictment becomes quite serious, because God severely judges Korah and his followers.[55] The Lord uses the events to establish the position of Aaron and the Levites as servants and intermediaries of Israel before Him.[56]

While reading through our *parashah*, I took special notice of how the act of falling on one's face and pleading for understanding or mercy—occurred an additional two times. The next time we witness this act of contrition and intercession is when God communicates the judgment that He is ready to deliver upon the congregation of Israel, for the people either following after Korah or considering his complaints:

"Then the LORD spoke to Moses and Aaron, saying, 'Separate yourselves from among this congregation, that I may consume them instantly.' But they fell on their faces and said,

---

[55] Numbers 16:5-35.
[56] Numbers 16:36-40; 17:1-18:32.

'O God, God of the spirits of all flesh, when one man sins, will You be angry with the entire congregation?'" (Numbers 16:20-22).

Just before, Korah and his cohorts, Dathan and Abiram, had leveled a series of serious charges against Moses (Numbers 16:12-14). Korah was a Levite[57] and he was not satisfied with his position of service in the Tabernacle. He wanted to have a similar position to Aaron's, if not replace him. Dathan and Abiram, who were Reubenites,[58] had a different motive. As descendants of the firstborn of Jacob, they must have thought that they deserved to be the leaders of Israel. They looked back at the recent failure to enter into the Promised Land, and blamed Moses for Israel's defeat by the Amalekites and the Canaanites (Numbers 14:39-45). Even though Moses had warned the Israelites that they had missed their opportunity to occupy the Promised Land, the blame was directed to Moses from these ungrateful rebels (Numbers 15:41-45). As the accusations came forth, Moses was angered and he made a request to the Lord:

"Then Moses became very angry and said to the LORD, 'Do not regard their offering! I have not taken a single donkey from them, nor have I done harm to any of them'" (Numbers 16:15).

Moses knew about his special relationship with God. He could recall all of the encounters with the Holy One back to the burning bush experience. But as you should remember, Moses was somewhat of a reluctant leader. He questioned his ability to articulate the words of the Lord, and was subsequently told to bring his brother Aaron onto the leadership team in order to effectively communicate to Pharaoh and the Israelites (Exodus 4:14-15). Yet these accusations were too much to bear. Moses was grieved with his accusers, and so he offered a challenge to the two hundred and fifty insurrectionists to take up a fire pan with incense and bring it before the Holy One (Numbers 16:6-7).

As the glory of God descended upon the Tent of Meeting, the Lord tells Moses and Aaron that He is going to pour out His wrath upon the congregation. It was at this word that the two men **fell on their faces** and pleaded for mercy for those gathered. At their request, the Lord gives them a way to separate out the rebellious from the somewhat innocent:

"Then the LORD spoke to Moses, saying, 'Speak to the congregation, saying, "Get back from around the dwellings of Korah, Dathan and Abiram."' Then Moses arose and went to Dathan and Abiram, with the elders of Israel following him, and he spoke to the congregation, saying, 'Depart now from the tents of these wicked men, and touch nothing that belongs to them, or you will be swept away in all their sin'" (Numbers 16:23-26).

By falling on their faces and pleading for mercy, Moses and Aaron received a temporary solution to keep the innocent from being swallowed up in the dramatic judgment that was shortly to follow. The ground opened up and swallowed those who were allied with Korah. It was followed by fire coming forth and consuming the two hundred and fifty who had offered up the incense:

"As he finished speaking all these words, the ground that was under them split open; and the earth opened its mouth and swallowed them up, and their households, and all the men who belonged to Korah with *their* possessions. So they and all that belonged to them went down alive to Sheol; and the earth closed over them, and they perished from the midst of the assembly. All Israel who *were* around them fled at their outcry, for they said, 'The

---

[57] Numbers 16:1a.
[58] Numbers 16:1b.

earth may swallow us up!' Fire also came forth from the LORD and consumed the two hundred and fifty men who were offering the incense" (Numbers 16:31-35).

Suffice it to say, Moses and Aaron were totally vindicated by these dramatic examples of God executing His judgment. But the exercise of falling on their faces was not complete. The very next day, the congregation of Israel decided to blame Moses and Aaron for the judgment meted out to Korah and his rebellious cohort:

"But on the next day all the congregation of the sons of Israel grumbled against Moses and Aaron, saying, 'You are the ones who have caused the death of the LORD's people.' It came about, however, when the congregation had assembled against Moses and Aaron, that they turned toward the tent of meeting, and behold, the cloud covered it and the glory of the LORD appeared" (Numbers 16:41-42).

This was not a good thing for the Israelites to be doing. Moses and Aaron definitely had the Lord on their side of the struggle for leadership, and He again communicates to them that additional judgment would be coming. Moses and Aaron fall on their faces before Him to intercede. Knowing that a plague would be spreading through the camp, Moses instructed Aaron to quickly take his censer with fire from the altar with incense, and appeal to God for mercy:

"Then Moses and Aaron came to the front of the tent of meeting, and the LORD spoke to Moses, saying, 'Get away from among this congregation, that I may consume them instantly.' Then they fell on their faces. Moses said to Aaron, 'Take your censer and put in it fire from the altar, and lay incense *on it*; then bring it quickly to the congregation and make atonement for them, for wrath has gone forth from the LORD, the plague has begun!'" (Numbers 16:43-46).

The intercession worked, but not until after many Israelites had died because of the plague:

"He took his stand between the dead and the living, so that the plague was checked. But those who died by the plague were 14,700,[59] besides those who died on account of Korah. Then Aaron returned to Moses at the doorway of the tent of meeting, for the plague had been checked" (Numbers 16:48-50).

Korah's rebellion was checked, but not without a significant loss of life. Not only did Israel lose two hundred and fifty leaders from the tribes of Levi and Reuben, but apparently, the insurrection also affected many more. *These were serious consequences for the people of Israel.*

## The Falling on Face Alternative

As I reflected upon these dramatic events, a number of thoughts came to mind. If you can place yourself back in time as a witness to these judgments, you should understand that there were very serious messages being communicated to Israel. Since this was taking place just a short while after the incidents concerning the twelve spies, and the subsequent aborted attempt to occupy Canaan without the protection of God (seen last week in *Shelakh-Lekha*), we see that there was a concerted attempt to challenge the leadership of Moses. When you contemplate watching the ground open up and swallowing Korah and his household and companions, this might conjure up images of a Hollywood production.

---

[59] Editor's note: Due to the ambiguity of the Semitic term *elef*, even if we were to view 14 *elef* 700 as fourteen *squads* of seven hundred, this would still equal somewhere around 9,800 people—more than three times those killed in the September 11, 2001 World Trade Center attacks.

Then, when you enhance this judgment with fire coming forth from the Most High to consume the two hundred and fifty who had been challenged to offer up incense—you can probably imagine special effects teams competing for an academy award.

Men and women of faith consider the scenes of *Korach* to be far more than just the fictional writings of some creative movie producer. *We believe that these were real life episodes in the history of Ancient Israel.* If you had been there as a witness, the images would never leave your memory. On top of seeing Korah and his associates swallowed up and burned alive, imagine the rapidity of a plague moving through the camp—the next day—with the loss of thousands of people! It is obvious that God was sending a very strong signal to Korah's contemporaries—and to generations yet to come—that a rebellious spirit against His chosen servants is not something one should have.

As I thought about all this, I was quick to be reminded of the humble character of Moses and how he displayed it during this defiant attempt to usurp his authority. Three times during the course of these trials, Moses fell on his face before the Holy One for understanding and for intercessory pleadings for his fellow Israelites. **To me, this was a great example of how Believers should react to crises that inevitably come our way.**

I then reflected upon the last time I went down on my face with intercessory, merciful prayers for my loved ones, friends, and acquaintances who are perishing. I was convicted that it had been far too long since the last time I had cried out for mercy for those who still, to this day, do not have a relationship with the Messiah Yeshua. In many respects, this is a chronic crisis because none of us knows when our loved ones' days on Earth are going to end. This is even more reason to take the time to fall on the face and implore God for mercy!

I have to often ask myself when the last time it was that I fell on my face and pleaded with the Lord, for understanding and wisdom for situations beyond my ability to fully comprehend. *It is usually not that often when I assume a prostrated position.* And yet, Moses' example—and many others throughout the Scriptures—are given to us as instructions to implement for our own walk with the Messiah.

How about you? When was the last time you humbled yourself and followed Moses' example of falling on your face—either seeking God for mercy for your loved ones, or for wisdom on how to handle various challenges? Is it possible that the Father will honor our humble, prostrated requests for compassion for the lost, and give us answers to predicaments that perplex us? In *Korach*, when Moses pleaded for mercy and wisdom, the Lord reacted favorably and gave him warnings about how to prevent any further loss of life. Perhaps there is something about falling on your face and admitting that you are totally dependent upon Him? Perhaps in His mercy, lost loved ones will be saved and solutions to life's challenges will usher forth? *It worked for Moses and Aaron.* Could it possibly have the same results for us?

# *Chukat* חֻקַּת
## Regulation
## "Speak to the Rock"

> Numbers 19:1-22:1
> Judges 11:1-33

*Chukat* includes some very important scenes, as well as some curious instructions. It begins with the mystery of the red heifer purification rites,[60] and concludes with a series of military conflicts that precede Israel's entrance into the Promised Land.[61] Also recorded are the deaths of Moses' two siblings, Miriam[62] and Aaron.[63] Once again, we find that students of the Torah have a number of important object lessons to consider, when examining this *parashah*.

For millennia, the enigma of the red heifer has baffled Torah scholars, the Jewish Sages, and even a few modern-day theologians and scientists. This mysterious rite seems to be beyond much human ability to comprehend, and subsequently, the Israelites were probably to just obey its prescriptions by faith. This they did in the ancient era, and they received the commensurate blessings of obedience.

In recent years, many have heard of the publicized birth of a red heifer named Melody. Some took this as a sign that the Temple could now be rebuilt, because the prerequisite sacrifice used for cleansing the Temple was now available. Of course, as many followed the frequent reports about the calf in anticipation of some dramatic end-time event, a few white hairs appeared on the young heifer. This disqualified her for the ritual, but did alert a considerable number of people worldwide, from a spectrum of backgrounds (even non-religious people), about this relatively obscure procedure. It also brought a number of evangelical Christians together, who believe it is only a matter of time before a qualified red heifer is born, and ultra Orthodox Jews, who believe it is only a matter of time before the Temple will be rebuilt. Both groups look to the coming of the Messiah.[64]

This small, inexplicable procedure lured thousands of Christians into the pages of the Torah and Tanakh, as many were prompted to seek answers to questions beyond their cognitive capability. *Some of them even got interested in their Hebraic Roots.*

Rather than dwell on the mysteries of the ashes of a sacrificed animal—as intriguing as they may be—*Chukat* reminds us of other things that relate more easily to the human condition, and some of the challenges we face as Believers. In the narrative of the Torah, thirty-eight years have passed since the failed attempt for Ancient Israel to enter the Promised Land without the protection of God (Numbers 13:26). The "Exodus generation" of the Israelites, who lacked the faith to take the land because they believed the bad report from the ten spies, had now died off:

---

[60] Numbers 19:1-22.
[61] Numbers 21:1-35.
[62] Numbers 20:1-6.
[63] Numbers 20:24-29.
[64] Cf. "Cattlemen of the Apocalypse," in Gershom Gorenberg, *The End of Days: Fundamentalism and the Struggle for the Temple Mount* (New York: Oxford University Press, 2000), pp 7-29.

"So the LORD's anger burned against Israel, and He made them wander in the wilderness forty years, until the entire generation of those who had done evil in the sight of the LORD was destroyed" (Numbers 32:13).

Much of what we encounter in *Chukat*, sadly, after the succeeding generation of Israelites has buried their predecessors in the wilderness, is nearly identical to what caused the delay. The general patterns of murmuring and complaining have been passed down by the Exodus generation to their children and grandchildren. In spite of very serious consequences of their disbelief in God, the descendants of the Exodus generation face their own discontentment, bitterness, and rebellion. The iniquity of the fathers seems to have been passed down to the group that should be preparing to enter into the Promised Land (cf. Exodus 34:7).

## A Water Problem, and Moses' Bad Works

As the narrative proceeds, the infamous incident at the waters of Meribah is detailed. Israel has arrived at the wilderness of Zin around Kadesh. Miriam dies and the lack of water becomes a crisis:

"There was no water for the congregation, and they assembled themselves against Moses and Aaron. The people thus contended with Moses and spoke, saying, 'If only we had perished when our brothers perished before the LORD! Why then have you brought the LORD's assembly into this wilderness, for us and our beasts to die here? Why have you made us come up from Egypt, to bring us in to this wretched place? It is not a place of grain or figs or vines or pomegranates, nor is there water to drink'" (Numbers 20:2-5).

When you read these complaints and sarcastic comments, you can almost hear the voices of the preceding generation who clamored very similar contentions (i.e., Exodus 14:11). It is difficult to believe that the hearts of this "Joshua generation" could be so similar to the preceding "Exodus generation." And yet, as you read their statements, the attitudes are almost identical. Derision and disgust pepper their remarks: "Would that we had died when our kindred died before the LORD!" (NRSV), is a reference to having died with Korah and his followers.

Questions about dying in the wilderness should remind us of the early days of Israel's travels, right after the people departed Egypt, when a similar water challenge was considered at the rock at Horeb:

"Therefore the people quarreled with Moses and said, 'Give us water that we may drink.' And Moses said to them, 'Why do you quarrel with me? Why do you test the LORD?' But the people thirsted there for water; and they grumbled against Moses and said, 'Why, now, have you brought us up from Egypt, to kill us and our children and our livestock with thirst?' So Moses cried out to the LORD, saying, 'What shall I do to this people? A little more and they will stone me.' Then the LORD said to Moses, 'Pass before the people and take with you some of the elders of Israel; and take in your hand your staff with which you struck the Nile, and go. Behold, I will stand before you there on the rock at Horeb; and you shall strike the rock, and water will come out of it, that the people may drink.' And Moses did so in the sight of the elders of Israel" (Exodus 17:2-6).

In this incident which had occurred nearly forty years earlier, the Lord instructed Moses to take the staff that he had been given to execute the judgments on Egypt, and to strike the rock. Miraculously, water flows forth from the rock, and the place is named *Massah u'Merivah* (מַסָּה וּמְרִיבָה; Exodus 17:7), actually rendered in the Septuagint with the adjectival designations *peirasmos kai loidorēsis* (πειρασμὸς καὶ λοιδόρησις) or "Temptation, and Reviling" (LXE).

In *Chukat*, the Ancient Israelites are almost forty years into their wilderness journey, and another water shortage is eliciting an almost identical response. This incident, to distinguish it from the earlier trial at Rephidim, is known as Meribah-Kadesh (Numbers 20:13-14). Moses is approaching 120 years of age, and he and Aaron are confronted by a mob of malcontents who are reverting to the patterns of their deceased parents and grandparents. As accusations come forth, Moses and Aaron resort to the persistent pattern of falling on their faces before the Lord for understanding and mercy:

"Then Moses and Aaron came in from the presence of the assembly to the doorway of the tent of meeting and fell on their faces. Then the glory of the LORD appeared to them" (Numbers 20:6).

God was faithful to answer their pleadings. Rather than repeating the message of some forty years earlier at Horeb, telling Moses to strike the rock for water to gush forth—God tells him instead to speak to the rock:

"[A]nd the LORD spoke to Moses, saying, 'Take the rod; and you and your brother Aaron assemble the congregation **and speak to the rock before their eyes, that it may yield its water.** You shall thus bring forth water for them out of the rock and let the congregation and their beasts drink'" (Numbers 20:7-8).

Moses and Aaron do as the Lord has directed them, assembling Israel before the rock. But rather than speak to the rock as instructed, Moses takes the staff and strikes the rock twice:

"So Moses took the rod from before the LORD, just as He had commanded him; and Moses and Aaron gathered the assembly before the rock. And he said to them, 'Listen now, you rebels; shall we bring forth water for you out of this rock?' Then Moses lifted up his hand and struck the rock twice with his rod; and water came forth abundantly, and the congregation and their beasts drank" (Numbers 20:9-11).

Why did Moses disobey the instruction of the Lord? Moses was told to speak to the rock so that water would come out—not strike it. A definite answer has alluded many readers of *Chukat* for centuries, but one of the reasons can probably be seen. In speaking to the crowds of Israelites, Moses begins his words with the command *shimu-na* (שִׁמְעוּ־נָא) or "Hear now" (RSV). In some ways, he appears to chide them: "Now listen, you rebels! Are we able to extract water from this rock?" (Keter Crown Bible). One is tempted to almost add "…or not?" to the end of Moses' sentence. The leader of Israel is certainly a bit frustrated with the people he has to lead.

Can you imagine what must have been going through Moses' mind as he looked down at the seething crowd, which could have been growing to a riot scene? How could these people be so ungrateful? Had they not seen the provision of the Lord as they grew up? Did they not know the consequences for questioning the authority of Israel's God-appointed leaders? Did they just forget what happened to their parents and grandparents because of their disbelief?

Moses was justifiably livid, but being angry—even righteously angry—does not justify deliberately disobeying the instructions of God, as seen here. Did Moses have a bit of a temper that was not totally under control? We can remember back some eighty years to the time Moses lost his temper and killed the Egyptian guard:

"Now it came about in those days, when Moses had grown up, that he went out to his brethren and looked on their hard labors; and he saw an Egyptian beating a Hebrew, one of his brethren. So he looked this way and that, and when he saw there was no one *around*, he struck down the Egyptian and hid him in the sand" (Exodus 2:11-12).

Now, in what would seem to be an uncharacteristic way, Moses does not simply speak to the rock, but instead he strikes the rock twice. This action was contrary to the explicit word of the Lord. Something must have overcome Moses, because by this point in his life and experiences, he knew how precise the Lord was in His instructions. He heard God's command to "speak to the rock," and yet for some unstated reason, he struck the rock. And he does not strike the rock only once, like he did at Horeb almost forty years earlier, *but twice*. The Lord was obviously watching, because shortly thereafter penalties upon Moses and Aaron are meted out:

"But the LORD said to Moses and Aaron, 'Because you have not believed Me, to treat Me as holy in the sight of the sons of Israel, therefore you shall not bring this assembly into the land which I have given them.' Those *were* the waters of Meribah, because the sons of Israel contended with the LORD, and He proved Himself holy among them" (Numbers 20:12-13).

This is such a difficult action to fathom. How can Moses and Aaron be guilty of not sanctifying the Lord in the eyes of the people of Israel? One simple slip of temper, or possibly even a senile moment—and Moses and Aaron are denied the opportunity to enter into the Promised Land. Apparently, the instructions of God were so specific here, that it was absolutely impossible for Moses not to understand that he was supposed to "speak to the rock" rather than strike the rock. The fact that he took his own initiative to strike the rock was obviously considered an act of his own will, which brought with it some serious judgment from God.

When reading this, I always wonder why Moses had reacted so violently to the rebels who were complaining about a lack of water. I try to remember that the rebellious Israelites were simply repeating a pattern that their forbearers had done a generation earlier. *Was Moses any different?* Had he not shown a disposition to lose his temper and strike out on his own? Perhaps Moses is simply a reflection of his Levite ancestors (cf. 1 Chronicles 23:6, 12-14). We can remember the last words spoken over Levi by Jacob on his deathbed, and how the Levites would be dispersed and scattered throughout Israel because of the bloodshed at Shechem (cf. Genesis 34:25-31):

"Simeon and Levi are brothers; their swords are implements of violence. Let my soul not enter into their council; let not my glory be united with their assembly; because in their anger they slew men, and in their self-will they lamed oxen. Cursed be their anger, for it is fierce; and their wrath, for it is cruel. I will disperse them in Jacob, and scatter them in Israel" (Genesis 49:5-7).

Is it possible that some of the effects of Levi's sin were passed down through the generations to Moses? Simeon and Levi had taken matters into their own hands hundreds of years earlier, when the prince of Shechem had compromised the honor of their sister Dinah. As a young prince of Egypt, Moses had taken matters into his own hands as he saw the mistreatment of his Hebrew kinfolk by the Egyptian slave masters.

Now some eighty years later, the pattern seems to have repeated itself. Moses is angry, frustrated, irritated, and probably sick and tired of watching the Israelites continue to make poor choices when it comes to not trusting in the Lord. Rather than simply speaking to the rock, he strikes it twice. Water rushes forth, but the price he will have to pay is very high: Moses will be unable to lead Israel into the Promised Land. What can we learn from this example of a great person, who pays a significant price for a single human failure?

## A Faith that Works

What has brought the Israelites to the point where they, yet again, have another altercation with Moses? **A lack of faith in God's provision.** Moses, with past examples in his life of acting rashly—has seemingly been able to keep his temper under control during his entire tenure as Israel's leader. Perhaps with some negative thoughts about the Israelites here or there, his actions in serving the people have been exemplary. But at Meribah-Kadesh, having to wait for the previous generation to be gone, the new generation of people are repeating old habits. *Moses reaches his proverbial wits end.* Moses is not vengeful or evil in his attitude toward either the Israelites or God, but he has had his fill of the wining and complaining.

I think that in *Chukat*, we can see a bit of a comparison and contrast between demonstrating faith and the *proper* works that are becoming of people who believe in God. Consider the mysteries of the red heifer, and the inexplicable procedure for purifying the Tabernacle and its accoutrements. No definite explanation, even today, has been offered for these things. The Israelites simply had to believe and follow the instructions—and yet, by faith and obedience to the instructions, the Tabernacle would be purified and the Lord would dwell in it.

Another example of faith and works is seen a little later in our *parashah*, as the Israelites begin again to complain—this time about a lack of water and a lack of variety of food. The Lord is again provoked to send judgment, this time in the form of poisonous serpents upon Israel:

"The people spoke against God and Moses, 'Why have you brought us up out of Egypt to die in the wilderness? For there is no food and no water, and we loathe this miserable food.' The LORD sent fiery serpents among the people and they bit the people, so that many people of Israel died. So the people came to Moses and said, 'We have sinned, because we have spoken against the LORD and you; intercede with the LORD, that He may remove the serpents from us.' And Moses interceded for the people. Then the LORD said to Moses, 'Make a fiery *serpent*, and set it on a standard; and it shall come about, that everyone who is bitten, when he looks at it, he will live.' And Moses made a bronze serpent and set it on the standard; and it came about, that if a serpent bit any man, when he looked to the bronze serpent, he lived" (Numbers 21:5-9).

Witnessed here is a very vivid example of a people judged by God. Yet because of Moses' intercession for them—and God's mercy toward them—they had just one simple thing to do if they wanted to avoid death: they had to look upon the brazen serpent. Those who looked upon the lifted standard, though bitten, would not die. In many respects, after being told the solution to the venomous bites, **the people had to have the faith to receive healing.** The standard did not heal them; it was necessity for them to look upon it which would. Think about how relatively easy this would be.

In a like manner, followers of Yeshua the Messiah have been instructed to look upon Him, who was lifted up to die for our sins. In His conversation with the learned Nicodemus, Yeshua made it clear that He would be lifted up, similar to the brazen serpent lifted up by Moses:

"As Moses lifted up the serpent in the wilderness, even so must the Son of Man be lifted up; so that whoever believes will in Him have eternal life" John 3:14-15).

Today, some have the same challenge that was presented to Nicodemus. **We have to believe in Him** and His accomplished work *in being lifted up* in order to receive eternal life. Then as we speak to the Rock, we can make our confession of faith from our hearts. The Apostle Paul writes, "[I]f you confess with your mouth Yeshua *as* Lord, and believe in your heart that God raised Him from the dead, you will be saved; for with the heart a person believes, resulting in righteousness, and with the mouth he confesses, resulting in salvation. For the Scripture says, 'WHOEVER BELIEVES IN HIM WILL NOT BE DISAPPOINTED' [Isaiah 28:16]" (Romans 10:9-11).

Additionally, it is important to understand that Moses, in spite of his mistake out of anger and being barred from entering the Promised Land, **did not lose his being counted among the redeemed.** Moses, like all human beings, simply had some flaws that cost him some temporary rewards. David and Paul and other characters throughout the Bible likewise suffered consequences because of previous sins. Most of us can relate as we have seen the consequences of sin in our lives, which have often caused us some aches and pains in Earthly living. But that does not mean that we lose our salvation or status as God's children. Moses never denied the supernatural acts of God in delivering Israel, or his own special calling into God's service; Moses was simply fed up with the bickering and immaturity of the Israelites.

Moses himself will be among the myriads of saints who spend eternity with us. Moses was, after all, present on the Mount of Transfiguration before Peter, John, and James—when Yeshua shone before them in all His glory (Matthew 17; Mark 9; Luke 9). Moses' presence at such an event assures us of His being numbered among the redeemed. Moses' legacy is a positive one that later generations looked to, most especially those within First Century Judaism such as Yeshua and the Apostles. Moses' choices and works indicate that he had great faith in the God of Israel, worthy of emulation by us. Consider what the author of Hebrews tells us:

"By faith Moses, when he had grown up, refused to be called the son of Pharaoh's daughter, choosing rather to endure ill-treatment with the people of God than to enjoy the passing pleasures of sin, considering the reproach of Messiah greater riches than the treasures of Egypt; for he was looking to the reward" (Hebrews 11:24-26).

As *Chukat* has indicated, some of the greatest of God's servants can be flawed. And yet, due to the mercy of a loving and compassionate Heavenly Father, we can have peace in the assurance that He has given us a way to approach Him and receive redemption by faith in His Son's sacrificial work at Golgotha. We have the choice—just like the Ancient Israelites had a choice to obey the laws of purification, or to look upon a brazen serpent in order to be healed—to cry out to the One who was lifted up on the bloody cross, slain to atone for our sins. One may not totally understand the reasoning behind any of these actions, but the result of being saved from sins should be in living a life of positive difference in the world (James 2:14-26).

Have you looked to the Risen Savior, speaking to Him as the Rock of your salvation? Do you have a faith that generates positive works—indicating that you truly have been redeemed? Do you continually operate in God's love and grace toward others, and perform good deeds? **May we all have faith that works, knowing that He hears our prayers and responds according to His mercy and grace!**

# *Balak* בָּלָק
## Destroyer
## "Consistent Blessings"

> Numbers 22:2-25:9
> Micah 5:6-6:8

Many Bible readers are quite familiar with elements seen in this week's Torah portion, *Balak*, even if they do not remember the chapters or verses where they appear. One of the main features seen in *Balak* is God using an animal to verbally communicate to a human being:

"And the LORD opened the mouth of the donkey, and she said to Balaam, 'What have I done to you, that you have struck me these three times?' Then Balaam said to the donkey, 'Because you have made a mockery of me! If there had been a sword in my hand, I would have killed you by now.' The donkey said to Balaam, 'Am I not your donkey on which you have ridden all your life to this day? Have I ever been accustomed to do so to you?' And he said, 'No'" (Numbers 22:28-30).

You may have heard the account of Balaam's donkey referred to, and someone quite seriously—or half-jokingly—say something like: *If God can speak through Balaam's a\*\*, He can certainly speak through me!* Even if you laughed at this, such an expression is certainly true, because many Believers can often recall points in their lives when the Holy Spirit used them in circumstances which in many cases were beyond their mortal comprehension. When they did not know what to say, the presence of the Lord took over, and communicated the proper words.

The focus for most people when they remember this section of Scripture is upon the miraculous incident of the donkey speaking to Balaam. Yet as memorable as it is to think about Baalam's donkey, too many forget the larger series of events in which this takes place. Baalam was some kind of prophet, who was to be hired by Balak king of Moab, who wanted him to curse the people of Israel.[65] However, the Lord would explicitly forbid Baalam from cursing Israel:

"God said to Balaam, 'Do not go with them; you shall not curse the people, for they are blessed'" (Numbers 22:12).

Baalam is permitted to see Balak, but he is not permitted to speak any words except those that God specifically would give to him:

"But the angel of the LORD said to Balaam, 'Go with the men, but you shall speak only the word which I tell you.' So Balaam went along with the leaders of Balak" (Numbers 22:35).

Balaam will only be permitted to speak the words that are given to him by God Himself (Numbers 22:38). This is a very interesting restriction, because even though Balak hires him (Numbers 22:41), what is spoken forth by Balaam are not curses upon Israel, but rather great blessings. While Balak expects Balaam to issue damning cries and laments upon the Israelites, Balaam instead declares great words of admiration, blessing, and prosperity (Numbers 23:1-30). As you read through the various utterances, one sees that Balaam is a

---

[65] Numbers 22:2-6.

mouthpiece for the God of Israel. Each of his three attempts to curse Israel (Numbers 23:7-10, 18-24; 24:3-9) turn out to be pronouncements of the Lord's great favor toward them.

## Balaam's First Attempt

The first attempt by Balaam to curse the Israelites comes from atop a hill overlooking the camp of Israel, after seven bulls and rams are offered up on seven altars[66] prepared by Balak and Balaam:

"He took up his discourse and said, 'From Aram Balak has brought me, Moab's king from the mountains of the East, "Come curse Jacob for me, and come, denounce Israel!" How shall I curse whom God has not cursed? And how can I denounce whom the LORD has not denounced? As I see him from the top of the rocks, and I look at him from the hills; behold, a people *who* dwells apart, and will not be reckoned among the nations. Who can count the dust of Jacob, or number the fourth part of Israel? Let me die the death of the upright, and let my end be like his!'" (Numbers 23:7-10).

This first utterance can be essentially summarized by the statement, "How can I damn whom God has not damned, how doom when the LORD has not doomed?" (NJPS). Balaam has spoken only what the Holy One has instructed him to say, and Balak is horrified. Shocked, he tells Balaam, "What have you done to me? I took you to curse my enemies, but behold, you have actually blessed them!" (Numbers 23:11).

## Balaam's Second Attempt

A second attempt is offered from another place, only where Balaam will not be able to see the entire camp of Israel. Again, seven bulls and seven rams are offered up before Balaam can speak:[67]

"Then he took up his discourse and said, 'Arise, O Balak, and hear; give ear to me, O son of Zippor! God is not a man, that He should lie, nor a son of man, that He should repent; has He said, and will He not do it? Or has He spoken, and will He not make it good? Behold, I have received *a command* to bless; when He has blessed, then I cannot revoke it. He has not observed misfortune in Jacob; nor has He seen trouble in Israel; the LORD his God is with him, and the shout of a king is among them. God brings them out of Egypt, He is for them like the horns of the wild ox. For there is no omen against Jacob, nor is there any divination against Israel; at the proper time it shall be said to Jacob and to Israel, what God has done! Behold, a people rises like a lioness, and as a lion it lifts itself; it will not lie down until it devours the prey, and drinks the blood of the slain'" (Numbers 23:18-24).

Once again, Balaam blesses rather than curses the people of Israel. In his declarations, the overriding thought is directed to the attributes of the Creator God. Balaam makes the categorical statement, **"God is not a human being, that he should lie, or a mortal, that he should change his mind"** (NRSV). Not only is Balaam respecting Israel's God in making these statements, but he declares forth how the words He causes him to speak will not be revoked. Unlike human beings, who will often say things that they will later renounce or alter—God's words about blessing Israel, spoken forth through Balaam, are not things He will renounce or alter. If anything, all Balak can witness is that things are

---

[66] Numbers 23:1-6.
[67] Numbers 23:13-17.

במדבר

going to be very good for Israel—by extension meaning that things are likely to be very bad for him!

Balak realizes that he has made a mistake in hiring Balaam, telling him to just stop speaking: "Do not curse them at all nor bless them at all!" (Numbers 23:25). But it is too late, because Balaam responds and reminds Balak, "Did I not tell you, 'Whatever the LORD speaks, that I must do'?" (Numbers 23:26). Balaam still has more to say about Israel.

## Balaam's Third Attempt

Balak realizes that Balaam has not finished speaking, so instead he takes him to another place where he can prophecy from, saying, "I will take you to another place; perhaps it will be agreeable with God that you curse them for me from there" (Numbers 23:27). For a third time, seven bulls and seven rams are offered up. This final time, Balaam issues a very special word, moved by the Spirit of God, that would impact not only future generations of Ancient Israel—but even Judaism until this very day:

"He took up his discourse and said, 'The oracle of Balaam the son of Beor, and the oracle of the man whose eye is opened; the oracle of him who hears the words of God, who sees the vision of the Almighty, falling down, yet having his eyes uncovered, how fair are your tents, O Jacob, your dwellings, O Israel! Like valleys that stretch out, like gardens beside the river, like aloes planted by the LORD, like cedars beside the waters. Water will flow from his buckets, and his seed *will be* by many waters, and his king shall be higher than Agag, and his kingdom shall be exalted. God brings him out of Egypt, He is for him like the horns of the wild ox. He will devour the nations *who are* his adversaries, and will crush their bones in pieces, and shatter *them* with his arrows. He couches, he lies down as a lion, and as a lion, who dares rouse him? Blessed is everyone who blesses you, and cursed is everyone who curses you'" (Numbers 24:3-9).

Certainly, one can see a bit of irony in how at the third time Balak asks Balaam to curse Israel—Balaam does exactly the opposite! Balaam can only declare how Israel has been blessed by God in abundance, and how He has been there to defend and guard His chosen people. Balaam was originally contracted to curse Israel, but was supernaturally prevented from doing so. It is easy to see in the Scriptures how devastating this would have been for King Balak. But, consider how even today the *Mah Tovu* is a traditional prayer that is used in the Jewish liturgy of the morning *Shabbat* service. These words, originally spoken by a pagan non-Israelite—speaking of the goodness of Israel's ancient tents and dwellings—remind pious Jews every week of the harmony that should be present in their lives on the Sabbath:

*Mah-tovu ohalekha Ya'akov*        מַה־טֹּבוּ אֹהָלֶיךָ יַעֲקֹב
*mishkenotekha Yisrael*            מִשְׁכְּנֹתֶיךָ יִשְׂרָאֵל

**How beautiful are your tents, O Jacob, your dwelling places, O Israel!** (Numbers 24:5, NIV).

This liturgical tradition of today's Synagogue, whether one is Orthodox or Conservative, intends to instill a connection between God's goodness and orderliness, and reverence that people are to show Him in the assembly place. The opening prayer when one enters into the sanctuary begins with exclaiming Numbers 24:5, and is then supplemented from various Psalm quotations:

> How fair are your tents, O Jacob, Your dwellings, O Israel! (Numbers 24:5).
> But I, through Your abundant love, enter Your house; I bow down in awe at Your holy temple (Psalm 5:8).
> O LORD, I love Your temple abode, the dwelling-place of Your glory (Psalm 26:8).
> As for me, may my prayer come to You, O LORD, at a favorable moment; O God, in Your abundant faithfulness, answer me with Your sure deliverance (Psalm 69:14).[68]

As you review the verses of the *Mah Tovu* prayer, perhaps you will discern that there is a thematic connection to be made between Israel being fair or goodly, and what the Prophet Micah declares is required by God of His people (Micah 6:8). Micah simply says that people are to do three things: (1) perform justice, (2) love kindness, and (3) walk humbly before the Lord. Is it possible that within the Jewish liturgical tradition, the Sages simply took Micah's description of *mah-tov* (מַה־טּוֹב), "what is good," and found some important verses from Psalms that would get people to continually remember that God requires much more than simply tents in straight lines? And by extension in more modern synagogues, would it help them demonstrate more than just reverent respect when the rabbi speaks?

When you consider the *Mah Tovu* verses from Psalms—or better yet, when you search intently into the counsel of Scripture about what doing justice, exhibiting lovingkindness, and walking humbly entails—there is much to inculcate into the mind and soul. This is to be a conformation process, where via the sanctification provided by the Holy Spirit, you can be transformed into the image of the Messiah Yeshua. The Apostle Paul taught, "do not be conformed to this world, but be transformed by the renewing of your mind, so that you may prove what the will of God is, that which is good and acceptable and perfect" (Romans 12:2). While the prophet-for-hire Balaam may have originally declared that Ancient Israel was "goodly," being good and proper involves far more than just being blessed by God. *Being blessed by God requires proper obedience and behavior becoming of Him.*

In order to prove, analyze, or examine what the perfect will of God is, His children must have their minds renewed by the indwelling presence of His Holy Spirit. The Spirit should be working in concert with a consistent, almost repetitious study of the Holy Writ. When Balaam type-figures, pagan persons, or irreligious individuals see you today—are the only things they can say about you are that you are blessed by the One you serve?[69]

## Balaam's Words to Balak

After Balaam makes this third, and rather significant blessing upon the Israelites—as he was "contracted" to do—Balak is furious. Balak sends Balaam away, but not without receiving a final prophecy delivered to himself. This prophecy against Moab has a message that will resonate to the end-times:

"Then Balak's anger burned against Balaam, and he struck his hands together; and Balak said to Balaam, 'I called you to curse my enemies, but behold, you have persisted in blessing

---

[68] All quotations for the *Mah Tovu* here are taken from the NJPS.
Cf. Hertz, *Authorised Daily Prayer Book*, pp 4-5; Harlow, *Siddur Sim Shalom*, 61.
[69] For some further thoughts, consult the author's article "God's '*Mah Tovu*' Requirements," appearing in the July 2009 issue of Outreach Israel News.

them these three times! Therefore, flee to your place now. I said I would honor you greatly, but behold, the LORD has held you back from honor.' Balaam said to Balak, 'Did I not tell your messengers whom you had sent to me, saying, "Though Balak were to give me his house full of silver and gold, I could not do anything contrary to the command of the LORD, either good or bad, of my own accord. What the LORD speaks, that I will speak"? And now, behold, I am going to my people; come, *and* I will advise you what this people will do to your people in the days to come'" (Numbers 24:10-14).

This prophecy was one that Balak did not bargain for, but by the end of the series of oracles, Balaam had no choice but to utter forth genuine words from God:

"He took up his discourse and said, 'The oracle of Balaam the son of Beor, and the oracle of the man whose eye is opened, the oracle of him who hears the words of God, and knows the knowledge of the Most High, who sees the vision of the Almighty, falling down, yet having his eyes uncovered. I see him, but not now; I behold him, but not near; a star shall come forth from Jacob, a scepter shall rise from Israel, and shall crush through the forehead of Moab, and tear down all the sons of Sheth. Edom shall be a possession, Seir, its enemies, also will be a possession, while Israel performs valiantly. One from Jacob shall have dominion, and will destroy the remnant from the city.' And he looked at Amalek and took up his discourse and said, 'Amalek was the first of the nations, but his end *shall be* destruction.' And he looked at the Kenite, and took up his discourse and said, 'Your dwelling place is enduring, and your nest is set in the cliff. Nevertheless Kain will be consumed; how long will Asshur keep you captive?' Then he took up his discourse and said, 'Alas, who can live except God has ordained it? But ships *shall come* from the coast of Kittim, and they shall afflict Asshur and will afflict Eber; so they also *will come* to destruction'" (Numbers 24:15-24).

In these the final words delivered by Balaam, generations of Israel could take comfort in knowing that foes like Moab would be defeated. Evil kings like Balak would be humiliated, and God's chosen nation would stand supreme. But this is not something that Israel itself would be responsible for, as instead someone coming forth from Jacob would accomplish it:

"I see him, but not now; I behold him, but not near; a star shall come forth from Jacob, a scepter shall rise from Israel, and shall crush through the forehead of Moab, and tear down all the sons of Sheth" (Numbers 24:17).

We believe that this reference is to Messiah Yeshua, the King of Israel. It is only by recognizing Him as the vindicator of Israel, that those who would cause harm to God's chosen nation can be discredited and conquered. But as our Torah portion from this week shows, individuals like Balaam had no choice but to recognize the supremacy of Israel and how God has blessed His people. When that future day comes when Moab, Edom, Amalek, Kain, Asshur, and any other enemies of Israel face a hopeless battle against the Lord—will many from those nations turn in repentance and acknowledge the King of Kings? If Israel does its job as is expected by the *Mah Tovu* prayer, then surely many will bow their knees in worship to Yeshua as Savior and be counted among the redeemed (cf. Philippians 2:9-11)!

# *Pinchas* פִּינְחָס
## Phinehas
## "Consuming Zeal"

> Numbers 25:10-30:1 [29:40]
> 1 Kings 18:46-19:21

Our Torah reading for this week, *Pinchas*, is entitled for the son of the high priest Eleazar, whose actions were actually more fully detailed in the closing verses of *Balak* (Numbers 25:1-9). As you begin your study, you might wonder why the incident regarding Phinehas was separated into these two different readings. The episode is described in detail at the end of *Balak*, and the resultant blessings that ensued for Phinehas are described in the *parashah* which bears his name. I would simply say that those who follow the annual Torah cycle are given two opportunities to reflect upon Phinehas—both his righteously indignant actions, and how the Lord promised him perpetual favor:

"Then the LORD spoke to Moses, saying, 'Phinehas the son of Eleazar, the son of Aaron the priest, has turned away My wrath from the sons of Israel in that he was jealous with My jealousy among them, so that I did not destroy the sons of Israel in My jealousy. Therefore say, "Behold, I give him My covenant of peace; and it shall be for him and his descendants after him, a covenant of a perpetual priesthood, because he was jealous for his God and made atonement for the sons of Israel"'" (Numbers 25:10-13).

With *Balak* having concluded with Phinehas' stoppage of a potentially wide sweeping plague, *Pinchas* records how a census of Israel is taken after the initial plague is stopped.[70] Following this are instructions regarding inheritance of property[71] and some of the specific offerings and sacrifices that are to be made during special days and the appointed times.[72] Although these are important passages, much of the focus for our *parashah* will understandably be considering the effects of the righteous deeds of Phinehas by stopping the spread of sin in the camp of Israel.

## Balaam's Advice

In *Balak*, our Torah portion from last week, the prophet-for-hire Balaam declared three distinct blessings over Israel (Numbers 23:7-10, 18-24; 24:3-9)—which were not well received by his benefactor, King Balak. Later in Numbers 31:16 it is stated that the council of Balaam to Balak was to get the Israelite men to curse themselves, which did occur as many of them consorted with Moabite prostitutes. The scene of Numbers 25:1-9 plays a role for further instruction that Yeshua's delivers to the assembly at Pergamum in the Book of Revelation. Apparently, there were teachers in Pergamum who taught things that would have the same negative effect of people cursing themselves, by cavorting in idolatrous places where sexual immorality was practiced:

"But I have a few things against you, because you have there some who hold the teaching of Balaam, who kept teaching Balak to put a stumbling block before the sons of Israel, to eat things sacrificed to idols and to commit *acts of* immorality" (Revelation 2:14).

---

[70] Numbers 26:1-65.
[71] Numbers 27:1-14.
[72] Numbers 28:1-29:40.

במדבר

Balaam's advice was simple, as He instructed Balak to encourage Moabite prostitutes to present themselves to the males of Israel. *Human nature and biology being what they are, many would fall into temptation.* Within a short period of time, the men of Israel will fall into sexual sin and gross idolatry, cursing themselves by demonstrating extreme disloyalty to their God. Sadly, as Moabite prostitutes entered into the camp of Israel, they had a considerable amount of success. Phinehas comes onto the scene, as an Israelite man and one of the prostitutes prepare to fornicate adjacent to the Tent of Meeting. He takes action and executes them both with a spear:

"While Israel remained at Shittim, the people began to play the harlot with the daughters of Moab. For they invited the people to the sacrifices of their gods, and the people ate and bowed down to their gods. So Israel joined themselves to Baal of Peor, and the LORD was angry against Israel. The LORD said to Moses, 'Take all the leaders of the people and execute them in broad daylight before the LORD, so that the fierce anger of the LORD may turn away from Israel.' So Moses said to the judges of Israel, 'Each of you slay his men who have joined themselves to Baal of Peor.' Then behold, one of the sons of Israel came and brought to his relatives a Midianite woman, in the sight of Moses and in the sight of all the congregation of the sons of Israel, while they were weeping at the doorway of the tent of meeting. When Phinehas the son of Eleazar, the son of Aaron the priest, saw it, he arose from the midst of the congregation and took a spear in his hand, and he went after the man of Israel into the tent and pierced both of them through, the man of Israel and the woman, through the body. So the plague on the sons of Israel was checked. Those who died by the plague were 24,000" (Numbers 25:1-9).

Reflecting on this scene, we see that the base desires and instincts of the flesh were inflamed. The Moabite women enticed the Israelite men with the promise of sexual pleasure. These acts of flagrant disobedience infuriated the Lord, and the punishment communicated to Moses was to be very swift and severe. The judges of Israel were to take the leaders, who succumbed to the Moabite women and joined themselves to Baal of Peor, and slay them. This direct judgment was to take place immediately, because the "the LORD's anger burned against them" (NIV) in the form of a plague that would ravage Israel.

As this command was given to the weeping judges at the doorway of the Tent of Meeting, the epitome of blatant sin was being exhibited right before their eyes. One of the young princes of Israel, from the tribe of Simeon, flagrantly brought a young Midianite woman right in front of Moses and those assembled at the Tent of Meeting. Then in an act of total disregard for his elders and the instructions of God, he took her aside to engage in sexual intercourse.

Our hero Phinehas jumped into action. He grabbed a spear and went over to the tent where the sin was taking place. He goes inside and impales both sinners. This dramatic execution astonished the crowd, but most importantly, it pleased God greatly. Almost immediately, the plague was stopped and only a limited number of Israelites died from the Divine fury.

## Phinehas' Reward

Now as we continue to this week's Torah reading, the reward to Phinehas for his actions to terminate the vile behavior is articulated:

"Then the LORD spoke to Moses, saying, 'Phinehas the son of Eleazar, the son of Aaron the priest, has turned away My wrath from the sons of Israel in that he was jealous with My jealousy among them, so that I did not destroy the sons of Israel in My jealousy. Therefore say, "Behold, I give him My covenant of peace; and it shall be for him and his descendants after him, a covenant of a perpetual priesthood, because he was jealous for his God and made atonement for the sons of Israel"'" (Numbers 25:10-13).

The Lord is greatly pleased with Phinehas. He states that Phinehas was "jealous with My jealousy," which elevated the execution of the two sinners to the level that He required for perfect justice to be delivered. As a result of responding with righteous indignation to the sin in the camp, Phinehas receives an eternal reward from God. He and his descendants will have a covenant of peace and be made a perpetual priesthood. The Lord was very moved when witnessing an individual who had the passion and zeal to operate on a level where sin and unrighteousness would be promptly dealt with. Centuries later, the Psalmist will reflect on Phinehas' actions:

"Then Phinehas stood up and interposed, and so the plague was stayed. And it was reckoned to him for righteousness, to all generations forever" (Psalm 106:30-31).

This is an interesting use of words, because it might remind us of how Abraham's faith in God was reckoned to him as righteousness:

"Then he believed in the LORD; and He reckoned it to him as righteousness" (Genesis 15:6).

The statement, "credited it to him as righteousness" (NIV), has become one of the most important themes seen throughout the Bible—most especially for those of us who have placed our trust in Messiah Yeshua. The Apostle Paul made use of Genesis 15:6 in his letters to the Galatians and the Romans:

"Even so Abraham BELIEVED GOD, AND IT WAS RECKONED TO HIM AS RIGHTEOUSNESS" (Galatians 3:6).

"For what does the Scripture say? 'ABRAHAM BELIEVED GOD, AND IT WAS CREDITED TO HIM AS RIGHTEOUSNESS'" (Romans 4:3).

James the Just, half-brother of Yeshua, also quotes Genesis 15:6, in trying to describe how faith in God and the right actions work together:

"You see that faith was working with his works, and as a result of the works, faith was perfected; and the Scripture was fulfilled which says, 'AND ABRAHAM BELIEVED GOD, AND IT WAS RECKONED TO HIM AS RIGHTEOUSNESS,' and he was called the friend of God" (James 2:23).

In many respects, the father of faith, Abraham, had his faith counted to him as righteousness because he fully believed in God's promises to him and acted accordingly. In a similar manner, Phinehas' actions to execute the fornicators not only halted a devastating plague upon Israel, but his actions were considered just and righteous. *God is greatly pleased when zealous people stand up and do the right thing.*

## Consuming Zeal

When Believers often think about zeal and zealousness for holy and righteous living, we are rightly reminded of the life and ministry of Messiah Yeshua. The words of Psalm 69:9, "For zeal for Your house has consumed me, and the reproaches of those who reproach You have fallen on me" (Psalm 69:9), may come to remembrance, as it embodies much of what guided Yeshua's actions. This very verse gives a witness to Yeshua's outrage with the Temple moneychangers, as they were often found to be shortchanging the people:

"The Passover of the Jews was near, and Yeshua went up to Jerusalem. And He found in the temple those who were selling oxen and sheep and doves, and the money changers seated *at their tables*. And He made a scourge of cords, and drove *them* all out of the temple, with the sheep and the oxen; and He poured out the coins of the money changers and overturned their tables; and to those who were selling the doves He said, 'Take these things away; stop making My Father's house a place of business.' His disciples remembered that it was written, 'ZEAL FOR YOUR HOUSE WILL CONSUME ME' [Psalm 69:9]" (John 2:13-17).

In this readily remembered incident, Yeshua is seen to have had a serious problem with the Temple moneychangers who made the House of God into a den of merchandising and business. We can see some definite parallels between Phinehas' act of summary judgment, and Yeshua taking matters into His own hands with overturning the tables in the Temple complex. The Lord discerned the motives of the enterprise that was being conducted, and without a great deal of warning, takes up righteous judgment on His own accord. Surely others had witnessed some of the hassling and intimidation of those who had come into the Temple to purchase animals for sacrifice, or exchange their foreign currency for Temple standard. Had there been those who had wanted to do something about it, but were too afraid? *Yeshua was not afraid to take actions in the Holy Place.*

## Modern-Day Zeal

As one contemplates the examples of both Phinehas' and Yeshua's zeal, it is important for us to consider our own level of passion for righteousness. When we examine *Balak* and *Pinchas* every year in the Torah cycle, do we really reflect on what we might do, when confronted with scenes of unrighteousness? Will we take the necessary action, or will we be scared of potential harm that might come to us? Admittedly, what Phinehas and Yeshua both did was not popular with many of the people. Yet, Phinehas inherited an eternal covenant of peace!

Perhaps each of us should take a good look at ourselves, before we consider to take action in an assembly. How are you presently dealing with any personal sin that impedes with your walk? Are you pursuing righteousness? Do you ever think about overturning the tables of sinful thoughts and attitudes that might manifest themselves in your heart? Are you willing to impale and execute that old unrighteous person, which may manifest itself from time to time?

The example of Phinehas should be a great inspiration to you as you seek to please our Heavenly Father, serving Him with a pure heart and with honorable motives. Does a zeal for things of the Lord *really* consume your thoughts and actions, or a zeal for self-pleasure, self-interest, and aggrandizement? It is my hope and prayer that a zeal for Him occupies your every waking moment!

# *Mattot* מַטּוֹת
### Tribes
### "Vows, Unity, Brotherly Love"

> Numbers 30:2[1]-32:42
> Jeremiah 1:1-2:3

The Book of Numbers is coming to a close as the Israelites gather on the plains of Moab, overlooking the Dead Sea and the Jordan River valley. Through His servant Moses, the Lord is continuing to prepare Israel for their taking of the Promised Land. *Mattot* or "Tribes" has three chapters that deal with three topics. Typically for calendar purposes, *Mattot* is coupled with the final reading in Numbers, *Masa'ei* or "Journeys," which has four chapters, but for our purposes in this commentary we will be considering each *parashah* separately.

The instructions delivered to Ancient Israel in *Mattot* first concern the taking of vows made by men and women.[73] Following this, a record of Israel's conflict with the Midianites is detailed, including a description of not only a successful campaign, but how the spoils of war were distributed.[74] The third chapter of *Mattot* covers how the tribes of Reuben and Gad request that they be allowed to settle in land east of the Jordan River.[75] In our Torah reading, the significance of honoring one's word, Israel seeking unity among itself, and the practice of tribal respect—are all critical components to consider as Israel prepares to enter the Promise Land and eject the Canaanites.

After almost forty years of wandering in the wilderness, the "Joshua generation" is being prepared for its journey across the Jordan River to occupy Canaan and establish Israel as a nation within its own territory. This is no easy task, because the land that God has promised Israel is occupied by six pagan nations who must be driven from it. We can remember how Moses gave explicit instructions to the Israelites soon after their departure from Egypt that these peoples were going to be driven out:

"Be sure to observe what I am commanding you this day: behold, I am going to drive out the Amorite before you, and the Canaanite, the Hittite, the Perizzite, the Hivite and the Jebusite. Watch yourself that you make no covenant with the inhabitants of the land into which you are going, or it will become a snare in your midst. But *rather*, you are to tear down their altars and smash their *sacred* pillars and cut down their Asherim—for you shall not worship any other god, for the LORD, whose name is Jealous, is a jealous God—otherwise you might make a covenant with the inhabitants of the land and they would play the harlot with their gods and sacrifice to their gods, and someone might invite you to eat of his sacrifice, and you might take some of his daughters for your sons, and his daughters might play the harlot with their gods and cause your sons *also* to play the harlot with their gods" (Exodus 34:11-16).

We know from our knowledge of Israel's history witnessed in previous Torah readings that the generation which received this instruction was not a faithful group of people. After over thirty-nine years, most of those of the "Exodus generation"—except Joshua and Caleb—who were twenty years or older at the time of the spies' bad report had died in the desert (Numbers 32:11). And yet on the plains of Moab, many of those of the "Joshua generation," as discussed previously in *Balak* and *Pinchas*, had succumbed to the temptations of Moabite prostitutes and their idolatry. Some of the warnings from Israel's early days of wanderings the desert, had not been obeyed. The Israelites exhibited a tendency to become involved with some of the cultures which surrounded them. This could have devastating, long-term consequences, because the Holy One of Israel does not want a people who are going to be associated with other gods. *He wants a people who are totally sold out to Him and Him alone.* In *Mattot*, we see some of how the Lord goes about preparing the "Joshua generation" for the task of taking the Promised Land.

Many of the Israelites had just died from a plague, incurred as a result of the entanglement with the Moabite women. Phinehas' zealous act abruptly stopped the plague

---

[73] Numbers 30:1-16.
[74] Numbers 31:1-54.
[75] Numbers 32:1-42.

and the Lord ordered Moses to conduct a census that would record the number of Israelites by tribe, just prior to crossing the Jordan. As our previous portion concluded, God once again had to reiterate the importance of observing His appointed times and the offerings involved in them:

"You shall present these to the LORD at your appointed times, besides your votive offerings and your freewill offerings, for your burnt offerings and for your grain offerings and for your drink offerings and for your peace offerings. Moses spoke to the sons of Israel in accordance with all that the LORD had commanded Moses. Then Moses spoke to the heads of the tribes of the sons of Israel, saying, 'This is the word which the LORD has commanded'" (Numbers 29:39-30:1)

But while *Pinchas* ended with an understanding that God's people are to take His sacred seasons very seriously, the instruction that follows it concerns order in the family.

## Vows and Oaths, Husbands and Wives

As *Mattot* begins, the Lord has Moses give some instruction to the leaders of the various tribes, about the importance of making vows and swearing oaths:

"Then Moses spoke to the heads of the tribes of the sons of Israel, saying, 'This is the word which the LORD has commanded. If a man makes a vow to the LORD, or takes an oath to bind himself with a binding obligation, he shall not violate his word; he shall do according to all that proceeds out of his mouth'" (Numbers 30:1-2).

The admonition to honor one's word is critical when it comes to maintaining cohesiveness among a group of people. The spoken word is something quite serious, as elaborated on throughout the Scriptures. Proverbs 18:20-21 asserts, "With the fruit of a man's mouth his stomach will be satisfied; he will be satisfied *with* the product of his lips. Death and life are in the power of the tongue, and those who love it will eat its fruit." James the Just similarly says, "So also the tongue is a small part of the body, and *yet* it boasts of great things. See how great a forest is set aflame by such a small fire!" (James 3:5).

In many cases, what someone agrees to do involves either family commitments or business agreements, things that sometimes have to be thought through and analyzed very carefully. If persons within the agricultural society of Israel agree to trade crops for animals, or their produce for a certain amount of gold or silver—such agreements should not be easily broken, but neither should they be made on a whim. The Lord did not want His chosen people entering into Canaan, establishing themselves, and then be dishonest with one another. In particular, should agreements or vows have to be broken, they should be broken with some specific guidelines in mind.

Numbers 30:3-15 includes some instruction which modern people admittedly have some difficulty with. The difficulty is not with the recognition that sometimes people speak without thinking, and that an authoritative voice has to come on the scene in protection, and be there to cancel a commitment that might be harmful. 1 Thessalonians 5:14 says, after all, "We urge you, brethren, admonish the unruly, encourage the fainthearted, help the weak, be patient with everyone." *Some people make stupid decisions and they need help.* What some Believers, Christian and Messianic alike, have difficulty with is that the power to annul vows in Numbers 30:3-15 is given to husbands and fathers. This is not to say that husbands and fathers are unimportant or to be disrespected—but it would appear here that men have some power that women do not have. In a time when women work alongside men in the workplace, and wives often have to provide for their families every bit as much as husbands, these instructions are often viewed as being a bit archaic. And being in

Messianic ministry, and having interacted with many Torah observant people over the years, I have personally witnessed a great number of abuses with these instructions.

The instructions in Numbers 30 themselves detail how vows and oaths can be made by husbands, their wives, their daughters, and even widows and divorcees. All readers agree that the Lord places a substantial amount of emphasis for people *to be careful* with the commitments that they make. The husband or father of a wife or daughter, who makes a statement which he believes is in error, has the authority to nullify and cancel such a statement when hearing about it:

"Also if a woman makes a vow to the LORD, and binds herself by an obligation in her father's house in her youth, and her father hears her vow and her obligation by which she has bound herself, and her father says nothing to her, then all her vows shall stand and every obligation by which she has bound herself shall stand. But if her father should forbid her on the day he hears *of it*, none of her vows or her obligations by which she has bound herself shall stand; and the LORD will forgive her because her father had forbidden her. However, if she should marry while under her vows or the rash statement of her lips by which she has bound herself, and her husband hears of it and says nothing to her on the day he hears *it*, then her vows shall stand and her obligations by which she has bound herself shall stand. But if on the day her husband hears *of it*, he forbids her, then he shall annul her vow which she is under and the rash statement of her lips by which she has bound herself; and the LORD will forgive her" (Numbers 30:3-8).

The way a great number of Messianic men have read this is that they need to not only be careful about what their wives and daughters commit themselves to, but that they are the final authority regarding what happens within their families. These commandments are viewed as being some kind of "reserve powers" that women do not have, affirming in their minds, albeit subconsciously, that men are ultimately superior to women—or that women are *inferior* to men.

There is a serious problem with this line of reasoning, which few Messianic people are usually are aware of: **What did these instructions mean for the Israelites against the social background(s) of the Ancient Near East?** Too many just read Numbers 30, and totally forget that these instructions regulated a social climate that was not at all the same as the Twenty-First Century West. Many Messianic and Orthodox Jewish men think that these commandments fully affirm the dominance of men over women. Yet, as Ronald B. Allen points out, the issue in Numbers 30 is actually how "In the male-oriented culture of biblical times, there were numerous complications that would arise when a woman would make a religious vow...we should not miss the fact that women did make vows, which shows that they really did participate in the worship patterns of Israel."[76] Far from Numbers 30 establishing some kind of male superiority over women, it actually extended some serious rights to women—*by the virtue of them even being allowed to make vows or commitments*—things which were largely unseen in the law codes contemporary to the Torah.

With Israel's Law allowing females the significant right to make commitments on behalf of the family (most likely in trade), it is understandable that within the largely patriarchal Ancient Near East, that some guidelines would need to be in place for husbands and fathers to protect their wives and daughters. A husband or father can cancel a vow made

---

[76] Ronald B. Allen, "Numbers," in Frank E. Gaebelein, ed. et. al., *Expositor's Bible Commentary* (Grand Rapids: Zondervan, 1990), 2:958.

by his wife or daughter, especially if agreements they made would cause some kind of harm to the family. *Such a principle should surely remain in place for today.* Messianic husbands and fathers need to be aware of what their wives or daughters are saying. If they hear something that is going to hurt the family, the effort should be expelled to see that their poor decisions be promptly stopped.

Once in Messianic ministry, I really had an opportunity to see how this instruction could work. When attending a gathering of Believers, I recall how a woman got up and made a declarative statement before a large audience of people, essentially bringing a curse or negative action upon herself and her husband. She said, in the presence of her husband and the crowd gathered, "If such-and-such occurs, then may God strike us dead!" There were some gasps in the audience, but by-and-large nothing was said. The husband let her statement stand and the meeting concluded.

Then the next day, a Messianic Jewish friend of mine, who grew up in a Conservative Jewish home where the Torah was honored, asked me if I had been at all disturbed by the comments made the previous evening. I said I was disturbed, but I had no control over the statements. At that point, he said that he believed that the husband had the opportunity to annul the statement his wife made and avoid any negative consequences. I encouraged my friend to tell the husband what the Torah said about his responsibility to annul a vow or oath. Unfortunately, the husband was unwilling to annul the remarks of his wife. Was he a bad husband in failing to consider that what his wife said could result in something bad occurring to both his wife *and himself?*

Everyone recognizes that a husband or father should be careful about what his wife or daughter says. **Husbands and fathers need to look out for their families.** Yet Numbers 30:3-8 says nothing about a father canceling a negative word made by a son, although a father as parent clearly does have the authority to nullify this. Likewise, does a mother have the authority to cancel a negative word made by a daughter *or* a son? I think that a mother as a parent surely does have the right to cancel the harmful words of her children, which can negatively affect the entire family.

The real challenge in applying Numbers 30:3-8 for Messianic Believers today is not that a husband should be looking out for the best interests of his wife should she speak without thinking—**but what happens when the husband errs by speaking without thinking.** Who is going to be there when he makes a vow or commitment that will bring harm to the family? Is his bad word just expected to stand because he is a male—or is his wife as his helpmeet and partner going to stand up for his defense, and see that his negative word be canceled?

This is an area that I have admittedly had difficulty with, because before marrying Margaret in 1994 I was married to a woman who was very dominating, and who totally ran our family. I had very little say in what we did, or in how my two natural daughters were raised. Unlike my current marriage, I was unequally yoked, and did not have the benefit of a spouse who really loved me and cared for me, just like I was supposed to love her and care for her (cf. Ephesians 5:25). When I married Margaret, I admittedly found my second marriage to be quite liberating, as I was able to have a definite say in the affairs of our new family, and in what John, Jane, and Maggie were doing. If Margaret or Jane or Maggie ever make a commitment that was in error, I have—according to the Torah—the right to cancel such a commitment. But it does not seem appropriate at all that female commitments which can be harmful can be nullified, yet male commitments made by John *or even myself* that can be harmful have to stand. I know that if Margaret too were not a co-leader of our family, always counseling me and letting me know about things, that I would have made some serious mistakes during our time together. I know of instances when Margaret has had to step in and nullify or correct remarks I have made that would harm our household. *She has saved me from experiencing negative consequences of some of my actions.*

I know of Messianic husbands today who would prefer that their words remain in force, *even harmful words*, just because it might prove some kind of male superiority or dominance over women. (Yes, a few might actually choose bad things to happen to their families just so their position of "authority" might stand.) Their wives frequently have no say in what goes on in their families. I would submit that their families are worse off because the wife does not have the ability to counsel her husband, and be there to guard him should he be in error.

The instructions of Numbers 30:3-8, far from asserting some kind of male superiority over women, originally extended rights to women that societies contemporary to Ancient Israel did not often have. Allen further describes how we see "a gradual shifting from the patriarchy to a more egalitarian relationship between women and men. The change is very gradual in biblical times, but the change is underway."[77] Now in the post-resurrection era, where males and females are definitely equal (Galatians 3:28), should wives and mothers have the authority of Numbers 30:3-8 as originally given to Israelite husbands and fathers, *halachically* extended to them? Many of today's Messianic Torah teachers would exclaim a resounding "No!" But much of the Jewish theological tradition itself has already answered this for us, recognizing how time has taken its course changing the applicability of these commandments originally delivered into a social setting that is largely gone. Jacob Milgrom points out, "by the time of the Talmud, the Sages limited the applicability of this law by restricting its time (the year between ages 11 and 12) and circumstances."[78]

In Messianic homes today, the issue is not so much whether the commandments remain relevant—*because they surely do*—the issue is whether a wife can look out for her husband to the same degree as a husband can look out for his wife. Do spouses share authority within the home? While I know many Messianic families will continue in thinking that husbands possess some kind of "reserve powers" in Numbers 30:3-8, I also know that if Margaret had not canceled some of my words in the past, I might not be writing this today, having chosen a different path for my pursuits. I know that not only is she stronger with me as her husband, *but I am stronger with her as my wife!* My position as a husband or father is not nullified or abolished if my wife is a co-leader of the family and an equal partner along with me. On the contrary, **we both look out for each other.** I pray that all husbands and fathers in today's Messianic community learn to value their wives, just as I have, and that some of the misapplication of Numbers 30:3-8 we have seen will come to an end.

## Unity Over the Midianites

After the instruction about making vows is delivered, the Israelites are commanded to take up war with the Midianites. The war plans are very explicit, and Israel complies accordingly:

"Then the LORD spoke to Moses, saying, 'Take full vengeance for the sons of Israel on the Midianites; afterward you will be gathered to your people.' Moses spoke to the people, saying, 'Arm men from among you for the war, that they may go against Midian to execute

---

[77] Ibid.
[78] Milgrom, in *Etz Hayim*, 942.

the LORD's vengeance on Midian. A thousand from each tribe of all the tribes of Israel you shall send to the war.' So there were furnished from the thousands of Israel, a thousand from each tribe, twelve thousand armed for war. Moses sent them, a thousand from each tribe, to the war, and Phinehas the son of Eleazar the priest, to the war with them, and the holy vessels and the trumpets for the alarm in his hand. So they made war against Midian, just as the LORD had commanded Moses, and they killed every male'" (Numbers 31:1-7).

Equal squads are taken from each of the twelve tribes, excluding Levi, for this military excursion. With tremendous unity of purpose and accompanied by Phinehas, the son of the high priest, and the holy vessels and the silver trumpets, the soldiers of Israel take on the Midianites and defeat them (Numbers 31:8-12). When the fighting is over, a census is taken of Israel's military force, and no one is found to have been killed in action:

"Then the officers who were over the thousands of the army, the captains of thousands and the captains of hundreds, approached Moses, and they said to Moses, 'Your servants have taken a census of men of war who are in our charge, and no man of us is missing'" (Numbers 31:48-49).

This was exceptionally wonderful news, especially in light of the invasion of Canaan that is seen later in the Book of Joshua. Unity of purpose and resolve is rewarded with an outstanding victory. The confidence level of Israel must have been sky high as the people pondered the humiliation of the Midianites, without losing a single combatant. *The Holy One was definitely preparing Israel for more battles to come.*

## Concern for Tribal Brethren

In Numbers 32, a challenge is presented to Moses. The Reubenites and Gadites have decided that they would like to settle on the east side of the Jordan, because the land there appears to be good for grazing their plentiful livestock. This request generates a lengthy tirade from Moses, who likens it to the judgment that came upon Israel as a consequence of the bad report from the ten spies:

"But Moses said to the sons of Gad and to the sons of Reuben, 'Shall your brothers go to war while you yourselves sit here? Now why are you discouraging the sons of Israel from crossing over into the land which the LORD has given them? This is what your fathers did when I sent them from Kadesh-barnea to see the land. For when they went up to the valley of Eshcol and saw the land, they discouraged the sons of Israel so that they did not go into the land which the LORD had given them. So the LORD's anger burned in that day, and He swore, saying, 'None of the men who came up from Egypt, from twenty years old and upward, shall see the land which I swore to Abraham, to Isaac and to Jacob; for they did not follow Me fully, except Caleb the son of Jephunneh the Kenizzite and Joshua the son of Nun, for they have followed the LORD fully.' So the LORD's anger burned against Israel, and He made them wander in the wilderness forty years, until the entire generation of those who had done evil in the sight of the LORD was destroyed. Now behold, you have risen up in your fathers' place, a brood of sinful men, to add still more to the burning anger of the LORD against Israel. For if you turn away from following Him, He will once more abandon them in the wilderness, and you will destroy all these people" (Numbers 32:6-15).

*This was a horrible rebuke.* Moses tears into the leaders of the tribes of Reuben and Gad. Yet at the end of his chastisement, the Reubenites and Gadites decide that they will indeed be among the Israelites who help secure the Promised Land with the other tribes, fighting alongside them:

"Then they came near to him and said, 'We will build here sheepfolds for our livestock and cities for our little ones; but we ourselves will be armed ready *to go* before the sons of Israel, until we have brought them to their place, while our little ones live in the fortified cities because of the inhabitants of the land. We will not return to our homes until every one of the sons of Israel has possessed his inheritance. For we will not have an inheritance with them on the other side of the Jordan and beyond, because our inheritance has fallen to us on this side of the Jordan toward the east'" (Numbers 32:16-19).

As it turns out, Moses not only places the Reubenites and Gadites on the eastern side of the Jordan, but he also discerns that it is the right place for part of the tribe of Manasseh.[79] In a great gesture of unity and camaraderie as a part of the polity of Israel, these two-and-a-half tribes commit to securing Canaan with the other tribes, before they return to establish lives for themselves in Gilead and Bashan. Their request for land east of the Jordan is granted, and they have made the decision to stand with the other tribes of Israel to take the land west of the Jordan.

## Being Ready for God's Purpose?

After nearly forty years in the wilderness, you would think that Israel is now ready to enter into God's purpose, and expel the pagan nations of Canaan, taking its inheritance in the Promised Land. But in reality, the final instructions that come in this Torah portion (and also those seen next week in *Mas'ei*), still indicate that the Israelites need some fine tuning. They are learning the valuable lessons of keeping their vows and oaths to one another. They are learning what it means to fight together. And, they are learning what it means to stand by one another.

Today's Messianic Believers often have a great amount of zeal for studying the Torah, and for following events in Israel. Sometimes this zeal is unbalanced and unbridled, and people think that the restoration of God's Kingdom is going to occur at a much faster pace than it actually will. Certainly, to one degree or another, I think Messianic Believers will always be in a mode where we are constantly being trained up in new instructions that are designed to help us become better, obedient servants of the Most High. We will always be challenged to accurately apply Scripture in new circumstances, requiring us to appeal to the Holy Spirit for guidance and discernment.

Whether we are learning to take on new responsibilities and approaches as husbands or parents—or we are learning how to watch out for fellow Believers—the benchmark should be that we are maturing in our walk with the Messiah Yeshua. Hopefully, in His time we will be able to attain the unity that will make our victory as God's people sure and complete. Such a unity begins in the home, and works outwardly into the local congregation, and then the greater Body of Messiah.

---

[79] Numbers 32:33.

במדבר

# Mas'ei מַסְעֵי
## Stages
## "The Effects of the Law of Israel"

> Numbers 33:1-36:13
> Jeremiah 2:4-28; 3:4 (A);
> 2:4-28; 4:1-2 (S)

The final Torah reading of the Book of Numbers is usually coupled with the previous Torah reading, *Mattot* (Numbers 30:2[1]-32:42), for the purposes of study and reflection. In many respects *Mas'ei*, just like *Mattot*, delivers a series of final instructions to the Israelites, prior to their invasion of the Promised Land. As *Mas'ei* begins, a summary of the forty-two stages or encampments of the Israelites is catalogued by name,[80] with details on how to rout Canaan of its current inhabitants.[81] The physical boundaries of Israel are described,[82] with the names of the leaders of the tribes recorded for posterity's sake.[83] Some definition about how the Land should be organized is conveyed, especially as it regards cities for the Levites[84] and specific cities of refuge to be available as safe places when someone has committed unintentional manslaughter.[85] Our *parashah* ends with some inheritance injunctions, on what was to be done in Ancient Israel when no male heirs were born into a family.[86]

All of what is seen in *Mas'ei* is important, because very steadily Israel is preparing to transition from being a desert-bound group of wandering "nomads," to an established nation-state within determined borders. The jurisprudence, of what it means to be an actual "country," is being spoken into the hearts and minds of the Israelites. Of all the instructions that God delivers, He is most concerned about the Israelites being loyal to Him, and in the pagan idolatry of Canaan being routed as they enter into their inheritance:

"Then the LORD spoke to Moses in the plains of Moab by the Jordan *opposite* Jericho, saying, 'Speak to the sons of Israel and say to them, "When you cross over the Jordan into the land of Canaan, then you shall drive out all the inhabitants of the land from before you, and destroy all their figured stones, and destroy all their molten images and demolish all their high places; and you shall take possession of the land and live in it, for I have given the land to you to possess it. You shall inherit the land by lot according to your families; to the larger you shall give more inheritance, and to the smaller you shall give less inheritance. Wherever the lot falls to anyone, that shall be his. You shall inherit according to the tribes of your fathers. But if you do not drive out the inhabitants of the land from before you, then it shall come about that those whom you let remain of them *will become* as pricks in your eyes and as thorns in your sides, and they will trouble you in the land in which you live. And as I plan to do to them, so I will do to you"'" (Numbers 33:50-56).

---

[80] Numbers 33:1-49.
[81] Numbers 33:50-55.
[82] Numbers 34:1-15.
[83] Numbers 34:16-29.
[84] Numbers 35:1-5.
[85] Numbers 35:6-34.
[86] Numbers 36:1-9.

Here the instructions are very detailed: completely eliminate the inhabitants and then let the lot determine who gets what parcels of land. After seeing a great victory over the Midianites with not a single soldier lost (Numbers 31), this sounds fairly basic. This remarkable victory allowed the Israelites to understand that the Lord is on their side, and that taking the Promised Land was only a simple matter of obeying His instructions. All God asks for in return is loyalty and fidelity to Him, as their job is to see the Canaanites' idols removed.

## Cities of Refuge

One of the most important aspects of what it will be like to live in the Promised Land, with God's Torah enforced as the law, is the establishment of cities of refuge. There were to be a total of forty-eight cities in Israel, specifically for the Levites (Numbers 35:7), with six of the cities being designated as cities of refuge or *arei ha'miqlat* (עָרֵי הַמִּקְלָט; Numbers 35:6). These cities of refuge were to be spaced between the eastern and western sides of the Jordan, three on the east and three on the west (Numbers 35:14), with the other forty-two cities sprinkled among the tribal territories.

The cities of refuge were designed to be places where those who committed unintentional manslaughter could come to avoid anyone seeking revenge, who probably had the assignment to avenge the death of a family member:

"These six cities shall be for refuge for the sons of Israel, and for the alien and for the sojourner among them; that anyone who kills a person unintentionally may flee there" (Numbers 35:15).

These instructions begin to formalize a code of justice on how Ancient Israel was to handle homicide, voluntary manslaughter, involuntary manslaughter, and accidental death. The establishment of various cities of refuge—safe places where people could go when there had been a homicide—is about as close as we see in the Torah to there being any kind of "prison system." While every community would have had some kind of jail, not everyone who is sent to jail is an accused murderer, as many are jailed as a penalty for unruly behavior or failure to pay a debt or for violating some kind of local ordinances. Here, the cities of refuge accomplish the role of some of today's maximum security prisons, where not only criminals can be held until trial, but where the state is supposed to keep them safe and unharmed until trial.

*Mas'ei* details how the cities of refuge were to function, in the determination of whether a homicide was intentional or unintentional, laying out some examples that would need to be considered in judging the accused:

"But if he struck him down with an iron object, so that he died, he is a murderer; the murderer shall surely be put to death. If he struck him down with a stone in the hand, by which he will die, and *as a result* he died, he is a murderer; the murderer shall surely be put to death. Or if he struck him with a wooden object in the hand, by which he might die, and *as a result* he died, he is a murderer; the murderer shall surely be put to death. The blood avenger himself shall put the murderer to death; he shall put him to death when he meets him. If he pushed him of hatred, or threw something at him lying in wait and *as a result* he died, or if he struck him down with his hand in enmity, and *as a result* he died, the one who struck him shall surely be put to death, he is a murderer; the blood avenger shall put the murderer to death when he meets him. But if he pushed him suddenly without enmity, or threw something at him without lying in wait, or with any deadly object of stone, and without seeing it dropped on him so that he died, while he was not his enemy nor seeking his injury, then the congregation shall judge between the slayer and the blood avenger according to these ordinances" (Numbers 35:16-24).

It is notable that here we see a real example of the Torah functioning as the Law. As serious as human death might be, with various examples of how tools or instruments can be used to murder, the ultimate judgment for guilt or innocence might still fall with a community's leaders. It is stated how "the assembly must judge" (Numbers 35:24, NIV). But more important than this is how the principle of convicting a murderer must have multiple witnesses:

"These things shall be for a statutory ordinance to you throughout your generations in all your dwellings. If anyone kills a person, the murderer shall be put to death at the evidence of witnesses, but no person shall be put to death on the testimony of one witness" (Numbers 35:29-30).

As you read Numbers 35, you should be able to easily discern how these verses have significantly influenced the Western legal tradition until our very day. The need to be able to not only read the Scriptures, but do so with a discerning mind, can be very important to see them applied properly.

## Inheritance Laws

As the Book of Numbers finishes, some information about the inheritance of property is detailed. Again, while Twenty-First Century people might think that these instructions seem a bit archaic, as they might be viewed as promoting a male-exclusive transference of property across the generations—with a few exceptions—what the Torah says must be viewed within the overall context of how property was kept in families in the larger Ancient Near East. The issue that Moses and Eleazar had to rule upon (Numbers chs. 26-27) allowed the daughters of Zelophehad to inherit from their father's estate, even though they were female:

"They stood before Moses and before Eleazar the priest and before the leaders and all the congregation, at the doorway of the tent of meeting, saying, 'Our father died in the wilderness, yet he was not among the company of those who gathered themselves together against the LORD in the company of Korah; but he died in his own sin, and he had no sons. Why should the name of our father be withdrawn from among his family because he had no son? Give us a possession among our father's brothers.' So Moses brought their case before the LORD. Then the LORD spoke to Moses, saying, 'The daughters of Zelophehad are right in *their* statements. You shall surely give them a hereditary possession among their father's brothers, and you shall transfer the inheritance of their father to them. Further, you shall speak to the sons of Israel, saying, "If a man dies and has no son, then you shall transfer his inheritance to his daughter. If he has no daughter, then you shall give his inheritance to his brothers. If he has no brothers, then you shall give his inheritance to his father's brothers. If his father has no brothers, then you shall give his inheritance to his nearest relative in his own family, and he shall possess it; and it shall be a statutory ordinance to the sons of Israel, just as the LORD commanded Moses""" (Numbers 27:2-11).

Later in *Mas'ei*, additional rulings are delivered. The Manassehites, recognizing how the daughters of Zelophehad inherited from their father's property, were concerned that they might marry Israelite men outside of their tribe of Manasseh. In doing so, the inheritance for the entire tribe might be jeopardized. After explaining the dilemma, Moses clarifies what actions should be taken:

"Then Moses commanded the sons of Israel according to the word of the LORD, saying, 'The tribe of the sons of Joseph are right in *their* statements. This is what the LORD has commanded concerning the daughters of Zelophehad, saying, "Let them marry whom they wish; only they must marry within the family of the tribe of their father." Thus no inheritance of the sons of Israel shall be transferred from tribe to tribe, for the sons of Israel shall each hold to the inheritance of the tribe of his fathers. Every daughter who comes into possession of an inheritance of any tribe of the sons of Israel shall be wife to one of the family of the tribe of her father, so that the sons of Israel each may possess the inheritance of his fathers. Thus no inheritance shall be transferred from one tribe to another tribe, for the tribes of the sons of Israel shall each hold to his own inheritance'" (Numbers 36:5-9).

Even though the daughters of Zelophehad affectively were treated like males, in being able to inherit from their father's estate—here we see that the need to maintain tribal distinctions was very important for the Ancient Israelites, *still yet to enter into the Promised Land*. It was ruled here that if any daughters had to inherit their fathers' property, that they could only marry within their tribe. But the issue here probably had more to do with tribal integrity within the Promised Land, than it had to do with women's' rights. Much of the property that would be inherited would not be in the form of a bank account, stock portfolio, or investments in a corporation—but rather in real estate within a tribe's territory and in agricultural assets. You cannot have a tribe of Israel within set boundaries, with all of the land within such boundaries actually owned by (absentee) people from another tribe. This is an excellent example of how the Torah's original setting and the needs of Ancient Israel have to be considered in our reading of the text, because presumably if a woman married outside of her tribe she would forfeit the right to having any inheritance which would pass into the family of another tribe. Allen observes,

"[T]he issue is not antiwoman but a concern for the integrity of the land....[But] women were still not considered as independent entities within the community; their definition continued to be in connection with their husbands (and sons)....Nonetheless, this sequence of events (chs. 27-31) is a significant entry in the history of women's issues. It is two steps forward and one step back; but there is movement forward—a countercultural thrust that has the blessing of God."[87]

The Torah gives us a glimpse into the legal process of ancient people who were chosen to be vessels of the Creator God, and *Mas'ei* has certainly given much for various rabbis, theologians, scholars, *and* lawyers to discuss and debate for several millennia. Applying these instructions in a modern setting might be a little difficult, as the modern world has a different kind of economy than did the ancient world. But these instructions can definitely inform us, as some of the first legal precedents set in the Bible. By reading and meditating upon them, we make sure that these instructions continue to have an influence on our reading of the Scriptures, being relevant to men and women of faith—even if just in the sense of being Biblical history. Even if we cannot follow everything in the Torah, because we do not live in the Ancient Near East, meditating on the Word of God will still teach us things about His character and dealings with people!

---

[87] Allen, in *EXP*, 2:1006.

במדבר

# COMMENTARY ON DEUTERONOMY

## *Devarim* דְּבָרִים
### Words
### "Review, Recall, Repent"

> Deuteronomy 1:1-3:22
> Isaiah 1:1-27

As the fifth book of the Torah begins, *Devarim* or Deuteronomy,[1] the reader is reminded of how Ancient Israel's forty-year journey in the wilderness is coming to a close. The punishment for the previous generation's having believed the bad report from the spies (cf. Numbers 14:33-35) is now over. Moses is in the waning days of his life, and he knows that he will not be able to enter into the Promised Land, because of his transgression at the waters of Meribah (Numbers 20:8-13), and also having been recently told that when the war with Midian is over, he will die (Numbers 31:1-2).

Recognizing that he has very little time remaining with Israel, Moses gathers the assembly together, and as leader repeats the events that have transpired to bring Israel out of Egypt to the very edge of the Promised Land. The Hebrew title for both our Torah portion and the entire book is *Devarim* (דְּבָרִים) or "Words," although there are many Jewish traditions that refer to the fifth book of the Pentateuch as *Mishneh Torah*, meaning "repetition of the Torah." In many respects, the Book of Deuteronomy is a repetition of much of what has been witnessed previously, repeating the Law that God has given Israel:

"Across the Jordan in the land of Moab, Moses undertook to expound this law, saying…" (Deuteronomy 1:5).

According to Rabbinical sources,[2] the Book of Deuteronomy records the last five weeks of Moses' life as he encourages the "Joshua generation" to remember God's instructions and His charge to them. Moses gives clarification to previously given commandments, and he prophesies concerning Israel's future. In *Devarim*, Moses reviews various leadership responsibilities,[3] recalls the bad report of the ten spies,[4] and then describes the calamity of attempting to enter the Promised Land without the presence of the

---

[1] The traditional title Deuteronomy is derived from the label given to the fifth book of Moses in the Greek Septuagint, *Deuteronomium* (ΔEYTEPONOMION), meaning "second law."

[2] Scherman, *Chumash*, 939.

[3] Deuteronomy 1:12-15.

[4] Deuteronomy 1:23-40.

Lord.[5] Then, recollection of the travels around the lands given to Esau, Moab, and Ammon is considered, as well as the victories secured over peoples in Gilead and Bashan.[6] Moses reiterates details about how the tribes of Reuben, Gad, and Manasseh are going to occupy lands east of the Jordan.[7] Our reading for this week concludes with a word of encouragement given by Moses to Joshua, his successor:

"I commanded Joshua at that time, saying, 'Your eyes have seen all that the LORD your God has done to these two kings; so the LORD shall do to all the kingdoms into which you are about to cross. Do not fear them, for the LORD your God is the one fighting for you'" (Deuteronomy 3:21-22).

## Timing is Everything

In many respects, Moses' orations witnessed in the Book of Deuteronomy are a summary review of the previous forty-year journey through the wilderness, allowing the people to consider where they have been—**but most importantly where they are going.** Moses knows how Israel has a propensity to disobey the Lord, and so a review of Israel's history is necessary so that the consequences of previous disobedience will not have to be repeated. God knows that His people need to spend some time remembering and reflecting upon their history. How does the saying go? *Those who do not learn from history are doomed to repeat it!*

As I pondered over our Torah reading for this week, the concept of reviewing the past, recalling some of Ancient Israel's transgressions and iniquities, and repenting of my own previous errors—reverberated throughout my thoughts. Human beings have a definite tendency to wander away from God. Just a few weeks earlier, near the close of the Book of Numbers, the Reubenites and Gadites had attempted to alter some of His plans in conquering the six nations of Canaan. Moses' rebuke of their request indicates a deep concern about Israel's ability to properly follow directions, even after forty years of sojourning in the desert (Numbers 32:14-15). Since he recognizes that his death is coming soon, throughout Deuteronomy he hopes to impart—through recollection and repentance—the qualities that will allow Israel to both persevere and prosper when they take the Land, entering into their inheritance.

As a Torah student, the concept of reviewing the past makes sense to me. Examining the weekly Torah portions every year, especially the days before Israel's conquest of Canaan, enables us to ask important questions of ourselves. The annual Torah cycle that has been in place for several millennia, and the repetition practiced by the Jewish people, have been used by the Lord to help maintain them as a coherent society. Somehow, through all the persecutions, pogroms, inquisitions, and the Holocaust itself—these people who have clinged to a study of the Torah, have been able to have a testimony of existence before the nations of the Earth. Perhaps the Divinely inspired wisdom of Moses, to review Israel's history, has been used by the Lord to create a repeated pattern that has preserved the Jewish people?

Thoughts about reviewing, recalling, and repenting percolated in my spirit as I read through our Torah portion—so I investigated some of the patterns established by the Jewish

---

[5] Deuteronomy 1:41-46.
[6] Deuteronomy 2:1-3:11.
[7] Deuteronomy 3:12-17.

Sages for a diligent study of the Torah. I discovered a few things that—what for me was new knowledge (2003)—were things that have been a part of Judaism for centuries.

## The Three Weeks and Shabbat Chazon

When *Devarim* arrives on the annual Torah cycle, with the Book of Deuteronomy winding down the yearly examination of the Torah—you are usually well into the Summer months on the Jewish calendar. It is during these Summer months that a number of important events have occurred within Jewish history, which have been memorialized for reflection and observance. These things are easy to overlook for many Messianics, as they are not explicitly mentioned in the Torah, although many Messianic Jewish congregations remember them to some degree.

The most recognized date during the Summer months is the Ninth of Av (Heb. *Tisha B'Av*). Next to *Yom Kippur*, the Ninth of Av is a day of great remorse accompanied with fasting and prayer. The Ninth of Av is an infamous day that commemorates the time when Ancient Israel believed the bad report from the ten spies (m.*Ta'anit* 4:6). The Ninth of Av is one of the saddest days on the calendar for the Jewish people, because *many more* tragic events have also occurred on this very day throughout history. Alfred J. Kolatch summarizes the main significance of the Ninth of Av in Jewish tradition:

> "Tisha B'Av, the ninth day of the Hebrew month of Av, is a day of mourning for the destruction of the First Temple in the year 586 B.C.E. by the Babylonians, and of the Second Temple in the year 70 C.E. by the Romans. (According to tradition, both Temples were destroyed on the same date.)
>
> "Next to Yom Kippur (a biblical holiday), Tisha B'Av (a post-biblical holiday) is the most important fast day in the Jewish calendar. It marks the final day of a three-week period of intense national mourning for the events that led to the loss of Jewish independence with the destruction of the holy shrines of Jewish life.
>
> "Aside from these two major historical events, other happenings in Jewish history have been said to have occurred on the ninth of Av. These include the fall of Betar (the last Jewish stronghold during the Bar Kochba rebellion against Rome) in 35 C.E. and the beginning of the expulsion of Jews from Spain in 1492. The importance of Tisha B'Av as a fast day was emphasized in the Talmud (Taanit 30b), where the comment is made: 'He who eats or drinks on the ninth day of Av must be considered as guilty as one who has eaten on Yom Kippur.' The fast of Tisha B'Av, like Yom Kippur, begins at sunset and ends the next evening with the appearance of the first three stars."[8]

There have been some other tragedies which have been associated with the Ninth of Av throughout history, but the most important have been the destruction of the First and Second Temples—which have been used to literally change the face of Israel in Biblical history. One might argue that the Ninth of Av is a time when the Jewish people have reflected on some of their specific faults before God—which caused the destruction of the two Temples—and have desired restitution for past errors. At the same time, remembering the Ninth of Av can be employed as preparation for the even more serious Day of Atonement.

---

[8] Alfred J. Kolatch, *The Jewish Book of Why* (Middle Village, NY: Jonathan David Publishers, 1981), 286; cf. Ronald L. Eisenberg, *The JPS Guide to Jewish Traditions* (Philadelphia: Jewish Publication Society, 2004), pp 304-305.

During the past two weeks, several significant Haftarah readings have been employed (Jeremiah 1:1-2:3; 2:4-3:4), which are supposed to admonish people to recall the impending judgment of Israel at the hands of its enemies—if it is unfaithful to God. Ronald L. Eisenberg notes how during these Three Weeks, traditional mourning rites are observed, including "abstention from weddings and other joyous celebrations, instrumental music, and entertainment and the prohibition against the purchase or wearing of new clothing or the eating of new fruit."[9] Indeed, even in a Messianic community that will often remember the Ninth of Av, very few of us are aware of how seriously Judaism has viewed this time in history.

On the third week prior to the Ninth of Av, the Haftarah reading is Isaiah 1:1-27, which corresponds with *Devarim*. All three Haftarah selections are to *drive people to repentance before God*. The weekly Sabbath which precedes the Ninth of Av has a special name, *Shabbat Chazon* or the "Sabbath of Vision." The Hebrew term *chazon* (חָזוֹן) or "vision"[10] is found in the opening verse of this week's Haftarah reading, where the Prophet Isaiah describes many of the reasons why the Temple was going to be destroyed:

"The vision [*chazon*] of Isaiah the son of Amoz concerning Judah and Jerusalem, which he saw during the reigns of Uzziah, Jotham, Ahaz *and* Hezekiah, kings of Judah. Listen, O heavens, and hear, O earth; for the LORD speaks, 'Sons I have reared and brought up, but they have revolted against Me. An ox knows its owner, and a donkey its master's manger, *but* Israel does not know, My people do not understand.' Alas, sinful nation, people weighed down with iniquity, offspring of evildoers, sons who act corruptly! They have abandoned the LORD, they have despised the Holy One of Israel, they have turned away from Him" (Isaiah 1:1-4).

So much of what I have witnessed in Messianic congregations over the past several years has frequently overlooked some of the rather serious, and sober themes, leading up to the Ninth of Av. We often attend weekly *Shabbat* services that are full of vibrant music, dancing, and laughter—**with no mention of the Three Weeks before the Ninth of Av.** Perhaps Believers think that because they possess forgiveness and redemption in Messiah Yeshua that they do not need to reflect on the consequences of sin, and fast at certain times of the year. Christian history is certainly replete with the examples of men and women who would go through rigorous times of introspection, fasting, and self-denial to appeal to the mercy of the Holy One. Even if we do have salvation—we still need to pray for those who do not! As always, the Ninth of Av is a perfect time to lift up our Jewish brethren in prayer *who do not yet know the Messiah of Israel!*

Discovering some new information about how important the Jewish community has considered the weeks approaching the Ninth of Av, I considered how this annual pattern has been incorporated into the Torah cycle to begin preparing hearts for the more serious Day of Atonement coming in just a few months. After the fast on the Ninth of Av, the Haftarah readings for the next seven weeks come from the Book of Isaiah,[11] and are more directed toward the redemption of Israel.

---

[9] Eisenberg, 304.
[10] More expanded definitions of *chazon* include: "*vision*, as seen in the ecstatic state," "*vision*, in the night," "*divine communication in a vision, oracle, prophecy*," and "*vision*, as title of book of prophecy; of other writings of prophets" (*BDB*, 302).
[11] Isaiah 40:1-26; 49:14-51:3; 54:11-55:5; 51:12-52:12; 54:1-10; 60:1-22; 61:10-63:9.

It is my hope that today's Messianics all learn to appreciate this season of the year, and its messages of both God's chastisement *and* forgiveness.

## Serious Conviction

Reflecting on the Three Weeks prior to the Ninth of Av, and how this time of the Summer is to prepare hearts for *Yom Kippur*—I am extremely convicted. I frequently find that even though I have read the Bible for years, *including the Old Testament*, that I really have had a limited amount of knowledge regarding traditional Jewish ways of reading the Torah (2003). Obviously, over the past several millennia, the Jewish people, who have been entrusted with the oracles of God (Romans 3:2), have been able to formulate some beneficial methods that enable the observant to focus on the history of Israel and its relationship with Him. *Messianic Believers can certainly benefit from this as well.* If we know that bad things have taken place in the past, in reviewing them and thinking about them, we can see to it that they are never repeated.

Over the years, I have known about the tragedies associated with the Ninth of Av and the destruction of the two Temples. As a non-Jewish Believer, who trusts in the redeeming work of the Messiah of Israel, my past thoughts have admittedly been a bit skewed by some teachings received over the years about my body *only* being the "Temple of God."[12] From my reading of Paul's teachings to the Corinthians, and from what I had been taught in the past, I was a little callous toward thinking about the destruction of the two Temples. I was told I had "a much better deal," because my body was to be considered the "real Temple of God." In fact, much of the "Temple teaching" I heard was really just designed to keep me from drinking, smoking, or abusing my body. As Paul writes,

"Do you not know that you are a temple of God and *that* the Spirit of God dwells in you? If any man destroys the temple of God, God will destroy him, for the temple of God is holy, and that is what you are" (1 Corinthians 3:16-17).

Some of the popular teaching that is witnessed in today's Christianity from these verses has been right to emphasize personal holiness regarding one's physical actions. But, as I think back on some of my previous instruction with a Messianic understanding, I realize how sophomoric some of it was. While I was correctly taught to not abuse my body and to consider myself a vessel of the Holy Spirit, I was not taught to heed the message of the destruction of the two Temples. Paul certainly wanted the Corinthians to understand how they were functioning on the same kind of level as the Jerusalem Temple, causing them to appreciate the Jerusalem Temple—not look down upon it.

*I was not taught to be empathetic to my Jewish neighbors about what the Ninth of Av might mean to them.* Because much of what I was taught came from a dispensational bias of believing that Israel and "the Church" were separate, my teachers rarely talked about the Temple in any other way except in regard to the fulfillment of future prophecy (after the pre-tribulation rapture, no less). We were not taught that the Temple contained important object lessons that mature Believers were to understand. We were not taught how to appreciate what the Temple represented, and then personalize it to some degree in our lives of faith. *I am glad that this has now changed.*

---

[12] And, even this has been challenged with me having to realize that the "in you" referred to in 1 Corinthians 3:16, *en humin* (ἐν ὑμῖν), is in the plural and not the singular—meaning that it is in reference to the corporate assembly of Believers, and not individuals exclusively.

In this day of restoration as the Messianic movement grows and matures, we can be reminded that the Lord is using things like knowing what the Ninth of Av is, to begin to bridge the gaps between all of His people. All Messianic Believers can use the Ninth of Av as a specific time to fast and intercede for Jewish people who do not yet know Messiah Yeshua. As we move ahead in our reading of the Book of Deuteronomy—we can review, recall, and repent for any of the sins we might have—which could be preventing us from entering into everything that the Father has called us to be. We can learn things about where we have been, but most importantly where we need to be going.

# *V'et'chanan* וָאֶתְחַנַּן
## I pleaded
## "Shema, O Israel!"

Deuteronomy 3:23-7:11
Isaiah 40:1-26

*V'et'chanan* is perhaps one of the more inspirational and instructional collections of statements that Moses conveys to Israel in any one Torah reading. Not only is the Decalogue reiterated, but also the *Shema*—which many consider to be Israel's pledge of allegiance—is articulated. As I read and meditated upon this motivating section of Scripture, many thoughts came to my mind about how the Lord is presently using many of these words to encourage His people to return to a disciplined and regular study of the Torah—as we are to all be instructed in His ways and in holiness. Today's generation of Messianic Believers possesses significant potential to make a concentrated difference in the lives of Jews and Christians today, if we are willing to submit ourselves to God's Word and allow it to mold our hearts and minds for His purpose.

## A Great Nation

One of the most profound things that is stated in *V'et'chanan*—that any person who has placed his or her trust in the God of Israel and His Messiah Yeshua **must commit to memory**—summarizes how obedience to Him manifests itself as His wisdom. Others can then witness this wisdom, and see how awesome God truly is:

"So keep and do *them*, for that is your wisdom and your understanding in the sight of the peoples who will hear all these statutes and say, 'Surely this great nation is a wise and understanding people.' For what great nation is there that has a god so near to it as is the LORD our God whenever we call on Him? Or what great nation is there that has statutes and judgments as righteous as this whole law which I am setting before you today? Only give heed to yourself and keep your soul diligently, so that you do not forget the things which your eyes have seen and they do not depart from your heart all the days of your life; but make them known to your sons and your grandsons" (Deuteronomy 4:6-9).

Here, Moses reminded Ancient Israel that they were indeed "this great nation" or *ha'goy ha'gadol ha'zeh* (הַגּוֹי הַגָּדוֹל הַזֶּה), but that such a great nation likewise has serious responsibilities. In order to be a wise and understanding people that other nations recognize and turn to for spiritual answers, Israel could not disobey the Lord. The kind of impact that Israel was chosen to make on the world would not happen all at once either, as Moses'

Teaching had to be taught to the succeeding generations. I think that one of the exciting features of the Book of Deuteronomy is that readers get to not only be reminded of the things that were to make Ancient Israel great—but that they are the same things which are to make *all of God's people today great!*

Today via the growth and expansion of the Messianic movement, many thousands of born again Believers—both Jewish *and* non-Jewish—are making a concentrated effort to make the Torah a firm foundation for their faith. As the Holy Spirit moves upon them, they want to make the statutes and commandments Moses delivered to Ancient Israel a part of how they think and act too. Just as Ancient Israel was admonished to be, they want others to witness their obedience to God, and use it as an opportunity to testify of the Father's goodness *and* the salvation He has provided in His Son.

## The Fundamentals Required

As you have been reading through *V'et'chanan*, you have no doubt seen how Moses is instructing the Israelites in how they can be a special, separated, holy nation unto God. One of the main reasons for heeding the instructions of the Lord is very clear: Moses wants Israel to live and prosper in the Land that He has promised to them. He details,

"Now, O Israel, listen to the statutes and the judgments which I am teaching you to perform, so that you may live and go in and take possession of the land which the LORD, the God of your fathers, is giving you" (Deuteronomy 4:1).

Moses knew that his days were numbered and that he would soon die. He also recognized that he had been used by the Holy One to communicate His words to the Israelites, which will allow them to ably take possession of Canaan. As he begins to reiterate many of the words and experiences from the previous forty years of Israel sojourning in the desert, he makes a strong admonition to remind his listeners about the imperative to follow God's instructions already given:

"You shall not add to the word which I am commanding you, nor take away from it, that you may keep the commandments of the LORD your God which I command you" (Deuteronomy 4:2).

This terse statement carries weight. It not only carries weight in terms of how authoritative the instructions of God are, but how the Israelites are to make sure that they do not carelessly nullify them. These words do not prohibit how in further history, God's Prophets would reveal more things to Israel, or that additional books of Scripture would be added to the canon. These words similarly do not prohibit how in later generations, religious authorities would need to make rulings and decisions on how the Torah was to be applied in complicated circumstances. What these words do more than anything else is to highlight how **God's Instruction is to force His people to follow and serve Him alone**—versus any other gods—as further specified:

"Your eyes have seen what the LORD has done in the case of Baal-peor, for all the men who followed Baal-peor, the LORD your God has destroyed them from among you. But you who held fast to the LORD your God are alive today, every one of you" (Deuteronomy 4:3-4).

As you read through *V'et'chanan*, the Israelites are reminded in summary form about many of their wilderness experiences. Moses specifies prohibitions against idolatry and making any idols of a created object for worship.[13] Moses restates the reality that the Lord is

---

[13] Deuteronomy 4:15-20.

a jealous God and a consuming fire.[14] Following this, Moses prophesies about the future when the chosen people, through willful disobedience, are going to provoke God to scatter them among the nations of the Earth. But, in spite of this anticipated punishment, He will restore them to the Promised Land when they will seek Him with all their hearts and souls. This is one of the most sobering parts of our *parashah* that you will read:

"When you become the father of children and children's children and have remained long in the land, and act corruptly, and make an idol in the form of anything, and do that which is evil in the sight of the LORD your God *so as* to provoke Him to anger, I call heaven and earth to witness against you today, that you will surely perish quickly from the land where you are going over the Jordan to possess it. You shall not live long on it, but will be utterly destroyed. The LORD will scatter you among the peoples, and you will be left few in number among the nations where the LORD drives you. There you will serve gods, the work of man's hands, wood and stone, which neither see nor hear nor eat nor smell. But from there you will seek the LORD your God, and you will find *Him* if you search for Him with all your heart and all your soul. When you are in distress and all these things have come upon you, in the latter days you will return to the LORD your God and listen to His voice. For the LORD your God is a compassionate God; He will not fail you nor destroy you nor forget the covenant with your fathers which He swore to them" (Deuteronomy 4:25-31).

In spite of future judgment that will come, Moses continued to encourage Ancient Israel by reminding them of the great things God had done for them:

"Indeed, ask now concerning the former days which were before you, since the day that God created man on the earth, and *inquire* from one end of the heavens to the other. Has *anything* been done like this great thing, or has *anything* been heard like it? Has *any* people heard the voice of God speaking from the midst of the fire, as you have heard *it*, and survived? Or has a god tried to go to take for himself a nation from within *another* nation by trials, by signs and wonders and by war and by a mighty hand and by an outstretched arm and by great terrors, as the LORD your God did for you in Egypt before your eyes? To you it was shown that you might know that the LORD, He is God; there is no other besides Him. Out of the heavens He let you hear His voice to discipline you; and on earth He let you see His great fire, and you heard His words from the midst of the fire. Because He loved your fathers, therefore He chose their descendants after them. And He personally brought you from Egypt by His great power, driving out from before you nations greater and mightier than you, to bring you in *and* to give you their land for an inheritance, as it is today. Know therefore today, and take it to your heart, that the LORD, He is God in heaven above and on the earth below; there is no other. So you shall keep His statutes and His commandments which I am giving you today, that it may go well with you and with your children after you, and that you may live long on the land which the LORD your God is giving you for all time" (Deuteronomy 4:32-40).

After this, Moses takes a break from the exhortative reminders, and chooses three cities of refuge on the east side of the Jordan River.[15] But, he quickly picks up where he left off, and reminds the Israelites about the words they received at Mount Horeb.[16] In fact, he just goes ahead and restates the Ten Commandments for the entire assembly to hear. Most

---

[14] Deuteronomy 4:23-24.
[15] Deuteronomy 4:41-43.
[16] Deuteronomy 5:1-21.

important, Moses wants the Israelites to know that these words were not only applicable to those who originally heard them, but to future generations also. The point is made that the covenant passes on to their descendants:

"Then Moses summoned all Israel and said to them: 'Hear, O Israel, the statutes and the ordinances which I am speaking today in your hearing, that you may learn them and observe them carefully. The LORD our God made a covenant with us at Horeb. The LORD did not make this covenant with our fathers, but with us, *with* all those of us alive here today" (Deuteronomy 5:1-3).

Moses mentions the great fear that the people of Israel demonstrated when they first heard the words of God being declared from the smoking mountain.[17] *The significance of the exhortations continues.* Moses encourages Israel with more instructions for those listening, and the generations to come:

"Now this is the commandment, the statutes and the judgments which the LORD your God has commanded *me* to teach you, that you might do *them* in the land where you are going over to possess it, so that you and your son and your grandson might fear the LORD your God, to keep all His statutes and His commandments which I command you, all the days of your life, and that your days may be prolonged" (Deuteronomy 6:1-2).

Following this, Moses gives Israel what is commonly referred to as the *Shema*, derived from the Hebrew verb *shama* (שָׁמַע) meaning "to hear." Throughout Biblical history, the *Shema* is believed to be the quintessential statement declaring not only a person's complete loyalty to the God of Israel, but also of monotheism. Observant Jews proclaim the *Shema* every day in their traditional prayers, and every *Shabbat* as the Torah scroll is pulled from the ark and ready to be canted. I personally like to refer to the *Shema* as Israel's "pledge of allegiance":

"**Hear, O Israel! The LORD is our God, the LORD is one!**[18] You shall love the LORD your God with all your heart and with all your soul and with all your might. These words, which I am commanding you today, shall be on your heart. You shall teach them diligently to your sons and shall talk of them when you sit in your house and when you walk by the way and when you lie down and when you rise up. You shall bind them as a sign on your hand and they shall be as frontals on your forehead. You shall write them on the doorposts of your house and on your gates" (Deuteronomy 6:4-9).

As you can see, the positive encouragements just continue to be made statement after statement in the *Shema*. By a variety of educational actions, including impressing the significance of Moses' Teaching on one's heart and mind, frequently discussing it, and actually placing it on one's hand, forehead, and doorposts (even if just figuratively, and not always literally)—people can be reminded to be loyal to God and to diligently follow after Him.

Finally in *V'et'chanan*, Moses tells Israel some of what they are to expect as they enter into Canaan, take the Promised Land, and defeat the seven nations which currently

---

[17] Deuteronomy 5:22-33.
[18] Heb. *shema Yisrael ADONAI Eloheinu ADONAI echad* (שְׁמַע יִשְׂרָאֵל יְהוָה אֱלֹהֵינוּ יְהוָה אֶחָד); also validly rendered as "Hear, O Israel: The LORD is our God, the LORD alone" (NRSV/NJPS), emphasizing Israel's exclusive worship of Him.
Consult the article "What Does the Shema Really Mean?" by J.K. McKee.

occupied it.[19] Of notable importance is how these nations are stronger than Israel, but how God will deliver them over to be defeated:

"When the LORD your God brings you into the land where you are entering to possess it, and clears away many nations before you, the Hittites and the Girgashites and the Amorites and the Canaanites and the Perizzites and the Hivites and the Jebusites, seven nations greater and stronger than you, and when the LORD your God delivers them before you and you defeat them, then you shall utterly destroy them. You shall make no covenant with them and show no favor to them" (Deuteronomy 7:1-2).

In the last verses of our *parashah*, we see a significant reminder from Moses regarding God's faithfulness to Israel and to His promises:

"For you are a holy people to the LORD your God; the LORD your God has chosen you to be a people for His own possession out of all the peoples who are on the face of the earth. The LORD did not set His love on you nor choose you because you were more in number than any of the peoples, for you were the fewest of all peoples, but because the LORD loved you and kept the oath which He swore to your forefathers, the LORD brought you out by a mighty hand and redeemed you from the house of slavery, from the hand of Pharaoh king of Egypt. Know therefore that the LORD your God, He is God, the faithful God, who keeps His covenant and His lovingkindness to a thousandth generation with those who love Him and keep His commandments; but repays those who hate Him to their faces, to destroy them; He will not delay with him who hates Him, He will repay him to his face" (Deuteronomy 7:6-10).

## Final Thoughts

As you read and consider *V'et'chanan*, Moses is delivering what is largely a very encouraging word to the people of Israel. Of course, the Israelites are being told of some of the challenges of disobedience to the Lord. But, the positive comments about the blessings they will experience *so outweigh the negative*—that any reader should walk away from this week's Torah portion with a great sense of relief for the love that God has for His people. **We should all want to obey the Lord.**

Thinking about these encouraging words, I naturally reflected back on my remembrance of the Ninth of Av this past week—as I fasted in remembering the destruction of the First and Second Temples. Reflecting upon *V'et'chanan*, Moses' words are quite uplifting and encouraging—especially for those who have been in mourning for the loss of the Temples. Those who are serious about their relationship with the God of Israel can be positively encouraged to seek Him with all of their being:

"But from there you will seek the LORD your God, and you will find *Him* if you search for Him with all your heart and all your soul. When you are in distress and all these things have come upon you, in the latter days you will return to the LORD your God and listen to His voice. For the LORD your God is a compassionate God; He will not fail you nor destroy you nor forget the covenant with your fathers which He swore to them" (Deuteronomy 4:29-31).

Moses says that God will remember His people like this *b'acharit ha'yamim* (הַיָּמִים בְּאַחֲרִית), or "in the latter days." For the generation that is alive today, many of the prophecies seen in the Bible have been fulfilled. In particular, in 1948 we witnessed the

---

[19] Deuteronomy 6:10-7:10.

rebirth of a sovereign Jewish State of Israel, with the Jewish people being returned to the Land of their ancestors. The possibility of rebuilding a Temple on the Temple Mount is debated every year. People are waking up and being stirred all over the world as they sincerely seek the Lord with all their hearts and souls, and pay attention to the Scriptures. The covenants promised to Abraham, Isaac, and Jacob are being remembered. *And, we all know how this will culminate with the return of Yeshua the Messiah as King from Jerusalem!*[20]

We have much to be grateful for as we learn to listen and obey the admonitions given to Ancient Israel three millennia ago. But what is to befall us in the future? I think understanding this begins with each of us falling on our faces before the Lord, and crying out to Him with that simple declaration: *Shema Yisrael!* or "Hear, O Israel!" Then we can allow our Father to answer our pleadings...

## *Ekev* עֵקֶב
### Because
### "Because of a Circumcised Heart"

> Deuteronomy 7:12-11:25
> Isaiah 49:14-51:3

*Ekev* continues Moses' monologue to the people of Israel as he is anticipating his death. He knows that his days are numbered, and how he is charged with preparing the Israelites to enter into the Promised Land. In many respects, the entire Book of Deuteronomy is Moses' last will and testament to his beloved Israel. Following Deuteronomy's recollections and instructions will be critical for a successful conquest of Canaan. Like any good leader, Moses knows the power of words—and as we saw last week in *V'et'chanan*, Moses is quite aware that he has been chosen to be the communicator of the voice of God to the people (Deuteronomy 4:2).

As we reflect on *Ekev* this week, one of the very first things we notice is that the term *ekev* (עֵקֶב), from which our *parashah* gets its name, begins the reading: *v'hayah ekev* (עֵקֶב וְהָיָה), "Then it shall come about, because..." (Deuteronomy 7:12). You might consider what I have to say on *Ekev* to be a bit of a stretch, but I do wonder if there is something about the Hebrew term *ekev* that might communicate important messages to Bible readers. While stylistically *ekev* can be translated a variety of ways throughout English Bibles, *TWOT* describes how it means "**consequence.** Usually occurs as an adverbial accusative, as a consequence of, because."[21] I simply ask, does this seemingly, insignificant connecting word have a more important meaning than just "because"?

Within our lives, we can probably all remember prefacing answers to questions with the word "because." We have certainly heard other people use "because" to justify various actions, saying "*Because* of such-and-such I did so-and-so," or "*Because* of so-and-so, such-and-such happened." How many times have you encountered an immature child, who has been caught in the wrong, use "because" as an excuse? Frequently in speech today, we see a term like "because" used—really exposing some of the negative reasons or causes because of an

---

[20] For a further discussion, consult the book *When Will the Messiah Return?* by J.K. McKee.
[21] J. Barton Payne, "עֵקֶב," in *TWOT*, 2:691.

action committed. Yet at the same time, the English term "because" can have positive uses as well. Within *Ekev*, is it possible that God is trying to get Israel to seriously consider the absolute root of their convictions, that they might take certain actions? Let us consider a variety of instances where *ekev* appears, so we can evaluate the function(s) it performs.

The opening verses of *Ekev* include a response to the final verses which concluded *V'et'chanan* last week. Recall how Moses ended his pleadings with a command to the Israelites: "Therefore, you shall keep the commandment and the statutes and the judgments which I am commanding you today, to do them" (Deuteronomy 7:11). This summary statement covers a broad range of instructions that have been given to Israel during the wilderness journey. Now this week as *Ekev* begins, we see a positive affirmation implied in the term *ekev* or "because," listing some of the blessings that the Israelites will receive as a result of obeying the commandments given:

"Then it shall come about, because [*v'hayah ekev*] you listen to these judgments and keep and do them, that the LORD your God will keep with you His covenant and His lovingkindness which He swore to your forefathers. He will love you and bless you and multiply you; He will also bless the fruit of your womb and the fruit of your ground, your grain and your new wine and your oil, the increase of your herd and the young of your flock, in the land which He swore to your forefathers to give you. You shall be blessed above all peoples; there will be no male or female barren among you or among your cattle" (Deuteronomy 7:12-14).

*Ekev* is employed to describe the blessings that the Israelites will receive if they obey the Lord. The term *ekev* is only used two times in our Torah portion,[22] and only nine other times in the rest of the Torah.[23] At the conclusion of Deuteronomy 8, Moses reminds Israel of the consequences they will incur if they do not listen to the Lord:

"But you shall remember the LORD your God, for it is He who is giving you power to make wealth, that He may confirm His covenant which He swore to your fathers, as *it is* this day. It shall come about if you ever forget the LORD your God and go after other gods and serve them and worship them, I testify against you today that you will surely perish. Like the nations that the LORD makes to perish before you, so you shall perish; because you would not listen to the voice of the LORD your God [*ekev lo tishme'un b'qol ADONAI Eloheikhem*, עֵקֶב לֹא תִשְׁמְעוּן בְּקוֹל יְהוָה אֱלֹהֵיכֶם]" (Deuteronomy 8:18-20).

What you discover between the two "*ekev* bookends" of our *parashah* (Deuteronomy 7:12 and 8:20) is a list of some of the benefits for Israel's obedience to God, and some of the serious consequences for disobedience. The blessings bestowed upon Israel—from fertility to disease prevention to expulsion of nations from the Promised Land[24]—are described. Details about how to deal with pagan idols,[25] and helpful reminders about the forty-year wilderness journey,[26] are included. Moses does this to remind the Israelites about the provisions that have been maintained by God since their departure from Egypt.

While pondering the two opposite results of listening versus not listening to the voice of God, a further look at some of the other uses of the Hebrew term *ekev* seemed

---

[22] Deuteronomy 7:12; 8:20.
[23] Genesis 3:15; 22:18; 25:26; 26:5; 27:36; 49:17, 19; Numbers 14:24.
[24] Deuteronomy 7:12-8:20.
[25] Deuteronomy 7:16, 25.
[26] Deuteronomy 8:2-5.

appropriate. I thought that perhaps some insight could be gleaned from other contexts where *ekev* is used.

The first time *ekev* appears in Scripture is where Abraham has not withheld his son Isaac for sacrifice. God will appropriately bless him because of his obedience:

"Then the angel of the LORD called to Abraham a second time from heaven, and said, 'By Myself I have sworn, declares the LORD, because you have done this thing and have not withheld your son, your only son, indeed I will greatly bless you, and I will greatly multiply your seed as the stars of the heavens and as the sand which is on the seashore; and your seed shall possess the gate of their enemies. In your seed all the nations of the earth shall be blessed, **because you have obeyed My voice** [*ekev asher shama'ta b'qoli*, שָׁמַעְתָּ בְּקֹלִי עֵקֶב אֲשֶׁר]'" (Genesis 22:15-18).

The second time *ekev* appears is where Isaac is warned by God not to travel to Egypt, but rather to remain in Canaan. Isaac, as the son of Abraham, will be an agent of blessing to the world because of the obedience of his father:

"The LORD appeared to him and said, 'Do not go down to Egypt; stay in the land of which I shall tell you. Sojourn in this land and I will be with you and bless you, for to you and to your descendants I will give all these lands, and I will establish the oath which I swore to your father Abraham. I will multiply your descendants as the stars of heaven, and will give your descendants all these lands; and by your descendants all the nations of the earth shall be blessed; **because Abraham obeyed Me** [*ekev asher-shama Avraham b'qoli*, עֵקֶב אֲשֶׁר־שָׁמַע אַבְרָהָם בְּקֹלִי] and kept My charge, My commandments, My statutes and My laws" (Genesis 26:2-5).

Finally, a third time, before this Torah portion where *ekev* is used, is in the description of the faith exhibited by Caleb, one of the two faithful spies:

"But My servant Caleb, **because he has had a different spirit and has followed Me fully** [*ekev hayatah ruach acheret immo v'yemalleih acharay*, אַחֶרֶת עִמּוֹ וַיְמַלֵּא אַחֲרָי עֵקֶב הָיְתָה רוּחַ], I will bring into the land which he entered, and his descendants shall take possession of it" (Numbers 14:24).

In these three examples of *ekev*, preceding our *parashah* this week, we see how "because" is used to describe either obedience to God or people faithfully following Him. Certainly, every usage of *ekev* in the Tanakh is contingent on context—and as I have previously mentioned, in speech today "because" is often used to self-justify one's sinful actions. But most important to us as people of faith is how *ekev* does indeed explain specific ways of how the Lord can demonstrate His favor to individuals who have heeded Him. And is this not one of the main points of *Ekev* that we are reading about? Is it possible that God was trying to get the Ancient Israelites—and by extension us today—to seriously consider following Him with their whole hearts?

Within *Ekev* Moses makes the serious point to Israel that God is going to drive out the inhabitants of Canaan, because of His previous promises made—and also because of the Canaanites' own wickedness and sin.[27] Interestingly enough, within these words Moses also declares to Israel that *they* are quite stubborn and discordant, frequently not wanting to follow the Lord:[28]

---

[27] Deuteronomy 9:1-5.
[28] Deuteronomy 9:6-29.

"Know, then, *it is* not because of your righteousness *that* the LORD your God is giving you this good land to possess, for you are a stubborn people...The LORD spoke further to me, saying, 'I have seen this people, and indeed, it is a stubborn people'" (Deuteronomy 9:6, 13).

After recalling how a second set of Ten Commandments had to be written, and how the Levites were separated out for duty as priests,[29] Moses reminds Israel of the critical duty that is required of them:

"Now, Israel, what does the LORD your God require from you, but to fear the LORD your God, to walk in all His ways and love Him, and to serve the LORD your God with all your heart and with all your soul, *and* to keep the LORD's commandments and His statutes which I am commanding you today for your good?" (Deuteronomy 10:12-13).

The Israelites must fear or revere the Holy One, walk in His ways, love Him, and serve Him **with all their hearts and all their souls.** *The problem was that too many had hard hearts.* Just how were they going to deal with those hard, stubborn hearts that they had? Moses provides an answer: a change of heart. The Lord demands that His people possess a circumcised heart, which will be sensitive to Him and to His ways:

"So circumcise your heart, and stiffen your neck no longer. For the LORD your God is the God of gods and the Lord of lords, the great, the mighty, and the awesome God who does not show partiality nor take a bribe. He executes justice for the orphan and the widow, and shows His love for the alien by giving him food and clothing. So show your love for the alien, for you were aliens in the land of Egypt. You shall fear the LORD your God; you shall serve Him and cling to Him, and you shall swear by His name" (Deuteronomy 10:16-20).

As you read this injunction for the Israelites to circumcise their hearts, you might consider the varied usages of *ekev* I mentioned—describing the obedience of Abraham and Isaac, and the faithfulness of Caleb. We cannot know whether these individuals consciously had heard of the idea to "circumcise" their hearts, but what we do know is that they were not stubborn and stiff-necked in their relationship with God. They knew of the Lord's supreme power, and they desired to accomplish His will and purposes, not resisting Him or disbelieving Him.

The command for people to circumcise their hearts is not the whole picture of what it means to submit to the Lord. Later in Deuteronomy, Moses asserts how the Lord Himself will have to circumcise hearts—indicating how this is not only a human action, but also a Divine action:

"Moreover the LORD your God will circumcise your heart and the heart of your descendants, to love the LORD your God with all your heart and with all your soul, so that you may live" (Deuteronomy 30:6).

To this may be added the Prophet Ezekiel's expectation of how in the era of the New Covenant, people will be given new hearts, filled up with God's Spirit:

"For I will take you from the nations, gather you from all the lands and bring you into your own land. Then I will sprinkle clean water on you, and you will be clean; I will cleanse you from all your filthiness and from all your idols. Moreover, I will give you a new heart and put a new spirit within you; and I will remove the heart of stone from your flesh and give you a heart of flesh. I will put My Spirit within you and cause you to walk in My statutes, and you will be careful to observe My ordinances" (Ezekiel 36:24-27).

---

[29] Deuteronomy 10:1-9.

Both a heart circumcision and transplant refer to how the Lord will give His people the desire and ability to fully obey Him and walk in His ways. This will come not out of compulsion, but rather be a positive result of the love people have toward Him and for the acts of deliverance He has accomplished. There is no greater act of deliverance that we can conceive of than the sacrifice of Yeshua the Messiah at Golgotha (Calvary), and how it results in us possessing eternal life:

"He saved us, not on the basis of deeds which we have done in righteousness, but according to His mercy, by the washing of regeneration and renewing by the Holy Spirit, whom He poured out upon us richly through Yeshua the Messiah our Savior, so that being justified by His grace we would be made heirs according to *the* hope of eternal life" (Titus 3:5-7).

Do you truly have a circumcised heart of flesh, that eagerly desires to obey the Lord and accomplish His tasks for your life? Do you receive of the blessings promised to those who follow the commandments? How will the Lord describe your life when you meet Him face to face? If there were any descriptions of your life employing the Hebrew word *ekev*, would they at all be similar to those of Abraham, Isaac, and Caleb?

## *Re'eih* רְאֵה
### See
### "Choices and Tests"

> Deuteronomy 11:26-16:17
> Isaiah 54:11-55:5

*Re'eih* continues where *Ekev* left off. Moses is persistent in encouraging the Israelites to obey the Lord with due faithfulness, so that they can prosper in the Land He is going to give them. **If** Israel chooses to listen to and obey the commandments of the Lord, **then** blessings will emanate from Him. On the other hand, **if** Israel chooses to disobey the commandments of the Lord, **then** curses will manifest themselves. Once again, the bottom line for Ancient Israel is how their choices—positive *or* negative—will affect them when they dwell in the Promised Land. Will Israel choose to follow Moses' Teaching? Or will Israel choose to abandon it? *Re'eih* opens with a rather critical admonition:

"See, I am setting before you today a blessing and a curse: the blessing, if you listen to the commandments of the LORD your God, which I am commanding you today; and the curse, if you do not listen to the commandments of the LORD your God, but turn aside from the way which I am commanding you today, by following other gods which you have not known" (Deuteronomy 11:26-28).

It is not difficult to compute how obedience to the Lord will result in people being blessed by Him, and how disobedience to the Lord will *at least* result in some kind of penalties being dispensed. If people desire to obey the Lord, then such obedience is a manifestation of one's love and loyalty to Him. What does it say of those who do not desire to obey Him?

In *Re'eih* this week, we are introduced to a variety of tests that the Lord will use to ascertain whether His people will truly choose to follow Him. The tests which are given are fairly challenging, as they will come not only in the form of false prophets, but even one's close personal relatives. False prophets, in particular, are said to be allowed to perform signs and wonders that come true:

"If a prophet or a dreamer of dreams arises among you and gives you a sign or a wonder, and the sign or the wonder comes true, concerning which he spoke to you, saying, 'Let us go after other gods (whom you have not known) and let us serve them,' you shall not listen to the words of that prophet or that dreamer of dreams; for the LORD your God is testing you to find out if you love the LORD your God with all your heart and with all your soul. You shall follow the LORD your God and fear Him; and you shall keep His commandments, listen to His voice, serve Him, and cling to Him" (Deuteronomy 13:2-5).

These visible and/or tangible signs and wonders have the intention of drawing people away to worship and serve other gods—especially when the signs or wonders the false prophets claim will occur, come true. But, because false prophets have every intention of leading people away from God's commandments, Israel is instructed to execute them:

"But that prophet or that dreamer of dreams shall be put to death, because he has counseled rebellion against the LORD your God who brought you from the land of Egypt and redeemed you from the house of slavery, to seduce you from the way in which the LORD your God commanded you to walk. So you shall purge the evil from among you" (Deuteronomy 13:5).

As serious as detecting a false prophet may be, even more hard-hitting is the fact that spiritual tests may come via one's own kin:

"If your brother, your mother's son, or your son or daughter, or the wife you cherish, or your friend who is as your own soul, entice you secretly, saying, 'Let us go and serve other gods' (whom neither you nor your fathers have known, of the gods of the peoples who are around you, near you or far from you, from one end of the earth to the other end), you shall not yield to him or listen to him; and your eye shall not pity him, nor shall you spare or conceal him" (Deuteronomy 13:6-8).

At this point, Moses warns Israel that siblings, children, best friends, and even wives can be used as vessels of temptation to get people to deny the Lord. God knows how intimate relationships with people who are *unfaithful toward Him*, can easily draw us away from Him. For Ancient Israel, at least, the answer was to similarly see that those close people would be put to death. And, the one who was tempted by a fellow family member, is the first one who had to throw stones:

"But you shall surely kill him; your hand shall be first against him to put him to death, and afterwards the hand of all the people. So you shall stone him to death because he has sought to seduce you from the LORD your God who brought you out from the land of Egypt, out of the house of slavery. Then all Israel will hear and be afraid, and will never again do such a wicked thing among you" (Deuteronomy 13:9-11).

*This is a difficult test.* After your loved one has been accused and convicted of enticing you away from serving the One God of Israel, you were required to be the first to cast a stone to initiate the capital punishment. **Thankfully, we now live in an era where Yeshua's sacrifice has absorbed such capital punishment** (Colossians 2:14). Yet, even if we might not stone false prophets or relatives who worship other gods—we still have to be very mindful of the deceptive influences present in our world. We have to avoid them and not listen to them! Each of us has to make the conscious choice to fully love and serve the Lord—or pursue other things that take us away from Him *and His promised blessings*. Such has always been the age-old question for the followers of the God of Israel.

During the ministry of Yeshua, we also see some tests present, similar to what is described this week in *Re'eih*. The Apostolic Scriptures warn about the coming of false prophets, with signs and wonders, which are again going to be used by God to test the hearts of those who have claimed faith in His Son. In His Olivet Discourse on the Last Days, Yeshua warned His Disciples about the eventual coming of false messiahs and false prophets who will arise to show great signs and wonders, saying,

"For false messiahs and false prophets will appear and produce great signs and omens, to lead astray, if possible, even the elect" (Matthew 24:24, NRSV).

The significance of such signs and wonders will be *to test the hearts of the elect*. The signs and wonders will be designed to mislead, and have the capacity to seriously disrupt how Messiah followers are to be exclusively loyal to Him. Taking Yeshua's warning to serious heart today, we should always question the motives of any minister or ministry that is actively (or exclusively) soliciting a following based on the manifestation of "signs and wonders." Are they the genuine activity of the Holy Spirit? Are they *really* confirming evidences of the work of the Lord, and in helping people be set free from their sins?

Just as *Re'eih* says that one's close family may be a source of temptation, Yeshua also told His Disciples that there will be division in families, because of belief in Him:

"Do not think that I came to bring peace on the earth; I did not come to bring peace, but a sword. For I came to SET A MAN AGAINST HIS FATHER, AND A DAUGHTER AGAINST HER MOTHER, AND A DAUGHTER-IN-LAW AGAINST HER MOTHER-IN-LAW; and A MAN'S ENEMIES WILL BE THE MEMBERS OF HIS HOUSEHOLD" (Matthew 10:34-36; cf. Micah 7:6).

In both Moses' and Yeshua's instructions, it is asserted how God's people are going to be tested. False prophets will arise with signs and wonders. Families will be at odds because of loyalty to God and to His Messiah. Sadly today, the reality of circumstances on the ground is that many people actually desire to hear ear-tickling and sensational words—rather than receive instruction which can aid them in their relationship with the Lord and spiritual effectiveness. As the Apostle Paul wrote his colleague Timothy,

"For the time will come when they will not endure sound doctrine; but *wanting* to have their ears tickled, they will accumulate for themselves teachers in accordance to their own desires, and will turn away their ears from the truth and will turn aside to myths" (2 Timothy 4:3-4).

## The Final Test and Choice

Within Deuteronomy the subject of prophets is seen multiple times,[30] but it is not exclusively about false prophets who will plague the Israelites. Moses will later speak of a Greater Prophet who will be raised up by God and speak definitive words that the people must heed. This Prophet will provide the ultimate test, and not heeding what He says will bring disastrous consequences:

"I will raise up a prophet from among their countrymen like you, and I will put My words in his mouth, and he shall speak to them all that I command him. It shall come about that whoever will not listen to My words which he shall speak in My name, I Myself will require *it* of him" (Deuteronomy 18:18-19).

The Apostle Peter knew who this Greater Prophet was, as he made a direct appeal to Deuteronomy 18:19—applying it to the ministry and work of Yeshua the Messiah:

---

[30] Deuteronomy 13:1, 3, 5; 18:15, 18, 20, 22; 34:10.

"Moses said, 'THE LORD GOD WILL RAISE UP FOR YOU A PROPHET LIKE ME FROM YOUR BRETHREN; TO HIM YOU SHALL GIVE HEED to everything He says to you. And it will be that every soul that does not heed that prophet shall be utterly destroyed from among the people'" (Acts 3:22-23).

Here, the test of believing in Yeshua is clearly stated. The consequences of unbelief are utter and complete ruin. **Have you placed your trust in Yeshua the Messiah, the Greater Prophet?** Anything else short of this, and you will have *chosen poorly*. Only by expressing true saving faith in the Messiah of Israel, can one also possess the wisdom and discernment to identify all of the false prophets and deceivers out there—which the world will throw at us!

## *Shoftim* שֹׁפְטִים
### Judges
### "Words Required for Life"

Deuteronomy 16:18-21:9
Isaiah 51:12-52:12 (or finish at **53:12**)

*Shoftim* continues to establish the constitution for the emerging nation of Israel. Moses addresses issues like the judicial system[31] and the inevitability of Israel having a monarchy,[32] and how all are to be subject to God's Law and authority. Specifics about the Levitical priesthood are also described,[33] and warnings are issued to Israel about some of the abominable practices that will be tempting the people as the conquest of the Promised Land proceeds.[34] Specifics about the cities of refuge are reiterated,[35] and further definitions about court proceedings are discussed.[36] Preparations for war with the obligations of the selective service or draft are outlined, with the rules of engagement for war included.[37] Finally, some specifics about how to handle homicide are detailed.[38] As you read and reflect upon *Shoftim*, you can easily see how the God of Israel is indeed a Master of order. He has laid out important aspects of the judicial, executive, and priestly functions that are to make His chosen nation be prosperous.

However, in the midst, of all of this instruction for the people of Israel, is a strikingly significant Messianic prophecy. Moses speaks of a Greater Prophet who will one day rise up with the words of God in His mouth. This Greater Prophet will speak all the words that God commands Him to speak. Not listening or heeding the words this Prophet will speak will incur a man or woman some severe consequences:

"I will raise up a prophet from among their countrymen like you, and I will put My words in his mouth, and he shall speak to them all that I command him. It shall come about

---

[31] Deuteronomy 17:1-13.
[32] Deuteronomy 17:14-20.
[33] Deuteronomy 18:1-8.
[34] Deuteronomy 18:9-14.
[35] Deuteronomy 19:1-13.
[36] Deuteronomy 19:14-21.
[37] Deuteronomy 20:1-20.
[38] Deuteronomy 21:1-9.

that whoever will not listen to My words which he shall speak in My name, I Myself will require *it* of him" (Deuteronomy 18:18-19).

This expectation has a degree of finality to it. Moses declares that this future Prophet will speak words that must be obeyed by those who hear them. If they are not obeyed, then God Himself "will call...to account" (NIV) those who ignored or disregarded them, holding those responsible who did not take seriously the words conveyed. Deuteronomy 19:18-10 is a powerful prophetic statement made by Moses, which pointed ahead to the eventual arrival of the Messiah. And yet, when the Messiah did come, how many chose to really believe His words?

One group of people who fully believed and acted on the words of the Greater Prophet were the Disciples of Yeshua the Messiah. Ten days after the ascension of the Messiah into Heaven, on the day of *Shavuot*/Pentecost, the Ruach HaKodesh or Holy Spirit was poured out upon the Believers. As it is recorded in Acts 3, the Apostle Peter confidently declared that Yeshua was indeed the Greater Prophet who Moses had foretold:

"But the things which God announced beforehand by the mouth of all the prophets, that His Messiah would suffer, He has thus fulfilled. Therefore repent and return, so that your sins may be wiped away, in order that times of refreshing may come from the presence of the Lord; and that He may send Yeshua, the Messiah appointed for you, whom heaven must receive until *the* period of restoration of all things about which God spoke by the mouth of His holy prophets from ancient time. **Moses said, 'THE LORD GOD WILL RAISE UP FOR YOU A PROPHET LIKE ME FROM YOUR BRETHREN; TO HIM YOU SHALL GIVE HEED** [Deuteronomy 18:19] **to everything He says to you. And it will be that every soul that does not heed that prophet shall be utterly destroyed from among the people.'** And likewise, all the prophets who have spoken, from Samuel and *his* successors onward, also announced these days. It is you who are the sons of the prophets and of the covenant which God made with your fathers, saying to Abraham, 'AND IN YOUR SEED ALL THE FAMILIES OF THE EARTH SHALL BE BLESSED' [Genesis 22:18; 26:4]. For you first, God raised up His Servant and sent Him to bless you by turning every one *of you* from your wicked ways" (Acts 3:18-26).

Peter directly quotes Deuteronomy 18:19, which details who the Greater Prophet is to be,[39] and identifies Him to be Yeshua the Messiah. But there is further amplification as to what the concept of "requiring" one to recognize Him actually means. Peter makes it much more succinct and to the point. He states that: **"Anyone who does not listen to him will be completely cut off from among his people"** (NIV). This statement is really to be taken seriously, because those who disregard Yeshua will have severe consequences leveled against them. The early Messiah followers understood that Moses was indeed foretelling of Yeshua—because before he was stoned, the young disciple Stephen likewise directly quoted from Deuteronomy 18:15, defending himself with the word,

"This is the Moses who said to the sons of Israel, 'GOD WILL RAISE UP FOR YOU A PROPHET LIKE ME FROM YOUR BRETHREN'" (Acts 7:37).[40]

Based on the prophecy delivered by Moses, and the confirmation offered by Peter and Stephen—**we must believe in and heed the message declared by the Greater Prophet**, Yeshua the Messiah—or the consequence will be eternal punishment. This might

---

[39] Kurt Aland, et. al., *The Greek New Testament, Fourth Revised Edition* (Stuttgart: Deutche Bibelgesellschaft/United Bible Societies, 1998), 418.

[40] Ibid., 433.

seem like a harsh word, but the author of Hebrews' words are even more direct than those witnessed in either Deuteronomy 18:19 or Acts 3:23:

"For if we go on sinning willfully after receiving the knowledge of the truth, there no longer remains a sacrifice for sins, but a terrifying expectation of judgment and THE FURY OF A FIRE WHICH WILL CONSUME THE ADVERSARIES [Isaiah 26:11]. Anyone who has set aside the Law of Moses dies without mercy on *the testimony of* two or three witnesses. How much severer punishment do you think he will deserve who has trampled under foot the Son of God, and has regarded as unclean the blood of the covenant by which he was sanctified, and has insulted the Spirit of grace? For we know Him who said, 'VENGEANCE IS MINE, I WILL REPAY.' And again, 'THE LORD WILL JUDGE HIS PEOPLE' [Deuteronomy 32:35, 36; Psalm 135:14]. It is a terrifying thing to fall into the hands of the living God" (Hebrews 10:26-31).

Reading this rather direct and stern admonition—born again Believers should recognize how they have the authority to not only rebuke those who have heard the knowledge of the truth and keep on sinning, **but also** those who completely turn away from the truth that the Messiah is Yeshua, the only Savior for humanity.

Brothers and sisters, you do not want to find yourself a sinner who fails to turn from bad habits, one who has known but has rejected the good news, or one who has just rejected the good news. While all of these negative predicaments are terrible—those who once professed to believe in, *but later deny*, the blood atonement of Yeshua on their behalf—are going to be punished even more seriously than those who just reject Him outright.

Have you truly believed in the words of the Messiah? Has the good news of salvation in Yeshua changed your heart, and truly enabled you to love God and neighbor like never before? If you have not experienced the supernatural power of the gospel—**now is the time to go before the Lord in prayerful repentance!** One must believe in the words of Yeshua to experience eternal life; it is not enough to only have the words of Moses.

## *Ki-Teitzei* כִּי־תֵצֵא
### When you go out
### "Be Well and Prolong Your Days"

> **Deuteronomy 21:10-25:19**
> **Isaiah 54:1-10** (or finish at **52:13**)

The final stretch of the Deuteronomy Torah portions through the month of Elul to *Yom Teruah/Rosh HaShanah* and the Fall feasts is now upon us (2003/5753). Our reading for this week, *Ki-Teitzei*, details many commandments that will directly apply to the Israelites upon their occupation of the Promised Land. A wide variety of unique subjects, ranging from how to deal with foreign women in the battlefields[41] to admonitions about those excluded from the assembly,[42] are covered. Reading and meditating about many of these different instructions can take Torah students to places in both spiritual reflection and Biblical examination that they may have not considered before. *Further investigation into the thoughts of different Rabbis, commentators, and scholars is often in order.* As you may begin to consider

---

[41] Deuteronomy 21:10-14.
[42] Deuteronomy 23:1-11.

some of the writings that have dissected many of these instructions over the ages, you will discover that the amount of material is voluminous.

Many of the instructions witnessed in *Ki-Teitzei* can only make sense when read in the context of Ancient Israel within the world of the Ancient Near East. Still, some of the instructions, such as covering up one's leavings (Deuteronomy 23:13), can be followed today (even if you just go out camping in the woods). One of the most perplexing yet intriguing instructions, is seen in how those who might take the eggs of a mother bird must make the effort to shoo away the bird before taking them:

"If you happen to come upon a bird's nest along the way, in any tree or on the ground, with young ones or eggs, and the mother sitting on the young or on the eggs, you shall not take the mother with the young; you shall certainly let the mother go, but the young you may take for yourself, in order that it may be well with you and that you may prolong your days" (Deuteronomy 22:6-7).

There is certainly a level of humanitarianism seen in shooing away a mother bird before taking her eggs. But, the Torah actually instructs people to do this "so that it may go well with you and you may have a long life" (NIV).

Also witnessed in our *parashah* is instruction on how a rebellious child was to be tried and stoned to death.[43] Many Bible readers have no idea what to do with this material in the Scriptures, and in Jewish history there is likewise considerable discussion as to how these instructions were to legally play out in the process of jurisprudence.[44] Since the Torah is the constitution of Israel, one can easily see why observant Jewish people have debated these instructions over several millennia.

As I pondered the text of our Torah portion, and reflected upon how the Holy One desires to be intimately involved with His children, I could not get the instruction I read about the mother bird and her eggs out of my mind. It is juxtaposed between prohibitions about cross dressing[45] and the need to build a parapet on the roof of one's house.[46] Catching my attention was how the blessing of a long life is attached to this commandment, and how the same will be incurred by honoring father and mother:

"Honor your father and your mother, as the LORD your God has commanded you, that your days may be prolonged and that it may go well with you on the land which the LORD your God gives you" (Deuteronomy 5:16).

Comparing these two commandments (Deuteronomy 22:6-7 and 5:16), I really did not see a connection. It seems far more logically important to honor one's parents rather than showing kindness to some random, female bird. After all, God Himself had included the command to honor one's parents as a part of the Decalogue—the Ten Commandments engraved in stone. The Apostle Paul further points out how the Fifth Commandment is the first commandment with a promise of blessing:

"HONOR YOUR FATHER AND MOTHER (which is the first commandment with a promise)" (Ephesians 6:2).

It is natural to ask yourself if there is any connection between honoring one's parents and showing kindness toward a female bird—both of which elicit the same blessing. Is it

---

[43] Deuteronomy 21:18-23.

[44] Scherman, *Chumash*, 1047 summarizes some of the Rabbinical discussions on this passage, including the thought of there being so many prerequisites in order for a rebellious child to be executed, that the inaction of capital punishment is effectively impossible (cf. b.*Sanhedrin* 71a).

[45] Deuteronomy 22:5.

[46] Deuteronomy 22:8.

possible that the Lord wants His people to demonstrate kindness not just to one's fellow humans, but also to those creatures that humanity has dominion over (cf. Genesis 1:26, 28)? Comparatively speaking, honoring one's parents is obviously more significant than being kind to a bird—but perhaps in showing kindness to an animal, we will be more akin to show kindness to *actual people?*

In the late 1990s, my family and I lived on a small, three-and-a-half acre country farm in North Texas. We had some goats, sheep, a donkey, and a number of free-range chickens that roamed around the barn area. I can remember the mornings when I would be on a search for eggs. It was usually a quiet time, when I would find myself reflecting upon the mercies of the Lord and giving Him praise for our many blessings. As I recall this delightful chore, I can remember the times when I would have to shoo away the hens to look for eggs. My heart occasionally considered the thoughts of the mother hen. Even though I was glad to have the eggs, the hen was going to have to go about her business and lay another egg after I left the barn. At the time, I thought shooing the hens was simply a practical matter of moving them away so that I could more readily access the eggs. I never really thought about the blessing that I was going to receive for treating the hen with human kindness. For whatever reasons, this approach to retrieving eggs was the way that the Father intended His people to do it. It seemed to come naturally to me without any extensive instruction. But apparently, based on the words of the Lord—by extending basic human kindness to our hens—I was receiving blessings, even without my knowledge of this particular Scripture.

Remembering this past experience this week, I then turned my thoughts to the Biblical requirement to honor one's father and mother, with its commensurate blessings. I reflected upon how natural my obedience to this instruction had been over the years—and I also remembered a period of time when I had a rebellious streak in me, which consistently dishonored my parents. Thankfully, the stubbornness was short-lived! My parents' love for me prevailed, and our relationship has been wonderful for decades.

Thinking about the material seen in *Ki-Teitzei* more and more, the reality of lovingkindness kept coming to mind. After all, is love not one of the principal attributes of our Heavenly Father? Is He not constantly working to have this attribute become ingrained into the hearts, minds, and souls of His people? **Is it possible that God wants us to be as tender hearted to mere birds as He is to us?** By using the example of the mercy we might show to a brooding hen, how truly significant is it that He wants us to extend a similar amount of mercy and lovingkindness toward *the people* we interact with? Extending love toward our neighbors is the most tangible example that we are diligently obeying the Lord. Remember how Yeshua reacted when questioned about the greatest commandment in the Torah:

"One of them, a lawyer, asked Him *a question*, testing Him, 'Teacher, which is the great commandment in the Law?' And He said to him, "'YOU SHALL LOVE THE LORD YOUR GOD WITH ALL YOUR HEART, AND WITH ALL YOUR SOUL, AND WITH ALL YOUR MIND" [Deuteronomy 6:5]. This is the great and foremost commandment. The second is like it, "YOU SHALL LOVE YOUR NEIGHBOR AS YOURSELF" [Leviticus 19:18]. On these two commandments depend the whole Law and the Prophets'" (Matthew 22:35-40).

Yeshua concludes that the entire Torah rests on the requirements for people to love God and their neighbors. If people can observe these simple commandments, then they will understand why God gave us His Law to follow. *The command to love one's neighbor is perhaps the most basic when it comes to human interaction.* Consider in tangible terms what loving one's neighbor actually involves:

"You shall not oppress your neighbor, nor rob *him*. The wages of a hired man are not to remain with you all night until morning. You shall not curse a deaf man, nor place a stumbling block before the blind, but you shall revere your God; I am the LORD. You shall do no injustice in judgment; you shall not be partial to the poor nor defer to the great, but you are to judge your neighbor fairly. You shall not go about as a slanderer among your people, and you are not to act against the life of your neighbor; I am the LORD. You shall not hate your fellow countryman in your heart; you may surely reprove your neighbor, but shall not incur sin because of him. You shall not take vengeance, nor bear any grudge against the sons of your people, but you shall love your neighbor as yourself; I am the LORD" (Leviticus 19:13-18).

The requirement to love one's neighbor goes back to the foundational instructions delivered by God about separating out a unique people for His own possession (cf. Exodus 19:5; Deuteronomy 4:20; 7:6; 14:2; 26:18). The Ancient Israelites were commanded to judge their neighbors fairly, and to not oppress, rob, slander, hate, bear grudges against, or take vengeance against them. Such is all summarized and made complete in the actions witnessed in the ministry of the Messiah Yeshua.

To what degree do you need to be reminded that we need to be treating a brooding hen the same way we might treat our neighbors? *If you show disrespect to animals, then it should not be surprising why you might show disrespect to human beings.* Each of us needs to heed the admonitions of Scripture, striving to have hearts and minds indwelt with the Ruach HaKodesh (Holy Spirit). We need to be people who can treat all of God's creatures with dignity and honor. Perhaps if we learn to extend loving kindness to the animal kingdom, then we will treat *people* properly. **If we can exhibit love to all those we encounter, then we can truly live long and blessed lives.**

## *Ki-Tavo* כִּי־תָבוֹא
### When you enter in
### "A Faithful Treasured Possession"

> Deuteronomy 26:1-29:8
> Isaiah 60:1-22

*Ki-Tavo* is frequently remembered for the lengthy lists of blessings and curses that are promised to Israel as a result of their obedience or disobedience to the Lord. In this season of repentance, which traditionally comes during the month of Elul as we approach the Fall high holidays, reflecting on such blessings and curses can be a sobering exercise. After all, God has declared many times throughout the Scriptures that Israel is a chosen people who have been designated as His own possession among all the peoples of the Earth—who are to in turn be a blessing to all they encounter. Here in our *parashah* this week, after we see instructions on how Israel should honor the Lord with offerings of first fruits and tithes,[47] Moses summarizes that the people are declaring their willingness to follow and obey Him fully:

---

[47] Deuteronomy 26:1-19.

"You have today declared the LORD to be your God, and that you would walk in His ways and keep His statutes, His commandments and His ordinances, and listen to His voice" (Deuteronomy 26:17).

This commitment receives a positive response from the Lord, who reiterates and amplifies just how treasured a possession Israel will be:

"The LORD has today declared you to be His people, a treasured possession, as He promised you, and that you should keep all His commandments; and that He will set you high above all nations which He has made, for praise, fame, and honor; and that you shall be a consecrated people to the LORD your God, as He has spoken" (Deuteronomy 26:18-19).

Being "the chosen nation" above all the nations of the world has some rather incumbent, serious responsibilities. Israel is required to be an example of a consecrated people, which fully submits itself to the will of God. He requires specific actions from His people to affirm that they are indeed His, and that they can truly be as prominent as He desires them to be.

Moses gives explicit instructions on what must be done once the Israelites have crossed the Jordan and entered into the Promised Land. In a very dramatic way, the Israelites are ordered to travel to the area around Shechem to perform a solemn ceremony on Mounts Ebal and Gerizim. There, the Levites will position themselves between the two mountains with six tribes on each side, and make loud declarations about curses that will come upon them as a result of deviant behavior.[48] Declarations about blessings as a result of obedience to God will be made,[49] but so will the consequences of disobedience be specified.[50] As all of these statements are ushered forth, the people will be expected to proclaim *Amein* (אָמֵן), issuing their agreement with what is said. Just imagine a scene of hundreds of thousands of people declaring forth *Amein* to words that will determine their future (cf. Joshua 8:30-35)!

As we review the different statements that Ancient Israel was to make when they entered into the Promised Land, there are some things that should really strike us. Moses said that if Israel was to diligently obey the Lord, that His blessings will just "overtake" them:

"Now it shall be, if you diligently obey the LORD your God, being careful to do all His commandments which I command you today, the LORD your God will set you high above all the nations of the earth. All these blessings will come upon you and overtake you if you obey the LORD your God" (Deuteronomy 28:1-2).

The lengthy list of blessings offered by the Lord (Deuteronomy 28:3-12) culminates in the ultimate elevation for Israel to always be the head and never the tail among those in the world:

"The LORD will make you the head and not the tail, and you only will be above, and you will not be underneath, if you listen to the commandments of the LORD your God, which I charge you today, to observe *them* carefully" (Deuteronomy 28:13).

*All that is required to attain this status is simply obedience to God.* But as the testimony of Scripture is clear, this is much easier said than done. The narrative and the tone shifts, because there is a much longer list of curses that will come upon Israel if the people choose to disobey God. Moses summarizes,

---

[48] Deuteronomy 27:1-26.
[49] Deuteronomy 28:1-14.
[50] Deuteronomy 28:15-68.

"But it shall come about, if you do not obey the LORD your God, to observe to do all His commandments and His statutes with which I charge you today, that all these curses will come upon you and overtake you" (Deuteronomy 28:15).

As you read curse after curse (Deuteronomy 28:16-65), you realize that these negative words touch almost every aspect of human life. After reading through these curses a number of times, you can understand why frequently—when this part of the Torah portion is often read in Jewish synagogues—it is traditionally read quickly and in an almost inaudible tone. So severe are the curses upon Israel that the Rabbis have sought to minimize even the contemplation of the possible curses. **And yet, in this time of personal and corporate repentance, is it not an ideal time to consider some of the consequences of disobedience?** Just consider some of the concluding remarks about just how the people of Israel will act once the effects of disobedience have taken their hold:

"So your life shall hang in doubt before you; and you will be in dread night and day, and shall have no assurance of your life. In the morning you shall say, 'Would that it were evening!' And at evening you shall say, 'Would that it were morning!' because of the dread of your heart which you dread, and for the sight of your eyes which you will see" (Deuteronomy 28:66-67).

Once all of the curses have taken their toll, life will be so miserable that one will not be comfortable with either the day or the night. *There will be no assurance of life at all.* One's existence will be in a sphere dominated by the power of death—a routine marked with incessant fear and loathing—especially since the people will have been scattered into the nations as a result of their disobedience.

With all of this being witnessed in our *parashah* this week, is there not a great incentive to be obedient to the Lord? Surely, as a part of His people today—even though we have experienced redemption in Messiah Yeshua—should we not recognize that we can only be blessed if we expel the effort to follow *and* obey? Sadly, much of religious history is marked by people who have made more of an effort to disobey God, or bend the rules with trying to do as little as possible, then people who have strived to love Him and His ways. Lamentably, the Lord has been quite true to His Word to enact curses and penalties upon disobedient people throughout the ages.

## The Faithful Remnant

Pondering this sad reality, I was also reminded that, thankfully, there has always been a faithful remnant of people throughout history who have chosen to diligently obey God to the best of their ability and understanding.[51] As a result, these people of faithful obedience have received the promised blessings, and have prepared the way for each successive generation. In His sovereignty the Lord has always had a group of people who are faithful to perform His Word, making a concentrated, positive difference in society—whether they be Jews *or* Christians. As the writer of Hebrews states it, faith is foundational to acts of obedience:

"Now faith is the assurance of *things* hoped for, the conviction of things not seen. For by it the men of old gained approval. By faith we understand that the worlds were prepared by the word of God, so that what is seen was not made out of things which are visible...And

---

[51] Editor's note: Of useful consultation would be the many people described in Robert G. Tuttle, *The Story of Evangelism: A History of the Witness to the Gospel* (Nashville: Abingdon, 2006).

without faith it is impossible to please *Him*, for he who comes to God must believe that He is and *that* He is a rewarder of those who seek Him" (Hebrews 11:1-3, 6).

Apparently, over the ages, it has been the faith of many men and women—who beyond a shadow of a doubt can be counted among the "treasured possession" of God's people—that has caused them to be obedient to the Lord. They have been responsible for demonstrating acts of kindness and mercy to others, fulfilling what James the Just calls, "Pure and undefiled religion in the sight of *our* God and Father is this: to visit orphans and widows in their distress, *and* to keep oneself unstained by the world" (James 1:27).

Considering the requirement of faith as a critical ingredient for generating obedience, my thoughts turned to some of the words of the Apostle Paul which address the requirement of God's people to function as a living sacrifice (Romans 12:1-2). Paul specifies how each person has been given a particular allocation of faith, requiring all Believers to work and serve together in the Kingdom of God:

"For through the grace given to me I say to everyone among you not to think more highly of himself than he ought to think; but to think so as to have sound judgment, as God has allotted to each a measure of faith" (Romans 12:3).

Reading this, I also had to recognize how Paul further says that faith is the means by which we receive salvation—not our human works:

"For by grace you have been saved through faith; and that not of yourselves, *it is* the gift of God; not as a result of works, so that no one may boast" (Ephesians 2:8-9).

But, too many people stop reading at Ephesians 2:9, because nowhere in his letters does Paul ever negate the need for the children of God to have good works. Instead, he asserts how Messiah followers have been created *for good works*, which come as a natural result of our faith demonstrated in action:

"For we are His workmanship, created in Messiah Yeshua for good works, which God prepared beforehand so that we would walk in them" (Ephesians 2:10).

James the Just is also noted for his description about how faith and works are to compliment one another. A true follower of the Messiah of Israel is to have a dynamic, active faith, that manifests itself in the appropriate deeds:

"Even so faith, if it has no works, is dead, *being* by itself. But someone may *well* say, 'You have faith and I have works; show me your faith without the works, and I will show you my faith by my works.' You believe that God is one. You do well; the demons also believe, and shudder. But are you willing to recognize, you foolish fellow, that faith without works is useless? Was not Abraham our father justified by works when he offered up Isaac his son on the altar? You see that faith was working with his works, and as a result of the works, faith was perfected; and the Scripture was fulfilled which says, 'AND ABRAHAM BELIEVED GOD, AND IT WAS RECKONED TO HIM AS RIGHTEOUSNESS' [Genesis 15:6], and he was called the friend of God. You see that a man is justified by works and not by faith alone. In the same way, was not Rahab the harlot also justified by works when she received the messengers and sent them out by another way? For just as the body without *the* spirit is dead, so also faith without works is dead" (James 2:17-26).

## More Faith

In these days of contemplation and repentance, as I have considered the different blessings and curses contingent upon obedience or disobedience to God—**all I can do is entreat Him to give me more faith.** *I ask the Father to increase my faith, so that I can have a heart desirous of serving Him.* In a day and age when temptation is rampant and is at clear odds with the will of the indwelling Holy Spirit—*I beseech the Lord to reveal more and more of Himself*, so that I can endure the trials and tribulations that have been thrust upon me in life. I want to live in accordance with His ways.

It is a great blessing to be given a significant measure of trusting faith. This gift results in one not only desiring to be obedient to the Lord, but it places one's total confidence in His will for the future. It lets me know that I, personally, am a treasured possession of His—who He loves and who He truly cares about!

What about you? Have you been turning your heart and attention toward God in this time of contemplation, in anticipation of the Fall high holidays? What about your actions toward your neighbors? Have they been consistent with what is expected of able Messiah followers? If not, I would recommend that you go before the Lord and truly seek Him with all of your being—remembering that He is faithful to reveal Himself to those who truly seek Him:

"'For I know the plans that I have for you,' declares the LORD, 'plans for welfare and not for calamity to give you a future and a hope. Then you will call upon Me and come and pray to Me, and I will listen to you. You will seek Me and find *Me* when you search for Me with all your heart" (Jeremiah 29:11-13).

*May you be found to be one of His faithful treasured possessions!*

# *Nitzavim* נִצָּבִים
## Standing
## "Prophecies Here and Now"

> Deuteronomy 29:9[10]-30:20
> Isaiah 61:10-63:9

The events of *Nitzavim* occur near the end of Moses' declarations to the Ancient Israelites, and contain some extremely profound prophecies. I believe that we are witnessing the fulfillment of some of these prophecies today. From the creation of the State of Israel in the Middle East to the emergence of the Messianic community of faith, elements of these profound realities are forecast in this Torah portion. In this season of repentance in the month of Elul, as we are preparing our hearts for *Yom Teruah/Rosh HaShanah* and *Yom Kippur*, I find it very encouraging to consider some of these passages.

As this section of the Torah commences, Moses specifies how the broad-sweeping influence that the covenant God has made with Israel affects every level of society. As you should notice from the opening verses of our *parashah*, the different groups of people range from the leaders of Israel, to wives and children, to those who perform menial labor, to those who are aliens or sojourners in the camp. We see how the God of Israel is an all-inclusive God, who wants all of humanity to be blessed by the covenant which has been established with His chosen nation. Perhaps most important for us to consider is that the agreement made between Himself and Ancient Israel is not only made with them, but is considered to have been made with future generations:

"You stand today, all of you, before the LORD your God: your chiefs, your tribes, your elders and your officers, *even* all the men of Israel, your little ones, your wives, and the alien who is within your camps, from the one who chops your wood to the one who draws your water, that you may enter into the covenant with the LORD your God, and into His oath which the LORD your God is making with you today, in order that He may establish you today as His people and that He may be your God, just as He spoke to you and as He swore to your fathers, to Abraham, Isaac, and Jacob. **Now not with you alone am I making this covenant and this oath, but both with those who stand here with us today in the presence of the LORD our God and with those who are not with us here today"** (Deuteronomy 29:10-15).

Remember that the group of Israelites which Moses addresses here are the second and third generations who have experienced the desert sojourn. The Exodus generation which first departed from Egypt—except Joshua and Caleb—have largely all died in the wilderness due to believing the bad report of the ten spies (Numbers 14:26-30). Their children and grandchildren are being admonished to obey the Lord and to keep His covenant. It is not just enough for the people to acknowledge His faithfulness in delivering Israel, but each successive generation of Israel has the responsibility of obeying His commandments.

Thinking about this, what might we really need to be considering today? What is most significant for us in the Twenty-First Century is the closing comment with how God's covenant is made "with the future generations who are not standing here today" (Deuteronomy 29:15, NLT). The message of Moses in the Book of Deuteronomy has relevance *for us living now*, as much as it did to its first recipients as Israel was preparing to enter into the Promised Land.

Moses was a prophet who had a unique relationship with the Creator, and so as he nears the end of his life, many of the words he delivers in Deuteronomy have tremendous prophetic significance for our times. He was very concerned for Ancient Israel, because already several times in Deuteronomy, he has said that they will not obey the Lord in the future—and will be punished and scattered accordingly:

"I call heaven and earth to witness against you today, that you will surely perish quickly from the land where you are going over the Jordan to possess it. You shall not live long on it, but will be utterly destroyed. **The LORD will scatter you among the peoples, and you will be left few in number among the nations where the LORD drives you.** There you will serve gods, the work of man's hands, wood and stone, which neither see nor hear nor eat nor smell. But from there you will seek the LORD your God, and you will find *Him* if you search for Him with all your heart and all your soul" (Deuteronomy 4:26-29).

"Moreover, **the LORD will scatter you among all peoples**, from one end of the earth to the other end of the earth; and there you shall serve other gods, wood and stone, which you or your fathers have not known" (Deuteronomy 28:64).

This week in *Nitzavim*, Moses once again communicates that Israel is going to be severely chastised for not obeying God and maintaining its covenant with Him. Moses again tells Israel that the people will be cast into other lands to live:

"Therefore, the anger of the LORD burned against that land, to bring upon it every curse which is written in this book; and the LORD uprooted them from their land in anger and in fury and in great wrath, and cast them into another land, as *it is* this day" (Deuteronomy 29:27-28).

We see how Moses has reiterated a tragic future for the Ancient Israelites as a by-product of their collective, future disobedience. Plagues and diseases upon Israel, and a curse upon the Promised Land, are just some of the penalties that will be incurred (cf. Deuteronomy 29). At the same time, not all hope is lost, because as Deuteronomy 29 comes to a close, we see Moses communicating a profound truth *which all generations* can take great encouragement from:

"The secret things belong to the LORD our God, but the things revealed belong to us and to our sons forever, that we may observe all the words of this law" (Deuteronomy 29:29).

There are many secret things that only God knows, but Israel as God's chosen people have been revealed things by Him—in order that they might follow His Instruction and be blessed. With such knowledge given to Israel by the Creator, they have a serious responsibility to be a blessing to others and be able representatives of Him in the world. The classic problem—as witnessed throughout the Tanakh, sadly—was that Ancient Israel was largely unable to follow God's Law. Even in spite of Moses' and the Prophets' warnings that if Israel disobeyed the Lord, punishment would come—disobedience still too frequently prevailed.

Following this, Deuteronomy 30 begins with one of the most important end-time prophecies regarding the future of Israel. This word not only considers how Israel will be scattered into the nations, but also how a future obedience of Israel will result in its return and restoration to the Promised Land:

"So it shall be when all of these things have come upon you, the blessing and the curse which I have set before you, and you call *them* to mind in all nations where the LORD your God has banished you, and you return to the LORD your God and obey Him with all your heart and soul according to all that I command you today, you and your sons, then the LORD your God will restore you from captivity, and have compassion on you, and will gather you again from all the peoples where the LORD your God has scattered you. If your outcasts are at the ends of the earth, from there the LORD your God will gather you, and from there He will bring you back. The LORD your God will bring you into the land which your fathers possessed, and you shall possess it; and He will prosper you and multiply you more than your fathers. Moreover the LORD your God will circumcise your heart and the heart of your descendants, to love the LORD your God with all your heart and with all your soul, so that you may live" (Deuteronomy 30:1-6).

This prophecy is to take place at a distant future time, when a scattered Israel remembers the words Moses delivered in Deuteronomy chs. 28 & 29, and as is declared, "you [will] come to your senses *while you are* in all the nations where the LORD your God has driven you" (HCSB).

If you are familiar with the broad history of Israel, then perhaps you can think about how the various blessings and curses Moses details have impacted the Jewish people—no matter where they have been scattered down through the centuries. Furthermore, the blessings listed in ch. 28 are noticeable in certain societies which have either directly or indirectly adhered to the morality and ethics of the Torah. On the other hand, the predominance of any disobedience to God, in and among the nations, is likewise readily discernible. Even if you do not know that much about the history of Ancient Israel or Judaism, the axiom of how obedience to God merits blessings and disobedience to God merits some kind of penalties—is quite easy to witness, if not just on a personal level.

In many respects, the prophecy of Deuteronomy 30:1-6 may have a direct correlation to much of what we are now witnessing with the emerging Messianic movement. Since the late 1960s, more Jewish people have come to faith in Messiah Yeshua than since the First Century. Also important is how since the 1990s, many evangelical Christians have been exposed to their Hebraic Roots and have started diligently studying the Torah of Moses. For the first time since the early decades of the Apostles' ministry, Jewish and non-Jewish Believers are coming together as one in the Messiah, and are submitting themselves to a regimen of considering Moses' Teaching every week (cf. Acts 15:21). Many Messianics think that Moses' prophecy of "…calling them to mind in the nations where the LORD your God has banished you…" (Deuteronomy 30:1b) is occurring in our day.

It is very true that our generation has witnessed a community of Messiah followers come forth who recognize Yeshua as the Savior of the world, *and* are considering a very high role for the Torah to play in their lives. While recognizing that Torah-keeping does not merit one eternal salvation, the emergence of a Torah observant sector of Believers does make one realize that God's Instruction is to mold men and women in ways of holiness and good works (Ephesians 2:8-10). Any born again Believer naturally wants God's blessings, and God's blessings can only come by a diligent and faithful obedience to Him. Yeshua may have been sacrificed to take away the capital penalties of the Torah (Colossians 2:14), but He still bids His followers to fulfill the Law (Matthew 5:17-19).

People around the globe today are desiring to fully return to the Lord, and are letting His Torah teach them about His holiness and what it means to be a part of a treasured people. Our own family—where two generations recognize the Torah as relevant instruction for Messiah followers—I believe is very much influenced by how "the things revealed belong to us and to our children forever" (Deuteronomy 29:29, NIV). While we do not know all of the future details of Moses' prophecy coming to pass, today's Messianic movement is doubtlessly going to be involved in the future return of scattered Israel to the Holy Land (Deuteronomy 30:4-5).

Many have rightly concluded that the formation of the State of Israel is a definite fulfillment of this prophecy. Many "outcasts" have been gathered from the ends of the Earth and brought back to reside in *Eretz Yisrael*. The remarkable achievements of the State of Israel are easily seen in how a primitive desert land can be turned into a productive and vibrant economy, and Israel today is one of the leading technological innovators in our world. We have already witnessed some prophetic fulfillment of Moses' words—although it is notable that most of Israeli society today is secular, and many do not acknowledge the existence of God. But as we move closer and closer to the Messiah's return, not only will more begin to acknowledge who God is, but they will also recognize Yeshua as their Savior. It should be our persistent prayer that the main essence of Moses' prophecy comes to fruition in the lives of all modern Israelis:

"Moreover the LORD your God will circumcise your heart and the heart of your descendants, to love the LORD your God with all your heart and with all your soul, so that you may live" (Deuteronomy 30:6; cf. 10:12-16).

Apparently, one of the challenges that Moses knows will plague Israel throughout history is the inability for them to willfully circumcise their hearts. At some future time, God will circumcise the hearts of Israel so that they will love Him, obey Him, and be empowered to perform some mighty deeds. Paralleling this, to be sure, are the words spoken by the Prophets Jeremiah and Ezekiel, in detailing the forgiveness provided in the New Covenant—and the supernatural ability to keep God's Law:

"'Behold, days are coming,' declares the LORD, 'when I will make a new covenant with the house of Israel and with the house of Judah, not like the covenant which I made with their fathers in the day I took them by the hand to bring them out of the land of Egypt, My covenant which they broke, although I was a husband to them,' declares the LORD. 'But this is the covenant which I will make with the house of Israel after those days,' declares the

LORD, 'I will put My law within them and on their heart I will write it; and I will be their God, and they shall be My people. They will not teach again, each man his neighbor and each man his brother, saying, "Know the LORD," for they will all know Me, from the least of them to the greatest of them,' declares the LORD, 'for I will forgive their iniquity, and their sin I will remember no more'" (Jeremiah 31:31-34).

"For I will take you from the nations, gather you from all the lands and bring you into your own land. Then I will sprinkle clean water on you, and you will be clean; I will cleanse you from all your filthiness and from all your idols. Moreover, I will give you a new heart and put a new spirit within you; and I will remove the heart of stone from your flesh and give you a heart of flesh. I will put My Spirit within you and cause you to walk in My statutes, and you will be careful to observe My ordinances. You will live in the land that I gave to your forefathers; so you will be My people, and I will be your God" (Ezekiel 36:24-28).

These two passages specifically describe how God will transform the hearts of His people, writing His Law onto them via the power of His Spirit. As those who have placed our trust in Yeshua the Messiah, we believe that His sacrificial work has already inaugurated this within the hearts of His followers (Luke 22:20; Hebrews 8:8-12). At the same time, the expectation of the New Covenant involves not only a cleansing from sins, but God's corporate people being brought back into the Promised Land. *When **all** this is going to take place is unknown.* It is safe to say that as the Messianic movement grows and matures, that the full realization of the New Covenant is going to come to fruition.

As our Torah reading for this week closes, Moses summarizes all of his teachings to one simple choice: life or death. Now that Israel has been given the Torah, will they choose an existence of being in God's plan and favor—or one dominated by separation and exile from Him?

**"See, I have set before you today life and prosperity, and death and adversity; in that I command you today to love the LORD your God, to walk in His ways and to keep His commandments and His statutes and His judgments,** that you may live and multiply, and that the LORD your God may bless you in the land where you are entering to possess it. But if your heart turns away and you will not obey, but are drawn away and worship other gods and serve them, I declare to you today that you shall surely perish. You will not prolong *your* days in the land where you are crossing the Jordan to enter and possess it. I call heaven and earth to witness against you today, that I have set before you life and death, the blessing and the curse. **So choose life in order that you may live, you and your descendants, by loving the LORD your God, by obeying His voice, and by holding fast to Him; for this is your life and the length of your days, that you may live in the land which the LORD swore to your fathers, to Abraham, Isaac, and Jacob, to give them"** (Deuteronomy 30:15-20).

Moses' summary statements bring his previous prophecies to a fitting conclusion—especially for those of us living today. Every single one of us can experience either life and prosperity, or death and adversity. We can love the Lord and walk in His ways, or we can choose not to follow Him and suffer the consequences of disobedience. *God gives each of us a free will to make these choices.*

If you choose obedience to God, He promises His blessings. If you choose anything else, He promises penalties. As God puts it, Heaven and Earth are witnesses against all who originally listened to Moses in the wilderness prior to crossing the Jordan—and all who are

דברים

reading and having to consider these passages today. Heaven and Earth have not gone away, and neither have these Divine principles. Now that these prophecies are becoming real to many, perhaps it is time to be serious about whether you are going to choose an existence dominated by the power of life or death!

The Prophet Isaiah affirms how eventually the prophecies of Moses will be fulfilled. In this week's Haftarah selection, the reality of these end-time events coming to pass is amplified, as Isaiah looked forward to the times which Moses' prophecies direct us to:

"I will rejoice greatly in the LORD, My soul will exult in my God; for He has clothed me with garments of salvation, He has wrapped me with a robe of righteousness, as a bridegroom decks himself with a garland, and as a bride adorns herself with her jewels. **For as the earth brings forth its sprouts, and as a garden causes the things sown in it to spring up, so the Lord GOD will cause righteousness and praise to spring up before all the nations**" (Isaiah 61:10-12).

The future time which Moses talks about is seen through a different set of eyes, as Isaiah sees righteousness and praise springing up before all nations—an emphasis on the worldwide effects of Israel's restoration. While we might still be some distance from this taking place, each one of us can experience the essential reality of the New Covenant in our lives today, and we can individually play a role in seeing God's goodness demonstrated to all in the world. As more and more of us commit ourselves to returning to the Lord *and* to His Instruction, the restoration of His Kingdom will accelerate.

I pray that whether we are the final generation—or even if these things occur ten generations from now—we will all experience the fullness of God's Kingdom, **and know the eternal life available through faith in the Messiah Yeshua!**

# *V'yeilekh* וַיֵּלֶךְ
## And he went
## "The Importance of Obedience"

> Deuteronomy 31:1-30
> Hosea 14:2-10; Micah 7:18-20; Joel 2:15-27

As the Book of Deuteronomy begins to come to a close, our annual cycle of Torah study begins to wind down. It is during these final words of Moses to Ancient Israel that we find some of his most compelling pleas. For the preceding discussions in the Book of Deuteronomy, Moses has been summarizing the events of Exodus, Leviticus, and Numbers. Now, as Moses' life is about to end,[52] his final exhortations to Israel are riddled with emotional appeals for the people to choose life (cf. Deuteronomy 30:19-20)!

For those of us studying these words today, who believe that by faith in Yeshua we are a part of Israel—we consider Moses' admonitions to apply to us and be just as relevant, as they are to the physical descendants of those who stood beside Joshua preparing to enter the Promised Land. *God's people are required to obey Him in order to be blessed.* Yet, over the centuries, many theologians and philosophers of religion have done their best to get around the Biblical requirement that God's people obey His commandments. Liberal branches of

---

[52] Deuteronomy 31:1-13.

Judaism relegate following the Torah to only be a part of Jewish culture. Varied branches of Christianity like to say that Jesus "fulfilled and thus abolished the Law,"[53] or that the Torah was "nailed to the cross."[54] Others simply do not take the time and effort to examine what the Torah says, and then falsely conclude that God's Law has no relevance for modern people.

I have found that all of these—and other arguments—are generally superficial. They are excellent tactics of our enemy to cause people to disobey the Lord, and at the very least, experience a very stifled and ineffective faith. It is my hope and prayer as a Messianic Believer that we would not find ourselves trying to make up excuses for ignoring the Scriptures. While there are certainly questions on applicability of various commandments in the Twenty-First Century, a widescale dismissal of Moses' Teaching is unjustified.

## Simply Obey

Messianic Believers today have some distinct advantages over the Ancient Israelites. We can read the words of Deuteronomy and recognize that many of Moses' prophetic statements have already been fulfilled to some degree.[55] From a Twenty-First Century perspective looking back in history, we can review tangible evidence from the record of Scripture in how obedience to God brings blessings, while disobedience results in curses:

"So it shall be when all of these things have come upon you, the blessing and the curse which I have set before you, and you call *them* to mind in all nations where the LORD your God has banished you, and you return to the LORD your God and obey Him with all your heart and soul according to all that I command you today, you and your sons, then the LORD your God will restore you from captivity, and have compassion on you, and will gather you again from all the peoples where the LORD your God has scattered you. If your outcasts are at the ends of the earth, from there the LORD your God will gather you, and from there He will bring you back. The LORD your God will bring you into the land which your fathers possessed, and you shall possess it; and He will prosper you and multiply you more than your fathers. Moreover the LORD your God will circumcise your heart and the heart of your descendants, to love the LORD your God with all your heart and with all your soul, so that you may live. The LORD your God will inflict all these curses on your enemies and on those who hate you, who persecuted you. And you shall again obey the LORD, and observe all His commandments which I command you today. Then the LORD your God will prosper you abundantly in all the work of your hand, in the offspring of your body and in the offspring of your cattle and in the produce of your ground, for the LORD will again rejoice over you for good, just as He rejoiced over your fathers; if you obey the LORD your God to keep His commandments and His statutes which are written in this book of the law, if you turn to the LORD your God with all your heart and soul" (Deuteronomy 30:1-10).

Certainly if you follow the history of Israel since the time of Moses for the past 3,300 years, you can see how God has been faithful to enact punishment on those who have disobeyed Him. Sadly, in spite of the warnings of either Moses or the Prophets, God has sent Israel into numerous exiles into the nations of the Earth.

---

[53] Consult the exegetical paper "Has the Law Been Fulfilled?" by J.K. McKee, examining Matthew 5:17-19.

[54] Colossians 2:14 specifically says "the certificate of debt consisting of decrees against us, which was hostile to us" was nailed to the cross. This comprises the capital penalties pronounced upon sinners who break the Torah, which Yeshua by His sacrifice absorbed in His death; it does not take away the standard of sin contained in God's Law.

[55] Deuteronomy 31:14-22.

We can be thankful that there is an anticipated time when scattered and dispersed Israel will return to the Holy One with all of its heart and soul. In our era, especially since the creation of the modern State of Israel, the restoration and gathering back to the Promised Land has become a reality. More is to be anticipated to be sure, but it is to all likely be preceded by a more concentrated return of individuals to God and to His ways *first*. The Lord is clear to say that obedience to His commandments is not at all something to be difficult or overbearing:

**"For this commandment which I command you today is not too difficult for you, nor is it out of reach.** It is not in heaven, that you should say, 'Who will go up to heaven for us to get it for us and make us hear it, that we may observe it?' Nor is it beyond the sea, that you should say, 'Who will cross the sea for us to get it for us and make us hear it, that we may observe it?' But the word is very near you, in your mouth and in your heart, that you may observe it. See, I have set before you today life and prosperity, and death and adversity; in that I command you today to love the LORD your God, to walk in His ways and to keep His commandments and His statutes and His judgments, that you may live and multiply, and that the LORD your God may bless you in the land where you are entering to possess it" (Deuteronomy 30:11-16).

Many Christians today investigating the Messianic movement, and seeing its emphasis on the Torah, often do not know what to do. Many have been inappropriately told or taught that following God's Law is a complete impossibility. *But the Lord Himself says that **it is absolutely doable.*** The problem is often with our human volition, and our widespread tendency to make a choice leading to death and adversity. We often do not want to commit the *little* time and effort it takes to obey our Heavenly Father the way He asks.

## Post-Resurrection Choices

The Apostle Paul understood how bad choices can lead to negative consequences, especially among many of his fellow Jews who had denied Yeshua as the Messiah in the First Century. If you will recall his comments throughout Romans chs. 9-11, Paul addresses many of his heartfelt concerns regarding his fellow Jewish people, who would be most familiar with the words of Moses:

"For I could wish that I myself were accursed, *separated* from Messiah for the sake of my brethren, my kinsmen according to the flesh, who are Israelites, to whom belongs the adoption as sons, and the glory and the covenants and the giving of the Law and the *temple* service and the promises" (Romans 9:3-4).

"Brethren, my heart's desire and my prayer to God for them is for *their* salvation. For I testify about them that they have a zeal for God, but not in accordance with knowledge" (Romans 10:1-2).

Paul knew that his own Jewish people, who had inherited the promises of God, and who exhibited a sincere zeal for His ways, did not largely comprehend the very essence of what the Torah was intending to communicate. Many deliberately blinded themselves to the message of the gospel, and were unable to see how the Torah's focus had always been the Messiah Yeshua:

"Since they did not know the righteousness of God and sought to establish their own, they did not submit to God's righteousness. Christ is the culmination [*telos*] of the law so that there may be righteousness for everyone who believes. Moses writes this about the righteousness that is by the law: 'Whoever does these things will live by them'" (Romans 10:3-5, TNIV).

Here as Paul addresses the zeal of his people, he references a concept that is found in Leviticus 18:5: "So you shall keep My statutes and My judgments, by which a man may live if he does them; I am the LORD." If you can keep the commandments as they have been given *perfectly*, then you will have a blessed life and will never have to suffer the Law's capital punishment. The problem is that if you disobey just one commandment, you have broken the entire Law and are subject to its penalties—**which is what all of us have done** (Romans 3:10). As James the Just reminds us, "For whoever keeps the whole law and yet stumbles in one *point*, he has become guilty of all" (James 2:10). What this human reality forces us to do is to entreat the mercy of the Lord, and it intensifies one understanding how the goal, acme, or aim of the Torah **is to point people to the Messiah Yeshua *and* the salvation He provides.** If in our quest to be obedient to the Lord, we find that we have erred—born again Believers can now have the comfort in knowing that they have been redeemed from any of the curses of the Torah.

Such a righteousness is based on faith—the same faith that Abraham exhibited when he believed God's promises to him (Genesis 15:6; Romans 4:3; Galatians 3:6; James 2:23). Paul's writing continues, as he specifies,

"But the righteousness based on faith speaks as follows: 'DO NOT SAY IN YOUR HEART, "WHO WILL ASCEND INTO HEAVEN [Deuteronomy 30:20]?" (that is, to bring Messiah down), or 'WHO WILL DESCEND INTO THE ABYSS?' (that is, to bring Messiah up from the dead).' But what does it say? 'THE WORD IS NEAR YOU, IN YOUR MOUTH AND IN YOUR HEART [Deuteronomy 30:14]'—that is, the word of faith which we are preaching, that if you confess with your mouth Yeshua *as* Lord, and believe in your heart that God raised Him from the dead, you will be saved; for with the heart a person believes, resulting in righteousness, and with the mouth he confesses, resulting in salvation" (Romans 10:6-10).

Here, the Apostle Paul describes a word of faith which confesses with the mouth that Yeshua is Messiah, and believes in the heart that He has been raised from the dead. The righteousness of faith is focused around His completed work at Golgotha, **recognizing that He came and paid the price for our sins.** Yeshua the Messiah fulfilled the Law perfectly for us, and paid the debt that we had incurred before the Father as Law-breakers. *Nowhere* does the Torah itself claim that by following its commandments a person will merit eternal life; at most the Torah promises a blessed life for those who follow its commandments on Earth. Eternal communion with God can only be a reality via the accomplished work of His Son.

Still, even though the Torah does not provide eternal life, obedience to its statutes and decrees is required if we intend to be the holy and separated people that God desires. The Apostle John reminds us that believing that Yeshua is the sacrifice for human sin is one thing; in order to signify that such a belief within us is real, we must demonstrate it via acts of obedience:

"[A]nd He Himself is the propitiation for our sins; and not for ours only, but also for *those of* the whole world. By this we know that we have come to know Him, if we keep His commandments. The one who says, 'I have come to know Him,' and does not keep His commandments, is a liar, and the truth is not in him; but whoever keeps His word, in him the love of God has truly been perfected. By this we know that we are in Him: the one who says he abides in Him ought himself to walk in the same manner as He walked" (1 John 2:2-6).

An indication that one truly knows Messiah Yeshua, is if one chooses to keep His commandments. **If one does not keep His commandments, then John indicates** that one is a liar who does not have the truth. This is very serious. If a person claims with his or her mouth and "believes" in the heart that Yeshua is the Messiah, and yet does not expel any effort to keep (any of) His commandments—notably those of loving God and neighbor—there is an obvious disconnect. Perhaps such a confession of faith was just some kind of lip service and not a true heart confession? *Thankfully, only our Eternal God can truly judge the heart intention of any person.*

How debilitating has it been for today's Christianity to often leave obedience out of the gospel message? While none of us can "earn" salvation, our being cleansed from sins and spiritually regenerated is to follow with our being obedient to the Lord. How can today's Messianics become a force of positive change, helping to not only see many Jewish people come to faith in Messiah Yeshua—but many Christians turn toward a path of diligent obedience to God?

These, and many other questions, should be reflected upon during this season of reflection and repentance, as we consider the themes of the Fall high holidays. As we each meditate upon the issues before us, and consider a future time when we will be standing before our Creator, **may we each be encouraged to choose the eternal life provided in Messiah Yeshua with all our hearts, minds, and souls!**

## *Ha'azinu* הַאֲזִינוּ
### Hear
### "The Rock of Salvation"

> **Deuteronomy 32:1–52**
> **2 Samuel 22:1–22:51**

Moses' approaching death has inspired him to make some very emotional appeals to the people of Israel, seen in the words of Deuteronomy 32. He knew how his days of leading Israel were soon coming to an end. As any good shepherd would be, he was very cognizant of his sheep's proclivities. For forty years he had observed the Israelites' behavior in a variety of circumstances, and he knew their inclinations. As is true of most sheep, they were prone to wander. Moses attests to this in some of his final statements:

"For I know your rebellion and your stubbornness; behold, while I am still alive with you today, you have been rebellious against the LORD; how much more, then, after my death?...For I know that after my death you will act corruptly and turn from the way which I have commanded you; and evil will befall you in the latter days, for you will do that which is evil in the sight of the LORD, provoking Him to anger with the work of your hands" (Deuteronomy 31:27, 29).

With Moses getting ready to depart, he delivered some final instructions about what was to be done with the *sefer ha'torah* (סֵפֶר הַתּוֹרָה) that had been compiled during his tenure of leading Israel. The teaching he had delivered from the Lord had been written down as a witness that could be referred to in the future—especially as it would remind Israel of their responsibilities before God, and what would happen if the people or their descendants disobeyed Him:

"Take this book of the law and place it beside the ark of the covenant of the LORD your God, that it may remain there as a witness against you" (Deuteronomy 31:26, 30).

The written testimony of the Lord, which has been communicated through Moses, was to be a permanent witness for His people to seek instruction and guidance. In one of his final acts, a song is delivered by Moses to the people of Israel, making up most of our Torah reading for this week (Deuteronomy 31:1-43).[56] After this message is communicated, Moses again admonishes Israel to take his words very seriously:

"When Moses had finished speaking all these words to all Israel, he said to them, 'Take to your heart all the words with which I am warning you today, which you shall command your sons to observe carefully, *even* all the words of this law. For it is not an idle word for you; indeed it is your life. And by this word you will prolong your days in the land, which you are about to cross the Jordan to possess'" (Deuteronomy 32:45-47).

Ancient Israel was commanded to seriously heed what Moses has told them, because their aged leader wants them to "live long in the land you are crossing the Jordan to possess" (NIV). Thankfully, this song—as well as the entire Torah—have been memorized and studied over the centuries by many followers of the God of Abraham, Isaac, and Jacob! Millions of people the world over have taken to serious heart the Biblical axiom of choosing the ways of the Lord—*the ways of life!*

## A Song of Moses

In a distinctively didactic ode, the song witnessed in *Ha'azinu* not only reviews some of Israel's past history, but also prophetically declares what will transpire to Israel in the days following its entrance into the Promised Land. Moses' words describe what will happen as "Jeshurun" waxes fat and forgets the commandments of God.[57] The required chastisement is softened, but perhaps only very little, by promises made to vindicate Israel in the future.[58] Veiled references to the future period when Assyria and Babylon will be used to punish Israel are seen.[59]

As you read the song Moses delivers in Deuteronomy 32, his words wax eloquently. One of the significant themes seen is how the Lord is referred to as the Rock or *tzur* (צוּר). The Hebrew term *tzur* appears in a number of distinct places to refer to God, and in one place to describe the pitiful "rock" of false gods:

- "The Rock! His work is perfect, for all His ways are just; a God of faithfulness and without injustice, righteous and upright is He" (Deuteronomy 32:4).
- "But Jeshurun grew fat and kicked—you are grown fat, thick, and sleek—then he forsook God who made him, and scorned the Rock of his salvation" (Deuteronomy 32:15).
- "You neglected the Rock who begot you, and forgot the God who gave you birth" (Deuteronomy 32:18).
- "How could one chase a thousand, and two put ten thousand to flight, unless their Rock had sold them, and the LORD had given them up? Indeed

---

[56] Please note that the Song of Moses referred to in Revelation 15:3 is most probably the Song of the Sea of Exodus 15, something employed in the daily liturgy of the Jewish *siddur*.
For a further discussion, consult the article "The Song of Moses and God's Mission for His People" by J.K. McKee.
[57] Deuteronomy 32:15-17.
[58] Deuteronomy 32:36-43.
[59] Deuteronomy 32:21-27.

- their rock is not like our Rock, even our enemies themselves judge this" (Deuteronomy 32:30-31).
- "And He will say, 'Where are their gods, the rock in which they sought refuge?'" (Deuteronomy 32:37).

When we look at how the term *tzur* is used, we get the impression that just as granite or limestone gives the presentation of firmness or majesty—so is our God steadfast and reliable. In delivering his song to Israel, Moses wants the people to look to the Lord as a Rock they can rely on. He wants them to have vivid recollections of their past, present, and future relationship with Him—so that they might persevere through the foreordained rough times. As you reflect on these significant verses in this Torah portion, are you reminded of any past saints who used these very verses in troubled times, to comfort them through affliction?

One who immediately comes to my mind is a young King David, as he avoided the efforts of King Saul to exterminate him. In 2 Samuel 22, we see that in a time of great turmoil, David turned what is communicated by the Deuteronomy 32 song to find solace:

"And David spoke the words of this song to the LORD in the day that the LORD delivered him from the hand of all his enemies and from the hand of Saul. He said, **'The LORD is my rock and my fortress and my deliverer; My God, my rock, in whom I take refuge, My shield and the horn of my salvation, my stronghold and my refuge; My savior, You save me from violence.** I call upon the LORD, who is worthy to be praised, and I am saved from my enemies. For the waves of death encompassed me; the torrents of destruction overwhelmed me; the cords of Sheol surrounded me; the snares of death confronted me. In my distress I called upon the LORD, yes, I cried to my God; and from His temple He heard my voice, and my cry for help *came* into His ears'" (2 Samuel 22:1-7).

This incident resulted in what became Psalm 18:

"For the choir director. A *Psalm* of David the servant of the LORD, who spoke to the LORD the words of this song in the day that the LORD delivered him from the hand of all his enemies and from the hand of Saul. And he said, 'I love You, O LORD, my strength.' **The LORD is my rock and my fortress and my deliverer, My God, my rock, in whom I take refuge; my shield and the horn of my salvation, my stronghold. I call upon the LORD, who is worthy to be praised, and I am saved from my enemies.** The cords of death encompassed me, and the torrents of ungodliness terrified me. The cords of Sheol surrounded me; the snares of death confronted me. In my distress I called upon the LORD, and cried to my God for help; He heard my voice out of His temple, and my cry for help before Him came into His ears. Then the earth shook and quaked; and the foundations of the mountains were trembling and were shaken, because He was angry" (Psalm 18:1-7).

The words of King David should encourage us to rely upon the Lord as our Rock—for strength, direction, protection, and deliverance!

## Testimony to the "Rock"

As I ponder these thoughts, I am reminded of an important testimony that my wife Margaret often shares. She has mentioned many times the tragic loss of her first husband, Kimball McKee, who died at 41 due to melanoma cancer. She frequently recalls some of the last words that Kim uttered to her in the hospital room just before he fell into his final coma. As a born again Believer and devoted evangelical Christian, Kim would often refer to Jesus Christ as "the Rock." In his walk with the Lord, frequently reading the Old Testament, the image of the Messiah as the Rock of Salvation was seriously impressed upon his heart.

During his final days, the cancer had spread to Kim's brain stem. Just before slipping away, Margaret was in his room, and Kim sat straight up and wide awake in his bed. He pointed through Margaret to an image that he was seeing beyond her. Kim looked straight into the eyes of his wife, and told her "I can see the Rock and hear the music!" Right at that point the ICU nurse came in and ushered Margaret out of the room. *These were his last words.* The monitors indicated that he had triggered a code blue and he was immediately put on a respirator. He was dying, but according to his last words, he had seen the Rock of his Salvation who was waiting for him with the chorus of Heaven playing, very similar to what Stephen experienced (Acts 7:55-60). While Kim doubtlessly wanted to live, the words of Paul, "My desire is to depart and be with Christ" (Philippians 1:23, RSV), were realized for him in 1992. Two days later, Kim McKee was released from the respirator and went to be with the Messiah Yeshua.

When Kim was buried next to his parents, his grave marker included the epitaph, **"Jesus Christ, the Rock of my Salvation."** As Margaret, John, Jane, and Maggie frequently remind me—they will all one day be able to touch the resurrected body of Kim McKee again, when Yeshua returns "with all His saints" (1 Thessalonians 3:13) at the Second Coming. Some of the most inspiring words we can remember, even if we do sincerely believe that our loved ones who knew the Lord are in Heaven with Him now, regard how the power of Heaven will come to Earth at the time of resurrection. As the Apostle Paul says,

"For our citizenship is in heaven, from which also we eagerly wait for a Savior, the Lord Yeshua the Messiah; who will transform the body of our humble state into conformity with the body of His glory, by the exertion of the power that He has even to subject all things to Himself" (Philippians 3:20-21).[60]

Thinking about the inspiring testimony of Kim McKee, we can be encouraged by how in the future—all of us as redeemed saints—will one day surround the throne of God **and will be singing praises to the Rock** (Revelation 15:3-4; cf. Jeremiah 10:7). The Rock of our Salvation is the Lamb of God sacrificed for our sins. As John the Immerser confessed, "Behold, the Lamb of God who takes away the sin of the world!" (John 1:29). Being a part of the company of redeemed from all ages and time periods, and being reunited with our loved ones and ancestors—should cause us to be so overwhelmed with joy, that we simply want to praise our Creator!

It is immensely beneficial for each of us to take some special time this week to reflect upon these foundational truths which are so imperative for our faith. Whether we get lost in the eloquence of a beautiful song that speaks of the marvelous works of the Lord throughout the ages, or whether we praise Yeshua for His work of redemption—the most important thing is that we understand how God has interjected Himself into our lives so that we might have salvation. **The Lord Yeshua is the Rock of our Salvation!**

---

[60] For a further discussion, consult the article "To Be Absent From the Body" by J.K. McKee. Also useful is Bruce Milne, *The Message of Heaven & Hell* (Downers Grove, IL: InterVarsity, 2002).

In these days of reflection and returning to Him, come to the Lord with all your heart, mind, soul, and strength. *His arms are wide open.* Turn and run to the One who is the Rock of our Salvation!

## *V'zot Ha'berakhah* וְזֹאת הַבְּרָכָה
### This is the blessing
### "Full Circle"

> Deuteronomy 33:1–34:12
> Joshua 1:1–18 (A); 1:1-9 (S)

The final Torah portion from the Book of Deuteronomy completes the traditional annual cycle which will begin again in the Book of Genesis, after the commemoration of *Shemini Atzeret* (Eighth Day Assembly) and *Simchat Torah* (Joy of the Torah). *Sukkot* or the Feast of Tabernacles has come to a close, and at this time it is a tradition in the Jewish community to celebrate the end of the yearly Torah readings. Frequently at this time, these extra days associated with *Sukkot* are believed to be an indication that the God of Israel is so pleased with the time of rejoicing and fellowship, that He desires to have one more day of fellowship with His people.

From a prophetic perspective, if the Feast of Tabernacles is symbolic of entering into the Millennial Kingdom with Yeshua reigning over the Earth, then the Eighth Day Assembly would be appropriately symbolic of entering into the eternal state and New Heavens and Earth. When people often think of the future resurrection and the redeemed being ushered into an existence that we can right now only speculate about—it is natural for us to think about the beginning, and the way things originally were in the Garden with Adam and Eve.

Hebrew readers are often keenly aware of how the last word of Deuteronomy, *Yisrael* (יִשְׂרָאֵל), ends in a *lamed* (ל), and the first term in Genesis, *b'reisheet* (בְּרֵאשִׁית), "in the beginning," begins with a *bet* (ב). When you put the *lamed* and *bet* together, you form the Hebrew word *lev* (לֵב) or heart. As the annual Torah cycle is completed, one might be reminded of how his or her heart must be committed to learning from Moses' Teaching with sincere intentions. The admonition of Deuteronomy 6:6 is, after all, "These words, which I am commanding you today, shall be on your heart."

If you consider the subject matter of *V'zot Ha'berakhah*, which is primarily devoted to blessing the tribes of Israel,[61] it is perfectly suited for the final study of the annual cycle. The final words of Moses are recorded as he blesses the Ancient Israelites, before his tenure as Israel's leader is complete and he is led to the plains of Moab and dies.[62] As you can imagine, a considerable amount of material about these last statements of Moses has been composed. After all, here is the man chosen by God for the incredible task of leading the people of Israel from the bondage of Egyptian slavery to the freedom of the Promised Land. As the narrative concludes, the final verses of Deuteronomy say it all:

"Since that time no prophet has risen in Israel like Moses, whom the LORD knew face to face, for all the signs and wonders which the LORD sent him to perform in the land of

---

[61] Deuteronomy 33:1-29.
[62] Deuteronomy 34:1-6.

Egypt against Pharaoh, all his servants, and all his land, and for all the mighty power and for all the great terror which Moses performed in the sight of all Israel" (Deuteronomy 34:10-12).

When a person dies, his or her last words may be some of the most meaningful ever spoken. This is especially true if one knows that the time of death is imminent, and that these will be the final statements made to loved ones. In the case of this Torah portion, we know how Moses is quite aware that he is about to die. In the previous reading, *Ha'azinu* (Deuteronomy 32:1–52), the beautiful song Moses delivers is drafted to give Ancient Israel a poetic reflection that would be easy to memorize and meditate upon for centuries to come. Not only did it speak back (1) to the times of the Patriarchs, but also ahead to (2) the immediate future after Israel's conquest of Canaan, (3) the consequences of disobedience several hundred years into the future (the punishment meted out by Assyria and Babylon), (4) and the end-time scenario which is still yet to come. Bible readers for millennia been able to consider this message, recognizing how Moses' prophecies have been extremely accurate with multiple fulfillments already chronicled.

## Moses' Prophetic Blessings

In his blessing of the Ancient Israelites (Deuteronomy 33), Moses repeats the pattern established centuries earlier by Jacob, when on his deathbed, he blessed his sons (Genesis 49). Here, in an almost farewell gesture, Moses places a parting blessing on each of the tribes of Israel, except Simeon, who goes unmentioned. Simeon's notable absence has generated speculation among Jewish commentators, ranging from the Simeonites being included within Judah's territory (cf. Joshua 19:2), or some kind of penalty being meted out because of being involved in the sin of Baal-peor (Numbers 25:3).[63]

Moses looks into the immediate future for Israel, but the blessings are *permanently* placed upon the specific tribes. A very interesting study can be done when you consider Moses' blessings and compare them with Jacob's previous blessings. When you combine these sets of blessings together, a prophetic picture of what either the individual tribes of Israel, or corporate Israel together, will likely be doing through time, is encouraging to consider. **Most important to reflect upon is God's faithfulness to His special, chosen nation.**

## Completing the Circle

The continuum of life continues from generation to generation. The Jewish Sages knew this, and centuries ago chose the beginning of the Book of Joshua for the corresponding Haftarah selection for *V'zot Ha'berakhah* (Joshua 1:1–18), which in the Jewish book order of the Tanakh begins the Prophets.[64] Here, as the baton is given to Joshua and his generation, we are reminded that as one generation passes away, it is up to the succeeding generation to carry forward. Joshua did just this, as he carried the anointing of Moses and continued to point Israel to obeying the words of the Lord:

"Be strong and courageous, for you shall give this people possession of the land which I swore to their fathers to give them. Only be strong and very courageous; be careful to do according to all the law which Moses My servant commanded you; do not turn from it to the right or to the left, so that you may have success wherever you go. This book of the law

---

[63] Cf. Scherman, *Chumash*, 1115.

[64] In the Christian book order of the Old Testament, Joshua is reckoned among the Historical Books.

shall not depart from your mouth, but you shall meditate on it day and night, so that you may be careful to do according to all that is written in it; for then you will make your way prosperous, and then you will have success. Have I not commanded you? Be strong and courageous! Do not tremble or be dismayed, for the LORD your God is with you wherever you go" (Joshua 1:6-9).

Joshua begins his work by pointing the Ancient Israelites to God's Instruction. He knows from his days as an apprentice to Moses, that obeying the Lord would manifest itself in Israel being blessed and accomplishing all that He desired. Upon admonishing the people to follow God's Torah, they concur that just as they followed Moses as leader, so will they follow Joshua:

"They answered Joshua, saying, 'All that you have commanded us we will do, and wherever you send us we will go. Just as we obeyed Moses in all things, so we will obey you; only may the LORD your God be with you as He was with Moses'" (Joshua 1:16-17).

Ancient Israel responded to the heed of Joshua to continue obeying the Lord in a very affirmative way. The people understood that the blessings of God would flow from obedience to His Instruction.

May we likewise, generations removed, be led as the Ancient Israelites to declare a similar refrain when we have the challenge put before us to continue in our study of the Torah, and commit ourselves to obedience to the Lord. As Believers in the Messiah Yeshua—filled up with the Holy Spirit with His Instruction supernaturally transcribed on the heart (Jeremiah 31:31-34; Ezekiel 36:25-27)—may such obedience truly be a manifestation of the love we have for Him! *In so doing, the circle of study and obedience to the Torah will continue to be followed, and we can pass it on to our posterity.*

# About the Author

**William Mark Huey** is the founder and director of Outreach Israel Ministries. Mark became a Believer in the Messiah of Israel in 1978, but it was a Zola Levitt tour to Israel in 1994 with his wife that sparked an ardent search for answers about the Hebraic Roots of our faith. By 1995, his family became members of a Messianic Jewish congregation in Dallas, Texas and their pursuit for truth intensified. Within a year, Mark formed a conference-producing enterprise called "The Remnant Exchange," a division of Third Race Endeavors, and began hosting prophecy conferences and seminars with increasing Messianic understanding and emphasis. Mark's business experience, owning a commercial real estate brokerage company, coupled with Margaret's ownership of a cross-stitch design company, led them to form a ministry consulting business that worked with a variety of Messianic ministries from 1997 to 2002.

By 2002, after years of exposure to tangible evidence that the prophesied "Restoration of All Things" (Acts 3:21) was becoming a reality, the impetus to focus energy and attention on Israel, the people, the Land, and Torah-centered Messianic teachings merged together. The outcome was the formation of **Outreach Israel Ministries**.

From the beginning of Outreach Israel Ministries, the need to educate and to minister to the expanding number of Messianics has always been at the heart of the mission. The technological tools made available through the Internet have allowed much of the communication and interaction to be affordable and extensive. Developing a website presence that was informational was essential to extending the outreach around the globe. The merger with TNN Online and TNN Press in 2003 substantially enhanced the website capabilities and teaching materials.

For years, Mark has had a fervent interest in Torah study. His "TorahScope" commentaries are e-mailed to those every week who are looking for a Messianic perspective on the weekly portions, and have been enhanced by "TorahScope Live" audio broadcasts. Additionally, Mark writes editorial commentaries under the byline "Hue and Cry" that are germane to issues involving Israel and the Messianic movement.

Contact with Messianics from around the world has generated a number of topics that need to be addressed from a Messianic perspective. At the founding of OIM, since there did not appear to be a broad overview of the Hebraic Roots of our faith, the concept of developing an introductory study guide appeared to meet an expanding need. In collaboration with J.K. McKee, editor of TNN Online, the workbook *Hebraic Roots: An Introductory Study* was produced. Mark has also written *TorahScope, Volumes I&II, TorahScope Haftarah Exhortations*, and *TorahScope Apostolic Scripture Reflections*.

Mark is a graduate of Vanderbilt University with a B.A. in history, with graduate studies toward a master's degree in aviation management completed at Embry-Riddle Aeronautical University.

# BIBLIOGRAPHY

*Articles*
Instone-Brewer, David. "Infanticide and the Apostolic Decree of Acts 15" in Journal of the Evangelical Theological Society Vol. 52 No. 2 (2009).
Coppes, Leonard J. "קָרַב," in *TWOT*.
Payne, J. Barton. "עָבַר," in *TWOT*.

*Bible Versions and Study Bibles*
Alter, Robert, trans. *The Five Books of Moses: A Translation With Commentary* (New York and London: W.W. Norton, 2004).
Garrett, Duane A., ed., et. al. *NIV Archaeological Study Bible* (Grand Rapids: Zondervan, 2005).
Green, Jay P., trans. *The Interlinear Bible* (Lafayette, IN: Sovereign Grace Publishers, 1986).
*Holy Bible, King James Version* (edited 1789).
*Holy Bible, New International Version* (Grand Rapids: Zondervan, 1978).
*Keter Crown Bible* (Jerusalem: Feldheim, 2004).
*New American Standard, Updated Edition* (Anaheim, CA: Foundation Publications, 1995).
*New English Bible* (Oxford and Cambridge: Oxford and Cambridge University Presses, 1970).
*New Revised Standard Version* (National Council of Churches of Christ, 1989).
Packer, J.I., ed. *The Holy Bible, English Standard Version* (Wheaton, IL: Crossway Bibles, 2001).
Scherman, Nosson, and Meir Zlotowitz, eds. *ArtScroll Tanach* (Brooklyn: Mesorah Publications., 1996).
Stern, David H., trans. *Complete Jewish Bible* (Clarksville, MD: Jewish New Testament Publications, 1998).
*Tanakh: The Holy Scriptures* (Philadelphia: Jewish Publication Society, 1999).
*Today's New International Version* (Grand Rapids: Zondervan, 2005).
*The Holy Bible, Revised Standard Version* (Nashville: Cokesbury, 1952).
Young, Robert, trans. *Young's Literal Translation*.
Zodhiates, Spiros, ed. *Hebrew-Greek Key Study Bible*, New American Standard (Chattanooga: AMG Publishers, 1994).

*Cited Books*
Gorenberg, Gershom. *The End of Days: Fundamentalism and the Struggle for the Temple Mount* (New York: Oxford University Press, 2000).
Kitchen, K.A. *On the Reliability of the Old Testament* (Grand Rapids: Eerdmans, 2003).
Strickland, Wayne G., ed. *Five Views on Law and Gospel* (Grand Rapids: Zondervan, 1996).
Wright, Christopher J.H. *The Mission of God: Unlocking the Bible's Grand Narrative* (Downers Grove, IL: InterVarsity, 2006).

*Cited Commentaries*
Allen, Ronald B. "Numbers," in Frank E. Gaebelein, ed. et. al. *Expositor's Bible Commentary* (Grand Rapids: Zondervan, 1990), 2:657-1008.
Ashley, Timothy R. *New International Commentary on the Old Testament: The Book of Numbers* (Grand Rapids: Eerdmans, 1993).
Bruce, F.F. *New International Greek Testament Commentary: Galatians* (Grand Rapids: Eerdmans, 1982).
Hagner, Donald A. *Word Biblical Commentary: Matthew 1-13*, Vol 33a (Nashville: Thomas Nelson, 1993).
Hays, Richard B. *Interpretation, A Bible Commentary for Teaching and Preaching: 1 Corinthians* (Louisville: John Knox Press, 1997).
Keck, Leander E., ed., et. al. *New Interpreter's Bible*, Vol. 10 (Nashville: Abingdon, 2002).
Metzger, Bruce M. *A Textual Commentary on the Greek New Testament* (London and New York: United Bible Societies, 1975).
Olson, Dennis T. *Interpretation, A Bible Commentary for Teaching and Preaching: Numbers* (Louisville: John Knox Press, 1996).
Sarna, Nahum M. *JPS Torah Commentary: Genesis* (Philadelphia: Jewish Publication Society, 1989).
Thiselton, Anthony C. *New International Greek Testament Commentary: The First Epistle to the Corinthians* (Grand Rapids: Eerdmans, 2000).

*Cited Theological Encyclopedias and Dictionaries*
Green, Joel B., Scot McKnight, and I. Howard Marshall, eds. *Dictionary of Jesus and the Gospels* (Downers Grove, IL: InterVarsity, 1992).
Hawthorne, Gerald F., Ralph P. Martin, and Daniel G. Reid, eds. *Dictionary of Paul and His Letters* (Downers Grove, IL: InterVarsity, 1993).

*Greek Texts and Lexicons*
Aland, Kurt, et. al. *The Greek New Testament, Fourth Revised Edition* (Stuttgart: Deutche Bibelgesellschaft/United Bible Societies, 1998).
Brenton, Sir Lancelot C. L., ed & trans. *The Septuagint With Apocrypha* (Peabody, MA: Hendrickson, 1999).
Danker, Frederick William, ed., et. al. *A Greek-English Lexicon of the New Testament and Other Early Christian Literature*, third edition (Chicago: University of Chicago Press, 2000).
Liddell, H.G., and R. Scott. *An Intermediate Greek-English Lexicon* (Oxford: Clarendon Press, 1994).
Rahlfs, Alfred, ed. *Septuaginta* (New York: American Bible Society, 1979).
Thayer, Joseph H. *Thayer's Greek-English Lexicon of the New Testament* (Peabody, MA: Hendrickson, 2003).
Vine, W.E. *Vine's Expository Dictionary of New Testament Words* (Nashville: Thomas Nelson, 1968).
Zodhiates, Spiros, ed. *Complete Word Study Dictionary: New Testament* (Chattanooga: AMG Publishers, 1993).

*Hebrew Texts and Lexicons*
Baker, Warren, and Eugene Carpenter, eds. *Complete Word Study Dictionary: Old Testament* (Chattanooga: AMG Publishers, 2003).
Brown, Francis, S.R. Driver, and Charles A. Briggs. *Hebrew and English Lexicon of the Old Testament* (Oxford: Clarendon Press, 1979).
Dotan, Aron, ed. *Biblia Hebraica Leningradensia* (Peabody, MA: Hendrickson, 2001).
Elliger, Karl, and Wilhelm Rudolph, et. al., eds. *Biblica Hebraica Stuttgartensia* (Stuttgart: Deutche Bibelgesellschaft, 1977).
Holladay, William L., ed. *A Concise Hebrew and Aramaic Lexicon of the Old Testament* (Leiden, the Netherlands: E.J. Brill, 1988).
Harris, R. Laird, Gleason L. Archer, Jr., and Bruce K. Waltke, eds. *Theological Wordbook of the Old Testament* (Chicago: Moody Press, 1980).

Jastrow, Marcus. *Dictionary of the Targumim, Talmud Bavli, Talmud Yerushalmi, and Midrashic Literature* (New York: Judaica Treasury, 2004).
Kelley, Page H., Daniel S. Mynatt, and Timothy G. Crawford, eds. *The Masorah of Biblia Hebraica Stuttgartensia* (Grand Rapids: Eerdmans, 1998).
Koehler, Ludwig, and Walter Baumgartner, eds. *The Hebrew & Aramaic Lexicon of the Old Testament*, 2 vols. (Leiden, the Netherlands: Brill, 2001).

*Jewish Reference Sources*
Cohen, Abraham. *Everyman's Talmud: The Major Teachings of the Rabbinic Sages* (New York: Schoken, 1995).
Cohen, Rev. Dr. A., ed. *The Soncino Chumash* (London: Soncino Press, 1983).
Eisenberg, Ronald L. *The JPS Guide to Jewish Traditions* (Philadelphia: Jewish Publication Society, 2004).
Harlow, Jules, ed. *Siddur Sim Shalom for Shabbat and Festivals* (New York: Rabbinical Assembly, 2007).
Hertz, J.H., ed. *Pentateuch & Haftorahs* (London: Soncino, 1960).
_____. *The Authorised Daily Prayer Book*, revised (New York: Bloch Publishing Company, 1960).
Kolatch, Alfred J. *The Jewish Book of Why* (Middle Village, NY: Jonathan David Publishers, 1981).
Lieber, David L. *Etz Hayim: Torah and Commentary* (New York: Rabbinical Assembly, 2001).
Encyclopaedia Judaica. MS Windows 9x. Brooklyn: Judaica Multimedia (Israel) Ltd, 1997.
Neusner, Jacob, trans. *The Mishnah: A New Translation* (New Haven and London: Yale University Press, 1988).
_____, trans. *The Tosefta: Translated from the Hebrew With a New Introduction*, 2 vols. (Peabody, MA: Hendrickson, 2002).
_____, and William Scott Green, eds. *Dictionary of Judaism in the Biblical Period* (Peabody, MA: Hendrickson, 2002).
Scherman, Nosson, ed., et al. *The ArtScroll Chumash, Stone Edition*, 5th ed. (Brooklyn: Mesorah Publications, 2000).
_____, and Meir Zlotowitz, eds. *Complete ArtScroll Siddur, Nusach Sefard* (Brooklyn: Mesorah Publications, 1985).

*Messianic Reference Sources*
McKee, J.K. *A Survey of the Apostolic Scriptures for the Practical Messianic* (Kissimmee, FL: TNN Press, 2006).
_____. *A Survey of the Tanach for the Practical Messianic* (Kissimmee, FL: TNN Press, 2008).
Stern, David H. *Jewish New Testament Commentary* (Clarksville, MD: Jewish New Testament Publications, 1995).

*Miscellaneous*
Charlesworth, James H., ed. *The Old Testament Pseudepigrapha*, Vol 2 (New York: Doubleday, 1985).
Wise, Michael, Martin Abegg, Jr., and Edward Cook, trans. *The Dead Sea Scrolls: A New Translation* (San Francisco: HarperCollins, 1996).

*Software Programs*
BibleWorks 5.0. MS Windows 9x. Norfolk: BibleWorks, LLC, 2002. CD-ROM.
BibleWorks 7.0. MS Windows XP. Norfolk: BibleWorks, LLC, 2006. CD-ROM.
E-Sword 7.0.5. MS Windows 9x. Franklin, TN: Equipping Ministries Foundation, 2003.
Judaic Classics Library II. MS Windows 3.1. Brooklyn: Institute for Computers in Jewish Life, 1996. CD-ROM.

TNN Press is the official publishing arm of TNN Online, and its parent organization, Outreach Israel Ministries. TNN Press is dedicated to producing high quality, doctrinally sound, challenging, and fair-minded Messianic materials and resources for the Twenty-First Century. TNN Press offers a wide array of new and exciting books and resources for the truth seeker.

TNN Press titles are available for purchase at

**www.outreachisrael.net** or at **amazon.com**.

*Hebraic Roots: An Introductory Study*
is TNN Press' main, best-selling publication, that offers a good overview of the Messianic movement and Messianic lifestyle that can be used for individual or group study in twelve easy lessons

*Introduction to Things Messianic*
is an excellent companion to *Hebraic Roots*, which goes into substantially more detail into the emerging theology of the Messianic movement, specific areas of Torah observance, and aspects of faith such as salvation and eschatology

**The Messianic Helper series**, edited by Margaret McKee Huey, includes a series of booklets with instructional information on how to have a Messianic home, including holiday celebration guides. After reading both *Hebraic Roots* and *Introduction to Things Messianic,* these are the publications you need to read!

> *Messianic Winter Holiday Helper*
> is a guide to help you during the Winter holiday season, addressing the significance of *Chanukah,* the period of the Maccabees, and the non-Biblical holiday of Christmas
>
> *Messianic Spring Holiday Helper*
> is a guide to assist you during the Spring holiday season, analyzing the importance of *Purim,* Passover and Unleavened Bread, *Shavuot,* and the non-Biblical holiday of Easter
>
> *Messianic Fall Holiday Helper*
> is a guide for the Fall holiday season of *Yom Teruah/Rosh HaShanah, Yom Kippur,* and *Sukkot,* along with reflective teachings and exhortations

# Additional Materials Available From TNN Press

*Messianic Sabbath Helper* (coming soon)
is a guide that will help you make the seventh-day Sabbath a delight, discussing both how to keep the Sabbath and the history of the transition to Sunday that occurred in early Christianity

*Messianic Torah Helper* (coming soon)
is a guide that will weigh the different perspectives of the Pentateuch present in Jewish and Christian theology, consider the role of the Law for God's people, and how today's Messianics can fairly approach issues of *halachah* and tradition in their Torah observance

Outreach Israel Ministries director **Mark Huey** has written Torah commentaries and reflections that are thought provoking and very enlightening for Messianic Believers today.

*TorahScope Volume I*
is a compilation workbook of insightful commentaries on the weekly Torah and Haftarah portions

*TorahScope Volume II*
is a second compilation workbook of expanded commentaries on the weekly Torah and Haftarah portions

*TorahScope Haftarah Exhortations*
is a compilation workbook of insightful commentaries on the specific, weekly Haftarah portions, designed to be used to compliment the weekly Torah reading

*TorahScope Apostolic Scripture Reflections*
is a compilation workbook of insightful reflections on suggested readings from the Apostolic Scriptures or New Testament, designed to be used to compliment the weekly Torah and Haftarah readings

*Counting the Omer: A Daily Devotional Toward Shavuot*
is a daily devotional with fifty succinct reflections from Psalms, guiding you during the season between the festivals of Passover and Pentecost

## Additional Materials Available From TNN Press

TNN Online editor and Messianic apologist **J.K. McKee** has written on Messianic theology and practice, including studies on Torah observance, the end-times, and commentaries that are helpful to those who have difficult questions to answer.

*The New Testament Validates Torah*
*Does the New Testament Really Do Away With the Law?*
is a resource examining a wide variety of Biblical passages, discussing whether or not the Torah of Moses is really abolished in the New Testament

*Torah In the Balance, Volume I*
*The Validity of the Torah and Its Practical Life Applications*
examines the principal areas of a Torah observant walk of faith for the newcomer, including one's spiritual motives

Confronting Critical Issues (coming soon)
*An Analysis of Subjects that Affects the Growth and Stability of the Emerging Messianic Movement*
compiles a variety of articles and analyses that directly confront negative teachings and trends that have been witnessed in the broad Messianic community in the past decade

TNN Press has produced a variety of **Messianic commentaries** on various books of the Bible under the "for the Practical Messianic" byline. These can be used in an individual, small group, or congregational study.

general commentaries:
*A Survey of the Tanach for the Practical Messianic*
*A Survey of the Apostolic Scriptures for the Practical Messianic*

specific book commentaries:
*Acts 15 for the Practical Messianic*
*Galatians for the Practical Messianic*
*Ephesians for the Practical Messianic*
*Philippians for the Practical Messianic*
*Colossians and Philemon for the Practical Messianic*
*The Pastoral Epistles for the Practical Messianic*
*1&2 Thessalonians for the Practical Messianic* (coming soon)
*James for the Practical Messianic* (coming soon)
*Hebrews for the Practical Messianic*

# Additional Materials Available From TNN Press

One of the goals of TNN Press is to always be in the mode of producing more cutting edge materials, addressing head on some of the theological and spiritual issues facing our emerging Messianic movement. In addition to our current array of available and soon-to-be available publications, the following are a selection of **Future Projects**, in various stages of planning and pre-production, most of which involve research at the present time (2012). Look for their release sometime over the next two to five years and beyond.

*Torah In the Balance, Volume II*
*The Set-Apart Life in Action—The Outward Expressions of Faith*
by J.K. McKee
will examine many of the finer areas of Torah observance, which has a diversity of interpretations and applications as witnessed in both mainstream Judaism and the wide Messianic community

*Honoring One Another*
*Mutual Submission and the Future of People in the Broad Messianic Movement*
by J.K. McKee
will consider the sizeable need for today's Messianic community to adopt a mutual submission ideology, where Jewish and non-Jewish Believers can all feel welcome and valued, and husbands and wives can be co-leaders of the home

*Messianic Kosher Helper*
will be a guide discussing various aspects of the kosher dietary laws, clean and unclean meats, common Jewish traditions associated with kashrut, and common claims made that these are no longer important for Believers

*Messianic Prophecy Helper*
will be a guide considering a proper approach to Bible prophecy, the end-times, the Second Coming, global events, the problem with date setting, and end of the world paranoia for today's Messianic Believers

*Salvation on the Line*
by J.K. McKee
is a planned two-volume work that will directly tackle the subject of apostasy in today's Messianic movement, considering both the Divinity and Messiahship of Yeshua (I) and then the reliability of the Scriptures and human origins (II)

Made in the USA
Charleston, SC
16 July 2012